ADVANCING THE
STORY

ADVANCING THE STORY

BROADCAST JOURNALISM

IN A MULTIMEDIA WORLD

Second Edition

DEBORA HALPERN WENGER and **DEBORAH POTTER**

University of Mississippi   NewsLab

CQ PRESS

A Division of SAGE
Washington, D.C.

CQ Press
2300 N Street, NW, Suite 800
Washington, DC 20037

Phone: 202-729-1900; toll-free, 1-866-4CQ-PRESS (1-866-427-7737)

Web: www.cqpress.com

Cover design: Anne C. Kerns, Anne Likes Red, Inc.
Typesetting: C&M Digitals (P) Ltd.

♾ The paper used in this publication exceeds the requirements of the American National Standard for Information Sciences—Permanence of Paper for Printed Library Materials, ANSI Z39.48-1992.

Printed and bound in the United States of America

15 14 13 12 11   1 2 3 4 5

Library of Congress Cataloging-in-Publication Data

Wenger, Debora Halpern.
   Advancing the story: broadcast journalism in a multimedia world / Debora Halpern Wenger and Deborah Potter. — 2nd ed.
       p. cm.
   Includes bibliographical references and index.
   ISBN 978-1-60871-714-9 (pbk.: alk. paper) 1. Broadcast journalism. I. Potter, Deborah (Deborah A.) II. Title.
   PN4784.B75A38 2011
   070.1'9—dc22

                                                              2010049469

*Dedicated to the outstanding journalists we learned from
and to future journalists who will uphold their standards*

About the Authors

Debora Halpern Wenger, a 17-year broadcast news veteran, is associate professor of journalism at the University of Mississippi and former associate professor at Virginia Commonwealth University. Prior to her academic appointment, she served as assistant news director at WFLA-TV in Tampa, Fla. She started her career as a reporter/anchor at KXJB in Fargo, N.D., moved on to producing at WBBH in Ft. Myers, Fla., and WMUR in Manchester, N.H., then became executive producer at WSOC in Charlotte, N.C. Wenger  conducts multimedia training in newsrooms across the country and is co-author of the broadcast and online journalism curricula for the Society of Professional Journalists' Newsroom Training Program. She has been invited to work as visiting faculty for the Poynter Institute. She has a BA from what is now known as Minnesota State University and an MA from the University of North Carolina at Charlotte.

Deborah Potter is a veteran journalist and educator who spent 16 years as a network correspondent for CBS News and CNN. She is executive director of NewsLab (www.newslab.org), a nonprofit resource for journalists in Washington, D.C., that she founded in 1998. She is a past executive director of the Radio and Television News Directors Foundation. Before joining CBS, Potter was a local TV news producer in Washington, D.C., and a radio news anchor at KYW in Philadelphia. She writes about broadcast news for American  Journalism Review, and leads workshops for journalists in newsrooms across the United States and around the world on writing, storytelling, ethics and news leadership. Potter previously taught journalism as a faculty associate at the Poynter Institute, and is the author of "Ready, Set, Lead: The Resource Guide for News Managers" and the "Handbook of Independent Journalism." She has a BA from the University of North Carolina at Chapel Hill and an MA from American University.

BRIEF CONTENTS

CONTENTS

TABLES, FIGURES AND BOXES

PREFACE

Every day it seems there's another headline that screams, "Journalism is dead!" And every day another pundit pronounces that there's never been a better time to be a journalist. We believe that this *is* a great time to be a journalist, and the second edition of our book is aimed at helping you be a better journalist by capitalizing on the opportunities that today's technology provides.

Journalists today have more options for telling stories to more people more quickly than ever before, but they need new ways of thinking and new skills if they're going to succeed. At the same time, they must uphold the time-honored standards of good journalism to establish their credibility and earn the public's trust.

This revised and updated edition of our book, its online learning modules (journalism .cqpress.com) and blog (www.advancingthestory.com) will take broadcast journalists well beyond the basics, while reinforcing traditional journalistic principles. One is that the story matters more than the medium you tell it in—or, to put it more bluntly, "It's the content, stupid." Another is that journalists still have a key role to play in a free society— to provide information that citizens need to govern their lives—a role that matters just as much today as it did when the United States was founded. And it matters just as much as it did more than 100 years ago, when the newspaper publisher Joseph Pulitzer wrote these words: "An able, disinterested, public-spirited press, with trained intelligence to know the right and courage to do it, can preserve that public virtue without which popular government is a sham and a mockery. A cynical, mercenary, demagogic press will produce in time a people as base as itself."

WHERE WE ARE GOING

Between the two of us, we have been teaching and training journalists for more than a quarter-century. We've often been asked to recommend a good advanced textbook about broadcast or multimedia journalism. What we've found is that there are few, if any, high-quality texts to help broadcast journalists go beyond the basics. And most multimedia texts are either theoretical or technical. Those books are useful, but not sufficient. We know this because our friends in newsrooms keep telling us how hard it is to hire journalists who understand both how to do a good TV or print story and how to enhance that story on the Web. So we wrote this book to fill the gap.

This second edition contains a number of significant updates and revisions that will help prepare journalists for jobs in today's newsrooms. We cover the essential topics for any journalist—researching, interviewing, writing, visualizing stories and adding depth, for example—but we begin with a clear message: It's a multimedia world and today's journalists must develop a multimedia mind-set. Throughout the book, we discuss how the multimedia approach to storytelling changes the newsgathering and news production process.

HOW WE GET THERE

Our goal is to provide a straightforward guide to what you need to know to practice journalism today. We've structured the book so that what you learn in each chapter builds on what you've already read. But we've written it in such a way that you can read individual chapters whenever they seem most useful.

In this second edition, we place even greater emphasis on the importance of understanding the audience. Today's news consumers want the news they want when they want it, and that's changing the way journalists gather, package and deliver content. But we believe that quality matters more than ever in this environment, so Chapter 1 focuses on how a multimedia approach can be used to produce better journalism.

Chapters 2 through 4 show you where to look for story ideas that work, and take you beyond the basics to improve your multimedia newsgathering skills. And because good journalism does much more than scratch the surface, we show you how to make your stories more meaningful by adding depth and detail.

Chapters 5 and 6 show you how to produce better-quality stories based on the content you've gathered, with an emphasis on story planning and structure. You'll learn how to make the most of sound and visuals—including graphics—in telling stories for any medium.

Chapter 7 breaks down the online writing process into a series of manageable steps, and the revised Chapter 8 is designed to spark creative thinking about the storytelling process by exploring what's possible online and with social media.

In the updated and renamed Chapter 9, "Producing for Multiple Platforms," we go beyond creating content for traditional television newscasts to explore mobile news delivery. We provide guidance on vocal delivery, stand-ups and live shots in Chapter 10, and we offer advice for print or online journalists who appear on TV. There's also a primer to help broadcast writers create print versions of their stories.

While practical skills are essential for journalists, they also need something more—a compass to make sure their actions are in line with their values. In Chapter 11 we explore the new ethical challenges faced by multiplatform journalists, as well as some of the ways a multimedia approach can help resolve ethical dilemmas.

In the revised Chapter 12 we discuss entrepreneurial journalism and the expanding field of hyperlocal news. You'll also find a wealth of information and resources for that all-important job search.

Throughout the book, you'll benefit from what other journalists have learned on the job. Each chapter includes two innovative features: "Know and Tell" reports typically focus on practicing journalists who share firsthand experience with issues discussed in the text; "Trade Tools" help you absorb best practices outlined in the text. In the second edition, we've added more than a dozen new examples of these features. At the end of each chapter, we include "Talking Points" to facilitate discussion, which can also be used as assignments to foster critical thinking.

In every chapter we have tried to be mindful of the need to encourage diversity in newsgathering and delivery. We suggest ways of finding diverse sources and include story examples with a strong diversity component. We've made sure to consult expert journalists from diverse backgrounds and perspectives to emphasize the importance of inclusiveness in high-quality journalism.

WHAT'S NEW?

This second edition of "Advancing the Story" includes substantial revisions but retains the essential strengths of the original text: clear instruction on reporting and producing for multiple platforms, real-world examples and advice from professional journalists, discussion questions and hands-on exercises. New screen shots, images and examples are included throughout.

The content has been updated to reflect the latest issues, trends and changes in journalism, including:

- A new focus on the use of social media to gather, promote and disseminate news content.

- The expanded coverage capabilities offered by mobile devices, as well as the impact of a growing mobile audience.

- New opportunities for journalists created by entrepreneurial, niche and hyperlocal news sites.

- The impact of a growing demand for multimedia content on the daily job of a broadcast journalist.

The online learning modules that accompany the text have been revised to allow students to download and work with video. We also provide new reference material, including video tutorials, screencasts and printable tipsheets.

AUTHOR BLOG AND ONLINE LEARNING MODULES

One of the biggest challenges in teaching and studying journalism today is staying current, because technology changes so rapidly. That's just one reason we believe our author blog and online learning modules are of immense value to anyone using this text.

"Advancing the Story" Blog

The author blog (www.advancingthestory.com) provides links to the latest research and news reports about multimedia issues, as well as examples of great reporting. We update it frequently and tag posts by chapter, so you can easily find the ones that apply to what you're reading in the text. Because we believe the best journalism is informed by conversation with the audience, our blog is open for comments. Please don't hesitate to let us know what you think.

Online Learning Modules

"Advancing the Story" has 12 online learning modules—one for each chapter in the book (journalism.cqpress.com). Individual modules can be purchased separately from the book, or as a package along with the book.

When students log in to the Web-based learning modules, they will have access to interactive exercises and learning resources and will automatically be set up with their own WordPress blog. The online modules can be used as a self-testing tutorial or as a teaching tool by instructors, who may assign exercises for credit or a grade. Also included is an instructor's resource area that provides teaching aids, including sample syllabi.

Each online module contains:

- **Skill building:** Exercises that test what you've learned and your ability to execute the techniques discussed in each chapter. Exercises include honing reporting and writing skills, creating a newscast lineup, testing ethical decision making and creating a multimedia portfolio to use as you enter the job market.

- **Discover:** High-quality work produced by journalists, including Web projects, slide shows, TV news stories and print articles. We provide explicit guidance on what to look for to help you get the most out of these projects.

- **Explore:** A guided tour of useful and relevant online material. These pages provide annotated links to skill-building tutorials, analysis from journalism experts, important research findings and more.

- **E-chapter:** Each online module includes a digital version of the chapter's text in full color, with active links.

The revised online modules also contain video tutorials and printable PDF tipsheets that students can use as reference tools. Screencasts demonstrate how journalists use Web applications to which students are introduced in the text. As the tools change, these online modules will change as well.

Ongoing Story

This unique module allows students to report and write a story from beginning to end. The "Ongoing Story" exercise for each chapter in the book draws on the skills you've learned from the text. Starting with a news release, you will plan and conduct virtual interviews, prepare for a one-day shoot, review data to add depth, log sound and video and write a package, as well as a stand-up and Web version. You will then develop a multimedia story plan. At every step, students can compare their work to that of the authors in developing, reporting and executing a multimedia story on the same topic.

ACKNOWLEDGMENTS

We could not have written this book without the help of many journalists who took the time to share their stories and wisdom. Colleagues, students, reviewers and editors who believed in the project worked to make this a better book.

We especially want to thank June Nicholson, Paula Otto and Jeff South of Virginia Commonwealth University. Sybril Bennett of Belmont University, Michael Cremedas of

Syracuse University, George L. Daniels of the University of Alabama, Don Heider of Loyola University Chicago, David Kurpius of Louisiana State University, Richard Moore of the University of South Carolina, Mary Rogus of Ohio University, Carol Schwalbe of the University of Arizona and Susan Smith of Ball State University reviewed the first edition and offered valuable suggestions, many of which we've incorporated here.

We are immensely grateful to all the journalists who made much of this text possible. Dan Bradley, Peter Howard and Donna Reed from Media General provided access to the people who work for them and authorized the use of multimedia examples in the text and online. So did Brian Bracco, Dan O'Donnell, Andrew Pulskamp and others at Hearst Television. In the area of social media, we owe thanks to social journalist Jeff Cutler, Amanda des Roches of Media General and Chip Mahaney of E. W. Scripps.

We'd specifically like to thank these journalists for their generosity and dedication to improving the profession:

Joe Adams	Bob Faw	Jacqueline Ingles
Nancy Amons	Mark Feldstein	Scott Jensen
Bryan Barr	Travis Fox	Demetria Kalodimos
Michelle Bearden	Joe Fryer	Sharon King
Mark Becker	Echo Gamel	Angie Kucharski
Kevin Benz	Jim Garrott	John Larson
Fred Brown	Michele Godard	Crystal Lauderdale
Joann Byrd	John Goheen	Victoria Lim
Nick Ciletti	Kim Griffis	Joe Mahoney
Roy Peter Clark	Tim Griffis	Jonathan Malat
Jennifer Coates	Jason Hanson	Dave Marcus
Candy Crowley	Larche Hardy	Regina McCombs
David Cuillier	Byron Harris	Josh Meltzer
Wally Dean	Michele Harvey	Charlie Meyerson
Lane DeGregory	Terry Heaton	Lane Michaelsen
Bob Dotson	Stan Heist	Jayne Miller
Mark Douglas	Gary Hill	Chris Mitchell
Darren Durlach	Steve Hooker	J. J. Murray
Dan Dwyer	Brant Houston	Eric Nalder
Mark Fagan	Boyd Huppert	Ted Nelson

Byron Pitts	Susie Steimle	Ann Utterback
Rod Rassman	Jane Stevens	Lynn Walsh
David Rosenbaum	Emerson Stone	Keith Weiss
Dale Russakoff	Steve Sweitzer	Dave Wertheimer
Corky Scholl	Christine Tanaka	Jason Whitely
Mike Schuh	Mackenzie Taylor	Robin Whitmeyer
Barry Simmons	Emily Timm	Amy Wood
Shreeya Sinha	Al Tompkins	Amanda Zamora
Sree Sreenivasan	Kevin Torres	Lauren Zimmerman

We couldn't have produced the "Ongoing Story" module without the help of Rich Murphy, senior Web producer at WTTG-TV, who shot and edited the video.

Finally, we would like to thank the people at CQ Press, who were ready to take a chance on a different kind of textbook. In particular, we would like to thank Charisse Kiino, who was the first to get excited about what we had in mind; Talia Greenberg, who copy edited the text; Gwenda Larsen, who oversaw production; and Dwain Smith and Jerry Orvedahl, who worked with us along the way and helped create online modules that we believe instructors and students will actually want to use.

Debora Halpern Wenger
Deborah Potter

1 THE MULTIMEDIA MIND-SET

The way news is gathered and delivered is evolving just as rapidly as audience expectations, technological changes and job descriptions for journalists. In this chapter, we'll take a look at what it means to be a journalist today and why you'll need to quickly develop your own multimedia mind-set.

It's 6:30 a.m. and your alarm is buzzing. You grab your phone and start scrolling through your Facebook live feed to see what's new in the world. If you have time, you reach for the TV remote to catch part of your favorite morning newscast. On the drive to work or school, you listen to a little radio news. While sitting at your computer, an alert comes in on an important breaking story, so you check out your favorite news website to get more information. On your way to the vending machines, a headline in a newspaper lying on the table catches your eye and you pick it up to scan the story. Heading out for an appointment, you notice a tweet on your phone about the latest developments on that story you heard about earlier.

It's a typical day in the life of a modern news consumer. But as a journalist, how do you deal with this multitasking, multiplatform, multiple-personality media world?

It's a challenge for many working journalists because they have spent a great deal of time learning how to tell stories to those news consumers using just one form of communication. But it's an incredibly exciting time to begin a career in the field because you now have more ways than ever to tell important stories. Learning to be an effective journalist in a multiplatform world requires an understanding of the ways in which today's news audiences are using media, as well as a thorough grounding in the story-telling tools and techniques available to you when you're working across platforms.

MULTIMEDIA BASICS

It's hard to spend any time studying journalism without reading or hearing the following terms—*multimedia, convergence, cross-platform* or *multiplatform journalism*. Continual advances in communications technology have forced journalists to come up with a new language to describe their storytelling. For the most part, this text will use the terms

KNOW AND TELL

A NEW TYPE OF JOURNALIST

Jacqueline Ingles got a job right out of school working as a multiplatform backpack political cor-respondent for MTV in conjunction with the Asso-ciated Press. She covered the 2008 presidential election in Illinois from a youth perspective. After a year as a one-woman-band reporter for WCTV, operating their Valdosta, Ga., bureau, Ingles was hired as a multiplatform reporter for KXAN, the NBC affiliate in Austin, Texas, where she pro-duces content for the Web, television and print daily.

"I am on continuous deadline," Ingles says. "Between the hours of 8 a.m. and 7 p.m., I am a reporter. Everything else, including personal mat-ters, is put on hold. My typical day involves start-ing the morning reading multiple newspapers

Source: Photo courtesy of Jacqueline Ingles.

both online and in print. Then I head into a morning meeting, typically via phone from my car or some random location, and pitch three story ideas for the day. By noon, I am

interchangeably to describe the practice of "communicating complementary information on more than one media platform."

A New Approach

If a television reporter and photographer go out to cover a high school football game, they might use live blogging software to report on the game as it plays out or post a few game updates on Twitter. They'll probably shoot far more video of the game and gather a great deal more information than they'll need to tell their story on the 11:00 news, so they may post online some of the unused video clips and key statistics from the game. That's

expected to have a preliminary Web script posted online including at least a few pictures. I usually write my script using my Droid phone and take pictures with my phone too. Once I post, I get back to my story, interviewing, shooting b-roll and shooting my own standup. Depending on the location of my story, I either head to the bureau or main station to edit. If those locations are not close, I upload my clips in the car to my laptop, log, track, write and edit, all while sitting in the driver's seat. Then I either FTP my work, feed it in or upload it to the server from a computer at the main station. Before the story airs, I must have a new version of the story with extended interviews and more information posted online. I commonly add more photos that I took throughout the day as well.

"Back in school, turning a story on deadline seemed like tackling a bear," Ingles says. "Admittedly, I often cried when I was first learning how to edit and shoot. I thought, will I ever be able to do this job? Many times in graduate school, my pieces were so bad, they didn't even make air! Despite being extremely discouraged at times, I forged on and took one day at a time. Fast-forward almost four years and my abilities as a multiplatform reporter shock me. What I can now accomplish with a computer and camera solo in the field is not something that seemed possible when I first started."

Ingles says she doesn't know where she'll be in two years, five years or two decades from now, but she does plan on being a journalist, learning new skills and new ways of telling important stories along the way.

multimedia journalism. They would be using more than one media platform—both television and the Web—and the information they broadcast would be complemented by the unique, additional information posted online or in various social media. The fact that multimedia allow you to communicate more information in new and different ways gets many journalists jazzed about the concept, whether they've been in the business for years or are just starting out.

A cross-platform journalist is one who is able to work effectively in more than one medium. For example, some television reporters regularly file separate stories for their stations' websites, and some print journalists appear regularly on television news programs because they communicate so well through the broadcast platform. All of these journalists are multimedia journalists.

Audience First

Most news consumers aren't content to get their news and information in one form—the same individual may routinely use television, print and online sources to get information from newscasts, podcasts, articles and social media. In fact, according to 2005 research from the Center for Media Design at Ball State University in Muncie, Ind., Americans spent 69 percent of their waking moments using some form of media, from radio to computers to magazines or books. And nearly a third of the time, they were media multitasking, using two or more forms of media at once.[1] Now that media multitasking trend has grown. In 2010 a Nielsen Company study found that nearly 60 percent of Americans surf the Web while watching TV.[2]

Though it's always been important for journalists to keep the audience top of mind, it's now even more critical because the platform used to deliver the news will affect what the audience gets out of it. As you begin to work on any story, you should be asking yourself what the best way is to deliver the information, what questions the audience will have and what answers you can provide.

Let's say there is major flooding in your community. Some may first learn about the rising waters from social media, but many won't stop there. Some people will tune in to a television newscast to see the impact of the flooding or how some of the worst-hit neighborhoods are being affected, as well as the weather forecast for the next few hours. At the same time, the online audience may be logging on to read and add their own comments to a live blog detailing what roads are currently blocked off or which shelters take pets and which don't. The audience for the

GO ONLINE

Module 1: Check out examples of strong multimedia reporting; decide what worked and what could have been better.

TABLE 1.1 MEDIA MULTITASKING ████████████████

Persons 2+ watching TV and using the Internet simultaneously at least once per month at home

	Dec. 2009	June 2009	Dec. 2008	% difference year to year
% of persons using TV/Internet simultaneously	59.0	56.9	57.5	2.7
Estimated number of persons using TV/Internet simultaneously	134,056	128,047	128,167	4.6
Time spent simultaneously using TV/Internet per person in hours:minutes	3:30	2:39	2:36	34.5
Average % of TV time panelists spent also using the Internet	3.1	2.7	2.4	29.7
Average % of Internet time panelists spent also using TV	34.0	27.9	29.9	13.9

People are multitasking with multimedia more than ever these days. Researchers at the Nielsen Company found that just under 60 percent of people use television at the same time they are surfing the Web.

Source: The Nielsen Company, http://blog.nielsen.com/nielsenwire/online_mobile/three-screen-report-q409. Used by permission.

████████████████

next day's paper will likely be looking for the big picture—did emergency preparation pay off, or how did this latest flooding compare with previous floods? Multimedia journalists will be thinking about all of these possibilities as they work on their individual stories; they will look for opportunities to use the tools of multimedia to provide many different pieces of information to several different audiences on multiple media platforms.

MEDIA ON DEMAND

In addition to having access to multiple news delivery systems, we are now also living in an "on demand" world. News consumers expect to get information when and how they want it—not on a timetable set by a television station or a newspaper operation. For a journalist, that means getting into a 24/7 mind-set. Instead of focusing all of your attention on one story that will air at 6 p.m. or appear above the fold in tomorrow's newspaper, you need to be thinking about the audience that's out there right now, hungry for information as soon as it has been verified and vetted.

It is quite likely that you will work—or perhaps already work—for a newsroom that breaks stories on the Web or sends breaking news directly to people using mobile devices first, and then worries about traditional content delivery platforms such as television or print. In the flooding example above, the multimedia journalist may first focus on getting the latest information out on Twitter or Facebook before writing a brief text version of the story to be posted online along with raw video. All that would happen before he or she begins putting together a more traditional TV story for the 5:00 news.

GO ONLINE

Module 1: Log your daily media use and track your multimedia multitasking.

The Multimedia Industry

More and more communications companies are taking a "get the consumers wherever they are" approach to providing information and content. ESPN, for example, is a multimedia powerhouse. From its cable TV channels to its print magazine to its website, the company has become synonymous with sports information by reaching out to sports consumers wherever they can be found.

The Food Network is another big multimedia player. What started out as a cable TV channel has expanded to the Web and even to the Wii game system. In 2009 the company released a video game called "Cook or Be Cooked." The Food Network also publishes a successful print magazine, hosts a recipe aggregator site called Food.com and has about a half-million fans on Facebook.

News organizations are also taking advantage of multimedia, of course. At Hearst Television, one of the ten biggest broadcast news companies in the United States, vice president for news Brian Bacco says his company is no longer focused on TV but also on the Web and cell phones. "Our audience is mobile, our audience wants their information now and wants it on three screens," Bacco says. "We need to deliver it on every one; we have to have that skills set."

WIBW-TV in Topeka, Kan., has a wide reach—and not just over the air. The station is a longtime market leader, but general manager Jim Ogle, a former news director, doesn't just want to own the television ratings. He wants to dominate every other platform WIBW is on, so he's pushed the station's presence on the Web and on social media. Everyone on staff posts to Facebook, Twitter and WIBW.com; most of them blog on the site as well. "It's a way of building rabid fans for the operation," Ogle says.

WFLA in Tampa, Fla., is one of many news organizations around the country that produces content specifically for a website. These websites provide a mix of top stories, weather, breaking news, blogs and interactivity that quickly bring viewers up to date all day long.

Source: TBO.com (accessed June 21, 2010).

Multimedia Journalists

Increasingly, strong news organizations are looking to hire journalists who fully understand this need to give consumers more ways to access information and more control over how they do it. The Associated Press (AP), for example, now has what it calls "1-2-3-4 filing." First comes a tweetable headline, then a brief synopsis of the story being filed, then the complete story, then an analytical and forward-looking piece.[3] The 140-character limit of

KNOW AND TELL

THE PROCESS OF NEWS

Technology has changed everything about the news business, from the way it's delivered to the way journalists do their jobs. Television reporters used to spend most of their day producing a complete package for the main newscast, with a live shot or two thrown in along the way. Not anymore.

"In today's world of journalism, you simply have to make 30 hours fit into a 24-hour day," says WIBW-TV anchor Melissa Brunner. "We still need to put a quality product on the air, but you also must incorporate social media and your website in general into your daily routine."

The station's general manager, Jim Ogle, expects everyone on the news staff to share information on stories all day long. "We've adapted to a world where people want to know where things stand," Ogle says. "It's not about that you produced a great Web piece and a great television piece. That's at the end of a process that you start sharing from the very beginning."

Source: Photo courtesy of the authors.

Brunner says that philosophy has changed everything in the newsroom. "When breaking news happens, you can't simply send a crew out the door and forget it," she says. "You must get the crew out the door, Tweet/Facebook the information, send a text alert, send a desktop alert and get a story on the website."

Constant sharing carries some risks, of course. Information the station puts out early on may turn out to be wrong. "That's all part of the process," Ogle says. "We acknowledge to people there's new information that changes things."

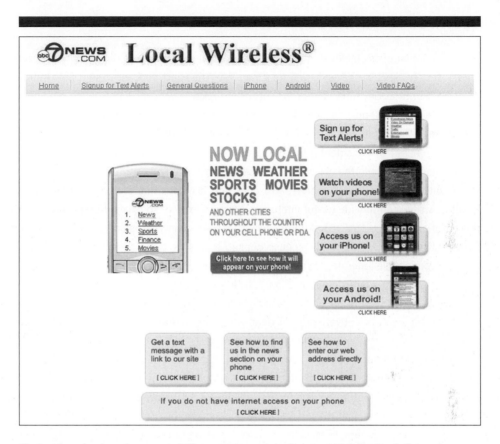

Technology is changing news delivery systems too. As more people stay informed through mobile devices, journalists like those at ABC7 in San Francisco must adjust to more immediate deadlines and develop new storytelling forms.

Source: KGO-TV/DT, ABC7, in San Francisco, Oakland and San Jose, Calif., http://cf.localwireless.com/wireless/signup.cfm?sid=22 (accessed July 8, 2010).

Twitter obviously requires a much different type of writing than the "think" piece at the end of the day.

So news organizations like AP want journalists who understand how the gathering and presentation of content change as the distribution of that content differs. Their writers have to know how to change their styles, depending on whether they are writing the Tweet or the Web version or the long-form story that may appear in local newspapers. In other words, as the medium changes, the best journalists will be versatile enough to know how the message should change as well.

TECHNOLOGY CHANGES CONTENT

Media are evolving so quickly that within a few years we'll probably be delivering news and information in ways we haven't even imagined yet. The word *podcast* wasn't in anyone's vocabulary until 2004; within a year, thousands of podcasts were available online. And who could have imagined how quickly Twitter would take off as a newsgathering and dissemination tool following its use in the 2009 Iranian election protests?

The concept of considering the best way to present content based on the delivery method goes far beyond the obvious differences, such as the fact that television news uses sound and video and a printed newspaper does not. It means that journalists must think about how they can provide useful information to people in all sorts of different ways. The presentation will obviously be different for a podcast, a newspaper article or an online story, and so will the content, because consumers using those media want different things. A podcast listener might want a headline summary with sound bites, a newspaper reader might want more details and an online news consumer might want to see the documents that underpin the story. Journalists have to know what elements they have to collect so they can effectively present news and information to consumers in all these media.

In addition, this means that the best multimedia journalists will stay on top of changes in communications technology. For example, the increase in the number of people with high-speed Internet connections is at least partly responsible for changing the thinking about the use of video and elaborate graphics online. Before high-speed connections were common, many news organizations hesitated to post multiple video clips and to create high-level, interactive graphics because the download time for people on dial-up connections made those features nearly impossible to use. Even more recently, the explosion in the number of people with mobile communication devices—from cell phones to BlackBerries to the iPad—has journalists rethinking the way they handle breaking news. These are just a few examples of the ways in which the development and increasing use of new technologies are having an impact on the way journalists do their jobs. We'll talk more about this phenomenon in Chapter 12.

Good Journalism Matters

Journalism is ripe with opportunity for storytellers, and learning how to take a multimedia approach to stories gives you the potential to reach a more diverse group of people with more important news and information.

Still, it's important to remember that good journalism skills are universal—they apply to all platforms. As the technology used to manage the content becomes easier to navigate, multimedia journalism is likely to become less about knowing how to post a story or stream a piece of video and more about the skills it takes to gather and present information that is relevant and compelling to an audience—regardless of whether that audience is watching, reading or interacting with the story. As Mike Wendland, who has covered technology for both the Detroit Free Press and NBC, puts it, "Our skill set as storytellers will be more in demand than ever."

In addition, adherence to journalism's best practices and ethical codes is also essential. As the speed increases and the methods of dissemination vary, your journalism must be sounder than ever. Your reputation and that of your news organization are only as strong as your credibility, so just because technology allows you to do something does not mean it's something you should do. For example, you may be able to post a horrific 9-1-1 tape on the Web, but you should still ask yourself about the journalistic purpose of posting that audio before taking advantage of the option.

The Power of Multimedia

Never before have journalists had so many storytelling tools with which to work. When you can take advantage of broadcast's powerful sound and imagery, print's depth and detail and online media's interactivity, you have the potential to reach more people with more of an impact. The key for today's journalists is to find a way to report information in the medium that works best for each individual news consumer.

In the most progressive newsrooms, journalists have the potential to do a better job of telling stories because they can now show, tell and invite the audience to interact with the information. For the rest of this chapter, we'll explore what broadcast, print and online media do best to give you the foundation you'll need to develop powerful multimedia stories.

GO ONLINE

Ongoing Story Module: Read the assignment and begin thinking about the reporting you could do for this multimedia story.

THE BEST OF BROADCAST

Ask people where they spent the most time learning about the impact of the 2010 earthquake in Haiti and they will likely mention watching television news. According to a study done by the Pew Research Center for the People & the Press, 69 percent

Some of the best broadcast journalism allows the audience to share in the experience of others. In a story about a home explosion and fire in Baltimore, Md., WBFF-TV viewers could hear and see for themselves how neighbors reacted.

Source: Photo courtesy of WBFF-TV.

of people it polled were primarily following the Haiti disaster on television.[4] TV technology allows broadcast journalists to present history as it happens. Television journalists can combine words, sound and pictures to create a sense of being there for the viewer. A great broadcast storyteller can make you feel like you know the person being interviewed, that you have been to the location being showcased or were at the event yourself. So when you begin to plan a multimedia story, you need to keep the strengths of broadcast journalism in mind.

On the Scene

Television news is able to let viewers watch events as they occur or to report on them within minutes, or even seconds, after they happen. Though social media and the Web allow for even greater immediacy at times, live trucks, satellite uplinks and cell phones allow television news crews to broadcast directly from the scene of breaking news events, showing viewers how big a fire is or taking them inside a courtroom to hear a judge read out a verdict in real time. Online, the live viewing experience can sometimes be erratic. Depending on connection issues, video can be jerky or fail to load altogether. For now, television generally provides the best live viewing experience to the greatest number of American news consumers.

For example, when the town of Austin, Minn., was inundated with several feet of water, anchor Pete Hjelmstad donned his hip waders and stood live in the middle of a flooded street to show viewers of KIMT-TV in Mason City, Iowa, exactly how serious the situation was in some parts of the city. From that vantage point, he acted as a narrator over live pictures of people trying to break into second-floor windows of their own businesses to salvage what little they could.

But this ability to disseminate information instantly or extremely quickly comes with risks. It is always better to be right than first and wrong, so "going live" or "getting on the air with the information" should be secondary to checking the facts.

Impact of Visuals and Emotion

Great print journalists are able to convey emotion and create pictures in the reader's mind through their writing, but broadcast journalists have an edge when it comes to this kind of reporting. Through the use of video, broadcasters can actually let viewers hear the mother's plea or see how swollen the river is at flood stage. TV journalists must still use words effectively to explain or supplement the video, but there is no substitute for great pictures combined with strong writing.

WBBH-TV in Ft. Myers, Fla., covered vast brush fires that were eating up thousands of acres in Collier County, a key part of the station's coverage area. In one story, a reporter-photographer showed the impact of the fire on a family-owned dog kennel. In his video we saw flames just a few yards away from the dogs and their cages as the owner of the kennel started opening the cage doors and urging the dogs to get out and run. The video of her frantically trying to save the animals and calling out, "Get out of here, go, go!" was one of the most powerful moments in the newscast—one that likely affected viewers in a way that few other stories did that day.

Again, this ability comes with responsibility. There will be pictures that are too graphic to use and sound that's too disturbing to hear. For example, some stations have policies against airing "moment of death" video or audio. If they get pictures of a fatal car crash as it's occurring or if officials release a 9-1-1 recording of a woman being beaten to death, these stations refuse to air the content. They believe the story can still be told without these potentially disturbing elements. Good journalists must always weigh the storytelling benefit against any potential harm the story might cause. We'll talk more about the ethical use of visuals in Chapter 11.

Audience Connection

Part of the reason why broadcast news has been so successful is that it is the medium in which a person is actually "telling" a story to the audience. Viewers make a personal connection with anchors and reporters. That may be one reason why so many newscasts begin or end with the statement, "Thank you for watching." Broadcasters realize that many people in the audience do feel as if they are inviting the newscasters into their homes, and that invitation comes with certain expectations.

"When is the last time a newspaper thanked its readers?" asks Michele Godard, general manager at KALB-TV in Alexandria, La. "As subtle as this seems, it works its way into viewers' mind[s], and they feel a greater stake in our lives."

Before she became the boss, Godard was one of the station's primary anchors, and her experience convinced her that television stations have an enhanced personal connection with the viewers. "When I was the evening news anchor I was pregnant twice," Godard says. "Do you know people still stop me in the street and sigh when they see how big my kids are? They chart their lives by the ups and downs of ours." For Godard, the connection works both ways. "I can tell you that as a result of the very personal connection I feel with our viewers I tend to take the information we provide more seriously," she says. "When our anchors read a story about a murder, I immediately wonder who the person was. Did that man or woman ever stop me in the store and ask about my children? It drives me to be more vigilant."

Social media outlets such as Facebook, Twitter and YouTube, and online interactivity such as the comments section or the reader ranking options following many stories, have made it easer for newspapers and online news organizations to create audience connections as well. But good television newscasts continue to provide the audience with important information presented in a compelling manner. That can include anchors and reporters who are good communicators, graphics that help better explain the stories and even music that helps set the mood or tone of a story.

THE POWER OF PRINT

Newspapers have a long and illustrious history in the United States. When the framers of the U.S. Constitution included the guarantee of press freedom, they understood that the dominant news medium of the time—newspapers—played a fundamental role in preserving the country's democracy. But newspapers are in crisis in America—advertising dollars and readership are declining, and that's translating into fewer newspaper jobs.

Even so, newspapers still cover local communities in far more depth than any other medium. The Project for Excellence in Journalism conducted a study in 2010 that looked at all the local news outlets in Baltimore, Md., for one week. It found that newspapers accounted for 48 percent of the original reporting in the market, followed by local TV with a little more than 30 percent.[5]

Newspapers also do much of the great investigative reporting in this country, and some of that may be attributed to the strengths of the medium. As you work on planning your multimedia stories, you'll want to remember the following print attributes.

Depth

In general, most newspaper articles are longer than the broadcast version of the same story. For example, "CBS Evening News" once did a story about a new treatment for asthma

In 2009 Seattle's Post-Intelligencer newspaper became an online-only publication. Commuters now have fewer choices; the Seattle Times is the city's only major daily printed newspaper. According to the Newspaper Association of America, the total number of daily newspapers nationwide has been dropping since at least 1980.

Source: AP Photo/Cheryl Hatch.

sufferers. The Washington Post reported the same story the next day. The CBS News story was approximately 2:00 long. When, in an experiment, the Washington Post's story was read aloud by a local TV news anchor, it was more than twice (4:40) as long. The essential elements of the story were reported by both news organizations, but the Washington Post's story included more background on the Food and Drug Administration's approval process for the drug, more information about how much the drug might cost and why it might not be right for everyone. The added depth would have made the story particularly relevant to someone considering using the drug.

Detail

Though similar to what we've outlined above, detail can also simply mean adding more specifics. For example, many print stories will include the age of a subject, the middle initial of an interviewee and specific numbers instead of a rounded figure. This additional detail can help in terms of ensuring accuracy and understanding. If someone's name is Peter Smith, then reporting on "Peter E. Smith, 52, of Mountain Lake, Va." makes it far less likely that someone will think the story refers to 19-year-old Peter W. Smith who lives in Richmond.

Since newspapers can't rely on video to convey information, television journalists writing print stories must be sure to incorporate significant details from the video into the text. Using the example of the fire threatening the kennel in Florida, the print version of the story might have included a paragraph like this:

> With the flames less than 10 yards away from the dogs in their kennels, Atwell started unlocking the cage doors one by one. With tears streaming down her face and a voice hoarse from inhaling smoke, Atwell pulled the dogs out, pointed them away from the fire and shouted, "Get out of here, go, go!"

Without video to help set the scene, the writer for print must be more specific about the nearness of the fire and must describe what the subject is doing and how she looks and sounds in order for the reader to fully experience the drama of the moment.

The risk of including too much depth and detail is that you bog the story down or make it boring and unreadable, but most television journalists writing newspaper stories easily avoid that trap.

Permanence and Portability

Ask avid newspaper readers why they like newspapers and many will mention the fact that they can take the paper with them wherever they go. The portability and permanence of a newspaper allow them to reread something that they didn't get the first time or to save it for later reference. This unique characteristic is important for those planning multimedia stories—anything that you think the audience may want to hold on to for any length of time might best be presented in print.

For example, the Sarasota Herald-Tribune, like many newspapers in the coastal areas of the United States, prints an annual hurricane guide for readers. These guides feature everything from evacuation routes to shelter locations to tips for protecting homes from high wind damage. If the lights go out and the TV and computer fail, readers can refer to their copies of the guide to get vital emergency information.

However, both permanence and portability are becoming part of the online experience—when you can routinely download and save content to a PDA or other device, permanence and portability may no longer be just newspaper strengths.

THE ORIGINALITY OF ONLINE

According to the Pew Research Center for the People & the Press, the number of people who go online for news three or more days a week stood at 46 percent in 2010, up from 37 percent in 2008. Looking at Figure 1.1, you'll notice it's the only news medium that has been consistently growing audience.[6]

Most likely when you turn to the Web for information, you go in search of something specific. You may choose to get news online because you don't want to wait for the nightly TV news or for the next day's paper. According to Pew, online news is valued most for headlines and convenience, not detailed, in-depth reporting. This "getting the information you want when you want it" is one of three key strengths of online journalism.

On Demand

With other media, the news consumer is essentially at the mercy of those who select what information to air or publish and when. In the online world, if the information is posted

FIGURE 1.1. TRENDS IN REGULAR USE OF NEWS SOURCES

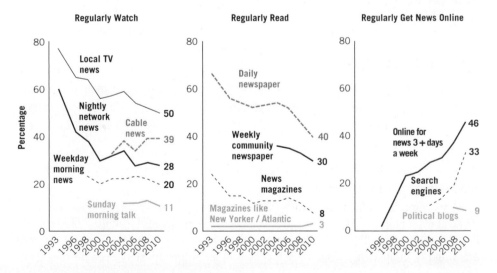

Source: "Americans Spending More Time Following the News," Pew Research Center for the People & the Press, September 12, 2010, http://people-press.org/report/?pageid=1792. © 2010 Pew Research Center for the People & the Press. Reprinted by permission.

somewhere, the savvy Internet user can usually find it. Even if the information will be included in a broadcast and in the newspaper eventually, if it's also online the user does not have to wait to access the information on someone else's timetable.

CBS News, for example, streams stories from its nightly newscast on the Web to gain viewers who can't or don't want to watch the broadcast during the time slots it airs on television. Like many other news outlets, CBS is trying to capture audience whenever it is available.

The Web also provides access to more information than could ever be aired in a single television program or published in a single newspaper. The "bottomless news hole" of the Web creates an opportunity to satisfy news consumers who want more than what the traditional media can offer.

Interactivity

Online media give journalists the opportunity to ask the audience to do more than passively read or watch a story—online users can be invited to explore information on their own, add perspectives to the storytelling or literally try something for themselves. This may be the real key to making multimedia stories powerful. For example, you may be working on a story about restaurants that don't meet state health standards. You will only be able to include a limited number of restaurants in your broadcast or print story, but if you add an online component, you can give users access to the entire restaurant report database so they can search for their favorite restaurants' ratings on their own. You could ask users to add their own restaurant horror stories or invite customer reviews of popular restaurants. If you have a creative online production team, you might work with the health department to create an interactive inspection game. The game might use a series of photos of a typical restaurant kitchen and ask users to spot the violations that health inspectors have set up for the purpose of this teaching tool.

Innovation

As you can see, the online medium allows us to combine the best of print and broadcast in innovative ways. Often journalists who don't understand the technical side of the Web are afraid to brainstorm the online component of a multimedia story because they don't know what's possible. The secret is to think from an audience perspective: How can I present the information in a way that's most helpful to the user's understanding? How can I make exploring this issue fun for the user? How can I find out what the user already knows or wants to know about this story?

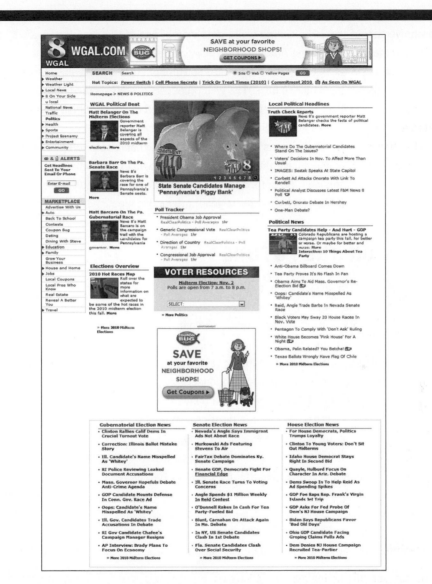

At WGAL in Lancaster, Pa., important stories are routinely enhanced online. During midterm elections, WGAL posted scores of text and video stories on local and statewide races, provided links to relevant election polling results, aggregated political coverage from other news sources and created an interactive element to help users find the information they needed to vote on Election Day.

Source: WGAL in Lancaster, Pa., www.wgal.com/wgalpolitics/index.html (accessed October 16, 2010).

When the Richmond Times-Dispatch was working on content to help commemorate the anniversary of the 1965 Selma civil rights march, one of the reporters involved discovered something called the Alabama Literacy Test. Blacks in Alabama had to take the test in order to vote, but the questions were so difficult that almost no one—white or black—would have been able to pass. The Web producers posted a series of the test questions, which helped people understand the type of discrimination that blacks were facing at the time.

GO ONLINE

Module 1: Test what you know about the strengths of each medium with our interactive game.

Sometimes you will want to create completely unique content but may not have the technical support to do exactly what you want. Even so, you'll be surprised how much you can accomplish if you can get people excited about a good, interactive idea.

FOCUS ON THE FUTURE

Although the news media are going through a period of rapid change and evolution, change itself is not new and should not be seen as a threat for journalists. It's important to remember that new media seldom, if ever, replace the old. We still read books, we still listen to the radio and we certainly still watch television; however, it's indisputable that most news media are trying to adapt to the changing technologies and a changing news consumer culture that is more fractured than ever. No longer can you count on the fact that a majority of adults in the United States will read a daily newspaper, and no longer can you be sure that the 6:00 newscast will be the most critical broadcast of the day. What you can be sure of is that journalists who are skilled in the journalism basics—researching, interviewing, writing and ethics—will be able to succeed in a changing media environment if they are willing to embrace the idea that it's the story that matters.

Media General, Inc., has been a key player in the area of multimedia journalism for more than a decade. Dan Bradley, vice president and general manager of WCMH, the company's TV station in Columbus, Ohio, embraced multimedia from the start.

"Journalists have to get over the idea that it's 'their story,'" Bradley says. "The story belongs to the audience and once reporters accept that, it doesn't seem to matter whether the story is published on the air, online or in print."

What Bradley and many other news managers are looking for are journalists who want to tell stories—regardless of platform. And those journalists who are already adept at telling stories in more than one medium are more likely to get jobs or to move up. Mike McMearty, news director at WTOP Radio in Washington, D.C., says, "If I have two candidates, each with the same skills and experience, but one of them is comfortable writing and working on the Web and one is not, I'm going to hire the one who knows the Web."

And beyond enhancing your ability to get a job in broadcast or print, learning about multimedia journalism may also jump-start a career for you in online journalism itself. In a study of all the jobs posted by the top TV and newspaper companies in the United States at the end of 2009, just under 6 percent of the positions available were for online-only jobs.

In addition to sites attached to traditional mainstream news organizations, jobs are available at nonprofit sites like ProPublica, which promotes investigative journalism, or online-only sites such as the Huffington Post, which is billed as an outlet for news from a liberal perspective. Sometimes journalists with a passion establish their own sites—for example, Brian Storm, who created MediaStorm.com, a website to showcase innovative multimedia storytelling.

As the Web audience grows, it's expected that Web staffs will grow as well, creating new opportunities for online producers, Web-only reporters, editors and videographers. Caroline Little is the former chief executive officer and publisher of Washingtonpost. Newsweek Interactive (WPNI), which operated washingtonpost.com, newsweek.com, Slate and Budget Travel Online. Little says journalism has fundamentally changed: "The method, the reach and the scope of how we communicate will never be the same." Today's journalists must remember that though the emphasis on solid newsgathering and story-telling skills remains, the future brings new challenges and new opportunities.

TAKING IT HOME

It is essential for today's journalists to understand how the audience is accessing and using news and information now, as well as the ways in which the message must change as the medium changes. Capitalizing on the strengths of each media platform available to you will make you a more effective storyteller and will help ensure that your audiences get the information they need.

This text is about preparing you for jobs that are changing and jobs that have not yet even been envisioned.

"With industry transformation and emergence of new technology, multimedia is now included in all of our job descriptions," says Virgil Smith, who heads up recruiting for Gannett. "We want multimedia journalists with solid basics—the ability to write, inquisitiveness, people who want to dig deeper, who know how to use the tools with an understanding of how their information will be used on multiple platforms."

We hope this text will help you do it all.

TALKING POINTS

1. Log on to the Pew Research Center for the People & the Press (http://people-press .org) and check out the latest research on how people are using news media. What implications does the research have on the way journalists are or should be doing their jobs? Pay particular attention to the demographic breakdowns for media use. What do the data suggest to you in terms of serving a diverse audience?

2. For one 24-hour period, track your news media usage. How much time are you spending with each medium? Are there stories that you saw mentioned on more than one platform? Are there stories that were unique to one platform? Did the news organization involved do anything specific to capitalize on the power of its medium?

3. Find a good multimedia storytelling example. Whether it's a broadcast story with a Web companion piece, or a print article that's enhanced online or a story that uses some other combination of media platforms, analyze how the journalists involved are leveraging the platforms included in the presentation.

ONLINE LEARNING MODULE 1

Activate or buy this chapter's online learning module at journalism.cqpress.com to get access to:

- SKILL BUILDING: Play our "Pick the Platform" game to test your knowledge of the strengths of each media platform in a fun and interactive way.

- DISCOVER: See examples of multimedia reporting and learn more about the tools used to produce the stories.

- EXPLORE: Learn more about current digital media issues and trends affecting journalists and their newsrooms.

- A template to log your media usage to see how much multimedia multitasking you do each day.

- A digital version of this chapter's text in full color with active links.

Also, begin your work on the ONGOING STORY MODULE. Start developing a multi-media mind-set by looking at the assignment and thinking about how you would report the story for multiple platforms.

2 FINDING THE STORY

If you're interested in the news business, you should be curious about the world around you and passionate about learning something new every day. Those traits are essential to generate story ideas, and the ability to find stories is one of the most valuable skills you can bring to any newsroom, no matter what your job. In this chapter, you'll learn how to find and develop better story ideas, gather useful background and research quickly, discover fresh sources and conduct better interviews, with an eye toward producing stories in a variety of media.

Police and fire scanners squawk loudly at the assignment desk as the editor monitors social media feeds. There's a steady stream of incoming phone calls and e-mails with news tips, press releases and announcements of scheduled events. The computer system chimes when the wire services file updates. In a typical broadcast, print or online newsroom, most of the day's stories will come from sources like these. But the scanners, e-mails and wires only provide reporters with a starting point.

Good reporters do much more than just get the facts, check them for accuracy and pass them along. It takes clear thinking and hard work to produce a television story worth watching, a print or online story that's a compelling read or an interactive element that helps the audience understand the story better. And in today's newsrooms, reporters may be asked to do all three.

It sounds like a lot of work to report for multiple media, but reporter Mark Fagan of the Lawrence Journal-World in Lawrence, Kan., says it's fun and rewarding. He often reports for the newspaper, a co-owned cable TV news operation and their websites. "You get a chance to tell your story to more people," he says. Fagan believes all journalists can succeed in any medium if they just know how to report.

STORY IDEAS

For years, journalists have based a story's news value on such factors as timeliness, impact, proximity, controversy, prominence and oddity. Those are good guidelines, but they don't really help you find newsworthy stories that aren't on the daybook, on the Web or in the newspaper. You have to get out of the newsroom, fine-tune your powers of observation and ask new questions to unearth the stories others may miss. The payoff is well worth the investment. "There are so many stories out there, you won't live long enough to do them all," says photojournalist John Goheen, who's done hundreds of stories for CBS and NBC, as well as local stations.

Cultivate Curiosity

The dictionary defines curiosity as "a desire to know," and it's an essential quality for journalists. Good journalists are a lot like 4-year-olds, always asking "why?" and "how come?" "Curiosity may be innate but it can be cultivated," says TV news manager Scott Libin. "It's a skill that improves with practice."

Cultivate your curiosity by taking nothing for granted. Ask why things work the way they do or how something got its name; you'll often find there's a story just waiting to be told. In fact, WTSP-TV in St. Petersburg, Fla., turned that idea into a successful morning news feature series, "Why Do They Call It That?," exploring how local towns, rivers, bridges and parks got their names.

If something strikes you as interesting or unexpected, try to learn more about it. That's what a Dallas reporter did when he noticed activity at a construction site on the way to work each day. The answers to his questions turned into a story about the phenomenal growth of megachurches.

Look and Listen

Pulitzer Prize–winning reporter Jim Schaefer advises journalists to "step away from the computer." He tries to take a walk every afternoon just to see what's going on. "The point is to be visible," Schaefer says. "You can be the smoothest talker, the funniest joker or the best-looking reporter in town. But the reporter who gets the tip, I think, is the reporter seen the most."[1]

Keep your eyes and ears open for what's important or unusual in your community. What are people talking about at the gym, the grocery store or the coffee shop? What do you notice on your way to school or work? Have you tried taking a different route and really looking around? Get outside your comfort zone and visit communities that are different from the one you live in to find stories that other reporters may have missed. "If we take the time when we're on a field trip with our kids or we're out to dinner with our husband and we are absorbing what people around us are caring about or talking about, that's where good ideas for feature stories come from," says Lane DeGregory, a reporter for the St. Petersburg Times. "That's how we reflect our community, not just what editors assign us to do."[2]

Former news director Jim Garrott once did a simple exercise to show his staff at WEEK-TV in Peoria, Ill., how to find stories. He took an hour, went home and had dinner, and then walked his daughter around the block. In that time he came up with 37 story ideas—including a story about downtown development and another about the growing popularity of home sales "by owner."

Of course, you'll also need to read a lot to spot good story ideas. Go beyond the obvious newspapers, magazines and news websites. Find and follow local Twitter users who can tip you off to developments in your area. Bulletin boards, church announcements, zoning notices, club notes, classified ads, community websites and school newspapers also can be sources of story ideas. One reporter found a great TV feature by following up on a classified ad that read, "For Sale: Fainting Goats."

Follow Up and Plan Ahead

Look back and see what's happened since the last report on a particular subject, or look ahead to see what might happen next. Some journalists make a habit of looking back at stories that were in the news a year ago or five years ago to see if there's a follow-up to be done. Look for a fresh angle on a predictable story that everyone will do, like the tax-filing deadline or Veterans Day. Find someone in advance to build your story around, perhaps a person from a segment of your community that is not often heard from in the news like the poor or racial or ethnic minorities.

Don't give up if your story idea doesn't pan out immediately. If you think you've found a nugget of a story, keep working to develop it further. Good reporters often track ideas for weeks before their story begins to take shape. We'll talk more about how to do this in Chapter 4.

Develop Stories from Topics

It's important to understand that a story idea is not the same thing as a topic. "Let's take a look at gas prices" is a topic. It's a starting point, but it's too broad and general to suggest

GO ONLINE

Module 2: Try your hand at turning a topic into a story idea.

what direction the story will take, and it fails the "so what?" test. Because you're not asking a specific question about the topic, you're not likely to find any useful answers. "Let's find out if the price of gas has people driving more or less" is an idea. It may not turn out to be true, but it's something worth investigating.

To develop specific story ideas from a broad topic, try brainstorming with a few colleagues to see what questions you might want your story to answer. Check the tips on how to do that in the box below. Or sketch out a story map, as writing coach Don Murray suggests. Put the topic in the center of a piece of paper and see where it leads. There's a story map example on the facing page. Each new idea can lead you to a different angle on the story. You might decide to pursue one or two of these ideas for your main piece while you collect information about other angles for use in a graphic or sidebar, or a story for another platform.

TRADE TOOLS

BRAINSTORMING BASICS

Brainstorming is a time-tested, collaborative way of generating lots of ideas quickly. It works best in groups of no more than a dozen. One person should take on the role of facilitator to establish ground rules, write down ideas and make sure that everyone participates.

- Anything goes and no one can criticize anyone's ideas. Don't even discuss ideas until the brainstorming session is over.

- Keep a record of all ideas, ideally on a flip chart where everyone can see them. Don't edit or elaborate.

- Everyone should participate. If people don't want to speak up, they can write ideas down and hand them in.

- Think fast and work quickly. The more ideas the better.

- Wild and crazy ideas can spark productive ones, so feel free to propose anything and everything.

- Give people time to look over the list and build on what they see. "Hitchhiking" or "piggybacking" on others' ideas should be welcome.

FIGURE 2.1 STORY MAPPING

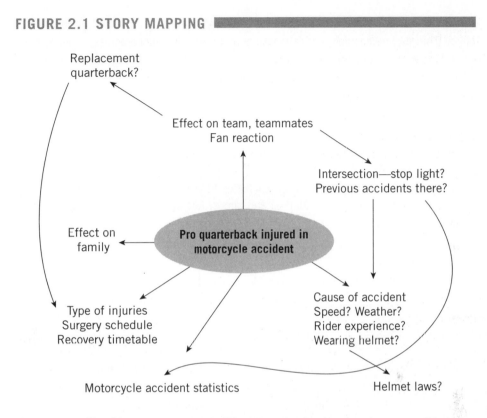

Replacement quarterback?

Effect on team, teammates
Fan reaction

Intersection—stop light?
Previous accidents there?

Effect on family

Pro quarterback injured in motorcycle accident

Type of injuries
Surgery schedule
Recovery timetable

Cause of accident
Speed? Weather?
Rider experience?
Wearing helmet?

Motorcycle accident statistics

Helmet laws?

A story map like this one can suggest different angles for reporters to pursue. Start with a news development—in this case, a motorcycle crash that injured a pro football quarterback—and see where it leads you.

STORY BUILDING BLOCKS

Every beginning reporter knows the basic questions any story must answer: the five Ws and an H. The reporter needs to know who did what, where and when, and if possible, why and how. But skilled reporters collect more than the essential facts so they can tell a compelling story. They dig deeper for the universal building blocks of great storytelling.

Character

Memorable stories feature people who are directly involved in the issue or situation, are directly affected by it or have a stake in the outcome. Good reporters build stories around strong characters whose experience illustrates a wider truth or the impact of an event or policy. They explore people's motivations in order to develop the characters in their stories. For example, the volunteer serving meals at the soup kitchen might have been homeless once herself. "Great stories begin and end with people," says former NBC correspondent John Larson, "not talking heads."

Place

Great stories transport the audience to give them a sense of what it was like at the scene. Experienced reporters know how to bring a scene to life by using all of their senses—not just looking and listening, but smelling and almost tasting a story so they can use their observations to bring it closer to the audience. They can tell us what burning rubber smells like after an accident, and how far away you can feel the heat of a fire. In some stories a place can become a kind of central character; in stories about conservation or climate change, for example, the main focus could be on a region like the Everglades or the Arctic.

Emotion

A story that speaks to a human emotion—whether it's anger, joy or empathy—is more engaging to the audience. Al Tompkins, broadcast and online group leader at the Poynter Institute, often says that people remember what they feel longer than what they hear. Good reporters look for the emotion in stories, even when it's not readily apparent. A dry sentencing hearing has significance to someone in the courtroom. You just have to find that person and let him or her talk.

Detail

Well-chosen details help the audience understand a story or character better. Reporters have to be keen observers so they can collect details that will enhance the story, not bog it down. It might be useful to know how long the city council members debated an ordinance, but only if they spent a particularly long or short amount of time doing it. On the other hand, it would be worth knowing that an American Indian doctor is the grandchild of a tribal healer in a story about the use of treatments that blend traditional and modern medicines.

Tension or Surprise

Stories should make the audience want to know what happens next, and how it will all come out in the end. Reporters should look for turning points and moments that illustrate

Imagine that you are covering this event. What might you notice, using all of your senses? Who might you want to interview? What questions would you ask?

Source: Photo by Flikr user Editor B, licensed by Creative Commons "Attribute" license, www.flickr.com/photos/editor/355146869 (accessed January 12, 2007).

the central theme of a story. A story about immigrants becoming U.S. citizens would likely explore these milestones along the way: deciding to leave their home country, learning English, passing the test and being sworn in. The surprise might be that many of the immigrants taking the oath on a given day are from the same country.

RESEARCH STRATEGIES

"Knowledge is the precursor of reporting," says reporter Byron Harris of WFAA-TV in Dallas, Texas. "I always felt I had to know more than anyone else to win." Harris is one of those reporters who is always researching. He reads everything he can get his hands on about all kinds of issues, from science to economics, looking for stories and learning as he goes. "The difference between reporters is energy," he says, "intellectual [energy] as well as pursuing the story."

GO ONLINE

Module 2: Watch two stories by Byron Harris and learn how he reported them.

It does take intellectual energy to think about stories in multiple layers, which is what you have to do if you're reporting the same story for different platforms. The need to collect material that plays to each medium's strengths makes research more important than ever for journalists today. The more you know about a story early on, the more efficient you can be in the field, whether you're shooting a TV story, gathering information for an interactive graphic or both.

Every story requires some research. On a breaking news story, you may not have time to do much more than get directions before you head out to the scene, but you'll probably need some background before you're done. On the other hand, if you're being sent to a news conference, you'll want to do some digging in advance so you can ask better questions and identify materials you'll want to bring back.

Let's imagine that you're covering the aftermath of a construction site accident that badly injured two workers. Here are just some of the avenues you could follow during the research phase.

Follow the Stakeholders

Find out who has a stake in the story—that is, who is most directly involved or affected. Think as broadly as possible at this point, because there's no way to know what information will turn out to be significant. In this case, you'd obviously want to know what companies were working on the site, who owns them and who owns the land, but you would also want to gather information about neighboring businesses. Learn all you can about the injured workers—were they union members or day laborers, experienced or new on the job? You'd definitely want to contact the workers' families about how the accident has affected them, and you'd follow up with their co-workers and any eyewitnesses who could shed additional light on what happened.

Seek Background and Data

Look into what may have happened in the past to see if you spot a cause or a pattern. You'd want to know whether there had been any safety problems at the site in the past, whether the construction company had been cited for safety violations at any other jobs, which permits the company had obtained and whether anyone had opposed granting those permits. You'd also want to know about any similar accidents that have happened in the past.

Search for related information that can help you put a story in context. How many construction workers are injured in accidents like this every year? Which government regulations—local, state or federal—cover construction sites? How many inspectors does the city have? How often do they inspect each site?

Consult Experts

Once you know some of the questions you need to have answered, find out who and where the subject experts are. In this case, you'd want to look for people who know the construction business and how it's regulated, such as current or former inspectors, builders, consultants or lawyers.

Look beyond the "usual suspects" for sources who will bring diverse perspectives to your story. For example, if the injured workers were not native English speakers, you might want an expert source who can talk about the particular challenges these workers face on the job.

RESEARCH TOOLS

The good news is that journalists today have more tools available to find the information they need quickly, thanks to computers and the Web. Many modern tools are just high-tech versions of the basic tools of the trade such as almanacs, encyclopedias, directories and maps, but the online versions can provide much more information faster than the hard copy ever could.

Clips and Scripts

One of the basic research tools journalists use has not changed in a century: previously published or broadcast stories are still a useful starting place. Most news organizations maintain extensive story archives; some make them available online free or for a fee. Many newsrooms subscribe to LexisNexis or Factiva, fee-based services that allow for exhaustive searches of newspaper and magazine archives.

Thanks to the Internet, it's also easier than it used to be to find and keep track of stories over time. Checking news.google.com or other news aggregators will give you the latest stories, and you can easily search for news about specific topics or sign up for an e-alert when new stories about that topic are added to the site.

Consider signing up for a social bookmarking site like Delicious or Digg so you can create your own online archive. But since many stories won't live on the Web forever, it's always a good idea to save copies of anything vital to your own hard drive or online storage service. Once you've saved electronic copies of stories, it's easy to find the information again by using a simple key word search.

Online Data

The Web makes it much easier to find databases and reports that in the past would have required a personal visit to a library or government building, or that might have been available only in Washington, D.C. If a plane crashes in your area, for example, you can quickly go online to the Federal Aviation Administration's website (www.faa.gov) and compare the plane's tail number with tail numbers in a government database of maintenance and repair problems. The information would be used in either a print or TV story, while an online version would include a link to the original data. The Census Bureau's website (www.census.gov) is a treasure trove of information that can help you quickly learn about a new community. But beware of depending too much on the Web. As technology guru Sree Sreenivasan of DNAinfo.com in New York puts it, "The Internet does not have all the answers. It has the clues to all the answers."

A reverse phone directory is another type of online database that works like a super-charged phone book. Not only can you find phone numbers and addresses by typing in someone's name, but you can also type in an address and pull up all the names of people or businesses nearby. This is particularly useful in breaking news situations when you are looking for people who might have pertinent information. Sites to try include www.switchboard.com and www.infospace.com.

Online "white pages" make it easy to conduct a "reverse lookup." You can search by street address to find nearby residences or businesses and their phone numbers, or enter a phone number to see what name it matches.

Source: MSN White Pages, http://msn.whitepages.com/reverse-lookup (accessed July 6, 2010).

Online maps also provide invaluable data for reporters. Sites such as Mapquest and Yahoo! Maps will generate driving directions to help you get to a story quickly; and, unlike GPS navigators, they can give you an advance feel for the lay of the land. They can help you locate nearby businesses and provide an instant satellite image. Understanding the geography might help you figure out a better vantage point for reporting or shooting your story or point you to a location where you're likely to be able to go live. And online maps can quickly be converted into graphics.

Social Media

A majority of journalists today use social media to do their jobs—mainly to find stories, sources and information quickly and to monitor trends. Twitter, Facebook and other social media tools, once used primarily in breaking news situations, have become a central part of the daily newsgathering process. TV anchor Amy Wood says she gets "*lots* of tips on breaking news" via her social media sites. One of her Twitter followers told her a hostage crisis at a local bank had been resolved before the police announced it.

"Every day, stories buzz and rumors emerge on social networks," says Lauren McCullough, manager of social networks and news engagement at the Associated Press. "Our editors make judgment calls on what merits further reporting. We won't report a story solely because it's trending on Twitter, but we will discuss it and weigh its popularity against its news value."[3]

Dozens of tools are available to discover what people are talking about on Twitter and to follow trends by location.

Because Twitter is an open platform, you don't even need to join to find information. But journalists who have Twitter and Facebook accounts can do a lot more. They can solicit story ideas, find specific

GO ONLINE

Module 2: Check out a tipsheet for journalists and a video tutorial on how to use Twitter.

types of sources and get feedback on stories they're working on. Let's say you are a reporter in Colorado, doing a story about autism. Because you know that memorable stories are centered around interesting people, you want to find a family willing to talk about their personal experience dealing with the disorder. A Twitter search turns up comments about autism from several users in your area. Reading through them could provide you with a starting point for finding a family to interview.

Reporter Daniel Victor says social media were absolutely critical to a story he reported for the Patriot-News in Harrisburg, Pa., about a planned school closing. In an interview with BeatBlogging.org, Victor said he joined an alumni group for the school on Facebook and posted a message explaining who he was and what he was working on, along with his cell phone number. Almost 50 alumni got in touch, and he interviewed about two dozen of them.

Searching Twitter for posts that include the words autism or autistic from users within 100 miles of Denver, Colo., turned up some potential sources for a local story. How would you evaluate these sources?

Source: Twitter, http://search.twitter.com/search?q=+autism+OR+autistic+near:"denver,+co"+within:100mi (accessed July 6, 2010).

"They ended up doing the work for me," Victor said. "It's amazing how much of a difference it made for my story. Everybody had a stake in it, and for them to all be in one place, and for me to have access to that, that's pretty powerful."[4]

Social media raise a host of ethical issues for journalists, including whether to "friend" sources on Facebook and how much to disclose on Twitter about stories they're working on. We'll discuss these and other concerns in Chapter 11.

Phone Calls

No matter how you go about finding background information, you'll probably still do a lot of your research by telephone. "The phone is still the most important tool, where you call as many people as you can," says award-winning TV reporter Joe Fryer of KING-TV in Seattle, Wash. One person will refer you to someone else, and eventually you'll find someone you want to interview or learn about an event you would never have heard of that provides great visuals for your story.

Reporting a story or doing an interview without having done any background research is like driving to an unfamiliar place without consulting a map. You might get where you intend to go, but it will take you longer and you'll probably miss a turn or two along the way.

SOURCES

Reporters typically use both primary and secondary sources when reporting news stories. A primary source could be an interview with a person who has direct experience of an event or topic, or an original document related to that topic. The journalist as eyewitness is also considered a primary source. Any other source is a secondary source, whether it's someone with knowledge that's relevant to the story or a written report based on the original document.

In the case of a fire, for example, the person whose house burned down would be a primary source. So would a firefighter who had been involved in putting out the fire. But the press release issued by the fire department the next day would be a secondary source, as would a newspaper story about the fire. Reporters always prefer primary sources. "Anything that's in the newspaper I don't report unless I heard it myself from the people who are quoted," says Fryer.

In a perfect world, a reporter would have access to several primary sources when working on a story, but that's often not the case. Secondary sources are most useful as a way of confirming information acquired from primary sources. Writing stories based solely on secondary sources can be risky. When a mine collapsed in West Virginia in 2006, news services reported that 12 of the 13 miners trapped inside had survived. They attributed the information to family members of the trapped miners. Elected officials, including the governor of West Virginia, talked on camera about the "miracle" rescue. But it wasn't true: Only one miner had survived. The journalists had relied on secondary sources (the family members) rather than primary sources (mine officials who were in communication with rescue workers inside the mine). NBC News anchor Brian Williams called it "an awful night for the news media."

Newspapers across the country relied on secondary sources and erroneously reported the survival of 12 miners after a West Virginia mine collapse. In fact, only one miner lived.

Source: © epa/Corbis.

Multiple, Diverse Sources

One rule of thumb reporters follow when researching a story is that no single source can provide all of the information they might need. Consulting multiple sources allows you to confirm information, add perspective and find new angles on the stories you're covering. As you expand your source list, pay attention to the diversity of your sources to make sure you get a range of opinions and avoid writing stories that rely exclusively on the "usual suspects"—most often white males.

Anyone with access to information can be a useful source for a journalist. Secretaries and clerks, for example, can provide copies of documents, and they often know who is the most knowledgeable person on a given topic. A reporter who treats them with respect may find that a request for an interview with the secretary's supervisor is accepted more quickly.

Source Credibility

Journalists need to evaluate the source of all information to determine whether it's credible enough to use in a news story. Sometimes sources are in no position to know what really

DIVERSE SOURCES

It's not always easy to find diverse expert sources for your stories, but there are tools available to help. The Society of Professional Journalists has an online resource guide—the Rainbow Source Book, at www.spj.org/divsourcebook.asp—that is a database of "qualified experts on key news topics from populations historically underrepresented in the news: people of color, women, gays and lesbians, and people with disabilities."

Another useful starting point is the Source Book of Multicultural Experts, at www.multicultural.com/experts, which lists experts by industry and demographic. You might also consult community directories such as the Hispanic Yellow Pages, www.hispanicyellow.com, to find sources in the Spanish-speaking community.

Minority and women-owned businesses can also be good places to look for sources; ask your local or state government for a list or search the online directory at www.sba8a.com. You can find expert sources at historically black colleges and universities, if any exist in your area.

For more suggestions on how to incorporate diverse perspectives in your stories, take a look at the Diversity Toolkit produced by the Radio Television Digital News Association (www.rtdna.org/diversity/toolkit/view/index.html).

TRADE TOOLS

happened, or they may have an axe to grind. To clear up confusion or discrepancies, reporters may have to see where the weight of the evidence lies or seek out original sources like documents to determine which version is true.

It's especially important to evaluate online sources of information before deciding if it's credible. Just because you can find something on the Web does not mean that it's true. Wikipedia, for example, may be a good starting point for basic information, but plenty of entries there contain errors that may or may not have been corrected. At least the site keeps track of revisions so you can see when changes have been made and by whom. But it's never a good idea to rely solely on one source of information, especially on the Web.

Evaluating online sources can require a little detective work. Begin by checking the "about" section for names and affiliations. If that information isn't easy to find, it should raise a red flag. Search for background on the companies or people behind the site, and check online registries like www.whois.com or www.domaintools.com. Is the publisher reputable? Is the writer qualified?

To assess a site's credibility, consider its purpose and presentation. If its primary aim is to sell products or to promote an agenda, the content may be slanted in favor of one point of view. If the content is not updated regularly and links are out of date, the site may not be a useful source. Grammar and spelling mistakes, exaggerated claims and sloppy design should also raise questions about accuracy and reliability.

TRADE TOOLS

EVALUATING SOURCES

Deciding what sources to use for a story is a large part of a journalist's job. Here are some useful questions for evaluating whether you have chosen the right source or the best source for your story:

- How well informed is this source? Is this person in a position—either personally or professionally—to know these things?

- Can you confirm this information through other sources or through documents?

- How representative is this source's point of view? For example, is this just one person who complains loudly about the landlord because of a personal problem? Or is this the most articulate voice speaking for an entire group with serious, legitimate problems?

- Has this source been reliable and credible in the past?

- Are you using this source only because it's the easy way to go or because you know you'll get a sound bite or quote you can use? Some people are reliably good interviews, but just because they are willing to speak with you doesn't make them the most knowledgeable source on a particular subject.

- What is the source's motive for providing information? Is this person simply trying to look good, or to make someone else look bad? Why is this source talking to you in the first place?

Source: Joann Byrd, "A Guide for Evaluating Sources," PoynterOnline, March 1, 2000, www.poynter.org/column .asp?id=36&aid=4352.

INTERVIEWS

Interviews are the heart of journalism, and each one is a little different from any other. A reporter might interview a candidate for governor one day and a 5-year-old the next. Obviously, you'd approach those two conversations differently, but there are some basic guidelines that apply to all interviews.

Remember that most adults associate the word *interview* with something stressful, like a job application, so try to avoid describing what you're doing as an interview, even when you're calling ahead to set it up. Instead, tell people you'd like to talk to them for a story. This may sound like a distinction without a difference, but experienced journalists say that using the right words can help people be themselves and result in a better interview.

GETTING AN INTERVIEW

Arranging an interview is not always easy. People may not want to talk with a journalist, especially if the story is controversial. When dealing with public officials, start from the premise that the public has a right to know what those officials are doing. Experienced reporters have found they can persuade even the most reluctant sources to agree to an interview by anticipating their concerns:

- They don't have time. The reporter can offer to meet at the most convenient time or place for the person they want to speak with. Limiting the amount of time requested may also help.

- They are afraid because they think the story will make them look bad. Treating sources with respect and telling them precisely why you want to talk with them will help them feel less anxious.

- They don't know what to say. Reporters need to be clear about why the story needs a particular person's point of view.

- They are hard to reach. Reporters often have to go through a secretary or public relations officer to contact the person they want to speak with. If they suspect that their request is not being forwarded, some reporters will write a letter to the source, or call during lunch or after business hours in an effort to get through.

TRADE TOOLS

INTERVIEW QUESTIONS

Questions are the backbone of an interview. They're the rudder, keeping the ship going in the right direction. Good questions can reward you with unexpected answers, rich information and surprises. Poor questions can leave you wondering why you bothered to talk to that person at all. Questions that are too general can let the person you are talking to get away with being unresponsive. Questions that are too specific can lead you down the wrong trail.

GO ONLINE

Ongoing Story Module: List people you might want to interview and top questions for each source.

Many reporters develop a list of questions or topics for discussion, which they may write down and take along with them but do not consult during the interview. Instead, they'll look at the list only near the end to make sure they haven't forgotten something important. The list also includes other information, documents or visuals they want to obtain from that source so they don't leave the interview without asking for everything they might need for the story. This step is particularly critical to make sure you have all the bases covered when you're planning to produce multimedia stories.

Open-Ended Questions

Most of the time, the best questions are open-ended questions that cannot be answered with yes or no. "Did the fire wake you up?" doesn't get you much. "How did you discover the house was on fire?" might be much more productive.

Robert Siegel, senior host of NPR's "All Things Considered," tells the story of an interview he did with a Turkish diplomat after Pope John Paul II was shot and wounded by a Turk in Rome. His first question, "Do you know any details about this man, Mehmet Ali Agca—where he lived in Italy, what he did there, what kind of visa the Italians gave him?" The answers were all no. After several more tries, Siegel paused, about to give up. And the diplomat filled the silence with this, ". . . except that he is the most famous convicted murderer in Turkey, who escaped from prison after assassinating the editor of one of our major newspapers." Siegel says he almost lost a good story by asking questions that were too narrow. He acknowledges that a better way to open the interview might have been, "Tell me about this man."[5]

Good questions are also nonjudgmental, in that they do not establish the reporter's point of view. It's the difference between "What do you think about that?" and "What could you have been thinking!" In most cases, avoid "double barreled" two-part questions because they give the interview subject a chance to answer only half of the question—usually the easy half. We'll discuss one exception to that rule in Chapter 3.

Openers and Closers

The first question in an interview is important because it sets the tone for what follows. A lot of journalists like to begin with an "ice-breaker" question that lets the source relax. It's something they're comfortable answering. It may, in fact, have nothing to do with the reason you are there. But often it helps to establish your credentials with the source, and that can create a sense of trust and openness. If you are interviewing a writer about her latest novel, your opening question could be about her previous book or her family to show you have done your homework and are well prepared for the conversation.

You may want to avoid opening questions that are too broad or too vague. One reporter tells of an interview he started with the question: "Why don't you tell me a little bit about what you have done?" The source just stared back and said, "If you don't know, why are you here?"

Whenever they conduct an interview, reporters usually have some general questions they save for the end. First, they may summarize the conversation to be sure they've understood what was said. Then they will ask if there is anything else the person being interviewed wants to add. They also ask for the best way to get back in touch with the person, especially after hours, and they thank the person for their time. And many journalists have one last question they ask at all interviews: "What else is going on?" It's amazing how many good stories you can find while you're out covering something else.

Tough Questions

Journalists often have to talk with people who have been through some kind of trauma. It's one of the toughest assignments you can get, but the right approach can pay off. Reporter Joe Fryer says his approach is "aggressive, in a nice way." "I hate to lose, but I never ambush someone," he says. "Without ever being intrusive or rude, my goal is still to get something no one else has." Instead of calling repeatedly to request an interview, Fryer will leave just one message for each person who might have something to say. When they are ready to talk, he says, "they remember that, and they talk to me first because I was the most respectful."

Fryer also keeps trying to find someone to talk to, long after another reporter might have given up. He once spent 40 minutes talking with the son of a 94-year-old woman who had died in a nursing home fire, hoping he would do an on-camera interview. When the man finally said no, Fryer asked if there was someone else he might talk to. The son put Fryer in touch with the woman's pastor who was planning her funeral service, and who turned out to be a terrific interview.

If you have difficult or confrontational questions to ask, it's a good idea to save them for about the last third of the interview. If you ask them first, the interview may be over

TRADE TOOLS

INTERVIEWING VICTIMS

People who have lost relatives or friends in a disaster are often the first target of journalists seeking to report on the event. How can journalists do their job of informing the public while showing sensitivity to victims? We compiled these tips on how to approach victims with the help of the Victims and the Media Program at Michigan State University (www.victims.jrn.msu.edu).

- Make sure the family has been notified. Check and double-check with officials before making your approach. Mistakes do happen. Decide what you will do and say if you become the inadvertent bearer of bad news.

- Have a plan. Know beforehand what you are going to say when you approach a survivor or relative. Decide precisely how you will phrase your request and practice it ahead of time.

- Leave your equipment behind. Announce who you are and what news organization you represent. Express regrets before asking if they'd be willing to talk.

- State your purpose. Explain that you are offering them an opportunity to share their memories and feelings, if they want to. Be clear about how much time you will need and whether you are live or on tape. Ask their help in choosing a location.

- Be prepared with alternatives. Offer a business card if they say they would rather talk later. Ask them if they would prefer that someone else speak for the family.

- Share control. Tell them they can choose to stop, to take a break or to keep some remarks out of your coverage.

- Thank them for their effort. Reliving trauma takes a toll. Tell victims how much you appreciate their willingness to share their stories.

before it begins. There are exceptions to this rule: If you have only a short time for the interview—say the person granted you five minutes only—or if you don't actually have a scheduled interview but are trying to ask a few questions "on the run." Then you don't have time for pleasantries, and you have to be direct from the start.

It's not always easy to get answers to tough questions, but Larche Hardy, former news director at WMBB-TV in Panama City, Fla., suggests this technique: Ask the question three times. "The first time you may get a nonanswer or an 'I'm not prepared to talk about that right now.' The second time, the interviewee will likely get a little huffy and say, 'I told you,

I'm not going to talk about that right now.' By the third time you will either get thrown out of the office or you may force the official to justify his answer—a natural reaction to being put on the spot. The answer to the third question is generally the best sound you're going to get."

CONFRONTATIONAL INTERVIEWS

Investigative reporters often have to interview people who don't really want to talk. In a courtroom, they might be described as hostile witnesses. For journalists, especially in television, these kinds of interviews require a lot of preparation or choreography, as former CNN reporter Mark Feldstein puts it.

Feldstein offers a "how-to" primer for confrontational interviews, especially for television, that includes these suggestions:

Source: Photo courtesy of Mark Feldstein.

- Take charge immediately [by] interrupting self-serving filibusters and carefully avoiding pleasantries that might weaken the necessary resolve to go for the jugular.

- Go for the tight shot. Zoom in slowly on the interviewee's face when the exchange grows heated. This cinematic effect visually reinforces the editorial goal of zeroing in on the quarry.

- Use props. As every good trial lawyer knows, such tangible exhibits—video, photos, documents—not only help buttress a cross-examination but also add theatrical flair.

- Set up targets to lie. You can't force them to do so, of course, but it is always better to give them the opportunity to tell a falsehood on camera before (not after) you pull out the smoking-gun memo that proves their culpability. A single lie captured on camera shakes the edifice of everything else they say afterwards.

Are any of these tactics unfair? Not at all, Feldstein says. "No more so than the carefully coached evasions, posturing, pontificating, stonewalling and outright lying that your target has perfected over a lifetime."

Source: Adapted from "Lights, Cameras, Gotcha," *American Journalism Review* (December/January 2009), http://ajr.org/Article.asp?id=4676.

KNOW AND TELL

Silence

While it's important to ask good questions, it's also critically important to be quiet and let the interviewee talk. Good journalists are good listeners, and often learn the most significant information by being silent. People naturally want to fill silences. Give them a chance to do so by responding with nonverbal cues that say, "I'm interested," such as leaning forward in your chair or taking notes in your notebook. What you hear can lead to additional questions that may not have occurred to you. But one word of caution: If you plan to use the audio or video, avoid verbal cues that are used in normal conversation. Saying, "mmm-hmmm" or "sure" or making other supportive noises is a good way to ruin a great sound bite. You won't be able to use it, either because the background sound is so distracting or because you can't risk letting anyone think that you were agreeing with the person you were interviewing.

NBC national correspondent Bob Dotson is a master of what he calls the "non-question question." He often finds that a comment or an observation can elicit a more natural response than a direct question. Instead of asking a tornado survivor, "How much damage did the storm cause to your home?" try saying, "Wow, what a mess!" People tend to respond as they would in a conversation, and instead of providing one- or two-word answers, they sound much more natural.

TYPES OF INTERVIEWS

Reporters today do interviews in all sorts of different ways—in person, on the phone, by e-mail or social media or even instant messaging. Sometimes the medium the story is destined for dictates the type of interview you'll do. Sometimes your choice will be based on the availability of the source. There are pluses and minuses to each type, so if you have a choice, make an informed decision.

In-Person Interviews

Obviously, interviewing in person is the best way to get on-camera sound bites for television or streaming video and the best-quality audio for radio or online news. It's possible to do TV interviews via Skype or to ask questions through a phone and have the answers recorded on site, but there is no substitute for being there. When you are on the scene, you can get a more complete sense of the person with whom you are speaking. What kinds of photos are on the wall? Is the desk messy or neat? What books are in the bookcase? Meeting in person also gives the reporter the ability to judge the source's credibility based on his or her demeanor. Does he look nervous or comfortable? Is she willing to look the reporter in the eye?

Interviewing in person also allows you to make adjustments to get the best technical quality for television, radio or the Web. Listen for background noise that could overwhelm your interview sound and relocate if you have to. Make sure the microphone is close enough to the source to capture crisp, clear sound. Avoid chairs that swivel or rock because random movement can be distracting on the air. We'll talk more about on-camera interviews in Chapter 3.

INTERVIEW PLANNING

You've come up with a great story idea, researched it thoroughly and decided on the key interviews you want to include. But just talking to people won't get you everything you need. Pulitzer Prize–winning reporter Lane DeGregory of the St. Petersburg Times says she looks for unfolding action to drive a narrative. When she's negotiated access to the sources she wants to interview, she asks herself seven questions:

Source: Photo courtesy of Lane DeGregory.

1. Can I go along for a ride or take a walk or be at a meeting, a trial or a funeral?

2. Is something going to happen?

3. Is the place important, the action important, or is the person important?

4. Will there be interaction between [the subject of the story] and others?

5. Do I want to tell the story around one scene or five minutes or a whole day, or perhaps follow someone over a period of time?

6. Do the characters experience an epiphany?

7. What's the big idea?

Knowing the answers will help you decide where and when to schedule interviews.

Source: Steve Weinberg, "Valuable Journalistic Advice Arises from Annual Gathering of Eminent Writers," Investigative Reporters and Editors, Inc., *IRE Journal* (July/August 2007), http://findarticles.com/p/articles/mi_qa3720/is_200707/ai_n19511157/pg_2/?tag=content;col1 (accessed January 30, 2010).

KNOW AND TELL

Phone, E-mail or Online Interviews

Interviewing by phone is often convenient for both the reporter and the source. You don't have to spend a lot of time in transit, and it's easier for a source to make time for a phone call than a personal appointment. Phone interviews are great for collecting basic information but less useful for interviewing in depth. Reporters often do "pre-interviews" by phone, getting background and other information before doing an in-person interview. This can be a time-saver, but it can also sap spontaneity.

E-mail and social media interviews are useful for reaching people in distant places, but the reporter can't listen to what's being said and follow up in real time. Instant messaging is more akin to a telephone interview. But both online methods raise the question of whether the answers are actually being sent by the person they appear to be from. It's important to confirm the authenticity of the answers before using them in a story.

Reporters using e-mail or other online forms of communication like direct messaging on Facebook or Twitter should follow the same professional standards that they would in any other form. They must identify themselves as journalists and tell what information they are seeking and why. And they need to exercise the same fact-checking and thinking skills they would apply to any other source of information. Many newsrooms have policies that require reporters to let the audience know when they use information that's been gathered via e-mail, especially direct quotes. The bottom line: Be aware that these interview methods have their limitations.

INTERVIEW GROUND RULES

Most interviews are conducted "on the record," which means the reporter can use anything that is said and attribute it directly to the person who is speaking. It is important to make sure the source knows this, especially when dealing with ordinary people who are not accustomed to being quoted by name. Even though your notebook, microphone and camera are in plain sight, it may not be obvious to some people that you intend to use their words, voice or image in a news story that everyone can see.

Occasionally, interviews are done under different ground rules. A whistleblower might not want to go on the record with a complaint about the company she works for, out of fear she might lose her job. A lower-level government official might resist going on the record if he's been told not to talk to the media. A Muslim teenager in the United States who wears a veil or a "hijab" headcovering at home but not at school might not want to be identified to avoid angering her parents. If an interview is not on the record, both the reporter and the source must agree in advance to the conditions under which the information can be used.

Background Interviews

An interview "on background" or "not for attribution" generally means the information can be used in a story and the source's words can be quoted directly but the source cannot be named. The source can be identified in a general way, however—for example, as "an administration official" or "a company engineer"—as long as both the source and the journalist agree on the description to be used.

Reporters should not be too quick to agree to talk on background because sources sometimes try to use it as a cover for a personal or partisan attack, knowing it cannot be traced back to them. And using an unnamed source makes it more difficult for the audience to evaluate the credibility of the information. But there are times when reporters have to get information on background because it's the only way a source will agree to talk. A source who fears for her safety if others learn that she has spoken to a reporter may agree to provide information only on background. Here are some general guidelines for deciding whether to accept and use background information:

- The story is of overwhelming public concern.

- There is no other way to get the information on the record.

- The source is in a position to know the truth.

- You are willing to explain (in your story) why the source could not be named.

Deep Background and Off-the-Record Interviews

Government officials sometimes want to talk to reporters on "deep background," which means the information can be used but not in a direct quote, and the source cannot be identified. For example, a top diplomat might be willing to tell a reporter on deep background that the government is close to reaching an important agreement with another country. The reporter could then write only that observers are "known to believe" an agreement is imminent. When you hear a story that begins, "CBS News has learned . . ." it usually means the information was provided on deep background.

Information that is offered "off the record" cannot be used at all, so most reporters will resist this arrangement unless they are fairly sure that the source is the only possible way they could get the information. Most reporters agree that off-the-record information cannot even be repeated to another source, but that it can tip you off to a story that is worth pursuing.

Interview Policies

Many newsrooms require that reporters have the approval of a news manager before accepting off-the-record information or information on deep background. The Media General Broadcast Group, which owns 17 network-affiliated television stations, takes this approach:

> It is Media General's policy to involve the News Director in any decision to grant anonymity to a source or to report the information from that source. While it is sometimes necessary to quote an unnamed source, it is important to remember that when we do so, we in effect, tell viewers: "Trust us." By not revealing a source, we vouch for the truth of what is said. That puts our own credibility on the line. Before using an unnamed source, you must be convinced that the story is of overwhelming public concern and that there is no other way to get the essential information on the record.[6]

Whatever the arrangement, it's up to the reporter to make sure both sides understand and agree to the ground rules before the interview. Sometimes sources try to change the rules in the middle, by telling the reporter something important and then adding, "But you can't use that, of course." That's why it's a good idea to spell things out at the beginning and not agree to withhold information unless a separate deal is reached before proceeding with the interview. Multimedia reporting raises other issues when it comes to agreements with sources. For example, if a person agrees to be interviewed for print, are they also agreeing to have their story posted online or recorded for television? We'll explore these questions further in Chapter 11.

Journalists also should be clear about how far they will go to protect the identity of a source. As we have seen in some prominent cases involving both print and broadcast journalists, reporters may risk going to jail rather than reveal information about a confidential source in a court of law. In 2004 Rhode Island television reporter Jim Taricani was sentenced to six months under house arrest after he refused to name the source who gave him an FBI surveillance tape that he used in a broadcast. On the tape, an aide to the mayor of Providence, R.I., was seen accepting a bribe from a government informant. After Taricani was found guilty of contempt of court, his source identified himself, but the judge still refused to lift the sentence. Taricani was willing to pay the price to keep his promise not to name his source. If journalists are not willing to face time in prison to protect a source, they should make it clear that their promise of confidentiality only goes so far.

GROUND RULES

Reporters and sources should agree in advance on how information provided can be used. Typically, on-the-record information can be attributed to a source by name. Make sure your source shares your definition of what "on the record" means, as well as these other types of information:

- Background: Information can be used in a story, and the source's words can be quoted directly, but the source cannot be named.
- Deep background: Information that can be used but not in a direct quote, and the source cannot be identified.
- Off the record: Information that is offered off the record cannot be used in a story at all.
- Embargo: Information is provided on the condition that it is not to be used until a specific time set by the source.

TRADE TOOLS

Embargoes

One other ground rule that is important for journalists to understand is the use of an "embargo" on information provided by a source. That means the information is provided on the condition that it is not to be used until a specific time. A government agency announcing a new policy may provide a written summary several hours in advance or even a day ahead. That gives reporters time to digest the information before the news conference making the policy official. Reporters who accept information under an embargo are bound to honor it unless the news becomes public somewhere else before the specified time.

NOTE TAKING

Some reporters consider their cameras or audio recorders to be the equivalent of a notebook and pen, but that can be risky and counterproductive. Electronics have been known to fail. If you're asked to go live on television, for example, you may not have time to review the tape of an interview to make sure you have the information straight. You will probably need more detail for a print or online story than you're likely to get during a taped interview, unless you record everything. And if you do that, you'll have so much tape you'll never have time to log it all. So it's important for all journalists to be skilled note takers.

Interview Notes

You won't take notes during an interview the way you would during a lecture because you'll want to maintain eye contact, but you should make a habit of writing down key words and phrases. If you're recording the interview, make a note of the time code or counter time when specific comments were said, or insert a digital marker or index point to save time finding those sound bites later.

Always put correctly spelled names and titles in your notebook, as well as contact information so you can easily get back in touch if you need more information. Don't depend on business cards alone; the information on them may be out of date, and they're easily lost.

Spell out interview ground rules in your notebook. Be clear about who said what and under what circumstances, especially if any of it was off the record.

Story Notes

In addition to taking notes on interviews, write down important facts and details as well as your own thoughts and ideas as you cover a story. Often, what you are thinking while observing a scene can be turned into a theme that holds your story together. Some journalists put brackets around all notes that reflect their own observations so they don't confuse what they've written with something a source might have said.

Draw diagrams or take photos of rooms, scenes or items in relationship to one another. This can help you remember and describe exactly what you saw, especially if you can't get it on video or if you need it for a print or online version of the story. These "visual notes" can be especially important in building accurate graphics.

Leave space for adding to your notes or inserting verbatim quotes later. Many reporters use their own shorthand for common words so they can take notes more quickly. As soon as the interview is over, they spell out any unusual abbreviations to avoid confusion later. They also will mark the most important information they have learned, anything they need to follow up on or check for accuracy, and questions that still need to be answered. Develop your own symbols to distinguish between these notations; you might underline what's most important, mark points to follow up on with an asterisk and insert a question mark wherever information is unclear. Whatever system you devise, use it consistently to avoid confusion.

GETTING IT RIGHT

Credibility is a journalist's most important asset, and accuracy is the best way to protect it. To ensure accuracy, reporters must check and double-check all of the information they collect for a news story. Mistakes will happen, but they should be rare.

Reporters are the news organization's first line of defense against errors. The best way to protect your credibility is to get it right during the reporting process. Consult multiple sources to nail down information that may be in doubt. Confirm that all numbers you have collected for a story are correct: addresses, telephone numbers, ages, dates and time references. Check the spelling of every proper name and make sure you have the correct titles for everyone you talked to.

Multimedia reporters should get in the habit of asking interview subjects to pronounce their names on tape. Get pronunciations for locations as well. Even words that are spelled the same may be said differently. For example, Beaufort, N.C., is pronounced "BO-fort," but Beaufort, S.C., is "BU-fort."

Context and Fairness

Getting the facts right is just one part of reporting accurately. You also need to make sure you have the facts in the right context, and that's sometimes more difficult. Researchers at Kent State University found that most stories on local TV news in Cleveland were factually accurate, according to people who should know best—people who were interviewed for those stories. But one interviewee in three said that important information was left out of a story, one interviewee in five complained that the interview was taken out of context and nearly one in five thought the coverage of the particular event was both overblown and sensationalized.[7]

To make sure you can put the facts in context, keep an open mind while you are reporting. Don't assume you know what someone means if there's any doubt at all. This is particularly important when you're reporting across cultures to avoid perpetuating stereotypes based on misunderstandings. Ask for a clarification, or consult another source. If you can't nail something down, it's perfectly acceptable to tell what you don't know as well as what you do. It's much better than going with information you can't confirm.

PITCHING THE STORY

Too many good stories never make it past the idea stage because they fail the "pitch test." With resources tight and time limited, news managers aren't going to green light every story idea. If you want the opportunity to tell a story, you have to know how to sell it. And that skill is even more important for independent or freelance journalists.

Crafting the Pitch

Know why the story matters to your intended audience. This means you must have done some advance reporting before you even bring up the idea. If you can't answer the "who cares" question, you likely won't sell the idea.

Be prepared to explain the story clearly and briefly. If you can't do that, your story idea probably needs more work. Rehearse your pitch ahead of time by trying it out on a colleague or friend to make sure you're being as clear as you think you are.

A good pitch for a multimedia story should describe what it might look like on the air or online. To do that, you should have an idea of the main characters and locations you would feature and what multimedia elements you could add. Come equipped with answers to logistical questions like how much time or how many people would need to be involved in producing the story.

If a newspaper article or Web story prompted your idea, make sure you can suggest how to advance the story. It's OK to pitch something you read in "a" newspaper, but not "the" (local) newspaper; in other words, don't suggest a story everyone in your area might already have read. If your pitch was inspired by an academic study or government report, make sure you've seen the original source.

Just like a good story, a good pitch needs to be focused and timely. If you can craft a captivating pitch, you'll be well on your way to telling a compelling story.

TAKING IT HOME

All journalists are reporters at heart, whether they have that title or not. They're always looking for good stories and for the opportunity to tell them well. The more broadly you think about what makes a good news story, the more good stories you'll find. Train yourself to be a story hunter, not an "order filler," and you'll succeed in any medium. Stay curious, even if you've lived somewhere for a long time. If you think something's unusual or interesting, look into it even if it doesn't seem newsworthy at first. Ask lots of questions and avoid assumptions as you pursue a story idea. When doing interviews, you'll learn more if you listen more than you talk.

No matter what story you're chasing, find a way to care about it because if you don't, no one else will. Be prepared to be persistent as well. It's hard work to find the stories that others miss, but the opportunity to tell stories that take the audience where they can't go, that give voice to the voiceless or that hold the powerful accountable, is always worth the effort.

TALKING POINTS

1. You've been asked to do a story about the increasing use of text messaging while driving. Brainstorm a list of questions you might ask to turn that topic into a story, or create a story map to see what angles you might follow. Write down the one story idea you want to pursue and summarize it in a single sentence.

2. Look at the local newspaper from two weeks ago, either in print or online. Find as many stories as possible that make you ask: What happened next? Suggest three stories that you think should be followed up and explain why. List three questions you would want answered in each follow-up story.

3. A new study indicates that breast cancer rates are increasing in the United States. The study provides detailed information broken down by race and ethnicity. You've been assigned to localize the story. How might you incorporate diverse sources into the piece? Why would that be important?

4. Choose a topic in the news and use a Twitter search tool like Monitter.com or Twitter's advanced search (search.twitter.com/advanced) to see what people in your community or nearby are saying about it. How might that be helpful in finding angles for stories?

ONLINE LEARNING MODULE 2

Activate or buy this chapter's online learning module at journalism.cqpress.com to get access to:

- SKILL BUILDING: Develop a story idea from a broad topic and decide what sources you would consult to begin reporting the story.

- DISCOVER: Watch two TV news stories and see how the reporter found and developed them. Consult tips for journalists on how to use Twitter.

- EXPLORE: Learn more about finding stories, evaluating sources and conducting better interviews.

- A video tutorial on how to search and monitor Twitter.

- A digital version of this chapter's text in full color with active links.

Also, continue your work on the ONGOING STORY MODULE. List people you might want to interview for this story and the top questions you'd want each source to answer.

CHAPTER 3 MULTIMEDIA NEWSGATHERING

To be successful in multimedia journalism, you have to keep the strengths of each platform in mind as you report. Even if you won't shoot video or build graphics yourself, you need to understand how it's done. In this chapter, we'll explain what it takes to gather the elements you'll need to tell stories well in multiple media, including crisp audio, vivid pictures and more.

You're heading out the door to cover a story for TV, but that won't be the only version you have to file. You may need to post updates on social media sites and write a separate story for the Web or the newspaper too. Knowing that in advance will change the way you report the story because you'll need different elements to do the story justice in each medium.

Approaching every story with a multimedia mind-set is a far better strategy than searching for elements you can use on different platforms after your reporting is done. A television reporter who gathers details and data along the way will be better prepared to write for print as well. A print reporter who thinks about video and sound from the start can more easily produce a TV version. And reporters who collect all of these elements and more, like original documents and graphics, will be all set to file for the Web. It's a good idea to get in the habit of reporting this way because many newsrooms now expect it.

THINKING ACROSS PLATFORMS

Multimedia reporters look for the same universal building blocks of great stories that we discussed in Chapter 2: character, place, emotion, detail and tension. But they may concentrate more or less on certain elements depending on the platforms they'll be using to tell the story. Let's take a closer look at the strengths and weaknesses of each medium to see how those qualities change the reporting process on one specific story.

Let's say you're reporting on the Census Bureau's announcement that the U.S. population hit 300 million at 4:46 a.m. today. To tell that story on TV, you'd probably want to contact hospitals in your area to find a baby born at about that time whose birth could illustrate the bigger picture and give the viewer a personal connection to the story. Because TV is a visual medium, you'd ask for video of the maternity ward and an interview with the family. You might also want to talk with a demographer on camera. Your story would include additional information about the population milestone, but not in great detail.

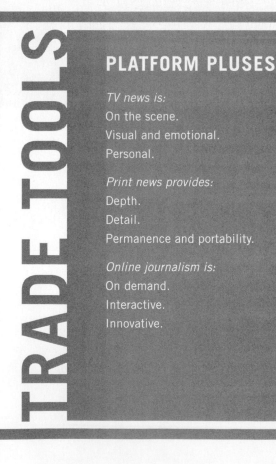

PLATFORM PLUSES

TV news is:
On the scene.
Visual and emotional.
Personal.

Print news provides:
Depth.
Detail.
Permanence and portability.

Online journalism is:
On demand.
Interactive.
Innovative.

Story Elements

The typical broadcast journalist who is asked to write a print or Web version of a story soon realizes something is missing—namely, enough detail to satisfy the print or online editor. While your TV story about the population milestone would mention that Hispanics are the fastest-growing minority in the country, it wouldn't include a lot of statistics. By contrast, your print or Web version would have to give exact percentages for all minorities, and compare the numbers with where they stood at a previous milestone— say, when the population hit 200 million in the 1960s. It would also explain how the Census Bureau counts the population, and how the U.S. population compares with other countries around the world. Get in the habit of collecting these specifics as you report to save yourself time and frustration later.

MSNBC's interactive population map allowed users to compare states by population change or density. Notice the timeline at the bottom with click-to-listen audio files of demographic experts describing the characteristics of different generations.

Source: "Made in the USA," MSNBC.com, www.msnbc.msn.com/id/15253291 (accessed August 16, 2007).

To tell the population story online, you might also want to use the data you collected to create interactive graphics. MSNBC, for example, created an interactive map. Different colors indicated which states had the greatest population growth and density. Users could select individual states to get more specific numbers. They could choose a decade on a timeline from 1770 to 2010 to see population estimates and a racial breakdown of the country at that time. Users could also click to listen to audio files of historians or demographers describing what life was like for people born at different times.

Reporters planning to tell a story on the Web need to collect elements like these that clearly go together, says Jonathan Dube, vice president of AOL News & Information and publisher of CyberJournalist.net. "Look for words to go with images, audio and video to go with words, data that will lend itself to interactives, etc.," he says. It's a good idea to get as much information as possible in digital form, including data you can use to create graphics. Try to get digital versions of charts, graphs and documents that you might want to post "as is." You'll also want to collect audio, photos and video for online use. We'll explain how to do this later in this chapter.

Story Development

Multmedia journalist Victoria Lim often reports the same story on multiple platforms. Her television stories are restricted by the amount of time and visuals she has, but she can use much more information online. Because she has that outlet, she reports differently than she used to. "Deeper, wider, longer interviews, much more background," she says. "[Multimedia] requires you to think about more than, well, I only have a minute thirty to give the nuts and bolts because you need more than nuts and bolts."

For a story about insurance companies refusing to write policies for people who own trampolines, Lim interviewed a woman who had been denied coverage, an insurance agent and the trampoline industry association. She also talked to the Consumer Product Safety Commission (CPSC) about trampoline safety and the state Office of Insurance Regulation to find out which insurance companies might cover trampolines. None of the reporting she did was wasted, but she developed each story differently based on the strengths of each medium.

GO ONLINE

Module 3: See how Victoria Lim reported a story about smoke alarms for multiple platforms.

Her television story opened with video of the woman's trampoline piled up in her shed, and we heard from the woman who was furious that her kids couldn't use it anymore. Lim then broadened the story to explain why trampolines are considered a bad insurance risk, and she included sound bites from the trampoline and insurance industries. Her print story included more statistics about injuries from trampolines and other sports equipment, plus advice about trampoline safety that didn't fit in her TV story. Both the print and TV versions were posted online, along with a Web-only video segment—a short stand-up with a little b-roll—in which Lim explained how to use a trampoline safely. She also compiled a list of insurance companies in Florida that might cover trampolines and posted that on the Web, along with a link to the CPSC. Lim's stories were built around the universal building blocks of character, emotion and detail, as well as the multimedia building blocks of sound, visuals and interactivity.

Obviously, to tell stories well in multiple media you'll need clear, crisp sound and compelling visuals. You may have to collect these elements by yourself, or you may work as part of a team. Either way, you need to know how it's done.

As we discuss the building blocks of multimedia stories, we'll pay particular attention to the way they're used in television news. But we'll also point out instances when you'd do things differently to accommodate the needs of online or print.

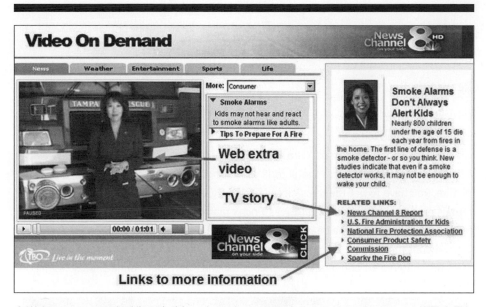

A Web extra report by Victoria Lim when she was senior consumer reporter at WFLA-TV in Tampa, Fla., offered tips on how families could prepare for a fire emergency. Users could click links for more information, to read Lim's newspaper column or to watch her TV story about how children often sleep through smoke alarms.

Source: "Multimedia/Convergence Reporting," www.victorialim.com/convergence.htm (accessed July 5, 2010).

SOUND

Sound is an essential element in multimedia journalism, whether you use it to accompany an online slide show, in a podcast, on the radio or in a television news story. Interview sound should be as clear as possible, so the user or viewer won't have to strain to understand what people are saying. Natural sound, recorded on site, is the other half of almost every picture. Compare a story with lots of natural sound with one that uses almost none and the difference is obvious. "Audio brings the story alive," says photojournalist Stan Heist. A story with natural sound lets the viewer experience something close to what it was like to be there in person. In television and online videos or slide shows, sound adds context and information that pictures alone can't convey.

Accomplished photojournalists often say they shoot with their ears. "If something makes noise and it pertains to my story, it draws my attention," says Ted Nelson of WTVF-TV in Nashville, Tenn. He listens carefully when shooting and makes sure to capture the sound that goes with every picture. Corky Scholl of KUSA-TV in Denver, Colo., is so attuned to sound that he often finds stories by following up on something he's heard while driving around with the car window down. The following tips from professionals will help you record better sound.

Recording Sound

Do not depend on any camera or recorder's built-in microphone to capture sound. Built-in microphones tend to be of poor quality and are liable to pick up mechanical noise. Use an external microphone and make sure you put it as close to the source of the sound as possible while keeping it out of the shot if you're shooting video. "If you want to hear the picture, you have to get the mics close," says longtime photojournalist Dave Wertheimer, former president of the National Press Photographers Association (NPPA). Mic the bird feeder and you can hear the beating of the hummingbirds' wings. For a story about National Guard troops in training, Ted Nelson taped a small wireless lavalier (lav) mic to the soldiers' cell phones to record both ends of their conversations with their families back home.

Photojournalist Dave Wertheimer always wears headphones when shooting. In some weather conditions, they do double duty as earmuffs.

Source: Photo courtesy of Dave Wertheimer.

For interviews or stand-ups using a lav, place the microphone just below collar level, if possible, on a tie or lapel. Stick mics should be placed about six inches from the person's mouth to keep the sound "on mic" and to avoid breathiness and popping. Shotgun mics can be held farther away, as long as you point them directly at the sound you want to capture. We'll talk more about the different types of microphones and their uses later in this chapter.

REPORTING CHECKLISTS

Many reporters use mental checklists to make sure they collect the elements they'll need to tell a story in multiple media. They ask the traditional reporting questions a little differently.

Television	Online
Who:	*Who:*
Who can speak most effectively on camera about the story?	Who can give me data, background or original documents to flesh out this story?
Whose personal experience will best illustrate the story?	
What:	*What:*
What visuals do I need to support the story?	What interactive elements can I add to this story?
What natural sound can I gather to tell this story?	What information could be told better in a graphic?
Where:	*Where:*
Where can I go to show what happened?	Where did things happen that I could put on a static or clickable map?
Where would it make sense to be on camera in this story?	Where can I refer people for more information?
When:	*When:*
When do I need to be at these locations?	When did things happen that I could put on a static or clickable timeline?

TRADE TOOLS

Never record audio or shoot video without listening to the output of the recorder or camera. Wear headphones and use both earpieces to be sure that what you're hearing is actually being captured. "Your mic hears differently from your ears," says Euan Kerr, an editor at Minnesota Public Radio. "Headphones can alert you to a loose connector, a bad mic and/or dying batteries," he says, not to mention the buzz of fluorescent lights and distracting background noise like traffic and air conditioners.

Ambient Sound

Whenever possible, record ambient sound or "room tone" for about a minute in every location. You may need it during editing to make smooth audio transitions. For example, you might want to cut from a sound bite from an interview conducted in a quiet room to a bite from a second interview conducted near a busy highway. If you sneak in the sound of the highway a few frames before you cut to the video, the change of sound quality won't be so distracting.

It can also be useful to carry and use a separate audio recorder to pick up "wild sound" while you are shooting video. If you're shooting a musical performance, you can capture entire songs on a separate recorder, leaving you free to stop and start your camera while shooting cutaways. TV photojournalist John Goheen often leaves a recorder rolling on the announcer or emcee of an event while he shoots the action. This play-by-play sound can help in the edit.

When KSTP-TV reporter Bridgette Bornstein reported live on a brutal Minnesota snowstorm, she wore a wireless microphone on her boot (right) to pick up the sound of ice crunching underfoot.

Source: KSTP-TV video courtesy of Bridgette Bornstein.

Photojournalist Joe Mahoney of the Richmond Times-Dispatch usually spends a couple of minutes recording ambient sound on location while he's looking for the people he will interview for his story. When covering a wedding involving a bride and groom of Indian heritage, for example, he recorded a few minutes of the wedding music to use as a second track on his story. You can't underestimate the importance of good audio, Mahoney says. "It doesn't matter how good your pictures are, if your sound is lousy, your story will be lousy."

Online Use

If you are recording audio to use with an online slide show, you can shoot pictures first and record sound later, but make sure you don't leave a scene until you have captured the sound that goes with it. You'll also want to ask specific questions about each person, object, activity and setting you've already shot. "If I have a really nice moment in a photo, I have to ask the person about that later, asking them how that happened or how they felt when it happened," says award-winning photographer Josh Meltzer.

Even experienced broadcast reporters have to think differently about how they do interviews when the audio also may be used on the Web. For the conversation to make sense, the audience has to be able to hear the reporter's questions as well as the answers, so it's a good idea to get in the habit of putting a mic on both the subject and the reporter. If you have only one microphone, move it back and forth to capture the conversation in full. And because your questions may wind up on the Web, approach all recorded interviews as you would a live interview on radio or television. Keep your questions short and to the point. Avoid using acronyms or jargon that your interview subject understands but the general public might not.

Print reporters need to think differently about interviews they do for online use as well. "Print reporters think they can go through and record a two-hour conversation and then go back and transcribe the entire thing and then they can take that, cut it up and put it together," says Seth Gitner, former multimedia editor at the Roanoke Times. "They don't understand that they need short, concise sound bites," he says. If you're used to doing print interviews, work on focusing your questions so you get answers that are on point for the online version. Remember, too, that partial quotes don't work on the air or in online audio or video, so one of your goals should be to get your interview subject to answer your questions in complete sentences. Some print reporters find it easier to do two interviews—one for print and a second, shorter one recorded for online use—but they have to make sure the interview subject agrees beforehand to answer some of the same questions twice.

KNOW AND TELL

CAPTURING SOUND

As a young child, Stan Heist listened to old-time radio shows like "The Shadow" that engaged his imagination. As a professional photojournalist, Heist preaches the gospel of great audio. "It's the audio that's a huge part of TV news that sometimes gets overlooked," he says. "Watching a story on TV is a passive act, but listening is how you get involved. Think about how many viewers watch our stories and they're

Source: Photo courtesy of Mike Buscher, www.buscherphotography.com.

making dinner or putting their pajamas on. Not everybody is going to be as engaged in our stories as we are. Audio brings the story alive."

Heist is one of those photographers who shoots with his ears, looking for "what's making interesting noise and who's making interesting noise. I don't waste a lot of time trying to find that perfect sound bite or convince anybody to talk. I shoot and move and move the mic to things that make sound, and to people who are doing something that makes sound. Maximize your moments with simple sounds. It doesn't have to be a siren. Be mindful of the natural sound you hear every day. The whiz-bang stuff is great but don't forget about the sound that is all around us."

Heist uses a wireless lavalier microphone most of the time. "A lavalier mic doesn't have to be pinned to a person. Put it on a rake, inside a port-a-potty or a Dumpster. Where there's a lot of movement and action, it's tough without a wireless, but you can still get a long cord and put a lavalier somewhere. You can zoom with your feet. Just being closer will make it sound better. [When I worked] in Richmond, I had a 50-foot cord and a lavalier mic. I wouldn't use it in high traffic areas, but you have to think about ways to get around the problem."

VIDEO

Whatever you shoot should be up to broadcast standards, whenever possible, whether you intend to use it on the air or online. Here are some tips from the pros on how to shoot top-quality video.

Framing

Pay close attention to the location of objects and people in each shot. Leave just a little space or "head room" between the top of a person's head and the top edge of the frame. Too little space and the person looks cramped; too much and the person looks lost. Frame your shots so there is space or "looking room" in front of people who are facing either screen right or left. The closer people are to being in profile, the more space you need to leave in the shot. As a rule of thumb, don't center a person in the frame unless he or she is looking directly at the camera. And try not to position the frame so that it cuts people off at the knees or ankles.

Watch out for distracting background objects that can draw attention away from the foreground. Position the camera so that trees and lamps do not appear to be growing out of people's heads. Be careful that horizontal lines like doorjambs or window frames don't slice across the top of people's heads.

Steady Shots

If your camera isn't steady, your video will be shaky and hard to watch. Use a tripod whenever possible, and make sure it's level. You can also use a solid platform like a chair or railing to steady the camera. "When you frame a shot and you like it, take your hands off the camera for a couple of seconds," says photojournalist Jason Hanson of KSTP-TV in Minneapolis, Minn. If you absolutely must shoot handheld or with the camera on your shoulder, get close to the subject and zoom out wide for steadier video. Keep your arms close to your body while holding the camera gently. If you grip it too tightly, the tension in your hands and arms may cause the camera to shake. On rare occasions you may want to move the camera while shooting, but only if you have a specific purpose in mind. For example, you might run behind an athlete in training to give the viewer a sense of what that person goes through to get in shape.

Hold each shot for at least 10 seconds. You can't edit if you don't have enough steady video to work with. Two-time NPPA television photographer of the year Darren Durlach

Photojournalist Jason Hanson of KSTP-TV in Minneapolis, Minn., insists on rock-solid shots, and gets them by shooting from a tripod. After he frames a shot and hits record, he'll take his hands off the camera to avoid accidentally shaking it, making sure his video is steady.

Source: Photo courtesy of Jason Hanson.

says he actually counts in his head while shooting. "It's very elementary and kind of stupid," he says, "but I still do it because I still get overexcited when I shoot spot news and I don't hold shots."

Always shoot more than you think you need. It's not unusual to shoot 20 minutes or more to produce a one-minute story. But don't shoot everything or you'll never find what you need in time to edit your story.

Get in the habit of zooming with your feet, not with the lens. "The human eye cannot pan, zoom or tilt," says photojournalist Dave Wertheimer, explaining why he avoids these camera moves. Using the zoom to get different shots from the same location is acceptable, but it's not sufficient. Once you have captured those shots, move to a different location and shoot again. Not only will your story be more visually interesting, it will be easier to watch. "If all of your shots come from the same spot, you get a 'vertigo effect' " similar to a jump cut when you edit them together, says award-winning video editor Brian Weister.

Sequences, Action and Reaction

A sequence is a series of shots of the same action taken from different perspectives or focal lengths. The most basic sequence consists of wide, medium and tight (or close-up) shots. You won't necessarily use them in that order, but you need to have them all: wide shots to establish the scene, medium shots to introduce characters and bring the viewer closer to the action, and tight shots to show details. For exam-

GO ONLINE

Module 3: Create a shooting plan from a fact sheet, and watch what a pro did with the same information.

ple, let's say you're shooting a story about a freight train derailment. The wide shot might show most of the train, with several cars off the track. The medium shot would show just the jackknifed cars. Tight and supertight (or extreme close-up) shots would show a crumpled section of rail and a leak from one of the tanker cars. Those shots also can be lifesavers in the edit room. "Tight shots, really tight shots, can help you get from here to there," says Brad Houston, a two-time NPPA editor of the year. To make it easier to find those shots when you start editing, Houston suggests shooting a lot of close-ups back to back.

When shooting action, position yourself so the action moves into and out of the frame; hit "record" several seconds before the action enters the frame and keep rolling for several seconds after it moves out of frame. If you plan to pan or tilt the camera to follow action, be sure to roll for several seconds on a static shot before and after the camera move. Let's say you're covering a parade. Roll on the empty street just ahead of the marching band and hold the camera steady as the band enters the frame. You can stay on a static shot or pan with the action, but once you've completed the pan be sure to hold another steady shot as the band exits the frame in the other direction.

Make sure you get the action, especially if it's developing quickly. Try to anticipate action so you can be in the right place at the right time to capture it. Covering an apartment fire, KUSA's Scholl noticed a piece of the roof fall in but missed getting it on tape. Figuring it would happen again, he set his camera up on the tripod and let it roll for five minutes until he captured "the money shot." But always remember that action is more meaningful to the viewer when it's connected to a reaction. "Reaction validates the action," says Scott Livingston, a former chief photographer who is now news director at WBFF-TV in Baltimore. The clowns in the parade may be funny in person, but what makes them hilarious on video is the reaction of the wide-eyed kids along the parade route.

Opens, Closes and Introductions

Look for shots that will draw attention to the beginning of your story and shots you can use at the end to reinforce the central point of the story. An opening shot can set the scene, introduce a main character or establish a tone. A closing shot wraps up the story. It should be the image that sticks in the viewer's mind once the story is over. A good closing shot often includes "negative action"—movement away from the camera as someone leaves the room or drives out of the shot. Keep shooting until you are sure that you have an opening and closing shot "in the can."

Make sure you have a head-on medium shot of any major characters you plan to introduce in your story. Boyd Huppert, a reporter for KARE-TV in Minneapolis, calls it a "handshake shot." "When I'm meeting someone, I'm going to look at them," he says. "Unless the subject of your story is in the witness protection program, there's no reason to introduce a character without looking him in the eye. I don't want to see the side of the head or back of the head or the person in a shot with other characters so I don't know who I'm supposed to be looking at."

Online Video

If you're shooting video or stills specifically for use online, a few additional considerations apply. Although technology is evolving quickly, the experience of watching video on a computer screen or handheld device still isn't quite the same as watching it on television.

It's even more important to keep the camera steady when shooting video for online use because shaky shots and shots with a lot of movement can look blurry on the Web. "Every change in pixels makes the encoder work harder and makes your picture fuzzier," says Regina McCombs, a multimedia producer-photographer. McCombs also says that when shooting video for use online, "remember your image will be quite small. This means you need to fill up your frame."[1] As a result, close-ups and medium shots work better online than wide, establishing shots.

You also want to minimize background elements that may be distracting to the online user. A study by the Nielsen Norman Group found that Web users' attention was diverted from a "talking head" at the center of an online video segment to a sign behind the person being interviewed.[2] Try to keep your framing clean and simple for online video. The foreground or background elements you might include to give TV video some depth just don't work as well online.

The splotches on this "heat map" show where people looked the longest when they watched a video story on CNN.com. Notice how they seemed to be distracted by the video controls and the signs in the background.

Source: "Eyetracking Study of Web Video," Jakob Nielsen's Alertbox, www.useit.com/alertbox/video.html (accessed December 5, 2005).

Online Photos and Slide Shows

Even for experienced news photographers, shooting stills for the Web is a little different. Former Roanoke Times photographer Josh Meltzer says that instead of looking for a lead photo and two or three detail shots for the newspaper, he would capture many more shots for use in a slide show. In addition, he had to think about transition shots that he would never use in the newspaper, like a shot of a sign to establish a location in a slide show.

Joe Mahoney of the Richmond Times-Dispatch says it's not unusual for him to take 200 to 300 photos when he's on a shoot. He looks through them all in a kind of rough edit and then selects 15 to 20 that he thinks might be good enough for a slide show. Then he puts them in a logical order so they tell a complete story. "A picture story is like any other, it needs a beginning, middle and end. Your first photo has to be something that grabs you," Mahoney says.

If you're not used to working with stills, you may need a refresher on the importance of composition and the role of captions. A well-composed still frame has a clear center of interest that draws the eye. According to the "rule of thirds," that center of interest should fall at the intersection of those imaginary lines that split the frame into thirds, horizontally and vertically. And just as you do in video, make sure subjects in close-up shots have enough headroom and "looking room" in the frame.

Notice how following the "rule of thirds" makes a difference in these photos. The picture with the woman doing Tai Chi centered in the frame (left) is less pleasing to the eye than the other. The elements in a photo that should draw your attention should be located at the intersections of the grid.

Source: Photos courtesy of the authors.

A text caption should convey basic information that helps viewers understand what they are looking at. It almost always tells the "who" and "where" of the image. Make sure you have this information for each photo before you leave a location. It's very difficult to play catch-up afterward. You'll need that same information for online metadata. If your camera or cell phone has geotagging capability, which automatically adds location data, make sure it's turned on.

LIGHTING

Cameras today are more sensitive in low light than previous models, so it's possible to shoot much of your work using available light and the camera's automatic iris. But the key to making video look really good is to manage the available light. "Control the canvas," says Steve Hooker, chief photojournalist at WIS-TV in Columbia, S.C. Knowing the basics of good lighting will improve your photography.

Technical Issues

Most digital cameras today can automatically adjust for color temperature so that white objects actually come out white, but the auto white balance function isn't always dependable. Test your camera under different lighting conditions (sunlight, clouds, incandescent-tungsten and fluorescent bulbs), and you're likely to see that the auto setting leaves something to be desired. Learn how to set the white balance manually to produce the best possible image. Fill the frame with a white object like a sheet of paper, set the white balance and be sure to reset it for each lighting situation.

A simple lens hood—a collar that surrounds and extends the lens—helps to exclude light you don't want in the frame, especially sunlight. Light coming in at an angle can distort or wash out part of the image, resulting in what is called "lens flare." A lens hood can prevent that. Even when your subject isn't backlit, you can get lens flare from sunlight that's coming from the side, especially when the sun is low in the sky. If you don't have a hood, you can shade the lens with your hand or a hat, but be careful to keep your fingers or hat brim out of the picture.

Placement

Whenever possible, position your subject so the main light source is facing that person and slightly to the side, not behind the subject. For example, you don't want to interview a person who's standing in front of a window. That kind of strong backlight will leave your subject in the dark. If you or the subject can't move, or if you need a particular object in the background, you can always adjust your exposure for the subject, but then the background will wash out. A better approach is to expose for the background, and then use an external light to illuminate the subject so its exposure matches the background.

If you do add light to a scene, make it motivated. That simply means adding light to supplement an existing source, whenever possible. For example, if you're shooting in a room with a window or a lamp, place your main light source so that the light in the frame appears to be coming from the window or lamp.

Using just one light can be harsh on your subject, especially if it's coming from directly in front. Avoid using a camera-mounted light, if at all possible. If you must use a single light, hold it off to the side so it hits the subject at an angle. Three-point lighting

GO ONLINE

Module 3: Watch a pro demonstrate how to set up interview lighting in a hurry.

is much more flattering. Use a key light placed about 45 degrees to the left or right of the camera as your primary illumination. Add a fill light on the opposite side to soften the shadows, and a back light (sometimes called a hair light) behind and above your subject to separate it from the background.

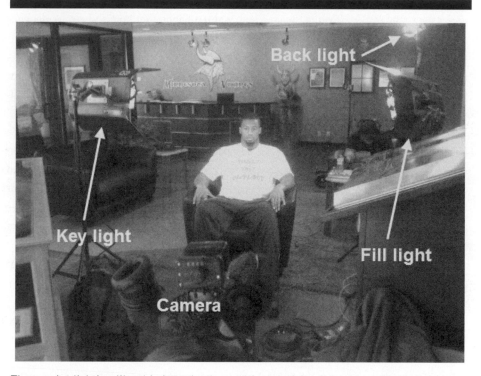

Three-point lighting like this is typically used for television interviews shot indoors.

Source: Photo courtesy of Dave Wertheimer.

ON-CAMERA INTERVIEWS

Take time to establish rapport with the person you are interviewing before you start asking questions. CBS photojournalist Les Rose suggests leaving the gear in the car when you go to say "hello." When you come back with the camera, he says, "You are a person with a camera, not a camera person. Big difference!" Other suggestions for establishing rapport include putting a microphone on the subject before setting up the camera and lights. This allows the subject to relax and get used to having the mic on.

While setting up, chat with the subject about something unrelated to the topic of your story, like what they had for breakfast or lunch. Get a mic level from what they say while you're chatting. The last thing you want is to remind them that you'll be recording by asking them to do something unnatural like counting to 10. For the same reason, ask people to spell their names at the end of the interview, not the beginning. And if you're working with a photojournalist, don't turn around to ask, "Are you rolling?" Set up a nonverbal signal in advance—a simple nod of the head will do—so you won't put your subject on edge.

Placement

The traditional way to shoot an on-camera interview is to have the reporter facing the subject from a comfortable distance, either sitting or standing. You want to be close enough to have a conversation in a normal tone of voice. The camera is then placed slightly to one side of the reporter, so the subject isn't looking directly into the lens. If you're doing multiple interviews for the same story, change the camera position for each interview so your subjects aren't all facing in the same screen direction. This makes editing easier and the finished product more attractive.

You don't always have to take what CBS correspondent Byron Pitts calls the "Dragnet" approach to interviewing. He likes to sit next to the person he's talking with. "Rarely do I have a 'conversation' with someone standing one foot in front of me," he says. If you're working with a photographer, just make sure he or she knows what you're up to if you decide to try this slightly unorthodox approach.

Active Interviews

Some on-camera interviews lend themselves to a different approach that's often called "active interviewing." Instead of sitting or standing while facing the camera, the subject in an active interview is doing something that is relevant to the story while at the same time talking about it. Let's say you're doing a story about a company in your area that has an innovative, on-site child care program. Instead of interviewing the company president in an office and shooting b-roll of the day care center later, you could talk to him or her in the center. As the president describes what makes the center unique, you can get video of those features.

KNOW AND TELL

LIVE INTERVIEWS

Live interviews are more difficult than interviews on tape, and not only because your time is limited. A live interview needs to stand on its own. Your questions have to include enough information for the audience to follow what's being discussed, but not so much that it appears you are showing off your knowledge or dominating the conversation. A good live interview also needs a beginning, middle and end, just like a story does, so you should have a mental road map for the interview before you start.

Former ABC "Nightline" anchor Ted Koppel is one of the best live interviewers ever. Quality live interviewing, Koppel says, requires adequate time and an ability on the part of the interviewer to mentally edit

Source: Photo courtesy of Bob Severi/Discovery Channel.

the interview as it is occurring. "The essence of journalism is editing," he told the Columbia Journalism Review. "And editing while you are on the air is extremely tough. It means sifting out the extraneous from the relevant, the new from the old" in your head, while also listening to what the person is saying and considering what else you want to know.

Koppel says he always tries to consider what the viewer or listener might be thinking and asks questions along those lines. He also believes that the audience should identify with the interviewer and see that person as representing viewers' interests. "You can lose that identification easily by losing control of the interview, or by being too aggressive or rude, or by not asking the right type of questions."

Source: Tom Rosenstiel, "Yakety-Yak: The Lost Art of Interviewing," *Columbia Journalism Review* (January–February 1995), http://archives.cjr.org/year/95/1/interviewing.asp.

Basically, an active interview involves shooting the conversation and the b-roll at the same time in the same location, which makes editing that much easier. You have to be nimble to make this work, of course. Put a wireless microphone on the subject, and be prepared to move the camera and tripod and even to shoot hand-held to get the video you need. For a two-person crew, shooting an active interview is obviously more challenging than a standard, sit-down interview. The reporter and photographer have to be on the same page throughout. The photojournalist must listen carefully to what's being said and make sure that when the subject says something important it's captured on camera. For the same reason, the reporter must pay close attention to what the photojournalist is shooting, taking care not to ask a crucial question while the camera is off the subject or moving.

Teams that do this well often develop subtle ways of communicating while shooting. For example, reporter Boyd Huppert and photojournalist Jonathan Malat, who work at KARE-TV in Minneapolis, Minn., have their own verbal shorthand. If Huppert hears a sound bite he knows he'll want on camera while Malat is shooting b-roll, he might interject a comment like, "I'm sorry, what's that?" These apparently offhand remarks are designed to get the subject to repeat himself, and they're a clue to the photographer that he needs to get the subject on camera. You'll notice that Huppert does not directly ask the person to repeat a comment because he's found that people tend to get self-conscious or ruin the sound bite by adding something like, "Well, as I told you before. . . ."

NONVISUAL STORIES

Not all stories are "made for TV," with eye-catching pictures and sizzling sound, but you can still tell those stories in a visual way if you think creatively. A metaphor or simile might help you convey the central point of the story. For example, in a story about hearing loss for WCCO-TV in Minneapolis, Minn., reporter David Schechter explained the damage that loud sounds cause to tiny hairs inside the ear by comparing it with the effect a crowd of playful children would have on a small field. The video of kids trampling the grass made the point quite clearly. Ask experts to compare complicated concepts to something simpler and more concrete, and you may be surprised by the visual possibilities. Comparing the electric grid to a row of falling dominoes might help explain how a power outage spreads and could give you a much better visual than static shots of electric meters.

Stories with lots of numbers are often challenging to tell on TV, but they can be made more engaging as well. Consider the government's monthly unemployment report. Reporter John Sharify made the dry statistics compelling in a story for KOMO-TV. He visited a food bank in Seattle, Wash., and took a long tracking shot of the people waiting in line, focusing in on a few individuals. Afterwards, Sharify asked those people about their employment status and told their stories in his narration to bring the statistics to life.

Just because there's nothing happening in front of your camera doesn't mean there are no visuals for your story. Home video, photo albums and yearbooks can yield great images. Government agencies routinely shoot video to document their work, and they may be willing to share it with you. When reporter Nancy Amons was covering a story for WSMV-TV in Nashville, Tenn., about a government dam project that failed, she realized that showing the dam just sitting there wouldn't be compelling. But it turned out the government had video of trial runs showing exactly why it didn't work, and officials gave her a copy to use on the air. Even documents can be brought to life for use on the air, if you shoot them with care.

TRADE TOOLS

SHOOTING DOCUMENTS FOR TV

Why would you want to shoot documents for a television story? Because showing the audience documentary evidence that supports what you're talking about can build credibility. The trick is to find a way to bring the documents to life.

- Instead of creating full-screen graphics, shoot the page, tight. Use highlights or lighting techniques to make the words stand out.

- Capture and use natural sound as you move pages or flip through documents.

- Be sure your narration repeats the words on the paper to reinforce their significance, but you generally won't read every word on the screen.

- If the volume of the documentation is part of the story, use it in a stand-up. For example, one reporter took a computer printout of DUI convicts who had never served their sentences and unrolled it along the jail's hallways. The sheer length of the list made the point that the city wasn't holding violators accountable.

- Have someone directly involved in the story read the documents aloud. This provides an opportunity for b-roll and brings the documents to life, sometimes with emotion that would be inappropriate in a reporter's narration.

Graphics

Charts, diagrams and maps can convey significant information visually in news stories in all media. As we've already mentioned, you'll want to collect any graphics you run across that you can use "as is" on the air or online. For example, a developer holding a news conference about a building project would likely have renderings to show what the development will look like once it's completed. If you can get a digital version, so much the better, but a good-quality paper version can be scanned and posted almost as quickly. Just make sure you're not violating any copyright protection.

While premade graphics are a time-saver, it's important to fact-check them just as you would a press release, so you'll still need the data that were used to build them. You'll also need raw data to construct interactive graphics for the Web. It's often easier to do that by starting from a data set than by extracting the data from an existing graphic. Instead of trying to decipher the color code on a complex world population map, for example, you could build your own map from a simple list of countries and their populations.

Get in the habit of asking for data whenever you cover a "numbers" story, whether it's the city budget or election returns. Make it easy for people to give it to you by carrying a USB flash drive so they can provide you with a copy on the spot. A promise to e-mail it to you later is often forgotten, but it's worth asking if all else fails. If you have a choice, ask for raw data in a format that's easy to work with, like Microsoft Excel or Access. We'll talk more about graphics in Chapters 6 and 8.

Natural Sound Stories

Some stories on television and especially online rely exclusively on pictures and sound, with no reporter narration (also called "track"). These natural sound or "nat sound" stories aren't easy to produce well. If the result is to be more than just a photo essay, you have to create a coherent narrative with the sound you collect. That can require more planning and just as much reporting as any other story. But the results can be powerful. Having a clear focus helps you decide what kind of sound and pictures you need to tell the story. "The sounds you record and the interviews you conduct are your only tools when you hit the edit bay," says photojournalist Tim King. Think story structure from the start. You need sound to introduce the issue and the people involved, explain it and demonstrate its resolution. Listen, as well, for sound that will give you a strong ending to tie up your story.

Interview Strategies

For a nat sound story, you'll conduct interviews differently than you would for other kinds of stories. As we've noted, in a traditional interview it's advisable to avoid two-part questions because the subject may just answer one part. But for nat sound stories,

TRADE TOOLS

10 RULES FOR VIDEO JOURNALISTS

Travis Fox is a talented video journalist who started his career as a still photographer. He's developed a list of 10 "golden rules" for shooting video, in reverse order, of course:

Source: Photo courtesy of Travis Fox.

1. Get "X-roll." X-roll is when you get your interviewee's money quotes in their natural environment.

2. Shoot within 180 degrees around a subject. In other words, don't walk around your subject when interviewing them.

3. Sequence your video with a variety of detail, tight, medium and wide shots as well as cutaway shots. 50 percent of shots will be tight, 25 percent medium and 25 percent wide.

4. Remember the 80:20 ratio (80 percent should be b-roll and 20 percent should be interviews).

5. Get close to the subject when interviewing them for audio purposes.

6. Stay quiet when shooting.

7. If you do not get the shot, you do not have it.

8. Do not move the camera when shooting (unless you are an advanced videographer).

9. Hold every shot for 10 seconds.

10. Wear headphones.

Source: Chrys Wu, "10 Golden Rules for Video Journalists," January 10, 2009, www.chryswu.com/blog/2009/01/10/10-golden-rules-for-video-journalists/.

double-barreled questions actually work well. For example, instead of asking people to identify themselves, you might ask who they are and what they're doing. "It's an easy way to introduce the subject and the story," says chief photojournalist Bryan Barr of WBFF-TV in Baltimore, Md. It's also a good way to get responses in complete sentences, containing complete thoughts, which photographer John Goheen believes are essential for nat sound stories.

Because the people you talk to will serve as your narrators, do active interviews in multiple locations. If you have one, put a wireless lav on your subjects and let them get used to it before asking questions. Then talk to them while they're doing something. Photojournalist Travis Fox calls this shooting "X-roll." Feel free to repeat your questions at several locations. "This gives me more options later in the edit room," says Goheen. Get more sound than you think you need. Goheen often conducts a more formal sit-down interview at the end of the shoot in a quiet location, just for audio purposes. This gives him additional sound he can use over the video he's already shot. The same technique works just as well if you're collecting audio for an online slide show.

Don't be afraid that asking the same question several times will make you look stupid. It may be necessary to get sound bites that will carry a story without narration. "If you ask someone to re-explain something, they will usually be a lot more descriptive," says Barr. Playing dumb also can elicit useful sound. Go ahead and ask what the score is and how much time is left in a game, even when the answer is obvious, because you may need that information on tape.

TEAMWORK

While journalists today do more and more of their work independently, television and multimedia news are still team sports. Reporters and photojournalists work together to collect the visual and audio elements they need to tell a complete and memorable story. Reporters, producers and graphic artists work together to develop charts, maps and other illustrations that will make the story more understandable.

Teamwork means sharing responsibility for what goes on the air or the Web. Photographers help reporters write, suggesting lines that go with the video or still photos they've shot. In the field, reporters help photographers spot great visuals to illustrate the main points of the story. Even when working in pairs, reporters and photographers must both be visual journalists, committed to understanding and telling a story together.

Story Planning

Reporters and photographers should suggest story ideas and touch base with each other as soon as they know they're working on a story together. A reporter making calls on a story can benefit from a photographer's perspective. Before the team leaves the newsroom, photographers can help reporters think about the video they might need. An early conversation about the story could tip the photographer to bring special equipment for the shoot. Don't wait until you are in the car!

In the Field

Longtime photojournalist Lane Michaelsen, now vice president of news and content at WTVJ in Miami, likes to joke that the root word in *reporter* is *porter.* Reporters should volunteer to carry equipment, put microphones in place and hold lights. Unless they're writing on deadline, they should not sit in the car while the photographer gets b-roll. By the same token, photographers shouldn't hang back while the reporter gathers information. Unless they've decided to split up in the field for efficiency's sake, reporter-photographer teams work side by side so they both know what elements they've collected and what they still need. And on breaking news, they stay together so they can watch each other's backs.

GO ONLINE

Ongoing Story Module: Develop a shooting plan, including times, locations and the elements you want to collect.

Mind reading only works in the movies, so teams need to communicate and collaborate from start to finish. Photographers need to tell reporters when they've captured a great shot, and if they have a line in mind to go with it, they should share that too. Reporters need to tell photographers whether there's a shot they definitely need in order to get a point across. Talk about what you'll use for opening and closing video while you're still at the scene. On breaking news, when there's no time to screen the video, photographers should make sure reporters know exactly what they have to work with before they write.

When concluding an interview, the reporter should routinely ask whether the photographer has any questions. Some photojournalists have a knack for rephrasing a question that was asked earlier so you get a better response. Photographers also should have the confidence to ask questions during a shoot. "A simple 'What's up?' may yield a good two-second bite," says KARE-TV's Malat. Photographer Juan Renteria of WFAA-TV in Dallas, Texas, says he tries to think like a reporter as well as a photographer. "I ask, 'What lines would I use here, if I use this image? What other shots do I need for a sequence?' Everybody should think like each other, and like a producer, to make the best story."

WORKING ALONE

For a long time, it's been common at small-market television stations for journalists to work as "one man bands" to report and shoot their own stories. But in recent years the practice has spread to larger stations and even to the networks. Whether you call them video journalists (VJs), solo journalists (sojos) or backpack journalists, the concept is the same: One person is responsible for reporting the story, shooting and editing the video, and producing the final product for television or the Web, or both.

VJs and Backpackers

Gannett-owned WUSA in Washington, D.C., made headlines in 2009 when it became the first major-market network affiliate to convert all reporters and photographers into multimedia journalists. The British Broadcasting Corporation (BBC) took a similar step at its local newsrooms. Other companies have introduced the concept more slowly. Since 2003 CNN has been deploying what it calls "video correspondents" and "all platform journalists," which the company describes as journalists "equipped with CNN's specially designed digital newsgathering kit to enable a single correspondent to shoot, edit and transmit reports from anywhere in the world." ABC News announced in 2010 that it would transition to using more "digital journalists," who can work alone or in pairs.

As we've already noted, technological improvements have made it more feasible for one person to do it all. Cameras are lighter and more foolproof than ever, so it's not as difficult as it once was to produce acceptable pictures and sound. Digital editing software is widely available and fairly easy to master. But that doesn't mean it's easy to be a sojo. "You learn very quickly that, while aiming to be a jack-of-all-trades, it's hard to be a master of one," says Preston Mendenhall, a pioneering sojo who reported extensively from Iraq and other hot spots for NBC News.

Pros and Cons

"The most rewarding part of working alone is knowing the package you created is completely yours," says backpack journalist Kevin Torres of KUSA-TV in Denver. The most difficult part? Getting everything done well and on time. "When you're a one man band, there are a million little things you have to keep in the back of your mind every day," he says.

Kevin Sites, who covered the Iraq war for CNN, later spent a year as a sojo covering "hot zones" around the world for Yahoo (http://hotzone.yahoo.com/). He told an Online News Association conference that he often felt he was stretched too thin. "When I first started this job it was really confusing because I was carrying a video camera, a still camera and a notebook and I wasn't sure which one I was going to use first," Sites says. "It took me three African countries to figure out, what do I need to focus on?" Eventually, he adopted a strategy of focusing on the text story first to get the details, then shooting video to document action and still photos to put a human face on conflict.

Backpack journalist Kevin Sites carried both a video and a still camera when reporting from Nepal in 2006.

Source: Photo courtesy of Dinesh Wagle, *Kantipur Daily,* Kathmandu, Nepal.

Mendenhall believes the sojo concept works best on feature stories. "Breaking news breaks the back of a solo journalist, and dampens quality," he says. But Lisa Lambden, formerly with the BBC, says an all-VJ newsroom can outperform a traditional one on breaking news by not asking one VJ to do it all. "When the bad weather hits and homes and businesses are flooded we can field five or six times as many cameras as our opposition. We are able to get really close to the people affected and our stories are more powerful as a result," Lambden says. "VJs can also outperform in terms of access. We've had many examples of where a VJ with a small camera can get access on a story where a conventional two-person crew can't."[3]

If you do work alone on breaking news, you have to establish some priorities. "Your video is the most important content you bring back from the field, so concentrate on your shooting," Mendenhall advises. His point is that if you miss a shot you may not get another opportunity to capture it. The old adage "shoot first, ask questions later" is good advice for sojos and photojournalists in breaking news situations.

Time Management

If there's one thing most solo journalists will agree on, it's that doing it all on your own requires terrific time management skills. Torres literally backtimes his entire workday, setting mini-deadlines for every step. That way, he knows when he needs to stop shooting, start writing and finish editing in order to make air. "I try to be as precise as possible," he says. "When I go over on time with one thing I cut from another."

Because a solo journalist is responsible for everything from transportation to transmission, another time-saver is to map the route to each location before leaving to avoid backtracking and other delays. It's also a good idea to search the Web in advance for locations with strong WiFi signals to save time feeding in the story. Solo journalists also save time by asking for help when they need it—enlisting a bystander to find people to interview, for example, so they can keep shooting b-roll.

KUSA-TV's Kevin Torres is a backpack journalist in every sense of the word. He carries all of his gear in a backpack everywhere he goes.

Source: Photo courtesy of Kevin Torres

TOOLS OF THE TRADE

In addition to a notebook and pens, many of today's journalists carry a gear bag stuffed with cameras (still and video), audio recorder, microphones, headphones and computer media like a USB flash drive or portable hard drive to capture all the elements they need to tell a story on different platforms. They're also likely to have a cell phone, iPhone or BlackBerry-type handheld and a laptop computer so they can file reports from the field.

Audio gear and camera equipment gets smaller, lighter and more sophisticated all the time. It may take a while to learn what your equipment can do, but it's worth the investment. "Read the manual," says Minnesota Public Radio's Kerr. "It could be some of those buttons on your machine could help you in gathering sound. Just as likely they could really mess you up." Trying to figure that out in the middle of a breaking news situation is foolhardy. Practice ahead of time so you know what to do when it counts.

Whatever you carry, it's important to be sure that your tools are in working order every day. There's nothing more embarrassing than arriving on the scene only to discover there is no tape or memory card in the camera or that the batteries are dead. It's a good idea to have an equipment checklist to make sure your gear is always ready to go, and to carry extra batteries and spares whenever possible.

Cameras

These days it seems that every person on the planet carries a camera at all times. Pocket-sized point-and-shoot cameras and cell phones can capture digital video. The quality gets better all the time, with even simple cameras now shooting high-definition video. In breaking news situations, cell phone video has proved to be more than acceptable for use online and on TV. When a small plane piloted by Yankees pitcher Cory Lidle crashed into a highrise in New York City in 2006, Fox News Channel streamed video from a Palm Treo smartphone on the air, live, until a better quality feed became available. Cell phone video of a woman who was shot to death during violent anti-government protests in Iran was uploaded to YouTube and shown on television around the world. It won a prestigious George Polk Award in 2010.

While a digital camera of any size can usually capture audio by way of a built-in microphone, the result is often muddy sounding at best. Some small cameras and mobile phones have inputs for external mics, which improve the audio quality substantially.

Thanks to the latest advances in technology, the mantra for at least some professional photojournalists is "one tool, many platforms," as they can now use the same camera to capture both stills and video. At the San Jose Mercury News, every photographer was outfitted with a high-definition Sony video camera. Instead of shooting separate still photos, they could simply grab still frames from the video they shoot and publish the pictures in the newspaper. Because the video is high-definition the quality of the stills was plenty good enough to print, even in fairly large formats. Not all photojournalists are convinced, however, and many who now shoot for both print and online outlets continue to carry a digital still camera as well as a video camera. The problem, of course, is that they can't use both at once, which means they may miss the "money shot" in one format or another.

Audio Recorders

Digital audio recorders come in a variety of shapes and sizes. The earliest digital format adopted by professionals was the DAT, or digital audio tape recorder, which was replaced by

SHOOTING TIPS FOR SMALL CAMERAS

When news breaks, the best camera to shoot with is the one you have on hand. One lesson learned from YouTube is that technical quality is secondary when it comes to newsworthy video. But it's always worth the effort to capture the best video possible under the circumstances, whether you're shooting with a cell phone or a pocket-sized digital camera.

- Keep the camera steady. Shaky video is hard to watch, but that's what you get from a lot of these small, lightweight cameras. The good news is that they all have a threaded tripod mount, so use it. Yes, it may look silly when you perch a Flip on a full-sized tripod, but it works. A flexible "gorillapod" is also handy to have. They weigh almost nothing and can be attached to lots of surfaces. If you have neither, rest the camera on a wall or the back of a chair to keep it steady.

- Avoid the zoom at all costs. While most of these cameras have zoom lenses, they're absolutely worthless. You can't zoom smoothly with any of them, and when you are zoomed in, the video quality goes from marginal to unacceptable. If you want a tighter shot, move in closer.

- Get close to get decent audio. If your camera has an external mic input, by all means use it. Many of them don't, so they'll only capture half-decent audio if you get close to the source. If you're doing an interview, try to find a quiet spot.

- Keep your camera charged and/or carry spare batteries. These little cameras can be power hogs, and they don't always warn you when they're getting low.

- Download what you've shot and clear your memory card on a regular basis. Video takes up much more space than still photos, so it's also a good idea to carry a spare memory card.

Finally, this may seem obvious, but make sure you know how to use the camera before you actually need to. The Flip and its ilk are simple enough, but it can take a few steps to get some cell phones and still cameras into video mode.

TRADE TOOLS

TRADE TOOLS

GEAR LIST

Most news organizations provide their journalists with gear, but if you decide to build your own kit, here's very a basic list:

- Digital video camera.
- Digital still camera.
- Digital audio recorder.
- Headphones.
- At least two good-quality lavalier mics.
- Handheld mic (may be a shotgun mic).
- Lightweight tripod.
- Portable, battery-powered light.
- Laptop with editing software.
- A wireless card so you can file from the field.

the smaller and less expensive minidisc recorder. Today, many journalists carry recorders that use flash memory instead of replaceable media, making it quick and easy to drag and drop the recorded audio files to a computer for storage and editing. Ideally, you want a recorder that lets you control the recording level manually and that has a separate microphone input.

With an audio recorder, you can begin experimenting with multimedia journalism without jumping straight into shooting video. Rather than trying to take pictures and record audio at the same time, Josh Meltzer started out by carrying a minidisc recorder and shotgun microphone in a waist pack in addition to his standard still camera. After shooting a story, he'd take out the recorder and ask people to talk about the moments he'd documented with his pictures. Or he'd go back to the paper, sit down in a quiet room and record his comments about the story. He'd then use the stills and audio to create a slide show for the newspaper's website.

Microphones

As we've discussed, built-in microphones are mostly worthless for recording clear, crisp audio. A professional gear bag usually includes at least two kinds of external microphones: lav and handheld, either a stick mic or shotgun. Knowing the difference between the various types of microphones can help you select the right one for the job and use it properly in the field.

A microphone's pickup pattern tells you where it's most sensitive. Different types work best in different situations. Lavs are small, unobtrusive and usually omnidirectional—great for ambient sound and interviews or stand-ups in relatively quiet settings. Make sure to place them as close as possible to the source of the sound, or background noise will be a problem. Hide wires inside clothing if you're shooting video. Stick mics have a more

MICROPHONES AND ACCESSORIES

Omnidirectional

Example: Lavalier microphone.

Picks up sound from all directions. Good for ambient sound, to give a sense of place. If used for interviews or stand-ups, must be placed close to the subject's mouth. A wireless lav can be attached to almost anything, from a squeaky hinge to the collar of a barking dog. Somewhat fragile.

Cardioid

Example: Stick microphone.

Directional microphone picks up sound mainly from the front in a heart-shaped pattern. Some have more of a figure-8 pattern, picking up sound from the back as well. Be careful when using hand-held as these mics can pick up vibrations. Extremely durable.

Hypercardioid

Example: Shotgun microphone.

Super-directional microphone must be carefully aimed to pick up sound. Can be used to pick up natural sound or for stand-ups in noisier situations. Can be placed farther away than a standard cardioid and still produce good-quality sound. Usually requires its own battery.

Specialty

Example: Lip microphone.

Designed for particular conditions, such as extremely noisy locations. A lip mic can cut out almost all background sound, even jet planes and the Indianapolis 500.

TRADE TOOLS

directional pickup pattern so they cut out more background sound. They're typically used for news conferences or office interviews. If you're shooting video, try to keep them out of camera range. Shotgun microphones are the most directional of all and do a good job picking up natural sound. They work well for stand-ups, too, in noisier settings.

A few mic accessories are also good to have. A wind screen that slides onto the microphone will reduce, if not eliminate, wind noise. It can also minimize popping consonants like "p" and "b." Stands and clamps can be set on or attached to a stable surface like a desk or podium, allowing you to keep both hands free.

If you're recording sound while also shooting video, wireless microphones offer the most flexibility, but they're expensive and their transmitter-receiver system can be tricky to work with. If you're using wired mics, make sure you have plenty of audio cable so you can place the microphone close, move the camera and still get good sound. All mics are sensitive to wind noise, so it's a good idea to use a windscreen whenever you're shooting outdoors.

TAKING IT HOME

Reporting for multimedia requires much more than the basic facts of a story. You need a lot of different elements to help you tell that story in a way that takes advantage of the strengths of multimedia. To construct a strong TV news story, you need to capture top-quality video, clear sound bites and crisp natural sound. An online story might also call for still photos, audio and interactive graphics. In today's multimedia newsrooms, journalists must think differently about every story in order to collect all the different elements they will need to tell it in print, on the air and online.

Chad Lawhorne, who covers City Hall for the Lawrence Journal-World in Kansas, says multimedia journalism is more work, but it's also liberating. "I feel I have more freedom to tell more of the story because I have the online edition," he says. "I have an outlet that can give more detail."

TALKING POINTS

1. A national report on drinking and drug use by college students has just been released and you are assigned to do a local version of the story. What images and

sounds would you want to capture to tell this story in video form for broadcast or online? Tell specifically how you would go about collecting those images and sounds.

2. Do you think VJs or sojos will be the standard in broadcast newsrooms within five years? Why or why not? What difference do you think this will make to the range and quality of broadcast journalism?

3. Find an audio slide show online and watch it. Would the story have been more effective as a video story? Why or why not? Now watch the slide show without listening to the audio. Does the story make sense? What's missing? Close your eyes and run the slide show again. Does the audio tell a complete story without the photos?

ONLINE LEARNING MODULE 3

Activate or buy this chapter's online learning module at journalism.cqpress.com to get access to:

- SKILL BUILDING: Decide how you would shoot a follow-up TV story based on newly available information, then watch what one reporter did with that same information.

- DISCOVER: See how one journalist reported a story for multiple media.

- EXPLORE: Learn more about photojournalism and multimedia skills.

- A video tour of a professional TV photojournalist's light kit, plus advice from award-winning photojournalists on how to shoot better stories.

- A digital version of this chapter's text in full color with active links.

Also, continue your work on the ONGOING STORY MODULE. Develop a shooting plan for this story, including times, locations and the elements you want to collect.

4 REPORTING IN DEPTH

Journalists who report in multiple media need to know how to do more than scratch the surface and meet a deadline. They must be able to report in depth, so they can produce meaty stories in any medium. In this chapter, we'll take a look at how you can go about digging deeper to report more fully on a community or a topic.

Network television correspondent Jeff Greenfield once compared news reporting to dry cleaning: In both cases, he said, it's often "in by 9, out by 5." But not all stories are one-day wonders, and even a "quick turn" can lead you to another story down the line if you keep track of the information you discover and the contacts you make along the way.

Digging for information to put the news in context and following stories over a period of time can add depth to your reporting in any medium. Journalists who can do this well are highly valued in their newsrooms. They're the beat reporters who break news on a regular basis and the investigative reporters who hold the powerful accountable. They're the multimedia reporters who always have enough information to build graphics or inter-active elements online.

One way to report in depth is to do it in "3D," with data, documents and diverse sources, says Randy Reddick, a pioneer in the field of computer-assisted reporting. Data and statistics allow reporters to make comparisons over time or between groups, which adds perspective to their stories. Documents can add background or validate or refute a claim, and diverse sources can add texture and authenticity. Data sets and original documents can be posted online to supplement your stories or can be used to create graphics to illustrate them. To acquire all this extra information and master the 3D approach, you'll need more than basic reporting skills.

MAPPING THE COMMUNITY

To report the news in depth you have to really know the community you cover. But journalism can be a transient business, so you may find yourself working in an area you know little or nothing about. It's incumbent upon you to learn your way around and figure out what makes the community tick. The military motto, "Time spent in reconnaissance is seldom wasted," applies just as well to journalists; the payoff in story ideas and sources is well worth the investment.

Research and Explore

Get to know the area you'll cover by doing some research. Look at government data on local demographics and the economy (the reference section at www.usa.gov is a good starting point). Find out who the largest employers are and whether they're thriving or hurting. Check with the local Chambers of Commerce, convention and visitors bureaus, and historical societies to get a sense of the area's past as well as its present. Drop by local libraries and talk to a veteran librarian. What are people here proudest of? What doesn't work as well as it should? Browse the classified section of the telephone book in print or online. Are there more restaurants than churches? More movie theaters than massage parlors?

As you build your background knowledge, buy a good map and spend some time exploring on your own. Don't be afraid to get lost—you never know what you'll discover. Walk around the downtown areas and drive through the neighborhoods. If it's available, ride public transit and listen to other riders. Take cabs and talk to the drivers. Ride a bike or jog and talk to locals who are out and about. Make a special effort to visit places where people who are different from you live and congregate. Eat at ethnic restaurants and chat with the owners and customers. What do the people you meet have in common? What divides them?

Read, Listen and Connect

It may seem obvious that you need to read the local newspaper, but don't forget to check smaller community newspapers or hyperlocal news sites that cover neighborhoods or the suburbs, or that serve different ethnic or minority groups. Be sure to scan the comments and letters to the editor—they often provide a glimpse into the community's values. Listen to local radio DJs and talk show hosts to see what the hot topics are. They often have a finger on the pulse of what matters most to the subset of the community they cater to. Watch as much local news on television as you can too. But don't stop there: See what local bloggers are writing about; search for local Twitter users and Facebook groups; follow those who seem most worthwhile.

Attend a few public meetings on your own time and introduce yourself to the people who seem most informed and involved. Arrange to meet community leaders for coffee and conversation, or ask them to give you a tour of their favorite places. Seek out places where people gather to talk—places like churches, synagogues, mosques and temples, community centers and parks, barbershops, diners or the sidelines at soccer or Little League games. Don't do any formal interviews; just listen to what different kinds of people are talking about and chat with them about what's important in their lives. Get contact information for the people who seem most plugged in and follow up with them. Ask them for the names of two other people they think you should know. In a few weeks, you'll be well on your way to building a diverse group of sources that will help you tell deeper, richer stories.

BEAT REPORTING

When Springfield, Mo., was searching for a new school superintendent, one reporter got the scoop everyone wanted: The leading candidate for the job had turned the offer down. John Shields broke the story on KYTV and sat back to watch the other stations and the local paper scramble to catch up. How did he do it? As the station's education reporter, Shields had developed sources who were in the know and who gave him the story first because they trusted him to get it right.

Many newsrooms assign reporters to beats or specialties, usually a geographic area or a specific topic. Beat system advocates believe there's no better way to encourage original reporting that has substance and depth. That's because reporters who specialize become experts in the subject they cover, so they know which questions to ask and where to look for answers. They are constantly expanding their knowledge of the issues and their sources, and they're persistent and organized enough to follow developments over time.

You may not have the opportunity to focus exclusively on one beat, especially when you're first starting out, but you can use the tactics and strategies beat reporters use to enhance your stories on any subject. Choose a topic that interests you and dig right in.

Getting Started

Beat reporters need the same basic reporting skills we discussed in Chapter 2, and more. They need the ability to develop sources and track information efficiently for months or even years. They often need to master a specialized vocabulary to decipher documents and data on the beat. And they need to really understand the institutions that dominate the beats they cover. Learning how systems work takes time and effort, but it pays off in stories that non-beat reporters can't match.

To develop these skills, you need to put in some study time. Read everything you can about the topic, including specialized publications that cover your beat. Look for mentions of government agencies, nonprofit groups and experts you can contact for more information. Check their websites and subscribe to e-mail lists or RSS feeds. Follow them on Twitter or Facebook. Most important, get up and go. Beat reporters have to spend time on the beat, meeting and talking with people. "No one ever got a story sitting around the newsroom," says veteran reporter Mike Mather of WTKR-TV in Norfolk, Va.

Get to know everyone who could be helpful—from officials to clerks—and pass out your business card to everyone you meet on the beat. Ask them to put you on the mailing list (e-mail or paper) for news releases and reports. Reporter Ann Notarangelo of KPIX-TV in San Francisco makes a point of handing out business cards and telling everyone she talks to that she'd love to hear from them again. "Most of those cards, I'm sure, get thrown out," she says. "But sometimes I get a call, even weeks or months later, about a story idea."

Collect budgets, organizational charts, directories, schedules and agendas from all the agencies and groups that touch on your beat. Attend public meetings even if you don't plan to report on them; it's a great way to get to know the players. Listen for any mentions of data or statistics, and ask for copies of documents, in digital form, if possible. Your goal is to learn how the institution is supposed to work, how it really does work and who makes the decisions.

Understanding the institutions and collecting data and documents are just the first steps to covering a beat well. Once you know your way around, look for the bigger picture. What are the most important issues these institutions deal with, and how do their decisions affect people in your community?

Finding Sources

Sometimes the best sources on a beat aren't official or even immediately obvious, says Jim Detjen, director of the Knight Center for Environmental Journalism at Michigan State

KNOW AND TELL

LEARNING A BEAT

"If our best stories are told through people, our toughest reporting tasks often involve cracking the associations they form," says Eric Nalder, senior enterprise reporter for Hearst Newspapers. He uses these questions to begin learning his way around an organization or institution:

Source: Photo courtesy of Eric Nalder.

- Who are the players? Get staff directories and newsletters; contact professional associations; check for government contracts, permits, complaints and lawsuits.

- Who is in charge? Check Dun & Bradstreet (www.dnb.com) for private companies, Edgar (www.sec.gov/edgar.shtml) for public companies and Guidestar for IRS 990 forms of nonprofits (www.guidestar.org).

- Who are the regulators? Most federal agencies have an inspector general (www.ignet.gov); contact state auditors, legislative oversight committees and watchdog groups.

- What are the rules? For government agencies, use the code of federal regulations (www.gpoaccess.gov/cfr/); for private companies, ask federal regulators which laws apply.

- How are things done? Follow the paper trail; get internal memos; talk to insiders.

- Where are the mistakes recorded? Learn how the organization monitors and tracks errors and ask for the documents.

- Where is the spending recorded? Obtain a budget, which outlines spending plans, and a balance sheet, which documents how money was actually spent.

- Who knows the story and how can I get it? Work your sources to gain access to significant events. Firsthand knowledge is always best. "Be there, and you will be aware."

Source: Adapted from Eric Nalder, "Breaking and Entering, How to Dissect an Organization," http://home.earth link.net/~cassidyny/breaking.htm.

University and a longtime environmental reporter. "When I've written about water pollution being discharged into a river by a chemical company, I've sometimes found it useful to interview anglers, swimmers or water skiers who utilize the river to get their views on the situation," he says. "When I've written about air pollution, I've interviewed window washers, city foresters and pilots."[1]

Covering a beat means getting to know people well enough so they will trust you, while still maintaining a professional distance. That can be a tricky balancing act. To serve the public, you need to be careful not to "go native"—that is, to identify more with the people you cover than with the audience you're supposed to serve. For example, all beats have their own specialized vocabulary, and you'll want to learn the terms used by the people you cover so you can talk with them knowledgeably. But you also need to remember that most of the audience might not be familiar with those terms, so you won't want to use them in your stories. For example, a hospital spokesperson might tell you that the victim of a mugging suffered "lacerations and contusions," but you'd want to use the phrase "cuts and bruises." Always define or translate insider language to make sure your stories make sense.

Language isn't the only challenge beat reporters face. The hardest part of being a beat reporter, says veteran journalist Chip Scanlan, is "dealing with sources you have to return to every day even if you've written a story they don't like." However, beat reporters who know their subject matter, and who tell accurate and fair stories, find that even sources who may dislike their stories will often respect them. As Celeste Ford, who covered education for WABC-TV in New York, says, "School officials know my stories may criticize them but they'd rather have the critical story come from me, because they know I do my homework."

Tracking the Beat

To cover a beat or to follow stories over time it's essential to be well organized. To keep track of developments, you'll need a basic calendar, a source list and a future file. Use the calendar to note meetings, hearings, anniversaries and due dates for reports or action. Check it daily, and make sure to look several days ahead so you can confirm details and get a jump on upcoming stories. Maintain a reliable, portable system for filing and retrieving contact information. And keep a file of future story ideas, with daily lists of things to follow up on.

Many reporters use computer programs for each of these tasks to make it easy to search for people, dates and information. They'll store contact information and documents online or synchronize files between an office computer and a laptop, personal digital

BEAT REPORTER RESOURCES

Building expertise on a beat takes time, but you can learn a lot from other reporters who cover the same issues. Check these journalism groups for online resources, membership and conference information:

Association for Women in Sports Media (www.awsmonline.org)

Association of Capitol Reporters and Editors (capitolbeat.wordpress.com)

Association of Food Journalists (www.afjonline.com)

Association of Health Care Journalists (www.healthjournalism.org)

Criminal Justice Journalists (www.reporters.net/cjj)

Military Reporters and Editors (www.militaryreporters.org)

National Association of Science Writers (www.nasw.org)

National Education Writers Association (www.ewa.org)

Religion Newswriters Association (www.rna.org)

Society of American Business Editors and Writers (www.sabew.org)

Society of Environmental Journalists (www.sej.org)

assistant (PDA) or smartphone like a BlackBerry or iPhone so they can access the information anywhere. Because technology can be unreliable, though, it's critically important to back up the information frequently.

Some people still prefer to track information on paper, using a pocket planner or even a wall calendar. Choose whatever system works for you—just be sure to use it and to update it regularly, at least once a week. If possible, try to set aside a few minutes every morning or evening to sort and save the information you've been collecting all day long. It takes time to get organized and stay that way, but it's a habit that can save you on deadline.

If you're like most people, you'll probably have some manila folders for hard copy and computer "folders" for electronic documents, data, digital recordings and e-mails. Use the same labels for each to avoid confusion. Don't let things build up in a general folder; sort them regularly by subtopic or you'll never find what you want. For example, you might begin with a file labeled "City Budget," but as you follow the story you'll probably create separate folders for the biggest budget categories. Don't keep entire newspapers or documents in a stack. Clip and select what you want to keep and file it by topic. Or find the online version of the article and store it in a digital file. Don't depend on social bookmarking alone to keep track of stuff you'd like to refer to later, because it likely won't stay online forever. Keep copies of stories, scripts and video and audio logs in the same places as your background information so you can quickly find file video or bites for follow-up stories.

Get as much contact information as possible for every source—not just an office address and telephone number but also cell phone and home numbers, and e-mail and instant message addresses as well. Move names and numbers out of your notebook, off press releases and business cards, and into your database daily. And don't stop at just names and contact information. Enter key words so you can find that person again: story topic, type of business, general location—anything that might help you find someone if you've forgotten the person's name or where they work. You may also want to note a source's race, ethnicity or languages spoken to help you build a "rainbow Rolodex" of experts in all sorts of fields. If you're working on a story over several days or weeks, you may want to make a master list of contacts and keep a copy in the story file.

GO ONLINE

Ongoing Story Module: Decide how you would add context and depth to this story with data, documents or details.

Working the Beat

Once you discover a helpful source of information for one story, stay in touch with that person over the long term. Good reporters "work" their sources regularly, contacting them to see what's going on. Reporter Bob Buckley of WGHP-TV in High Point, N.C., makes what he calls a "five and three list" on Sundays—five people to visit during the week and three people to call each day. "People give information and stories to those they're comfortable with," he says. "And they'll get that way when you visit them some time other than when you need something from them."

When you make routine "beat checks" by telephone, don't just ask whether there's anything new and then hang up when the answer is no. Take time to get to know your sources and demonstrate your interest in the subject, and it will pay off over time. "I know that when I have seven calls on my voice mail about the same crime, I return the calls of reporters who make regular beat checks," says Susan Rossi Medina, former public information officer for the Arvada (Colo.) Police Department.[2]

CBS national correspondent Byron Pitts is an expert at keeping track of good sources. Every time he interviews someone, he makes a note of things he has learned about that person. Maybe the person likes to fish or has a daughter who plays basketball. Mentioning that the next time he calls can help him resume contact or give him a lead on a related story. Say, for example, that when he interviews a military expert about defense spending, they happen to have discussed the pictures of horses he noticed in her office. Pitts will make a note of that in his handheld computer or PDA. Then let's imagine he's assigned to do a story about equine virus. He would run a search for "horses" in his electronic contact list and pull up the military expert's name. Even if she is not an expert on equine virus, she might be able to help him find the right person to talk to for his story.

TOPICAL BEATS

Topical beat assignments are common at newspapers and even in some broadcast newsrooms, despite their relatively small staffs and high turnover rates. It's not unusual for TV reporters to be responsible for tracking news on a beat in addition to covering everyday news. Many online news sites are niche publications for audiences with special interests, so everyone who reports for them is effectively a beat reporter. That makes the ability to work a beat more valuable than ever.

Many newsrooms assign reporters to cover issues that are of particular interest or importance in the local community, so you won't find the same beats everywhere. In Orlando, Fla., for example, a beat reporter may cover transportation and tourism; in South Dakota, he or she might be assigned to cover issues involving the state's large American Indian population; and in communities with big defense installations reporters often track the military beat. That said, the following beats are among the most common in newsrooms today: crime and justice, government and politics, education, business, and health and medicine.

Crime and Justice

Few reporters have any training in criminal justice, but veterans on the police beat recommend taking at least one course in the subject. Police officials are notoriously reluctant to provide information to journalists, says crime reporter Caroline Lowe of WCCO-TV in Minneapolis, Minn., but if you know their rules, regulations and procedures, she says, you can ask better questions and improve your chances of learning what you want to know. Lowe herself didn't take just one criminal justice course; she has a graduate degree in law enforcement and says her studies gave her insights that helped her build relationships with police sources and tell stories that make a difference. "Nothing is more satisfying than doing a story that helps a victim or leads to positive change in the system," says Lowe.

Spending time on the crime beat means hanging out at police stations, firehouses, and with emergency medical technicians, getting to know their problems and procedures. Reporters who cover crime make it a habit to listen to the scanner and read the "blotter" or daily police log as well as any incident reports they can get their hands on to get a sense of what's happening in the community. To begin learning your way around the beat, arrange for a ride-along or ask a homicide detective to walk you through an unsolved case.

Nancy Weil of IDG News Service in Boston advises reporters to play by police rules when covering cops. "Don't be rude to them, especially at crime scenes. If they tell you to move back, do it," she says. Avoid at all costs getting them angry at you for any reason, Weil advises. "I have found that cops can hold grudges for all eternity. If one of them gets it in for you, that can infect others and you can be hosed when it comes to trying to build other relationships. If you treat them with respect and handle the stories you write with respect and let them know that you think what they are doing is important, you'll do a lot to earn their respect in turn and their trust."

Police reporters obviously need to know exactly how crimes are defined. A burglary and a robbery are not the same thing, for example. Developing a glossary of essential terms can prevent embarrassing mistakes.

A police news release may provide the basic facts about a crime, but good reporters dig deeper. Whenever possible they go to the scene to look for details and to talk with neighbors or eyewitnesses. They connect not only with police officials but also with Neighborhood Watch captains and activist groups, such as those that oppose drunk driving or domestic violence. Covering crime and public safety is not just a matter of reporting on incidents as they occur; to do it well, you have to look for patterns and trends, and always look for the impact of crime on individuals and communities.

Reporters who cover crime also need to pay attention to the potential impact of the coverage itself. Research has found that news reports tend to feature more minorities as

CRIME GLOSSARY

Assault: Threatening bodily harm.

Battery: Causing bodily harm to a person by any means.

Burglary: Illegally entering a building to commit a crime.

Homicide: Unlawful killing of a human being.

Larceny (theft): Taking money or property.

Manslaughter: Unintentional homicide.

Murder: Premeditated homicide.

Robbery: Taking money or property by force or threat of force.

TRADE TOOLS

perpetrators of crime and fewer as victims of crime than the actual data would support. According to several studies, the disparity is greatest when it comes to violent crime. "The absence of Black victims, coupled with the repeated presence of Black suspects across different sources of news, reinforces stereotypes about African Americans as a group audiences should fear," say researchers Lori Dorfman and Vincent Schiraldi.[3] They suggest that reporters broaden their sources, provide more context in crime stories and conduct periodic content audits to make sure their coverage reflects reality.

Crime reporters also dig for data they can use to develop stories and supplement their coverage online. Crime data is a key feature of the mash-up created by online journalist Adrian Holovaty at EveryBlock.com. (Mash-ups are websites or software applications that combine data from other sources.) Holovaty started by merging a database of all crimes reported to the Chicago police department with a Google map of the city and then expanded it to include other public information and to cover other cities. Users can search and sort the data by type of crime, date or location, and then pinpoint the information on a map.

EveryBlock.com describes itself as "a newsfeed for your neighborhood." It's a searchable mash-up of civic information, like crime reports and building permits, in multiple U.S. cities. This map shows crimes reported in the month of June 2010 in one Chicago neighborhood.

Source: EveryBlock.com (accessed July 6, 2010).

To cover courts, reporters must understand the judicial process from beginning to end. They should know what happens when a suspect is arrested, charged, arraigned, makes bail, is tried and sentenced or released. Experienced reporters say the best way to learn the process is to spend time at the courthouse. Begin with the court clerks, who keep track of the docket (the list of cases) and the calendar. Find out how to get copies of the court record, filings and testimony. Some of it will likely be online, but even today much of it will exist only on paper at the courthouse. Read the case files, including motions and pleadings before trial, and keep track of what's reported about the case if you can't be in court every day, which is more typical than not.

Some of the best sources of information on the justice beat are defense attorneys, who are often more willing than prosecutors to talk with reporters about cases they are working on. Do your best to understand legal jargon, but avoid using it in your stories. "Lawyers are counseled to use big words to confuse journalists," says S. L. Alexander, author of "Covering the Courts: A Handbook for Journalists." "If you don't know what something means, ask the person you're interviewing to explain it," she advises.

Government and Politics

Reporters who cover government need to understand its inner workings and keep a close eye on the impact of government actions. Reporters who ask the basic question, "Who cares about this?" when covering government at all levels are able to find people whose lives are affected by what government does; stories that feature those people are much more interesting to the audience.

Much of the business of government is conducted in meetings, so reporters on the city hall or state or national capitol beat can expect to cover plenty of them. Just remember, a dull meeting does not justify a dull story. The audience depends on the journalist to tell them only what's important, not everything that happened in chronological order. And the best stories about meetings focus not on what happened in the room but on the results of the decisions that were made.

On the government beat, it's critically important for journalists to know how to read and interpret a budget and other financial statements. "Follow the money" is good advice for all journalists, but particularly for those covering government and politics. Stories about government funding may seem dry, but taxes and spending affect the audience directly, and people need to know where their money is going. Documents in general are the lifeblood of government, so beat reporters must be able to obtain them, understand them and interpret them for the audience.

KNOW AND TELL

FACT-CHECKING

One way to hold politicians and government officials accountable is to monitor the factual accuracy of what they say in speeches, debates, interviews and campaign ads. PolitiFact.com, a project of the St. Petersburg Times, was designed to do just that.

Editor Bill Adair says PolitiFact is his way of atoning for what he calls the lazy coverage of politics in the past. "We spent too much time writing about polls, too little writing about the things that matter," Adair says. "We need to help voters sort out campaigns, not just tell them who's ahead in the battleground states."

Inspired by FactCheck.org, a nonprofit "consumer advocate" for voters, Adair's team developed a "truth-o-meter" to rate the veracity of statements by candidates and politicians. Instead of "he said," "she said" coverage that never reaches a conclusion, Adair says, "We made a commitment that we would make the call. We'll be the umpire to say the runner is out or safe at home."

"This is about accountability journalism, holding elected officials responsible for what they say," Adair says. "It gets to the core of what political journalism ought to be."

Source: St. Petersburg Times, PolitiFact.com, www.politifact.com (accessed July 7, 2010).

Good reporters don't just cover government from the top down, however. Charlotte Grimes, a longtime political reporter and now Knight Chair in Political Reporting at Syracuse University, says government action also "bubbles up from the public." So beat reporters need to pay attention to local concerns that could or should be addressed by elected officials.[4]

Political reporters basically have one central mission: to provide citizens with the information they need to make an informed choice among the candidates for elective office. To do that, journalists need to examine the candidates' backgrounds and qualifications, their positions on the key issues, and what they're saying in campaign appearances and advertising. Reporters who cover politics also look at the candidates' supporters, because their interests can often shed light on what a politician will do if elected.

Good political reporters do not simply tell where the candidates stand on the issues; they also ask what the candidates have done about those issues in any previous elected office they have held. And to bring the issues to life, reporters look for people whose individual stories can illustrate why the issues matter and what difference it would make to them if one candidate or another wins the election.

When it comes to campaign issues, journalists should pay attention not only to what the candidates say but also to what the voters want to know. Many news organizations conduct "issue polls" or focus groups to see which topics are of greatest interest to the public during an election year. Online forums can serve much the same purpose, although it's important to remember that they're not statistically reliable and may not fairly represent the views of diverse groups in the community.

Education

The education beat is a wide umbrella, covering everything from preschool through higher education, and from school funding to learning outcomes. The beat has become even broader and more complex in recent years, in part because of the expansion of charter schools, the increasing popularity of homeschooling and federal achievement standards. These days, education stories are often political stories as well, and reporters on the beat frequently have to navigate overlapping layers of authority to get the information they need to understand what's really happening in the schools.

If you're on the education beat, you'll probably spend time attending school board and PTA meetings, not so much to report on them as to look for sources and story ideas. Celeste Ford once found a story by scanning the agenda for an upcoming meeting and noticing a proposed city resolution that would ask the state to tighten beeper requirements

TRADE TOOLS

REPORTING ON POLLS

Public opinion surveys are a staple of campaign coverage, but journalists need to look closely before deciding whether a poll's results are worth reporting. The National Council on Public Polls suggests asking these 20 questions:

1. Who did the poll?

2. Who paid for the poll and why was it done?

3. How many people were interviewed for the survey?

4. How were those people chosen?

5. What area (nation, state or region) or what group (teachers, lawyers, Democratic voters, etc.) were these people chosen from?

6. Are the results based on the answers of all the people interviewed?

7. Who should have been interviewed and was not? Or do response rates matter?

8. When was the poll done?

9. How were the interviews conducted?

10. What about polls on the Internet?

11. What is the sampling error for the poll results?

12. Who's on first?

on school buses. At the time, the state required back-up beepers only on buses built after 1990, but thousands of city school buses were older than that. Ford located statistics through the Board of Education and the Department of Motor Vehicles. She did the math, determined how much it would cost to install beepers on the buses that lacked them, and then took that number to a city official for comment. Her story included the voices of schoolchildren, parents, a deputy chancellor of city schools, a school bus company

13. What other kinds of factors can skew poll results?

14. What questions were asked?

15. In what order were the questions asked?

16. What about "push polls"?

17. What other polls have been done on this topic? Do they say the same thing? If they are different, why are they different?

18. What about exit polls?

19. What else needs to be included in the report of the poll?

20. So I've asked all the questions. The answers sound good. Should we report the results?

"Horse-race" polls that tell what percentage of voters support each candidate are of limited value as a snapshot of the race on any given day. Some journalists believe these polls may actually bias voters in favor of the leading candidate because people want to be on the winning side. But researchers have discovered that voters who pay attention to polls also learn more about the issues involved in the campaign. The study suggests that journalists should continue to report the results of legitimate "tracking" polls throughout the campaign, but not make them a major focus of the coverage.

Sources: List is excerpted from Sheldon R. Gaweiser and G. Evans Witt, "20 Questions a Journalist Should Ask about Poll Results," National Council on Public Polls, www.ncpp.org/?q=node/4; the concluding paragraph is from Philip Meyer and Deborah Potter, "Making a Difference: Covering Campaign '96," University of North Carolina at Chapel Hill, School of Journalism and Mass Communication, 1997, www.unc.edu/~pmeyer/meyrpot1.htm.

executive and a representative of a school where a student was killed when a bus without a beeper backed over her.

Reporters covering education need to understand the structure, staffing and economics of the school systems they cover, which may vary widely. They should be prepared to decipher statistics and to compare budgets over time to see where the money goes and what happens as a result. Covering education also means tracking statistical data such as dropout and graduation rates, teacher retention and vacancy rates, principal turnover and the results of high-stakes testing. Many news organizations use these kinds of data to produce interactive online features. The Philadelphia Inquirer's annual "report card" on local schools, for example, provides data on teacher salaries, student diversity and test scores on a clickable map so users can easily compare their district with others in the area.

This interactive lets online readers of the Philadelphia Inquirer search for schools based on what they offer and compare districts on measures like spending per student and class size.

Source: "Report Card on the Schools," www.philly.com/inquirer/education/school_report_card (accessed June 3, 2010).

COVERING EDUCATION

Longtime education reporter Dave Marcus says the best stories are found in classrooms. "They have to do with the way teachers teach; with the way students soar and struggle; with the way some parents pressure their kids while others ignore their kids," he wrote in a column for the Casey Journalism Center on Children and Families. Here are some of his tips for education reporters:

Source: Photo courtesy of Dave Marcus, retrieved from www.davemarcus.com/content/contact-me.

- Cover what the kids and the best teachers are talking about—avoid the agenda of the district's public relations office.

- Spend a few days in a school, even volunteering as a mentor or writing teacher (but be honest and constantly remind everyone you're really a reporter).

- Follow the money. "Plenty of education software, test-prep tools and other gimmicks impress taxpayers, but much of it is junk," Marcus says. Keep an eye on the soaring costs of basics as well. At budget time, ask what a district spends on heating and health insurance. Then ask what special education services must be provided because of federal laws and pressure from parents' lawyers.

- Don't be hemmed in by artificial constraints like county lines. Why not look at innovative programs in middle schools throughout your readership or viewership area?

- Write about parents, parents, parents. You can usually judge a school by its parents. If they're involved, the school probably will have higher standards. What can poorly performing schools do to draw in parents?

Source: Dave Marcus, "The Secret of the Education Beat," Casey Journalism Center on Children and Families, November 14, 2005, www.cjc.umd.edu/jcommunity/articles/Marcus_11.14.htm.

KNOW AND TELL

Some news organizations use education data to create their own measurements, like the Washington Post's "challenge index" that ranks high schools based on the percentage of students who take Advanced Placement, International Baccalaureate or other college-level tests.

When education reporters cover policy issues like the certification process for teachers or efforts to end social promotion, they need to know how these issues have been handled in the past or in similar school districts, and what research has shown about the effectiveness of these policies. When they cover test results, they need to examine the details behind the data. Ranking schools' performance without considering demographics like race, income or parents' education, for example, will produce a misleading story.

One of the toughest challenges many education reporters face is a lack of access to schools and students; superintendents often cite privacy concerns to keep reporters out. It's difficult to put a human face on education stories if you can't shoot pictures in classrooms or talk to students and teachers on school grounds. Reporters who invest time in developing relationships with individual students, parents, teachers and administrators can eventually earn their trust and gain the access they need to tell compelling stories on the education beat.

As an education reporter, you should read school newspapers and websites, subscribe to parent newsletters and e-mail discussion lists, and check local university alumni reviews to see which issues are bubbling up. To stay abreast of national developments so you can put local stories in context, make a habit of reading Education Week (www.edweek.org) and the Chronicle of Higher Education (www.chronicle.com).

Business and Economics

The business beat may sound as dull as can be, but stories about business and economics touch almost everyone's life. Unemployment, the cost of food and gasoline, personal savings and investment—all of these topics matter not just to business leaders but also to workers and consumers. Covering the local business beat means reporting on jobs, construction and property sales, as well as the business sectors that keep the local economy going, whether it's farming, manufacturing, mining or health care.

Reporters covering business and economics have to make their stories accessible to a general audience. They must understand economic concepts and terms and be able to define them or restate them in plain language. This is good practice even for reporters working for specialized publications, websites or broadcasts, whose audience might be expected to be familiar with business jargon. The Wall Street Journal, for example, is aimed at business-savvy readers, but it still spells out the meaning of common terms like *gross national product*—the total value of a nation's output of goods and services. Over time, business reporters develop their own list of concise definitions they can plug into their stories. They also become skilled at explaining why all of this matters to individuals and not just to corporations and governments.

Multimedia features are a great way to make business stories more accessible to a general audience. For example, when reporter Paul Salopek decided to track the flow of crude oil from producers around the globe to one suburban gas station, his online story for the Chicago Tribune included a "Travelogue of Addiction" that allowed users to follow his reporting journey to the sources of the oil.

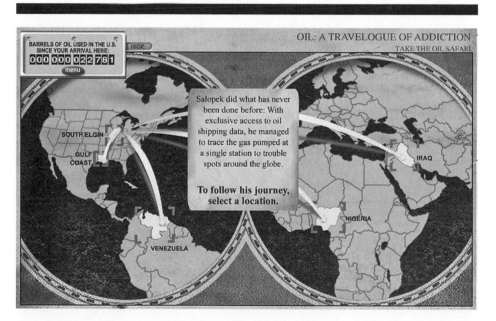

To supplement a four-part newspaper series on America's "mighty thirst for gasoline," the Chicago Tribune invited online users to take an "oil safari." This Flash animation let users follow reporter Paul Salopek's journey to trace the source of the gasoline at one suburban gas station.

Source: Paul Salopek, "A Tank of Gas, a World of Trouble," *Chicago Tribune,* www.chicagotribune.com/news/specials/broadband/chi-oilsafari-html,0,7894741.htmlstory (accessed August 23, 2007).

Business reporters need to be able to read and understand financial statements, balance sheets and annual reports. They often find stories by looking at year-to-year changes in income or spending that seem unusual. They compare companies with others in the same industry or the same region. For example, when a business closes, reporters want to know how many people have lost their jobs and what impact the shutdown will have on the community. To answer that question, they need to know whether the company was one of the largest employers in the area, whether other local companies provide the same product or service, what the local unemployment rate is, and so on.

The business beat requires a deeper knowledge of math and statistics than most other topic areas. But business reporters should use numbers sparingly in their stories because too many figures make a story dry and dull. The most compelling business stories show the significance of developments by putting them in human terms, telling how individuals have been or will be affected.

Health, Science and the Environment

Stories about health and the environment have a direct impact on people's lives. Reporters who cover AIDS know that ignorance is almost as big a killer as the disease itself; their stories can educate people so they can protect themselves. Journalists on the health, science and environment beat may report about everything from avian flu to the mapping of the human genome and the effects of damming rivers.

In large newsrooms, reporters may specialize in only one of these three areas. But in all cases, the underlying issues are complicated and the journalist's job is to explain them clearly. Multimedia features can convey complex information in an interactive form. For example, MSNBC created simple Flash animations to explain how illegal street drugs affect the human body. And the Las Vegas Sun developed an interactive map and timeline to show how the abuse of prescription drugs had spread across the country and increased during the course of a decade.

When dealing with these kinds of stories, journalists need to be familiar with the language of scientists and medical researchers, which can be confusing to say the least. Like business reporters, science writers develop their own list of definitions and explanations for complicated terms so they can write stories that make sense to the general public.

Reporters who cover scientific subjects need to understand the scientific method as well as basic math and statistics so they can double-check the results of research studies. They should always ask for and compare results for different demographic groups. If the

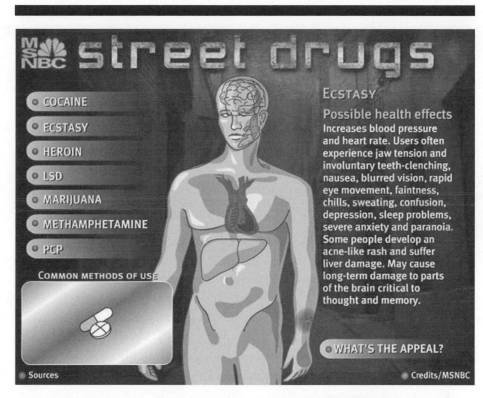

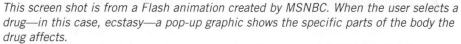

This screen shot is from a Flash animation created by MSNBC. When the user selects a drug—in this case, ecstasy—a pop-up graphic shows the specific parts of the body the drug affects.

Source: "How Drugs Affect the Body," MSNBC.com, www.msnbc.msn.com/id/12423004 (accessed June 23, 2007).

study looked only at white patients, for example, the findings might not apply to other groups. At the same time, reporters should resist the urge to turn every development into a breakthrough, or to press for yes or no answers instead of accepting probabilities. Their stories may not seem as dramatic, but they will certainly be more accurate.

Journalists who are trained to report all sides of a story often fall into a trap when covering science. Giving equal coverage to differing scientific opinions can actually mislead the audience. For example, the overwhelming majority of scientists believe that exposure to lead can harm children's intelligence levels; only a few researchers dispute

ENVIRONMENTAL REPORTING

Demetria Kalodimos is a full-time anchor at WSMV-TV in Nashville, Tenn., who reports in her "spare time." She won an award from the Society of Environmental Journalists for an investigation into tricholoroethylene (TCE) pollution in a rural Tennessee county. The contamination had been reported before, she says, but officials insisted the levels were considered "safe." "To be honest, hearing that phrase parroted over and over just caused my journalistic senses to tingle," Kalodimos says. "I decided to look a little closer."

What she found were stories of human suffering: "a family's dream home lost to contamination they should have been told about, the almost cavalier attitude of a summer church camp that continued to fill its swimming pool with contaminated spring water because it was cheap, the heartbreak of 19 families whose children were born with cleft lip/palate, defying the epidemiological odds."

Source: Photo courtesy of WSMV-TV, www.wsmv.com/video/23787477/index.html (accessed July 7, 2010).

the connection. You could mention both viewpoints in a story about lead exposure, but you'd have to be careful not to suggest that the science is really in dispute.

Carol Rogers, longtime editor of the journal Science Communication, has two useful tips for health and science beat reporters. First: identification matters. Journalists often don't identify the experts they quote in a meaningful way. For example, a story about an international conference on climate change quoted the head of the White House's Office of Science and Technology but never mentioned that he was a respected climate scientist. Leaving that out made his comments seem politically motivated.

Second, Rogers says, audiences don't bring anywhere near the background journalists do to any kind of story, much less to complicated ones. That means if you're covering a science conference, for example, you can't assume your audience has heard or read

Her advice to other reporters wanting to tackle a similar story?

- Do not be afraid of what seems like a technical issue, or something "out of your league." Chances are very good that an expert is willing to give you a thorough science tutorial. And, believe it or not, starting with a mere layman's understanding can help you explain the difficult material more effectively to viewers who are in the same boat.

- Go back [and] look at property deeds, old hearings, old minutes. It was fascinating to learn how concerned people were with one of the contaminated springs 30 years before the TCE problem surfaced. This context helped me build a stronger story.

- Be ready and prepared to get no official comment or cooperation. These days municipalities, even the feds, seem to have no qualms about just not playing ball at all on an issue. It's difficult for us to imagine telling a story without the traditional balance we are used to, but there are ways to be fair and skeptical without interviewing folks in suits.

Source: Mike Dunne, "Top TV Reporters Say Don't Fear the Technical," SE Journal (Fall 2006): 1, http://notes.sej.org/sej/sejourna.nsf/21fd4c7bbafa1be5862568a50017a819/183a8a1cd7b2f6f7862571f60017662f/$FILE/sej_fa06.pdf.

yesterday's story, or that they will tomorrow's. Give them the background they need to understand a story as if that will be the only information they will ever hear or read on the subject. It may well be.

INVESTIGATIVE REPORTING

Investigative reporting is by definition in-depth reporting, requiring extensive research and interviewing. But investigative stories often begin the way ordinary stories do, with a phone call or a conversation. When a waitress at a diner in Charlotte, N.C., mentioned her grandson's unpleasant experience at a local dental clinic to WCNC-TV photojournalist Doug Stacker, he passed her name along to reporter Stuart Watson, one of the station's investigative journalists, who decided to check out the story.

The first step was to talk to the child's mother and get her son's dental records. The records showed that 4-year-old Brandon Dillbeck had 16 of his baby teeth drilled and capped with stainless steel crowns—all in one three-hour session. Watson knew he was on the trail of a good story, but his reporting had only just begun. To find out whether the boy's treatment was typical or excessive, Watson needed a dentist to review the dental records. He needed background on the clinic where the work was done, and he needed pictures to tell Brandon's story on television. He also had to try to get a response from the dentists who treated the boy.

"We put that story on the air," Watson says, "and then, as is the case when you find systemic problems, the phone starts ringing." More than six months later, one woman's complaint had led to a series of 13 reports about dental treatment for children on Medicaid. The station's investigative team obtained and analyzed thousands of dental records, Medicaid billing records, and corporate and property records for the series that eventually won both a Peabody and a duPont-Columbia Award—two of broadcast journalism's most prestigious prizes.

GO ONLINE

Module 4: Watch one of Stuart Watson's award-winning investigative stories.

So what makes a story "investigative"? It's not just the time that's spent developing a story nor the length of the finished product, although investigative reporters usually do get more time to research and write, and more air time or space than general assignment reporters. And it's not just that investigative reporting is enterprising—that is, it requires original work and effort. Lots of daily stories do too. What sets investigative reporting apart is its focus on mistakes or wrongdoing that affect the public. True investigative stories are about corruption, mismanagement, dysfunction, dishonesty, system failures or fraud, and they hold the powerful accountable. Because of that, investigative reports require more stringent verification and more disclosure about the sources of information. Investigative reporters often use specific techniques to obtain and decipher the information they need for their stories, such as using Freedom of Information laws, computer analysis or going undercover.

Using FOI

The federal Freedom of Information Act (FOIA) and state open records laws are tools that reporters can use to find stories that won't show up in a news release. These laws basically protect the public's right to know what the government is doing by providing access to records, data and documents. Beat reporters and investigative reporters use FOI laws routinely to search for stories and to document what they hear from their sources.

ANSWERING THE "WHY?"

Jayne Miller, a longtime investigative reporter at WBAL-TV in Baltimore, calls investigative reporting "the answer to the why — why did this happen, who screwed up, who greased a palm?" Miller works hard to find those answers, and she's broken her share of big stories. How does she do it?

Source: Photo courtesy of WBAL-TV.

"I always have something brewing on the back burner. I am notorious for that. I work on stories for 12, 18 months before they get on the air. I'm always collecting. Sometimes when you seek information it takes time to get it.

"The money in investigative reporting is the money story, the one everyone will talk about. Knowing how to follow that is what we need to work on. By 2 p.m. everyone knows the news of the day. The only reason they'll come to your news organization is to get something good or something they won't find anywhere else."

Miller believes the art of newsgathering has become a lost art. How do you get information? she asks. The answer: Know where to find it. And for Miller, that means knowing who has the information and how to reach them.

"The first thing I ask [students] is, 'How many of you at 3 a.m. can call the fire chief . . . by hitting a contact number on your phone?' Measure your value by how many contacts you have in your phone. What makes you unique are the human sources you have."

KNOW AND TELL

To make the best use of government data, learn your way around. What databases exist on your beat or in your area of interest? What information is included? What form is it in? Who keeps the records? For example, a local government reporter would want to have a list of public employees and their salaries, contracts and disciplinary records; disclosure forms for elected officials; accident and inspection reports for businesses regulated by local government agencies; and any audits and investigations conducted by and of those agencies. Most of that information is public, so Brant Houston, former executive director of Investigative Reporters and Editors, Inc. (IRE), says your first step should be to check the Internet to see whether it's been posted online. If you can't find it, then just ask for it. Only if that doesn't work, Houston says, should you file a formal FOI request.

Planning and follow-up are critical to a successful FOIA request, Houston says. Begin by asking what information is really needed for the story. Keeping your requests reasonable and targeted will improve your chances of success. Then figure out who has the record you're looking for. It's not always obvious, so find out who tracks the specific data you want before you make a request. It's also a good idea to determine who else might have the information, so you know where to go if the first agency says no. Local crime statistics, for example, are usually shared with state and federal agencies, including the FBI. "The farther away you go from the 'official custodian,' the more likely the record will be released," says Houston.

It's useful to know if the kind of record you're after has ever been released before. Knowing whether there's a precedent can help you make a case that you should be allowed to have the information you're requesting. You should also know what exemptions might apply to the records; under the law, exemptions may keep some information from being released to protect national security, individual privacy, business interests and efficient government operations. But the FOI law says that even if part of a document is exempt, the government still has to let you have the rest of it. Take what you can get, Houston advises. If you're looking for trends in Medicaid spending, for example, you may not need to know the names of individual patients.

Not all public records are documents or data. Videos, training tapes, recordings and e-mails can be considered public under certain circumstances. For example, information the state turns over to defense attorneys in a criminal case can be released if you ask for it. Joe Adams, author of the "Florida Public Records Handbook," advises searching online for specific file types, like .ppt for internal PowerPoint presentations, or .avi or .mov for video.

Adams says every journalist should know the public records laws and file requests for records on a regular basis. "Ask for records long before you are going to need them," he advises. And always pick up the records you requested, even if your deadline has passed. "Custodians won't take you or your news organization seriously if you don't," he says. "And they won't go out of their way to help you next time."

Computer-Assisted Reporting

The term *computer-assisted reporting* or CAR has been used to refer to everything from creating multimedia to gathering databases. For the purposes of this text, we'll confine our discussion of CAR to the use of computer programs to analyze information, especially data. CAR isn't just useful for major reporting projects; it can also be used to add depth to daily stories and even to uncover quirky features, like the fact that on the 13th of every month, the number of marriage ceremonies performed in North Carolina drops by 40 percent. The (Raleigh) News & Observer discovered that little gem about love and luck in the state's marriage database.[5]

Government data is a journalist's gold mine. Police incidents, highway patrol citations, medical examiner reports, state university payrolls, political contributions—reporters have used all of these records and more to develop stories and track down sources they would never have discovered any other way. When a child in Florida was killed by her family's pet Burmese python, reporter Mark Douglas asked the state fish and wildlife commission for a database of all permits to own venomous reptiles. He found more than 40 for Burmese pythons, along with the owners' names and phone numbers—a goldmine of potential sources.

Nancy Amons of WSMV-TV in Nashville, Tenn., is a skilled database reporter who describes herself as a pack rat, always fighting for more file space. "I save data longer than the city does," she says. She's uncovered dozens of stories by crunching the data. One of her favorite stories involved a 20-year-old man who had killed a woman in a traffic accident and had never been prosecuted. "I stumbled on the story by looking at speeding ticket records, hoping to profile the driver with the most tickets," she says. It turned out that driver had a vehicular homicide on his record and had never gone to court. After her story aired, the young man went to prison. That same data set of speeding records had a field showing whether violators' tickets had been erased after they attended traffic school. Amons crunched the numbers again and reported that some people were getting away with going to traffic school half a dozen times a year.

Amons advises reporters to find out how the data is kept before requesting it. "If you want court information, for example, start by asking for the form that the clerks use to do data entry from." Knowing the fields and the record layout will help you formulate a request that's easy to fulfill. Then ask for the data in a form you can use. Microsoft Excel, for example, uses .xls files, while Access files have the extensions .mdb or .dbf. It's sometimes safer to ask for a text file or ASCII file,[6] delimited by comma, space or tab, which allows you to import the data into almost any spreadsheet or database program. Obviously,

Who's Keeping Exotic Animals?

Many of the most dangerous species in Florida aren't in zoos or sanctuaries. They are in people's houses, at private animal attractions, or in once-rural settings now surrounded by housing developments. Use this database and map to see the 400 Florida businesses and residents holding permits for the wildest and most lethal species. Enter a category to narrow your search or search "all" to see the complete database.

Back to search

License type	Business name	Licensee ▲	Address	City	Class I	Class II	
ESB	Primate Products, Inc.	Bradford, Donald A	34200 Dr. Hammock Road	Immokalee	C	C	Map it
ESA	Kozlow, Dan	Kozlow, Dan	6015 Green Blvd.	Naples	A	A	Map it
ESA	Rinehart, Pamela G	Rinehart, Pamela G	2861 4Th. Avenue S.E.	Naples		A	Map it
ESA	World Exotics, Inc.	Rosenblum, Gary	221 Griffin Road	Naples	A	B, C, A	Map it
ESA	Rue, Gracelyn	Rue, Gracelyn	2861 4Th. Avenue S.E	Naples	A	S, A	Map it
ESB	Shy Wolf Sanctuary	Smith, Nancy J	1161 27Th. Street S.W.	Naples	A	A, O	Map it
ESB	Naples Zoo	Tetzlaff, David L	1590 Goodlette-Frank Road	Naples	E, L, T, A	C, Q, A, R	Map it
ESA	Wooten'S Alligator Farm	Wooten, Gene	32330 E. Tamiami Trail	Ochopee	B, A	B, A	Map it

TBO.com, the website of WFLA-TV and the Tampa Tribune, has a vast collection of searchable databases, including this one that lists individuals and businesses with state licenses to keep exotic pets.

Source: TBO.com, www2.tbo.com/static/news-special-reports-data-bay/tbo-special-reports-florida-wildlife-permits/?appSession=328163235660614 (accessed July 7, 2010).

your best bet is to get data in digital form, but if the information is available only on paper, you'll need to enter it into a program by hand so you can sort and compare the information efficiently.

Once you have the data in your computer, make sure it's "clean" and complete. Check for inconsistencies in spelling and see if any pieces of data are missing. After that, it takes only a few clicks to perform the most basic analysis, such as sorting the numbers in ascending or descending order. That's how Amons determined who had the most speeding tickets in Nashville.

If you're working with budgets, you can program Excel to perform calculations, like the difference between last year's spending and this year's and the percent change from one year to the next. Then, by sorting the numbers, you can easily see which budget categories increased, which were cut and by how much. As you become more experienced at using CAR, you can begin to compare data sets using a "relational" database program like Access. Just by asking the right questions, you could learn how many convicted felons have hunting permits, for example, or how many sex offenders live near day care centers.

The key to good computer-assisted reporting, says Amons, is to remember that the data is not the story. The people and the problems you uncover are the story. The data is evidence, which you will refer to in your story for print or television and then post online so the audience can check the facts for themselves.

GO ONLINE

Module 4: Try your hand at computer-assisted reporting by looking for story ideas in a data set.

Undercover Reporting

Investigative journalists sometimes go undercover to report stories that would be difficult or almost impossible to confirm any other way. Reporting undercover is a controversial practice that should be considered only as a last resort. That's because going undercover almost always involves some deception and raises ethical concerns, so it should not be undertaken lightly. "Hidden cameras are not unlike weapons and power tools that should be kept away from the unskilled and the reckless," says the Poynter Institute's Bob Steele, a leading expert in journalism ethics.[7] News organizations usually have strict rules governing the use of undercover techniques, and reporters should always have management approval before using them.

To decide whether going undercover or using a hidden camera is justified, reporters and news managers should consider whether the story they're covering is of vital public importance. Will it prevent substantial harm or expose a major system failure? By that standard, the stereotypical TV sweeps story about valet parking attendants stealing loose change simply doesn't measure up.

Pam Zekman, a longtime investigative reporter at WBBM-TV in Chicago, has broken some of her biggest stories by going undercover. As a reporter for the Chicago Tribune and later the Sun-Times, she shared in two Pulitzer Prizes for local reporting. She urges reporters to think and plan carefully before attempting an undercover assignment. Make sure your superiors are on board and are willing to commit the personnel and money it will cost. Undercover reporting is not a shortcut and can require weeks or months of extra work. "Remember that going undercover is just an additional tool; it shouldn't serve as an alternative to good old-fashioned digging," Zekman says. "The best undercover reports are bolstered by public records research, human sources and interviews with experts before and after anyone goes undercover."[8]

The Multimedia Advantage

The ability to tell a story in multiple media is a huge advantage for investigative reporters. They can use information in print or online that would never fit in a TV story because of time limitations or the need for visuals. Print and online graphics can be more detailed than the television versions, and additional video and supporting documents can be posted online to bolster a story's credibility. And reporters say that because stories told in multiple media reach more people, they can pay off in new leads and additional sources.

Reporter Mark Douglas put the multimedia advantage to work when he learned that parts of Tampa Bay's Sunshine Skyway Bridge were corroding just 10 years after it was built. Over a period of months, Douglas accumulated thousands of pages of technical and engineering records for the stories he eventually reported on WFLA-TV, in the Tampa Tribune and for TBO.com online. "It was quite a relief to have different ways of telling it to make optimum use of all of that research," he says.

The online story became an outlet for raw video of the corrosion and for documents that that didn't work in either the newspaper or TV versions. The print version allowed Douglas to explain some of the technical details of the corrosion problem that he couldn't get into on television. "I also had the ability to develop a narrative style of storytelling about events in the corrosion investigation that I couldn't discuss in such detail on TV because I didn't have the pictures and it was just too lengthy," he says.

Telling the story in three dimensions made the topic hard to ignore, held state officials accountable and gave news consumers choices in how they wanted to digest the information, Douglas says. The print story had a wider impact as well. "Quite frankly, writing a story or two for the Tampa Tribune opened some doors in state government that probably would have remained shut if this had 'just' been a fleeting story in the six o'clock news," Douglas says. "Newspapers get the attention of the high and mighty in [the state capital in] Tallahassee in a way local TV can't compete with sometimes."

TAKING IT HOME

Reporting in depth is hard work. It's time-consuming and labor-intensive, but it can be enormously rewarding. One of the criticisms of daily journalism is that it barely scratches the surface. Covering events and incidents in isolation doesn't help the audience make sense of the world around them. Reporters who dig deeper are able to connect the dots and tell stories that have an impact by focusing attention on problems that might have been overlooked and forcing action to remedy those problems.

Some journalists say there's not much room for this kind of reporting in today's news media. They point to budget cuts at news organizations and a society that seems to value immediacy over quality. But journalists who bring passion, persistence and skill to work every day are able to report in depth, even if they have to do it in between other assignments. And reporters who do this kind of work in multiple media can use more of the information they uncover and make it available to a wider audience by presenting that information in different and more engaging ways.

TALKING POINTS

1. This chapter discusses some typical beats that journalists cover. You also read that some newsrooms have additional beats, determined by the makeup of the community they serve. Think about your community and suggest several specific, nontraditional beats for a local newsroom to consider. What sources would you need to connect with to cover those beats? What stories might you find?

2. Choose one of the beats discussed in detail in this chapter and explore several sources of information about that beat. What can you learn from specialized publications and groups related to the beat? How would it help you to be a member of a beat reporters' association?

3. Imagine that you have acquired the following data sets for your community:

   Public school bus drivers.

   Registered handgun owners.

   Drunk-driving violations.

   Vehicle recalls.

   Campus liquor law violations.

   What questions might you ask to analyze and compare these data sets in search of possible stories?

ONLINE LEARNING MODULE 4

Activate or buy this chapter's online learning module at journalism.cqpress.com to get access to:

- SKILL BUILDING: Practice basic computer-assisted reporting skills to analyze a data set and develop story ideas.

- DISCOVER: Watch and analyze an award-winning investigative story.

- EXPLORE: Learn how to use freedom of information laws to find and request public records.

- A digital version of this chapter's text in full color with active links.

Also, continue your work on the ONGOING STORY MODULE. Decide how you would add context and depth to this story with data, documents or details.

5 WRITING THE STORY

No matter what medium you're writing for, stories that are overstuffed with information are harder to understand. In this chapter, we'll discuss how to take your writing to the next level by sharpening your focus, organizing your material before you write and choosing your words with care. We'll also show how you can improve your work by using time-tested strategies to revise your writing, quickly and effectively.

For many journalists, the most difficult part of telling a story is <u>deciding what to leave out</u>. All news stories are created from a mass of facts, observations, comments and details. Reporters work hard to collect all of that information, so their natural impulse is to use as much of it as possible in their stories. But airtime and print space are limited, and even online, there's a limit to the audience's attention.

Good journalism involves selection, not compression. Cramming in all the facts that will fit rarely results in a well-told story that will engage the audience. What the painter Georgia O'Keefe said about art applies just as well to writing: "It is only by selection, by elimination, by emphasis that we get at the real meaning of things."

A reporter who tries to explain everything in one dense story may succeed only in confusing the audience. Multimedia reporters can put additional elements online that won't fit in a print or broadcast version, but they're still selective about what they use. Good reporters use their news judgment and experience to decide what is most important to include in a story and what order to put it in. They also take a systematic approach to writing, whether they call it that or not. Their first step is to choose a central point or a theme for the story, also called a focus.

FINDING THE FOCUS

The focus of a story is basically the answer to the question, "What is this story really all about?" That sounds simple, but it's not. To decide on a focus, you have to sort through the information you've collected and figure out what's at the heart of it. You need to know what the news is, of course, but often that's not enough. For a story to be memorable, it also needs to have a central point. The news might be that a candidate won an election. The point might be what the voters' choice of that candidate says about the community and its future.

Experienced reporters don't wait until the end of the day, after they've done all their research, interviews and observation, before finding a focus for their stories, especially if they're working on tight deadlines. As we've discussed, they may actually start the reporting process with a focus in mind, which helps them decide where to go and whom to interview. Veteran TV reporter Joe Fryer compares it to a grocery shopping trip when you have some idea of what you'll be serving before you go to the store. "You can't buy apples, lemons, pears and kiwis, and when you get back decide your story is about peaches," he says.

Of course, the focus can change as you collect more information, and it often does. Reporter Victoria Lim says she tries to keep an open mind in the field. "When you go in thinking you know what the story is all about you don't leave yourself open to other possibilities that could come out of it," she says. KARE-TV reporter Boyd Huppert says he looks for a focus from the moment he starts reporting, which he defines as "a concept, a character or emotion that can tie the disconnected pieces of a story together." The focus is often the answer to this simple question: If nothing else, what do you want people to remember about this story?

What's most important is to decide on a focus before you start writing. That may seem obvious, but it's astounding how many reporters skip this step and start scribbling as soon as they're done reporting. Small wonder they often turn in stories that are boring, confusing or both.

Focus Questions

One way to find a focus is to ask yourself why you care about the story, and why the audience should bother to watch or read it. After all, if you don't care, there's no reason anyone else should. Your story ought to answer the question, "So what?" To focus a complicated story, ask the question several times. Let's say you are reporting on standardized testing in your state's high schools. So what? Students will have to pass tests in five subjects in order to graduate. So what? Last year, almost 40 percent of seniors who took practice tests failed

KNOW AND TELL

WRITING WISDOM

Reporter Boyd Huppert of KARE-TV in Minneapolis has won dozens of awards for his writing, including multiple national Edward R. Murrow Awards from the Radio Television Digital News Association. Huppert works hard to focus his stories while he's still out reporting. "Writing a focus statement often gives me an opening or a closing line," he says. "If I don't know what the open is going to be when I'm heading back, I start to panic. I'm always asking, 'Where should this start?'"

Source: Photo courtesy of Boyd Huppert.

Many of Huppert's most memorable stories are built around unusual characters, and he pays special attention to the way he introduces them to the audience. "I try to find at least one meaningful detail I can tell you about that person right away," he says. For an amusing story about a man who can play three trumpets at once, Huppert introduced Wally Pickal as "a man who shares his name with a gherkin." "I went to the grocery aisle to find a word that sounded funny," he says. "A meaningful detail."

Stories have layers, Huppert says, and he makes it his job to find them. "Even the best story can be better if you look for the other layers," he says. Take his story about the high school janitor who for 14 years has manned the public address system at the prom, introducing each couple as they arrive. Cute story, right? But much more meaningful when you learn that Duane Ammann already knows almost every kid in the school by name, and that the kids love him for it. After he had a heart attack a few years back, students pooled their money to buy him an exercise bike. Huppert carefully structures his stories so each layer builds on the one before. "I map out the things we're going to reveal. What are my moments, what are my layers?" Once he's made a plan, he says, the rest comes easily. "My job is writing transitions."

Huppert honed his writing skills by reading voraciously and listening to other good TV writers. "There are certain things that good writers do," he says. "Putting the most important part of the sentence at the end. That way, when you slow down as you're reading, at the end of a thought, you slow down and stop at the most important word."

How to get better? "Go to seminars, study good writers, read a good novel, go to a good movie. Get people to critique your work. Make relationships. I'm still learning."

at least one of them. So what? Schools are having trouble preparing students for a test that will shape their futures. Now you have a focus.

When Bruce DeSilva was at the Associated Press he sometimes gave reporters what he called the bus stop test for focus. "Suppose you are at a bus stop and someone leans out the bus window and shouts, 'What is that story you are working on?' The bus engine starts and begins to pull away from the curb. What are you going to shout?"[1] This forces reporters to break down the action in the story by stating it in a simple sentence: subject-verb-object. Who is doing what to whom? See if you can do it in three to six words. For example, the focus of the testing story might become: "Schools fail students."

Let's take it one step further. Imagine that you're covering a fast-moving wildfire. You've been out talking to people and observing the damage all day. Now you need to focus your story before you begin writing.

- What's the news?
A fire destroyed two houses in the mountains east of the city, but no one was injured and the city business district was spared.

- What's the point?
Two families are homeless but grateful to be alive.

- How can I tell it in three to six words?
Fire destroys homes, not spirits.

- So what?
Property damage from a dangerous fire was limited.

This is not meant to suggest that every story has only one acceptable focus. On the contrary, reporters for different news organizations may take the same basic facts and write their stories quite differently because they have decided on a different focus. In the case of the wildfire story, a reporter could use the same questions to come up with a different focus:

- What's the news?
Businesses in our city escaped damage from a wildfire that destroyed two houses in the mountains east of downtown.

- What's the point?
Business owners are grateful the fire spared them this time.

- How can I tell it in three to six words?

Fire doesn't stop business.

- So what?

Economic impact of a dangerous fire was limited.

The first story would concentrate on the families who lost their homes in the fire and use sound bites from the people directly affected. The second would pay more attention to the businesses that were spared, including the reactions of business owners. Both stories would contain the same basic information—that two houses were destroyed while businesses were unaffected—but their emphases would be different. You don't want to focus a story so narrowly that you miss the big picture, but as long as you cover the most important points somewhere—in the story itself, the anchor intro or Web summary—there's nothing wrong with your story having a different focus from someone else's.

Focus for Multiple Media

We've said it before, but it bears repeating—if you're reporting for multiple platforms, keep the strength of each medium in mind as you decide on a focus. As we've discussed, a TV story is well suited to sharing experience and emotion, while a print story can provide more depth and context, and an online story can offer elements of both.

Let's say you're covering a protest march in your city. Everything is peaceful until the marchers close in on City Hall and police decide to use tear gas to break up the crowd. On television, you might choose to tell what happened and why through the eyes of a demonstrator and a police officer. Your focus statement might be something as simple as this: "Chaos at City Hall." The focus of your print and online stories would likely be broader and include the impact of the march and its aftermath on demonstrators, bystanders, government workers and downtown businesses. The focus statement in this case could be something along these lines: "Protest paralyzes city."

GO ONLINE

Module 5: Practice finding a focus for some well-known stories.

For a video story, your focus statement also helps you decide what to shoot, which can be a huge time-saver both in the field and in the edit room. You don't have to run from place to place, shooting video or stills you won't end up using. And you don't have to sort through all that excess material when it comes time to edit. Take a KARE-TV story about the aftermath of a tornado that focused on the loss of trees in one community. Photojournalist Jonathan Malat framed every interview for that story with a damaged tree in the shot.

You may not think you have time to focus your story before writing. It seems like an unnecessary extra step when you're already in a rush to make deadline. But that's when it's most critical to have a focus. Knowing what to emphasize before beginning to write helps the reporter decide which facts, images and sounds to include and which to leave out. "The less time you have to write, the more time you should take to think about it," says CNN chief political correspondent Candy Crowley. Thinking time helps you make sense of all that stuff you have collected, which saves time when you start to write. You wouldn't shoot video without making sure it's in focus; you shouldn't write stories without focusing first.

PLANNING YOUR STORY

Having a focus in mind is just the first step in preparing to write a story. You now know what you are trying to say, but you still have to decide how you are going to say it. That means you need to get organized. Here is a step-by-step guide to planning your story.

Review

Flip through your notes and look over any background material you've collected. Mark the key points that fit your focus—information that absolutely must be in the story for it to make sense. Use any system that works for you. Some writers like to use colored highlighters; others use a mix of stars, asterisks, underlining and brackets to isolate the good stuff. If you do this as you go along, you can quickly home in on the best material.

If you've piled up a lot of notes and documents, make a list of all the facts and details you expect to use. Obviously, when planning a report for multiple media, you'll need to consider the audio, video and graphic elements you've collected that you might include in different versions of the story. We'll talk in detail about how to do this in Chapter 6.

Don't worry about putting any of your elements in order yet; you'll get to that soon enough. At this point, you just need to get a handle on what you've collected during the reporting process, and tease out anything that will help you deliver on your focus statement.

Select

When you've narrowed the list of possible bites and quotes, get them down on paper word for word. If you left space in your notebook as we suggested in Chapter 2, you can simply insert any missing words. At this point in the planning process, many reporters choose to type the quotes or bites into a document so they can easily cut and paste them into their stories. You need to know exactly what a person says in order to write what goes before and after. Remember that while sound bites for TV and radio will be short, you may be able to use a longer segment in an online audio or video clip. You may want the exact or verbatim text of those clips as well, so you can post it on the Web.

REVIEWING NOTES

Great reporters often cover the same stories everyone else does, but somehow they do it better. David Rosenbaum of the New York Times was one of those reporters whose stories left competitors muttering to themselves, "Why didn't I see that?"

"David beat all of us by noticing things that were in plain sight, but that we somehow missed," said Dale Russakoff, a longtime reporter at the Washington Post, at Rosenbaum's memorial service. "He'd look at the same documents and talk to the same people. But where we saw trees, David saw a forest."

Source: Photo courtesy of Marcus Rosenbaum.

Russakoff had always wondered how Rosenbaum could be so efficient, how he managed to stay on top of things while everyone else was running around. On a slow news day in the Senate press gallery some 20 years ago, she asked him to show her how he organized his notes before writing. "I tried it the next time I wrote a story and was stunned at how much easier it was," Russakoff said. "His system doesn't just organize your notes; it organizes your mind."

Here's the Rosenbaum method:

- Number every page of your notes.
- Go through each page and mark every fact, quote or detail you want to use in your story.
- Create an index of this information on a separate page—just a couple of words for each element and the number of the page where it's found in your notes.

That's all there is to it. "The process of thinking about the things that matter, and boiling them down to a word or two, allows you to store information better," Russakoff says. Colleagues sometimes wonder why she spends all that time reading over her notes, she says. "The truth is it makes the rest of it go faster."

Russakoff says she uses the Rosenbaum method on every long story, and sometimes on daily ones too, because it helps her feel organized when she starts writing.

Rosenbaum was murdered in January 2006, just weeks after he retired from the Times. Sharing his note-taking strategy will help keep his memory alive.

KNOW AND TELL

Choose quotes or sound bites that fit your focus, and follow this basic rule: Don't plan to use a bite or quote if you can say it better. The best quotes and bites are subjective, offering opinion, reaction, experience or emotion. They add insight and perspective to stories, not just facts. Too many news stories are stuffed full of quotes and sound bites that fail this test; often they come out of the mouths of officials. There's no need to let the mayor say, "We expect to have a decision at the council meeting later this week on contingency plans for the distribution of funds to low-income residents in the Brentwood area." That kind of information would be much better stated in clear, concise language by the reporter. In this case, the reporter might write, "According to the mayor, people in Brentwood won't find out if they'll get any money from the city until later this week." Then he could use the mayor's words explaining why it's taking so long or reacting to complaints about the delay.

Don't feel obliged to use a quote or sound bite for the wrong reasons. Maybe it took a lot of effort to set up the interview, or it was a long drive to the location. That's no excuse for using a worthless bite. No one knows or cares how hard you had to work to get it. If it's bad or it doesn't fit the focus of your story, leave it out. And resist the temptation to include a quote just to avoid upsetting the interviewee. If you think they've called every living relative to tell them to watch or read your story, let them know as soon as possible that they're not in it. Better yet, make parts of the interview available online and point them there.

Organize

Once you have the key points, details, quotes or sound bites and scenes isolated, group them by topic and put them in a rough order and see if one point or scene leads logically to the next. Jack Hart, former managing editor at the Oregonian newspaper, recommends what he calls a "jot outline"—four or five words or phrases that summarize the main points of your story. Here's what your initial jottings might look like for the protest march story:

Focus: Protest paralyzes city.

—Protestors demand hike in minimum wage.

—Marchers converge on City Hall.

—Police spray tear gas.

—Businesses close.

—Traffic is jammed.

Once you have all the main topics on paper, rearrange them until the order makes sense. In the case of the protest, you might choose to begin with the tear gas and then explain why the protestors were in the streets. You may change the order several times before you start writing, but it's worth the trouble. Your finished outline will serve as a kind of road map for your story that you can consult as you go along to make sure you haven't skipped anything important.

GO ONLINE

Ongoing Story Module: Write a focus statement and "jot outline" for this story.

Consider the Extras

You may use the same information in stories for different media, but the way you use it may change. You'll usually include more information in a print or online story than you will in a TV or radio piece, but that additional information doesn't have to be folded into the narrative. Now is the time to consider what you can break out into graphics, bullet points

STORY PLANNING

- Review your notes.
- Select the best parts of your interviews.
- Organize your information.
- Consider the extras.

Deborah Potter made this jot outline for a story she reported from New Orleans about the aftermath of Hurricane Katrina. Notice how she rearranged some of the elements to produce a road map to consult as she wrote the story for the PBS program "Religion & Ethics NewsWeekly."

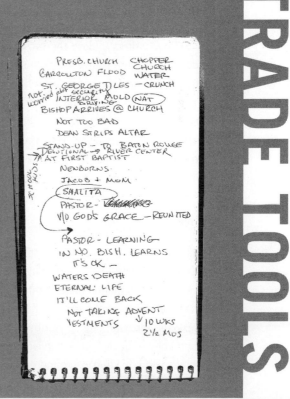

TRADE TOOLS

or timelines. Think about interactive elements you could add to the online story in the form of links, searchable databases or surveys.

Let's go back to that protest at City Hall again. Your TV story is going to be tightly focused on the experience of one protestor and one police officer. But you may want a more detailed map of the protest route for your print and online versions, highlighting businesses that had to close as a result of the chaos. You might also include a list or timeline of previous downtown demonstrations, a link to the city ordinance regulating police use of tear gas and another link to public health information about the potential effects of "riot control agents."

STORY STRUCTURE

All stories have a structure in the same way that people have a spine—or at least they should. Without a structure, stories would be a jumble of facts with nothing to hold them together. Structure is essential for stories to be understandable and meaningful. Choosing a structure before you write can help you decide what goes where—the logical next step in the planning process that makes the actual writing go more smoothly.

Good writers choose the most suitable shape for the story they are telling and the medium they are using. As you'll see, some structures are more appropriate for breaking news or features, and some work better on television than in print or online. The last thing you want to do is to follow a formula that makes your stories all seem alike. "Approach every story differently," says TV reporter Joe Fryer, who says he got into a rut of beginning every story the same way, with short voice tracks and lots of natural sound. "It's not bad to start a story with a longer track if it's well written," he says. "You don't always have to have that same pattern."

Inverted Pyramid

Many stories begin with the most newsworthy information, following the classic "inverted pyramid" structure. This form puts the most important information at the top, followed by additional information in descending order of importance. A report on a massive storm, for example, would likely begin with the death toll and the location of the heaviest damage. Next, the reporter might describe the scene of the worst devastation, and then include a sound bite or quote from a survivor or a rescue worker. Supporting paragraphs would fill in details and provide background on the storm.

Some journalists argue that this structure is outdated and dull because it requires writers to tell stories backwards. Using this structure, they say, is tantamount to telling

FIGURE 5.1 STORY STRUCTURE: INVERTED PYRAMID

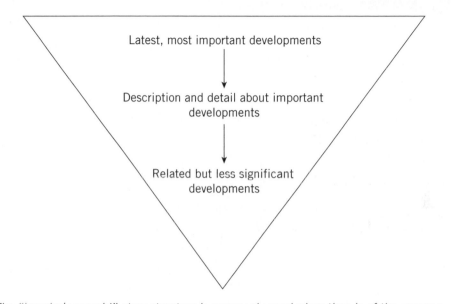

Latest, most important developments

↓

Description and detail about important developments

↓

Related but less significant developments

The "inverted pyramid" story structure is commonly used when time is of the essence. If you start with what's most important, the audience knows immediately what your story is about.

a joke by starting with the punch line because the audience knows how the story will end from the very beginning. But the inverted pyramid survives because it makes sense in some circumstances, especially when reporting important or breaking news when timeliness is of the essence, and especially when writing for the Web, as we'll discuss in Chapter 7. If you are the first to report a significant development, you'll want to tell the audience what has happened right at the top. Reporters who resist using this structure when it is called for may be accused of "burying the lead," making it more difficult for the audience to determine the importance of the story.

Hourglass

A modified form of the inverted pyramid, frequently used in broadcast, is known as the "hourglass" structure. It begins in a similar fashion with the latest and most important information, but after a few paragraphs it takes a turn and becomes a narrative told in chronological order.

FIGURE 5.2 STORY STRUCTURE: HOURGLASS ▰▰▰▰▰▰

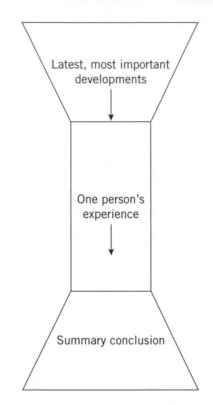

Latest, most important developments

One person's experience

Summary conclusion

This "hourglass" story structure is a modified form of the inverted pyramid. It still begins with a summary lead, but then becomes a more focused narrative before broadening out to a summary conclusion. In broadcast, the lead and conclusion may be read by the anchor, leaving the reporter to tell the story in narrative form.

When you're on deadline on a breaking story, chronology can be a lifesaver. Just start at the beginning and write until you've told everything that happened, putting the most recent information last. Sticking with the example of the story about the massive storm, a television reporter could provide the anchor with a hard lead, and then tell the story of the storm as witnessed by one survivor. This structure allows for a summary ending, either by the reporter or the anchor in a tag. On the Web, this structure can be used to create a story timeline, either static or interactive. In print, the summary information could be placed in a box or subhead, so the story itself could stay focused on the survivor's experience, told in chronological order.

Diamond

A reporter using the "diamond" structure would begin with an anecdote, introducing a character whose experience illustrates what the story is all about. This small story would then broaden out to show its wider significance. Toward the end, the reporter would return to the individual character's story as a way of concluding the narrative. These stories are most effective if you don't abandon your character in the middle.

Reporter John Larson likes to structure stories by thinking about them as quests, in which someone is trying to do something. This helps him choose a central character to build his story around as well as an action to illustrate the story. It also provides some tension because the viewer doesn't know whether the character will succeed in his quest.

For example, a reporter might begin a story about a new AIDS treatment by introducing a patient who desperately needs the treatment, then describe the person's experience with an experimental drug, explain how it works and conclude by noting that doctors give the patient we met at the beginning only a limited time to live if the new treatment is not effective. This story form "hooks" the audience by presenting an individual's dilemma first. The important information that follows is more interesting because it's clearly relevant to that individual. The diamond structure is often used for stories that might otherwise seem dull. You can apply it by remembering that every "policy issue" is really someone's personal problem, writ large.

FIGURE 5.3 STORY STRUCTURE: DIAMOND

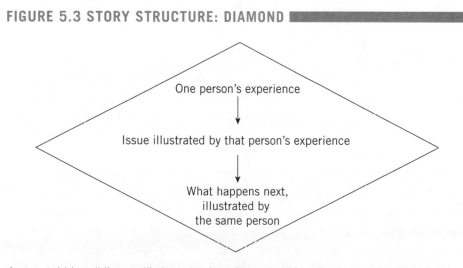

A story told in a "diamond" shape begins with an individual's story and weaves that person's experience throughout. It's a useful way of approaching "issue" stories, since issues are just personal problems on a bigger scale.

KNOW AND TELL

THE STORY "QUEST"

For a National Press Photographers Association workshop, reporter John Larson wrote this story about growing fears of an economic recession to demonstrate how one individual's "quest" can become the backbone of a topical news story:

Source: Photo courtesy of John Larson.

BOB TAYLOR HASN'T SLEPT WELL FOR WEEKS.

FOR ONE THING, HE HAS TO GET UP AT ONE IN THE MORNING JUST TO BAKE TOMORROW'S DOUGHNUTS.

BUT HE WORRIES THAT NO MATTER HOW HARD HE WORKS, NO MATTER HOW CAREFULLY HE MIXES THE BATTER, THE RESULT MAY NOT BE SWEET.

BECAUSE SOMETHING HAS CHANGED.

LAST YEAR, BUSINESS WAS SO GOOD, HE BOUGHT NEW OVENS. THIS YEAR, HE IS DIPPING INTO SAVINGS JUST TO KEEP HIS BAKERY OPEN.

THE PROBLEM?

THE WAREHOUSE ACROSS THE STREET HAS LAID OFF 20 PEOPLE. THEY'RE NO LONGER BUYING HIS DOUGHNUTS. AND HIS COSTS HAVE RISEN.

SO NOW, WHEN BOB TAYLOR'S ALARM GOES OFF, HE FINDS HE IS ALREADY AWAKE. AND HE IS WORRYING.

OFFICIALS IN WASHINGTON SAY WE ARE NOT IN A RECESSION. THEY SAY THERE IS NOTHING TO WORRY ABOUT, YET.

BOB SAYS HE DOESN'T HAVE TIME TO LISTEN TO THE NEWS. AND HE WONDERS, WOULD WE LIKE TO BUY A DOZEN DOUGHNUTS? OR EVEN ONE?

—JOHN LARSON, FOR THE WORKSHOP.

You can see how Larson was able to focus his story by centering it around Bob the baker, whose personal experience reflects that of many Americans. Bob's quest was to bake his doughnuts, and that action became the visual narrative for the story. But the point of the story is that Bob's experience illustrated the bigger topic of people fearing recession. Larson built his simple story out of three elements that are a storyteller's grail: character, action and tension.

Christmas Tree

This story shape might suggest a kind of random approach, considering the haphazard way many people stick decorations on Christmas trees. But "Christmas tree" is really a structure that helps the writer build tension and release it several times as the story moves along. KARE-TV's Huppert says he uses this structure in many of his longer-form stories. He focuses tightly at the top, introducing a character or a place, then broadens out to provide more context. Each time the tree narrows before widening again represents a turning point or unexpected moment in the story. Keeping the tree shape in mind, Huppert says, helps him construct a story that keeps the audience engaged. "Let them catch a breath," he says, "then build to the next surprise."

You could apply this structure to the AIDS story by introducing the patient right at the top, then revealing that he's fighting the disease. He's tried many treatments that have worked for others but (turning point) not for him. Now he's looking desperately for a new approach and (turning point) his doctor learns there's an experimental drug that could help. The patient has signed up for a study of the drug but (turning point) nobody knows if it will really work. If it doesn't (conclusion), the patient's future looks grim.

FIGURE 5.4 STORY STRUCTURE: CHRISTMAS TREE

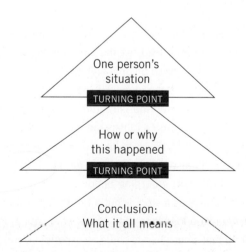

A story in the shape of a "Christmas tree" has multiple turning points. This structure is useful for longer-form stories because it makes sure there are "moments" or surprises all along the way to keep the audience engaged.

BEGINNINGS AND ENDINGS

Knowing what your structure is helps you decide where to begin your story and how to end it, which just happen to be two of the most difficult decisions any writer has to make. Experienced reporters are able to decide on a beginning and end while they are still in the field, but this takes lots of practice. Your opening needs to make the audience sit up and take notice. Your conclusion needs to button things up. Once you've settled on a beginning and an end, the middle is much easier to write. Think of each story as a journey that you're inviting the audience to take with you. The opening should make them want to go along. The ending should make them glad they did.

"When I sit down to write, I sit down like a lover planning a seduction," Robert Krulwich, who has reported for ABC News and National Public Radio, told Current magazine. "My job is to make them notice me—find me interesting, tantalizing. Like any lover, I want their attention first, I want to get them comfortable. I want to get them in the mood—not prone, not right away—just relaxed, willing to let me go further, and then I want to put my hands on their minds—and get 'em excited, bit by bit, so they want a little more."[2]

Leads

Choosing a lead is one of the most important jobs any writer has to do. If the lead doesn't make people want to keep going, they'll never get to the rest of the story. There's no formula for writing a great lead but there are lots of options—hard or soft, anecdotal or delayed, for example. Check the box on page 139 for a quick summary of the most common types of leads. Make sure your lead fits the structure you've chosen for your story. Inverted pyramid? You'd probably write a summary lead. Diamond? You could choose to write an anecdotal lead. Sometimes the idea for a lead comes to your mind first and the structure follows. Just be sure to keep that structure in mind as you put the rest of the story together or you could end up with a mushy mess that's either repetitious or missing significant information.

The style of lead you write also depends in part on the subject matter. A story about five pets being rescued alive from a burning building wouldn't need to begin with the same hard news angle or gravity as a story about a fire that killed three people.

Another way to decide on a lead is to think about what your story is trying to accomplish. You'd begin a story that's designed to share an experience with the audience differently than you would a story that's aimed at explaining why something happened. For example, let's say it's Election Day, and you're doing a story about voter turnout. Election officials have told you the turnout is the lightest they've ever seen, about 23 percent. You've talked to people who didn't vote today, asking them why, so your lead might say: "Less than a quarter of the registered voters in our county voted in today's election. What kept the rest of them away?" That's a hard lead, providing the news right up front that you'll explain in the story. But if your story is focused on what happened at one polling place, where only three voters showed up during a two-hour period, you might write a lead along these lines: "The noisy and expensive campaign for governor has ended with a whimper." In this delayed lead, you have introduced the topic, but you'll give the facts about voter turnout in the story.

Whatever type of lead you choose, make sure it's honest. Don't bait the hook with a promise on which the story can't deliver. For example, a story about a woman who found a paper clip in her breakfast cereal should not begin with a warning that breakfast cereals can be deadly. If you pump up the lead just to draw attention and the story doesn't measure up, you may simply annoy the audience, leaving them feeling like they've been victims of a bait-and-switch sales pitch.

One last important point about leads for television and radio: Remember that the lead to your story is whatever the viewer or listener hears first, whether you read it or the anchor does. The anchor intro should set up what comes next, not repeat it. Make a habit of writing your intro first and then your package so your entire story holds together. Don't leave the intro for someone else to write. You know your story best, so you won't give it all away. A good broadcast lead grabs the viewer's attention and gives a sense of what the story is about but leaves the audience wanting more. You can't do that if your lead is an afterthought.

TRADE TOOLS

TYPES OF LEADS

- Anecdotal (or narrative): Introduces a person as well as the individual's experience, which illustrates what the story is about.

- Delayed (or blind): Establishes the central facts of the story, without immediately identifying the person or event at its center.

- Descriptive: A type of delayed lead that sets the scene for the story by describing a situation, setting or event before revealing its significance.

- Summary: General synopsis of the most important facts of the story, used in the inverted pyramid structure.

- Umbrella: A listing of several equally important elements, each of which will be elaborated in turn.

Endings

It's a good idea to have an ending in mind when you begin writing, much as it's helpful to have a destination in mind when you set out on a journey. As Yogi Berra famously said, "If you don't know where you're going, you might wind up someplace else." This is particularly important for television stories because of the linear nature of the broadcast media. Viewers can't jump ahead in a TV or radio story to find the parts they're most interested in the way they can in a print or online version. Besides, research has found that viewers tend to remember best what they hear last. For that reason, many broadcast stories conclude with a kind of summary ending, reinforcing the story's main point or restating its focus. Print stories often achieve that same goal by ending with a "wrap-up" quote—something for the reader to ponder. This technique is less successful on TV or radio because each story is followed by something else—either another story or a commercial—so there's no time for a final sound bite to sink in.

Endings often echo beginnings in that they return to an important place, person or theme. Boyd Huppert began a flood story that aired on a Sunday night with this line: "On the Lord's Day in Granite Falls, life along the river went to hell." He concluded by echoing the same theme, referring to people in that town "not knowing what will be left when the unholy waters recede." Huppert says he looks for something that ties the story up. "Sometimes, I'm holding back a little information that could be a final surprise," he says. "Something that says, 'The story's over.' It's kind of like shutting the lights off as you walk out of the room."

In a chronological narrative, the ending is what happens last. If a story has raised a problem, the ending might offer a solution. Endings frequently look to the future, to what might happen next. These approaches work equally well in all media, presuming that you've written a story compelling enough for the audience to make it all the way to the end.

WATCH YOUR WORDS

No matter which medium you're using to tell a story, the words you choose matter. As Tom Stoppard put it in his play "The Real Thing": "Words are sacred. They deserve respect. If you get the right ones in the right order, you can nudge the world a little." Choosing the right words and putting them in the right order is the basic task of any writer. Here are some universal keys to writing stronger stories in all media.

Keep It Simple

You've heard this advice a million times, but if you read or watch a lot of news you'll notice that it's frequently violated. A story about a house fire might call it an "inferno" or a "conflagration," or it might describe "firefighters battling the blaze." There's nothing wrong with using a simple word—*fire*—more than once. In fact, it's better because it's so much easier to understand. Charles Osgood of CBS News put it this way: "Bloated words and phrases don't penetrate. Well-chosen, well-ordered ones do."

Simple writing means avoiding jargon—specialized language or technical terms unfamiliar to the general public. If a technical term must be used for accuracy, it's a good idea to include a definition as well. For example, the term *fossil fuels* in a story about global energy issues should include a short list of what those fuels are: coal, oil and natural gas. Steer clear of bureaucratic euphemisms—words or phrases that may confuse or mislead the audience. If the city council votes to approve a new interment facility, your story should tell residents that the city plans to build a new cemetery.

Stay Active

Write simple, declarative sentences in the active voice: subject, verb, object. In the active voice, the person doing the action comes first. "Police found the body," for example, is written in the active voice. Who (police) did what (found) what (body). Using the passive voice means putting the object first: "Shots were fired," for example, or "Mistakes were made." This kind of structure often begs the question: Who did it? When you spot the passive voice, it may be a clue that you need to do more reporting to fill in the blanks.

That doesn't mean you should never use the passive voice. You may want to begin a sentence by naming the most important person in the story. For example, you'd probably write, "Kurt Cobain's body was discovered at his home by a workman," because the rock star's name is an attention grabber. On television, you'd also use this construction to make your words match your pictures. Just be sure that when you do use the passive voice, you're doing it on purpose.

And one more thing: using the present tense does not make your writing active. "Shots are fired," for example, is still in the passive voice.

Use Powerful Words

Nouns and verbs give writing power. Adjectives don't, especially empty adjectives that tell people what to feel. A murder is always "brutal" or "horrifying." A fire could be "shocking" or "devastating." Broadcast writers fall into this trap all the time. In a 15-minute span one morning, reporters and anchors on one channel promised "stunning new developments" that weren't in the least bit astonishing, described a Vatican gathering of visibly

TRADE TOOLS

WRITING TIPS FROM CNN'S CANDY CROWLEY

1. If you don't understand it, don't write it.

2. The less time you have to write, the more time you should take to think about it.

3. Stories should have a beginning, an end and a middle. Not necessarily in that order.

4. The way you would tell a story to your Mom is probably the way you should write it.

5. Write seamless stories—woven so tightly there is no place to cut.

6. Sound bites are not production techniques to break up the sound of your voice. Think of them as part of your narrative.

Source: Photo courtesy of CNN.

7. It is important to remember that grammar counts.

8. The harder you try to be clever, the less likely your writing will be.

9. Et tu, Brutus?

   I think therefore I am.
   I have nothing to offer but blood, sweat and tears.
   I have a dream.
   I am not a crook.
   The Eagle has landed.
   Take adjectives and adverbs out of your story.

10. Style is not something you seek. It is something that happens when you write it right by following the rules.

11. Break the rules.

12. Good writers read. Superb writers read more.

delighted members of the College of Cardinals as a "solemn ceremony" and discussed the possible punishment for a "heinous crime" without ever mentioning what had actually happened.

Great writers seek and use specific details, not shopworn generalities, to convey information and emotion. Instead of telling the audience that there has been a tragic accident, provide the facts: Six members of one family were killed. The only survivor is a 6-month-old boy, now in critical condition. And it happened on Christmas morning. Let the audience decide if that's tragic. Boyd Huppert put this principle into practice in a story about a spreading grass fire. Instead of telling viewers that the situation was terrifying, he described the scene through the eyes of the fire chief: "He had men out there, and he couldn't see them."

Sometimes adjectives are simply redundant. Close proximity. Shower activity. That kind of writing makes a journalist sound ignorant. It undermines credibility and wastes time besides. Does this mean all adjectives must go? Of course not. Just the ones that add no meaning, or worse yet, distort the truth. If you habitually describe all victims as "innocent," for example, you'll be wrong when it turns out one particular victim was wanted for armed robbery in four states. Don't waste time on worthless adjectives. Think of words like this as fat, and put your writing on a diet.

Be Conversational

In broadcast writing especially, tell the story to the audience the way you would tell it to a friend or family member. You're writing for the ear, not the eye. What you write will have to be read out loud, so pay attention to the sound of the words and the rhythm of the sentences as you write. That doesn't mean it's OK to use slang or bad grammar. But it does mean writing copy that is conversational, as opposed to the stilted journalese that reporters often use. If the victims were taken to a hospital far away, that might be news and worth mentioning, but why bother telling us they went to a "nearby hospital"? And where is this "area" that "area-man" comes from, anyway?

Surely you wouldn't call home and describe your dinner at a "60-year-old family-owned eatery," but that's what a local reporter said on the air one night. If a person or an institution's age is important, by all means include it, but put it in a separate sentence. Instead of referring to "the ailing 82-year-old prime minister," break out the information this way: "The prime minister is 82." By the way, it's perfectly fine to use a pronoun on second reference. Martin Luther King Jr. could be referred to as "he" instead of "the slain civil rights leader." Wouldn't that be more conversational? If your words are so stilted they call attention to themselves, you've failed as a writer. As the English author George Orwell put it, "Good prose is like a windowpane. It does not draw attention to itself. It makes the reader see the story, not the words."

Preserve Surprise

The late BBC reporter Alistair Cooke once said: "To write a dull sentence, a sentence without suspense, a sentence that doesn't make you want to know what is coming next—that is the only gross incompetence in broadcasting." That's a tough standard but a welcome reminder of the importance of surprise in storytelling.

GO ONLINE

Module 5: Compare structure and word choice in two versions of the same story.

People remember what surprises them. Before you write any story, think about what you learned that surprised or moved you. It could be the most memorable part of the story. Make sure to include it, but be careful not to spoil the surprise by announcing it. For example, if your Veterans' Day story will include the unplanned reunion of two long-separated shipmates, don't just tell what happened and say how pleased they were to see each other. Let the audience discover their delight through quotes, sound bites or images, and your story will have a lasting impact. As reporter Peter Rosen puts it, "I want people to experience the story, not have it explained to them."

ACCURACY

As you already know, there's nothing more important in journalism than getting it right. In Chapter 2 we talked about the importance of accuracy in reporting. But even if you've captured everything accurately in your notes, errors can slip in during the writing process.

Sometimes mistakes happen when you translate complicated information, especially numbers, into simpler terms the audience can understand more easily. Make sure that when you round off a number you're not making too big a leap. For example, $1.6 billion is not "almost $2 billion," but rather "just over $1.5 billion." You may also raise doubts about the accuracy of your information if you don't let the audience know as much as possible about where you got it. When you're writing, pay close attention to calculations and attribution to avoid questions about accuracy.

Attribution

Attribution is critically important in news stories in all media because it answers the question, "Who says?" Identifying the source of the information allows audiences to judge its credibility for themselves, particularly when it comes to controversial statements. For example, a report that North Korea has decided to suspend its nuclear program could be seen as more or less credible depending on who is quoted as saying so: a visiting Chinese scientist or a team of United Nations officials.

Another reason for attribution is to place responsibility for a controversial statement where it belongs: with the person who said it, not with the reporter or the news organization. This does not imply immunity from lawsuits, of course. But it is good journalistic practice to make clear who is making allegations or taking a particular stand.

Attribution can be explicit or implied. Print stories typically use explicit or direct attribution, for both direct and indirect quotes. For example, a newspaper reporter might write: "The man was arrested and charged with murder, Montgomery County police sergeant Roberto Perez said." For broadcast and online, the sentence would be rewritten using implied or indirect attribution to read, "Montgomery County police arrested the man and charged him with murder." In both cases, the audience can tell that the source of the information is the police.

Not all information in a news story needs to be attributed, however. Naming the source of every bit of information would make stories almost incomprehensible. Information that a reporter observed directly can be stated without attribution. Indisputable or well-accepted facts do not need to be attributed, either. For example, a reporter could say which team won a football game without attribution because the final score would not be in doubt. But writing that one candidate won a political debate would need to be attributed; without attribution, it would be seen as the reporter's opinion.

Numbers

A journalism teacher once described her students as "do-gooders who hate math." Most journalists will never come to love math, but they need it. Numbers may look solid and factual, but they are not infallible. Journalists need numerical competence in order to tell the difference between a meaningless number and a significant one. If they can't, they risk writing stories that are misleading and confusing at best, and at worst flat out wrong. Just ask any reporter who's ever been fooled by the numbers in a city budget or a federal spending bill.

Journalists need math intuition so they can tell when the numbers they're looking at just don't add up. They need math mechanics to find the meaning behind figures and data. They need math concepts so they can understand banking and business, bankruptcy and boom times. Simply put, journalists need math skills to make sense of numbers the way they need language skills to make sense of words.

Competent journalists are both capable and careful with numbers. They're quick to spot an implausible number, and they have a basic working knowledge of arithmetic and statistics so they can confirm their suspicions. Now that every smartphone and laptop has a built-in calculator, journalists should use them. Just because a number or percentage is in a press release doesn't mean it's correct. Calculators can also help you translate numbers into terms readers and viewers can relate to. For example, when reporter Steve Daniels was covering a plane crash, he learned how many tons of fuel the aircraft had on board. For his story, he converted tons to gallons of fuel, a measurement anyone could understand.

Percentages, ratios, rates of change and other relationships between numbers tell far better stories than raw data can. A story about a $13 million increase in school spending would be more understandable to viewers if the reporter translated the raw numbers into the additional amount that will be spent per child—$500. If that amount is 95 percent more than it was 10 years ago, you could write that it's almost doubled in 10 years.

In television and radio news, when it comes to writing with numbers, the rule of thumb is the fewer the better. Numbers that are used should be rounded off for simplicity's sake, and put in context for clarity. Remember the election turnout story we mentioned earlier in this chapter? We didn't use the specific number, 23 percent, but instead referred to a turnout of "less than a quarter" of registered voters. As we mentioned in Chapter 1, print and online stories usually provide more exact numbers, but not always in the story itself. You can keep the text clear and relevant by rounding off numbers and using the specific data to create a graphic or interactive element.

Journalists with numerical competence are more important than ever in today's highly technical world. They are the writers and editors who can assess and explain scientific, medical, technological and economic developments. They are the journalists who can find stories in databases by crunching numbers themselves, instead of waiting for someone with a vested interest to do it for them.

GO ONLINE

Module 5: Find math tools, and check your math skills with an interactive exercise.

Journalists who fail to master math lack a basic skill needed to decipher much of the information in the world around them, such as crime statistics, pollution standards, real estate taxes and unemployment figures. Without math skills, journalists are bound to fall short in their quest for accuracy. The good news is that there are tons of online tools to make math easier for journalists.

REVISING YOUR STORY

Revising is a lost art in many newsrooms. Reporters say they don't have time to revise their stories because they work right up to deadline every day, and besides, isn't it a supervisor's job to make any changes that need to be made? Don't bet on it. The story approval process in many broadcast and online newsrooms amounts to a quick read to make sure the facts are right. There really isn't time for supervisors to improve reporters' writing on deadline. That's something a reporter needs to do before submitting the story.

Building in just a little time for revision will make your writing stronger. Set yourself a deadline that's a little earlier than it needs to be, so you can spot problems and fix them before submitting a final story or going on the air. As little as five extra minutes will help.

Don't start revising as soon as you get to the end of your first draft. If you start revising immediately, you may see what you meant to write rather than what you actually put on the page. Take a short break, walk away from your desk, clear your mind. When you come back, read the story from start to finish as if you know nothing about it. Does it make sense? Are the elements in the right order? Is any crucial information missing?

Read Aloud

Spot jargon and journalese by reading your story out loud. Not under your breath, but really out loud. If you're writing for broadcast, it's the only way you will notice things that look fine on paper but sound silly when you hear them. When Lynn Swann, a former pro football player, announced that he was running for governor of Pennsylvania, one reporter referred to him as the 53-year-old Swann. Not good if you're writing for the ear. As you read aloud, try adding an extra phrase to the beginning of each sentence: "Hey, Mom . . . guess what?" Or "You won't believe this, but. . . ." If what follows that opening line is stilted or convoluted, you'll notice it right away and you can revise your copy to make it more conversational.

Reading aloud also gives you a good sense of a story's rhythms. You don't want every sentence and paragraph to be the same length. Variety maintains interest. But you also want to avoid using long strings of modifiers. "Allegheny College sophomore and budding electronic musician Paniya Ly . . ." is hard to read without picking up speed like a freight train. Derail those phrases by breaking them up. "When she's not in class at Allegheny College, Paniya Ly writes electronic music. . . ."

Nuke Wasted Words

Well-written news stories are not vague, ambiguous or repetitious because every word counts. As E. B. White notes in his classic book "The Elements of Style," one of the basic rules of writing is simply "Omit needless words." A "marathon seven-hour operation" is redundant. Here's another example from a local TV script: "In Mecca, Saudi Arabia, thousands are gathering in the city for the annual Muslim pilgrimage there." The sentence has

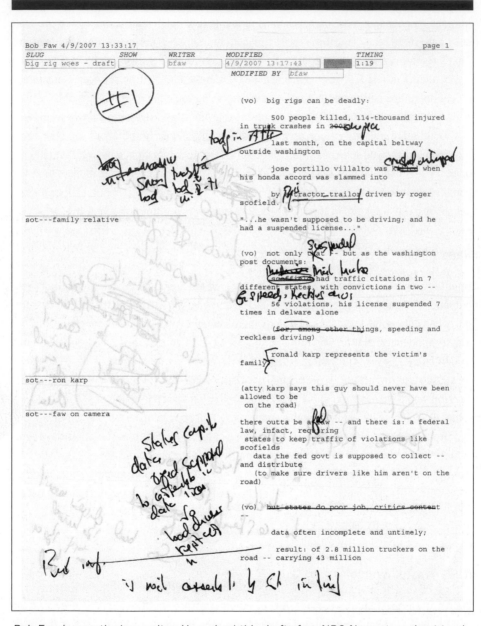

Bob Faw is a meticulous writer. He revised this draft of an NBC News story about truck safety four times before it aired.

Source: Photo courtesy of Bob Faw.

three references to the location: Mecca, city and there. One would do. Unless you are repeating something for emphasis or clarity, don't do it.

"Reporters tend to fall in love with their own words and the words they need to fall in love with are those of the subjects," says WJZ-TV reporter Mike Schuh. "I think people use too many words and try to overexplain, and I think it's lazy." It's hard work to pare your own writing down, but keeping the narration short can make the story more engaging. One caution, however: This only works if you've chosen strong sound bites that don't run on so long that they become boring.

Look closely at any use of superlatives, and when in doubt, leave them out. They're red flags, says Alice Main, former executive producer at WLS-TV in Chicago, Ill. "Just

ACCURACY CHECKLIST

1. Confirm information that could be in doubt. Check any unattributed information to make sure it's solid. Be sure that all attributed information is credited to the correct source.

2. Clarify context. Make sure the sound bites or quotes you use fully capture what each person meant to say.

3. Look for what might be missing. Review your story with an eye to significant information or points of view that have not been included.

4. Review for focus. Make sure your story backs up your lead. Restate the focus of your story and reread to see if you're still on target.

5. Check names, places, titles. Make sure all are correct and up to date. Don't depend solely on business cards or a Web search.

6. Check spelling, grammar, usage. If you are not positive about a spelling, look it up. Read out loud to find and fix grammar and usage problems. If in doubt, ask a colleague or check a reference guide.

7. Do the math. Make sure the numbers add up. Recalculate percentages, percent change and ratios, no matter where you got them. Check with an expert not involved in the story if you have any questions about how the numbers were calculated.

TRADE TOOLS

think of the potential for error when you declare something is the best/worst/most/largest/ smallest thing." Her advice: If you're going to say it, make sure you can prove it.

Wasted words often show up at the ends of sentences, oddly enough in three-word phrases. A story about a chrysanthemum show said it featured "51 varieties of the flower." Another story talked about people living "miles apart from each other." Those last three words aren't necessary, are they? Try to end your sentences with a strong word, not a weak phrase. Look again at how Boyd Huppert did it in his flood story: "On the Lord's Day in Granite Falls, life along the river went to hell." That's a sentence that ends with punch.

Revise your entire story by going over it backwards. Take your script, cover up the final sentence and work back to the beginning, sentence by sentence. You may find that your story actually ended long before you finished writing. Cutting back makes a story stronger, just as it does a rose bush.

Check for Errors and Accuracy

Look closely at dates, addresses, quantities, URLs and all the other details. Getting someone's name or age wrong is the kind of error that can erode a journalist's credibility. Make sure your story is grammatically correct. Pay particularly close attention to subject-verb agreement and misplaced modifiers. And check for spelling errors too. Broadcast journalists used to joke that spelling didn't count on the air, but it certainly does now, with scripts being used for closed-captioning and adapted for posting online.

An accurate story tells a complete story, not just one side or another. That doesn't mean that any single story can include everything there is to say about a topic, but it does mean that reporters must not leave out key information that could distort the story's meaning. For example, writing that a new test makes it easier to detect oral cancer suggests that the old test was unreliable. If the new test is merely faster, the reporter should say so.

TAKING IT HOME

Journalists today have more tools and options for telling stories than ever before, but the words they use still matter. As the late CBS News correspondent Eric Sevareid once said, "One good word is worth a thousand pictures." A big part of the job is to choose the right words and put them in the right order to tell a story that is both clear and meaningful, whether you're doing it on television, online or in print.

Good writing is not magic. It's a skill that can be learned and improved with discipline and practice. If you want to become a better writer, read, watch and listen to great writers in all media. Take their stories apart and figure out what makes them work. Challenge yourself to find a clear focus for every story you write. Be ruthless about leaving things out that don't fit your focus. And if you choose to do only one thing to improve your writing, make time for revision.

TALKING POINTS

1. Take a script or story you've written and look for wasted words. How many words can you remove without losing the meaning or power of the story? Is the story better after you've taken those words out? Why or why not?

2. Choose a script or story and review it for attribution. List all the statements that include either direct or indirect attribution. Are there elements of the story that should have been attributed but were not? What questions would you need to have answered in order to include more attribution in the story?

3. Watch and record a local TV or radio newscast, paying close attention to the writing. Make note of what you would have changed if you'd been in charge of editing copy before air.

ONLINE LEARNING MODULE 5

Activate or buy this chapter's online learning module at journalism.cqpress.com to get access to:

- SKILL BUILDING: Practice writing focus statements of six words or less for some well-known stories.

- DISCOVER: Read and watch two versions of the same story to see how conversational writing can add power and meaning.

- EXPLORE: Find online grammar help, writing checklists and math tools.

- Tips on writing from award-winning journalists.

- A digital version of this chapter's text in full color with active links.

Also, continue your work on the ONGOING STORY MODULE. Write a focus statement and "jot outline" for this story.

CHAPTER 6 MULTIMEDIA STORYTELLING

Multimedia journalists tell stories with audio, video, photos, text, graphics, data and documents that complement rather than repeat each other. They choose these elements carefully and combine them to present information in the most appropriate way for the medium and the audience. In this chapter, we'll describe how to select and write to the sound and pictures you've gathered, and how to add other elements to create stories that are both informative and engaging.

Once you've captured all the elements you need to create a compelling story, you still need to choose the best of those elements and decide how to use them. If the foundation of great writing is selection not compression, great multimedia storytelling depends on your choice of images, sound and interactives, and the way you put those elements together with the words you write, either text or narration.

Every element you choose to include should enhance the story's impact and credibility. Do it well online, and you can offer the audience multiple ways to experience and explore a story.

Multimedia journalist Travis Fox says the key is finding the right balance among the different media. For example, in an online report for washingtonpost.com about the fence Israel built in the West Bank, Fox used video stories, panorama still photos and a Flash graphic showing the route of the fence. Fox says his successful projects all have some things in common. "Those would probably be ones where you took the various media and combined them in a way that was logical," he told the Online Journalism Review, "using a blog for user feedback and conversation; using the panoramas to give you a sense of place; and using videos to give you a sense of people, the character, the location, and then combining [them] to give you a full picture of the story."[1]

152

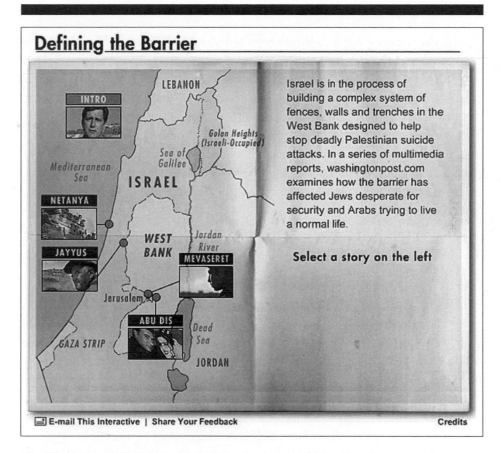

Defining the Barrier

LEBANON

INTRO

Golan Heights (Israeli-Occupied)

Sea of Galilee

Mediterranean Sea

ISRAEL

NETANYA

WEST BANK

Jordan River

JAYYUS

MEVASERET

Jerusalem

ABU DIS

Dead Sea

GAZA STRIP

JORDAN

Israel is in the process of building a complex system of fences, walls and trenches in the West Bank designed to help stop deadly Palestinian suicide attacks. In a series of multimedia reports, washingtonpost.com examines how the barrier has affected Jews desperate for security and Arabs trying to live a normal life.

Select a story on the left

E-mail This Interactive | Share Your Feedback   Credits

The Washington Post gave online users multiple ways of experiencing a story about Israel's security barrier. Each hot spot on the map led to a Flash animation showing the barrier's path and a video essay featuring local residents; some also had 360° panorama still photos of the area.

Source: "Defining the Barrier," *Washington Post,* 2005, www.washingtonpost.com/wp-srv/world/interactives/israel/israelFence.html (accessed August 15, 2007).

MULTIMEDIA STORY TYPES

As you prepare a multimedia story, consider what you want the end result to look and sound like. What form will your story take? Will it have narration or not? Some story types exist on multiple platforms; others are more common on the air than they are online and vice-versa.

Audio Story Types

Several story types are common in both radio and podcasting. A voicer is a reporter narration, using no additional sound. A wrap includes at least one sound bite, sometimes referred to as an "actuality," and may also include natural sound. Stories that are narrated on scene rather than in the studio may be called ROSRs (pronounced "roser," short for "radio on-scene report"), the audio equivalent of a television live shot. Short clips from interviews edited together are often called "vox pops" in both radio and television. Longer clips may be used online. Both radio and TV air Q-and-A interviews, either live or edited. Long-form audio stories, sometimes called "mini-docs," are used on radio and online, and may be produced with or without narration. We'll talk more about long-form stories later in this chapter.

Visual Story Types

Some video styles commonly used on television are rarely seen online. The V/O (voice over, or video with narration) and V/O-SOT (voice-over-sound-on-tape, or video with narration followed by a sound bite) are staples of TV news but almost never used on the Web. Both platforms use packages—self-contained stories with narration, sound bites and natural sound—but while TV packages daily news stories, online packages tend to be longer-form stories. Both platforms also use raw video and excerpts from interviews, although these also tend to run longer on the Web. The "nat sound" story, complete with video and sound but without narration, is another story type that's used on both platforms but is more frequently found online than on air. Audio slide shows are typically an online-only story type. We'll discuss nat sound stories and slide shows in more detail later in this chapter.

PLANNING

As we made clear in Chapter 5, you can't construct a story without knowing exactly what you have to work with. For a multimedia story, you need detailed notes on all the video, still photos and audio you think you might use on the air, online or in print. You also need to decide what information you want to convey in graphic form in each medium.

Screening and Logging

Even if you recorded all the audio and video for your story yourself, you should still review it to make sure you captured exactly what you think you did. Don't fall into the trap of

```
    schuhm              Tue Dec  3 16:03  page    3
                                          TAPE ONE 9:14
                                          RUNS:01

  T/1   9:45 CU MANHOLE COVER MOVE


  T/1   9:57 DRIVE DOWN STOPPED CARS <

  ENG/SOT                                 ENG/SOT
                                          BUSINESSMAN
                                          DAVID COHEN
                                          TAPE ONE 10:24
                                          "WELL THE WAY THEY..... MIDDLE OF
                                          DAY... IMPOSSIBLE TO GET AROUND
                                          RUNS:08


  ENG/SOT                                 ENG/SOT
                                          BUSINESSMAN
                                          DAVID COHEN
                                          TAPE ONE 10:57
                                          AND I DON'T KNOW WHY THEY CAN'T DO IT
                                          AT NIGHT
                                          RUNS:04


  T/1   11:23 LO EW STAND AROUND PAVERS

  T/1   BBBB :04 KOMP WORKER NAT WIPE

  ENG/SOT                                 ENG/SOT
                                          NATS
                                          JACKHAMMER ECU W/ NAT WIPE
                                          TAPE ONE BBB :47
                                          RUNS:01


  T/1 BBB 1:24 EW TRUCKS BACKHOE

  T/1  BBB 1:35 BACKHOE OPERATOR

  T/1  BBB 2:24 NO PARKING ECU MACRO

  T/1  BBB 2:36 BARREL

  ENG/SOT                                 ENG/SOT
                                          RIDE ALONG
                                          TAPE ONE BBB 2:42
                                          WE'RE GOING TO BE AT THEIS LIGHT FOR A
                                          WHILE
                                          RUNS:02

  ENG/SOT                                 ENG/SOT
                                          RIDE ALONG
                                          TAPE ONE BBB 3:03
                                          OH IT'S HORRIBLE REALLY....
```

WJZ-TV reporter Mike Schuh's log notes for a story about construction in downtown Baltimore, Md. Notice how detailed his log is, with tape number and time codes, a shorthand description of each shot and the exact running time of sound bites and "nats."

Source: Courtesy of Mike Schuh.

TRADE TOOLS

LOGGING SHORTHAND

CU: Close-up.

XCU: Extreme close-up.

MCU: Medium close-up.

MS: Medium shot.

WS: Wide shot.

LS: Long shot.

>:   Screen direction right.

<:   Screen direction left.

INT: Interior.

EXT: Exterior.

RF: Rack focus.

writing a script based solely on your recollection of what you observed at the scene, or you may have to rewrite or re-edit when you discover you don't have the pictures or sound to make it work. If you've taken good notes in the field, you can quickly find and screen just those segments you think you'll use. It takes a little time, but investing it at the front end will pay off in a quicker edit.

As you screen, create a detailed log of your material. If you've captured digital video or audio clips, note the name and location of each file or bin and what's in it. If you're working with linear video or audio, note the exact time code or counter time so you can cue it up for digitizing or editing. You'll also need a description of the pictures and a word-for-word transcript of the audio, both sound bites and natural sound "pops."

Not everyone does this the same way, but good writers tend to be meticulous loggers. Reporter Mike Schuh of WJZ-TV in Baltimore, Md., logs in two columns— visuals on the left and audio on the right. He uses his own shorthand to describe the video: EW-2 means an extreme wide two-shot, for example, and OOF stands for "out of focus." KOMP tells him the shot was taken with a long lens, so the video is compressed. He uses the symbols < and > to note the direction people are facing on the screen, so when he writes he doesn't call for back-to-back sound bites in which everyone is looking in the same direction.

Schuh logs all the audio he might use "up full," whether it's nat sound or a bite from an interview. If the sound is off-camera and he plans to use it as a V/O (voice over), he draws a squiggly line—his symbol for "radio."

Timing

If you've interviewed a slow talker, what looks short on paper may actually take a long time to say out loud. You definitely need to know the total running time (TRT) of each bite before you write a television or radio story, and before you decide which clips to post online. The Internet may not have any built-in time limits, but most users do. "One of the hardest things to learn in editing video or audio is discipline," says multimedia producer Regina McCombs, who has worked for both newspapers and TV. "Sometimes—many times—shorter is better."[2]

If you're doing an online or print version of your story and you have enough time, transcribe segments of sound that are longer than the bites you'd use on the air. You can use the transcript to select quotes for print, to post online in its entirety, or to help you create short natural-sound videos or slide shows with audio for the Web. We'll talk more about how to do that later in this chapter.

CHOOSING SOUND

Sound is a critical element in many types of multimedia stories, from online slide shows and podcasts to TV and, obviously, radio. "It's what brings people into a story," says radio news executive Robert Garcia, who has worked at ABC, CBS, CNN and NPR. "If somebody's in a Pakistani village you're going to be listening to [what it sounds like] and you can practically taste the dust on the road."

Selecting the best sound for a multimedia story takes more effort than choosing quotes for print. As we discussed in Chapter 5, you'll narrow down your choices by reviewing and transcribing the best sound bites, but you can't make a final decision about what to use by looking at a transcript. Something that looks great on paper may not work on the air or online. And you still have to consider all the other sound you might want to include to bring your story to life.

Sound Quality

Too many stories include bites that are off mic, muffled or so thickly accented that they're hard to decipher. A good sound bite has to be perfectly clear and understandable, whether the person is on camera or not. For radio or a podcast, sound quality is even more important because there's no video to help convey the meaning of what's being said. To make sure each bite is good enough to use, listen to the audio with your eyes closed, and if you have any doubt about the quality, ask someone who wasn't involved in the story to listen for you. Reporters and photographers who hear a bite on the scene and then hear it again in the edit room may think it's easier to understand than it really is.

Sometimes a bite that's hard to decipher is still essential to the story you're telling. For example, you might have emotional sound from a person who is not a native English speaker but was the only eyewitness you could find to a natural disaster. Don't reject the bite out of hand. Instead, consider using the bite with subtitles or a translation so your audience can both experience the emotion and understand the content. At the same time, make sure you discuss whether doing so could be seen as disrespectful.

Sound Bites

Bites should not only be clear, they should sound authentic. Avoid using bites in which people sound like they're robots reading from a script. As we've discussed, the best sound bites are subjective and provide insight, not just facts. Great sound bites have passion, says reporter Tony Kovaleski of KMGH-TV in Denver, Colo. "During interviews, try and capture the passion," he says. "During writing, make sure not to miss it."

There's no rule about how many sound bites you need for any given story, nor how long or short each bite should be. Some terrific stories have been told without a single bite; others are told almost entirely in sound bites with very little track. "Not every package needs three sound bites," says news director Mark Ginther of KING-TV in Seattle, Wash. "Every package needs to make sense."

Even so, most beginning reporters tend to let their bites run too long, especially when they think everything being said is important. It's often more effective to paraphrase a portion of a long bite and use the information to set up a shorter bite. When three climbers were stranded on Oregon's Mt. Hood, the local sheriff talked to the media about the ongoing search. "We've been searching all week—but when an opportunity opened up because of the weather, [it] gave us a break to be up there this morning," said Sheriff Joe Wampler.

What's going on—what our strategy is today, and it's going to continue through the weekend, is we've got teams on the mountain right now that basically started at 4:00 this morning—and our strategy is to get a summit team from the south side of the mountain, from Timberline, and this is totally dependant upon avalanche conditions, which are extreme on the mountain right now. As you can see, even from right here, we have some wind on the mountain now to the east and there's a lot of fresh snow and there's blowing snow up there. But that's OK, we're able to operate in that environment today.[3]

There's a lot of good information in that sound bite, but it runs 35 seconds. In a case like this, you might want to apply the "12 second rule"—if the bite runs longer than 12 seconds, it had better be riveting. In this case, it isn't. The first part of the bite is just factual information you can summarize, so the last part of the bite, where the sheriff shares a personal opinion, works best:

> As you can see, even from right here, we have some wind on the mountain now to the east and there's a lot of fresh snow and there's blowing snow up there. But that's OK, we're able to operate in that environment today.

Generally speaking, a sound bite should convey a complete thought, be easily understood and keep the audience's attention. If a bite is too short, it may be hard to absorb. Keep in mind that the human brain takes a few seconds to adjust to a change in voice before it can process what's being said. So bites that run only a few seconds can't really convey much useful information, but that doesn't mean they're always worthless. Long bites can be boring, but they can also be compelling. The best advice on how to make good decisions about sound bites is to focus primarily on content, as we discussed in Chapter 5, not length.

Natural Sound

Natural sound serves three basic functions in a story. It gives the viewer or listener the sense of being closer to the action, it helps vary the pace and it provides information. Review your material for other sound you can use in your broadcast stories or online. Some audio may have been captured on the fly. For example, when covering a flood you might put a microphone on a volunteer while he's stacking sandbags to keep a river from overflowing. Your mic could pick up the comments he makes to the volunteer next to him, including this one: "These things are getting mighty heavy." Using that comment in your story would bring the audience closer to understanding the experience of those volunteers. "Nat pops" like these will likely be short, but they can reinforce what's in your narration or video. If you intend to use this kind of sound "up full," apply the same standards you would for an interview bite and make sure the words are clear and understandable.

Listen as well for other sound you can use to reinforce the theme of your story or move it forward. In the flood story, for example, you'd probably want to include the sound of the river rushing by, water pumps chugging to keep the river from overflowing its banks, the hiss of sand being poured into bags and so forth. As you log, make a note of where these sounds occur.

You also may have audio from other sources that will help the audience better understand your story. Mark Bowden, who wrote the Philadelphia Inquirer series that turned into the book and movie "Black Hawk Down" about U.S. forces fighting in Somalia, obtained radio transmissions of soldiers during the battle. He posted that audio as part of the online version of his story, sounds that he said "captured the frenzy and terror of the fight."[4]

CHOOSING VIDEO

Selecting the best video or photos to tell your story isn't as easy as it sounds. Sure, there are some stories where the choice of pictures is obvious. You wouldn't tell a breaking news story about a warehouse fire without shots of flames and smoke. But you'll also need the establishing shots and reaction shots we talked about in Chapter 3. And make sure the video you plan to use to begin and end the story is as good as you think it is. "The opening needs to say, 'watch me' and the close needs to say, 'the end,'" says Sharon Levy Freed, director of the NPPA Television NewsVideo Workshop.

Moments

Make note of what many photojournalists call "moments" in the video—images or sequences that capture the real impact of the story. Scott Jensen, an award-winning TV news photographer, says the best moments are spontaneous, and typically symbolize joy or struggle. "What moves you will probably move your audience," he says. "What you remember from a shot is likely going to be what your audience remembers."

The "moment" in this WTVF-TV story about the dedication of a new statue in Nashville wasn't the predictable unveiling (left) but the unexpected (right)—when the cable used to remove the tarp broke.
Source: Courtesy of WTVF-TV.

Sometimes you won't even be aware of these moments until you review what you've shot. As he screened video for a story about a house being moved across a frozen lake, photojournalist Jonathan Malat of KARE-TV in Minneapolis was surprised to discover a shot of the ice almost breaking under the house trailer's wheel. He'd shot a close-up of the wheel to use as a cutaway, but didn't notice the movement of the ice until he was in the edit room. Using that shot allowed him to prove just how dangerous the move really was.

The audio you've chosen will dictate some of the video you'll use to tell your story. If you've selected a sound bite from an active interview, you'll probably want some b-roll shot in the same location. Look for pictures that prove the point of the narration or sound bites. When the volunteer in your flood story says the sandbags are getting heavy, you'll want to cut to video that proves he's right—for example, a shot where he accidentally drops a sandbag while trying to hand it to the next person in line.

WRITING TO SOUND

Now that you've chosen your best audio, decide which bites you'll definitely use. Eliminate sound bites that duplicate information unless you're using them on purpose to emphasize a statement or fact. NBC's Bob Dotson warns, "Don't use sound bites as substitutes for more effective storytelling." Reporters who simply string bites together are often taking the lazy way out. On the other hand, don't write your script first and then look for sound to plug in. Remember what CNN's Candy Crowley said: "Sound bites are not production techniques to break up the sound of your voice." Your goal is to create a seamless narrative, to keep the audience's attention from beginning to end, and your success depends to a large degree on the way you write in and out of each sound bite.

Leading In

Look closely at the beginning of each bite you've decided to use. Your goal is to write a line just before the bite that prepares the audience for what they're about to hear. Because the best sound bites express opinion or emotion, they often don't make sense without a good setup line, and a bad setup line can leave the viewer confused. "It's like putting the ball on the tee," says Mike Schuh. "I try to write as little as possible going in, make it as clear as possible, and all I'm doing is the setup."

Let's say you're reporting on a candidate for political office who has promised not to take money from lobbyists. You could write: "Eric Chao signed a pledge not to accept gifts from lobbyists," but if you follow it with this sound bite—"We should be able to expect that they're going to enrich us and not themselves"—you'll leave viewers wondering why anyone should expect that lobbyists would "enrich us." That's because the pronoun "they" in the sound bite appears to refer back to the noun in your script that's closest to the bite, "lobbyists." What the candidate meant was that elected officials should not enrich themselves. You'd have served the audience better by writing: "Eric Chao signed a pledge not to accept gifts from lobbyists, saying it's wrong for politicians to line their own pockets." Write so that the ear gets the information needed to decode what's coming next.

You also don't want to write lead-in lines to sound bites that echo or repeat what the person says. You'll bore the audience and steal the thunder from the characters in your story. Let them say how they feel or what they learned. You don't have to say it for them. There's nothing more annoying than a story full of lines like this: "Many parents were upset they weren't notified," followed by sound bites from people saying, "I was upset" and "It made me angry." One way to avoid this is to think of sound bites as reactions to the action in your script or video, or as punch lines that you set up in your script. Use your narration to tell what happened—"Many parents weren't notified"—and leave it to the parents themselves to describe how they reacted.

In most cases, you'll want to identify the person speaking before the sound bite is heard. Many television reporters rely on lower-third graphics to provide that information, but that presumes the audience is actually watching the screen. Because that's often not the case, many journalists believe it's always a good idea to name the person in narration. It's advisable to at least write something before the sound bite that makes the person's role in the story clear. Tell the audience they're a parent or teacher, for example, even if you don't name him or her.

For radio and audio podcasts, you'll typically set up each sound bite with the person's name and some information that explains why they're worth listening to. In a story about the unemployment rate, for example, NPR's Tamara Keith identified one person she interviewed this way: "Lisa Lynch is dean of the public policy school at Brandeis University, and a former chief economist at the Labor Department."[5] If the bite is short, you can sometimes put that kind of information after the bite.

Leading Out

Repetition may not be the best way to set up a bite, but it's often effective to repeat words from a bite in the line that follows it. Let's say you have a bite from a hurricane survivor who says, "Insurance isn't going to do me any good, so I'm in big trouble here." You might be tempted to write out of the bite this way: "That's because it only covers flooding, not wind damage." But you'd be better served to repeat the word *insurance* in your narration to avoid any confusion as to what "it" stands for, so you'd write, "That's because her insurance only covers flooding, not wind damage."

You can also repeat the very last words in a sound bite for emphasis or clarity, as correspondent Jim Wooten did in a story about integration for ABC News. A person he spoke to in Oxford, Miss., described adults in the community this way: "They're not used to being around the other color, the other races, and they want their kids to grow up that way too." His next line said, "That way meant that when integration began, the annual prom ended."

Some sound bites may convey complete thoughts, but the person speaking may not come to an obvious stop at the end. Some people seem to end every sentence with an upward inflection so their statements sound almost like questions. You can still use these bites if you're careful about how you write out of them, so your line completes the person's unfinished thought. For example, let's say your hurricane survivor says something that sounds like this: "The cops came through with a bullhorn. They wanted us to leave?" Her inflection makes her sound uncertain, even though she's making a statement of fact. Your line coming out of the bite can make that clear to the audience. The simplest solution is to begin with a conjunction like "and" or "but." In this case, you could write, "And they left immediately" or "But they decided to stay."

One more point about using sound bites: They usually need company. "When you use a sound bite to either open or close a piece, pair it with a line of track," says reporter Wayne Freedman of KGO-TV in San Francisco, Calif. "If you close with a sound bite, it should be stronger than any other words you might write." That's a high standard most sound bites just don't meet.

Using "Nat Pops"

Using nat sound for pacing can keep your story moving, but it can also be overdone. You've probably seen stories that bring sound up almost at random in the middle of lines of track, making it harder for the audience to follow the story. Reporter Boyd Huppert says that thinking of nat as punctuation helps him put it in where it makes sense. A very short nat could be used where you'd pause for a comma. Longer nat works as a period at the end of a sentence. Put a longer nat where a short one belongs and you create what Huppert calls a "Knievel," named for the stuntman known for his daring motorcycle jumps. "If it's too long," Huppert says, "you can't get to the other side."

Nat sound is often used to prove a point made in narration. Huppert once described a man as "part preacher, part Wal-Mart greeter," and proved it by inserting a short bite

KNOW AND TELL

MAKE IT MEMORABLE

NBC national correspondent Bob Dotson is a brilliant visual storyteller who regularly shares his insights at the annual TV workshop of the National Press Photographers Association. He uses the term *commitment* to describe a story's focus. "The commitment should be stated as a complete sentence with subject, verb and object," Dotson says. "Prove the commitment visually."

Source: Photo courtesy of Bob Dotson.

His story checklist includes these additional tips:

- Write your pictures first. Give them a strong lead, preferably visual, that instantly telegraphs the story to come. Ideally, the ending is also visual.

- Write loose. Be hard on yourself. Say nothing in script your viewers would already know or that the visuals say more eloquently.

- Build your report around sequences. Two or three shots of a guy buying basketball tickets, two or three shots of a husband and wife drinking coffee at a kitchen table, etc. Sequences demand matched action.

- Strong natural sound. Some reports merely let you watch what happened. The best reports let you experience what happened.

- Short sound bites. Short bites prove the story you are showing. Don't use sound bites as substitutes for more effective storytelling.

Source: Adapted from Bob Dotson, "Story Checklist," National Press Photographers Association workshop.

from the man after each phrase. After Huppert said "part preacher" he used a bite of the man saying "Amen," and after "part Wal-Mart greeter" the man said, "Thank you."

Like every other element in your story, nat sound should move it forward and not interrupt the flow. Use nat sound to glue your story together, like "mortar between bricks," says photojournalist Tim Griffis, not to "break up" your narration.

WRITING TO VIDEO

As you write your multimedia story, think video first. It's a simple rule, but that doesn't mean it's easy to follow. Thinking video first means you should never write more narration than you have video to cover. It also means you must consider what the audience will be looking at before you decide what audio or narration should go along with the pictures. That's because pictures are powerful—so powerful they can trump words. Studies have found that when the video and audio in a television news story are not in sync, people remember what they see much better than what they hear.[6]

CBS News correspondent Lesley Stahl says she learned that lesson when covering the White House in the 1980s. She used video of President Ronald Reagan visiting nursing homes and speaking at the Special Olympics in a story that detailed the administration's plans to cut benefits for the elderly and handicapped. Far from being unhappy, the White House loved the story. In her book, "Reporting Live," Stahl says an official told her why. "Nobody heard what you said," he explained. "When the pictures are powerful and emotional, they override if not completely drown out the sound."

Keep that in mind when deciding what video to use when. If you have compelling images, pause for a few seconds and let the pictures tell the story. If you put critical facts in your narration at that point, no one will hear them anyway.

Build Sequences

Put the video for your story in order, scene by scene, and see if you can let each sequence play out before you move on to the next. Jumping back and forth between locations and going backward and forward in time makes a story choppy, not seamless.

For example, let's say you're doing a story about those missing mountain climbers. You have shots of the search team heading out of base camp before dawn, a midmorning news conference by the sheriff, daytime video of the mountain with helicopters overhead and two interviews with family members of the missing men. You'd probably start with the search team video because everything else was shot in daylight and you wouldn't want to go from day to night and back to day again. Bring the family members into your story to have their say, and then say goodbye to them. And once you've introduced a main character like the sheriff, don't feel obliged to use a shot of him on camera every time you refer to something he's said—especially not a silent shot of him talking. Lip flap is almost always a bad idea. If you want to mention the sheriff's plan to keep the helicopters flying all weekend, stick with the video of the choppers and keep your story moving smoothly along.

Show, Don't Tell

One key principle of news writing is to show the audience what happened rather than tell about it. For example, instead of saying that family members attending a funeral were grief-stricken, a well-written story would show their grief by describing or using video of them hugging and sobbing. "You can say she's a devoted mother, or you can show a child jumping into her lap," says Mike Mather, a reporter at WTKR-TV in Norfolk, Va. "Which is more effective?"

That sounds obvious enough, but it gets tricky when reporters try to write something to go along with the video. Too many take the old TV news maxim, "See dog, say dog," literally, and what they write just repeats what the viewer can already see. Of course, if you have a sound bite of someone talking about her dog you should show video of it. But narration should enhance the visual elements in stories by adding context or meaning. There is no point in showing video of a country road and writing a line that describes the road. Instead of telling viewers what they're looking at, tell them why they're looking at it.

GO ONLINE

Ongoing Story Module:
Log raw video and audio for this story, and write a TV package.

For example, in a story for WTVF-TV in Nashville, Tenn., about National Guard troops preparing to head for Iraq, reporter Barry Simmons used video of soldiers in their barracks and in tanks, but he didn't talk about their training routine over those pictures. Instead, he referred to what the soldiers had left behind: "Just six weeks ago, they had careers, woke up in their own beds and drove to work on wheels." Some reporters call this technique "writing to the corners of the picture," because the words convey what the viewer can't see.

Draw Attention

On rare occasions, you may want to refer directly to what the viewer is looking at to underline the significance of something on the screen that otherwise might be missed. For example, in a story about a bear roaming a suburban neighborhood, you might write: "You can just see the bear's nose poking out of those bushes." Or if the bear can be seen clearly, but only for a few seconds, you could say, "Neighbors watched for hours and *this* is all they saw," matching the word *this* to the video of the bear's brief appearance.

Your words can also help avoid confusion in the viewer's mind. If you're writing to a shot of two people but referring to just one of them in your copy, it's a good idea to identify that person as being on the left or right. Years ago, the only video of accused serial killer John Wayne Gacy showed him dressed in a clown costume doing charity work. Using that video without explanation would have been puzzling to say the least.

Parallel Parking

Another way to create a seamless narrative is to "parallel park" part of your narration between sound bites that occur in one continuous shot. Instead of removing a relatively long pause or stumble in a sound bite you want to use and covering the edit with a cutaway, let the video roll and insert a short line of narration during the pause.

For example, when reporter Matt Barcaro was covering the story of a one-time boxing champion charged with arson, he interviewed people who had known the man in better days. In his story for WGAL-TV, Barcaro used a bite from one of them, complete with pauses in which he "parked" his narration:

WORDS AND PICTURES

When words and pictures work well together, the result is a stronger, more memorable story:

- Pictures should illustrate the story, not dictate the story. Great pictures don't make a story newsworthy. A lack of pictures doesn't mean the story shouldn't be told.

- Use words to add a further dimension to pictures. Don't describe the obvious. Explain the significance of what the audience is seeing or the implications of the pictures.

- Use words to draw attention to pictures. Words can tell the audience: "This matters," or "Look at this."

- Understand the value of silence and natural sound. Let the audience see and hear what it was like to be there. Give them time to feel something.

- Let the pictures reveal surprises. Use words to set them up. Don't steal the thunder from your pictures.

TRADE TOOLS

"Oh man, I didn't know that. [*BARCARO: It left his former partner*] Oh, I didn't know that. [*BARCARO: searching*] No. [*BARCARO: for something to say*] Wow.

"It's not hard to do," Barcaro says. "I first look for sound with pauses, time out the pauses and then think of some words that can fit the space and also make sense there. I play the tape a couple of times and say what I want in the pauses to see if it fits." Obviously, if you're not editing your own story, you need to clearly communicate what you have in mind to the person doing the edit so the narration winds up precisely where you want it.

EDITING

As an editor, you have a lot of power over the way a story will be received. You can change the order of events, shrink or expand the time it took for them to unfold and increase or reduce their impact, just by the way you put the elements together. When editing news audio or video, take care to follow the same ethical guidelines you would when reporting or shooting in the field. Staging is a cardinal sin in journalism. You wouldn't ask someone to say something just so you could record it, or do something just so you could shoot it, unless you plan to explain that in your story. So you shouldn't manipulate video or audio in the edit room unless you plan to explain that too. We'll talk more about the issues raised by digital manipulation in Chapter 11.

The editing process varies widely, but most editors follow some general principles to produce a story that will keep the audience's attention from start to finish.

Video Edits

Always open with strong video, but avoid the trap of using all your best video off the top. "If you do, what's left?" asks television reporter Joe Fryer. "And will the viewer have enough background to care about it?" Instead of starting your story with people weeping at a funeral, for example, you'd serve the audience better by setting the stage for that scene, offering some details about the person being buried or how he or she died. By the time you use the video of people crying, the audience will understand why.

Rather than using all the best video and sound at the top, skilled editors often put together a sequence that pulls the viewer into the story. Quick edits and nat sound can create a sense of urgency for a breaking news story—for example, while a series of static "beauty shots" sets the tone for a feature.

By combining careful editing with adept writing, you can let the audience discover surprises in your stories. A story about a wheelchair basketball team could open with

Photojournalist Stan Heist opened a breaking news story about an explosion in a Baltimore neighborhood with a quick montage of pictures and sound that set the scene and established an urgent pace.

Source: Courtesy of WBFF-TV.

a wide shot of the court, but that would give away the surprise that the players are in wheelchairs. Instead, you could begin with tight shots of dribbling, a ball going through the hoop, and players' faces, to establish that your story is about basketball. Then you can let the video reveal what makes this game different from others.

As you build video sequences, let shots last as long as they have "energy," says award-winning editor Jon Menell. For example, if you have a shot of a girl yawning, cut to the next shot when her mouth is opened the widest. One of Menell's watchwords is to avoid pointless cutaways. "A cutaway is the right name for it," he says, "because it cuts the viewer's attention away from the story. You want to take their attention to the next thing." So don't feel that you have to cover part of every sound bite with b-roll. The long-term success of CBS News' "60 Minutes" proves that viewers are more than willing to watch "talking heads" if they're saying something interesting.

Don't forget the basics when editing video. A jump cut—from one shot to another that's similarly framed—is still a jump cut, even if you insert a dissolve. And remember the rule not to cross the axis, the imaginary line that divides a scene in two. Characters or elements in the same scene should always have the same relationship to one another. What starts on the left should stay on the left. If the video has been shot from one side of a 180-degree line, you won't have a problem in the edit. But if you have shots taken from both sides of the line, be careful how you edit them together or you can wind up with moving objects that appear to reverse direction.

Digital editing makes it easy to add effects like wipes and color adjustments, but try to resist the temptation. "When you have a bad story and you put all these effects in it to jazz it up, it's like [the MTV show] 'Pimp My Ride,' " says award-winning video editor Josh Shea. "You can put as much stuff on it as you want. You can put on nice rims, but you're still driving home in a Pinto."

When editing video for use online, it's often advisable to split your story into chapters or topics. You might want to post a short video segment on each of the main characters in your story, or construct segments around different themes. For example, a crime story might be broken into segments on the details of the crime, the investigation, the trial and the sentencing. Multimedia journalist Angela Grant says she edits video segments that run only two or three minutes to make her video presentations more interactive. "The user gets to choose which topic interests them, and only watch that video if they want," she says. "Also, if they choose one and then think it's boring, they don't have to just drop my story like a hot potato. They may choose another video instead."[7]

Audio Edits

When working with natural sound, let the type of sound determine how you should edit it into the story for radio, television or the Web. Award-winning editor Brian Weister says he'll cut directly to a sharp, crisp sound like a hammer hitting a nail, but he'll bring up a droning sound like a circular saw about 20 frames ahead of where he wants it up full, and then will fade it back down. Weaving this kind of audio in and out of the story helps to create a seamless narrative.

Audio can help you make transitions from inside to outside, or from location to location. Photojournalist Stan Heist uses a foreshadowing technique, sometimes called an "L-cut," that involves bringing audio in before making a video edit. "You hear the sound before you're there," he says. For example, he might use audio of a door creaking open under video of the exterior of a house, then cut to an interior shot of the door closing. "Dissolve with your audio, not your pictures," Heist says, "and your story will feel smoother and have more energy."

ONE EDITOR'S WISDOM

Shooting video is hard work, says photojournalist Jason Hanson of KSTP-TV in Minneapolis, Minn., kind of like cutting down trees. But editing is like woodcarving, he says; that's where you can truly be creative. "Watch raw footage and you'll be blown away at how dull it is," he

Source: Photo courtesy of Jason Hanson.

says. "We shoot hours of stuff that we whittle down to nothing. Editing can save the day almost any time."

Hanson's editing skills earned him the National Press Photographers Association 2006 Editor of the Year award. He says the key to excellent editing is to assume ownership of the story. "If you think of something that might work, try it," he says. "It's only TV news. If you're editing nonlinear you can always change it."

For Hanson, pacing is king. The best stories vary the pace, he says. "Give the audience one shot where they can see what's going on," he suggests. "Sit on a wide shot. If it's all fast, you lose the sense that it feels fast." He also advises against using all the best shots right out of the gate because "you'll run out of steam. People remember endings. If you want to dazzle the audience, save it for the big finish."

Hanson is not a big believer in visual effects. "Dissolves waste time," he says. He almost never uses them in spot news. In features, he'll use dissolves for effect, and in long-form, in-depth stories he uses them for pacing. On the other hand, Hanson's stories are packed with sound. He'll even add sound to graphics, just to keep stories moving. "Graphics are made up anyway," he says. "Find creative ways to add sound."

When there's an emotional reaction to a story, Hanson says, the sense of time goes away. So he never tells producers how long a story is before they see it. He'd rather show them a finished story and ask what they want to cut. "The kudos don't happen until the editing is done," he says. "I don't show a rough cut. They always go for the weak spot. I make it a point to finish, even if they want to see it 15 minutes before air."

KNOW AND TELL

SPECIAL STORY TYPES

Some specialized types of stories can be particularly challenging to produce. These include radio "mini-docs," which are long-form audio stories, video stories told with natural sound and sound bites but without narration, and online slide shows, with or without sound.

Long-Form Audio

Radio stories and podcasts that run longer than the average news piece are particularly challenging to structure because they depend on sound alone to maintain the listener's interest. Ira Glass of public radio's weekly program "This American Life" says he abides by a "45-second rule" when producing the hour-long show. "It turns out that we public radio listeners are trained to expect something to change every 45 to 50 seconds," he says. "And as a producer you have to keep that pace in mind. For example, in a reporter's story, every 45 or 50 seconds, you'll go to a piece of tape. So if you have a four-minute story, you figure you're going to have four quotes or maybe five."[8]

Without pictures to hook the audience, long-form radio stories and podcasts must use words and sound at the start to make the listener want to know what happens next. As journalist Nancy Updike puts it, "A radio story has to be a little sluttier with its charms: It can't be coy and get to the most interesting stuff a couple of minutes in. It has to frontload the drama, and not be too subtle about it." A story she wrote about a flour mill demonstrates the point. It begins this way: "A man is vacuuming the inside of a machine about half the size of a Volkswagen . . . that grinds wheat into flour. Every visible hair on Alex Melnikov's body—head, eyelashes, eyebrows—is dusted with flour, as though he's been cast as an old man in a low-budget play."[9] On television, the viewer could see the scene, so most of that description would be redundant, but for radio, the details Updike uses paint a vivid word picture that draws the listener in.

Natural Sound Stories

As we discussed in Chapter 3, you can only tell powerful stories without narration if you've collected the necessary elements with that kind of story in mind. Begin by creating a story outline just as you would for a scripted story. Because the nat sound approach is particularly suited to stories that unfold in chronological order, identify the high points in the story and select the sound bites and nat sound that go with them. Put your sound bites in a logical order from start to finish.

Remember that you can't depend on narration to fill in the blanks or clear up confusion; the sound you have must tell a complete story. Photojournalist Bryan Barr says he usually asks a reporter or producer to screen his nat sound stories before air to make sure he's accomplished his goal. "They weren't [at the scene], and if the story makes sense to them, you did it," says Barr.

Opening sound is critically important in a nat sound story. It has to get the story started by setting the scene or introducing a central character. A nat sound story about a Christmas program at a local mall that Brian Weister produced for KMGH-TV in Denver began with a woman saying, "This is our first ever holiday challenge," one line that explained what the story was about.

GO ONLINE

Module 6: Watch and analyze a nat sound story.

A piece Tom Aviles shot for WCCO-TV in Minneapolis started with this sound bite: "I'm just one voice. I've never really been a man of many words. I never thought I could make a difference." The story was about a man named Tom, who waved an American flag near a highway after the 9/11 terrorist attacks in 2001 and stirred a patriotic response from everyone passing by.

Your final sound should leave the viewer in no doubt that the story has come to a close. Tom's flag story ends with him saying simply, "God bless America." A story John Goheen shot about the annual wedding dress sale at Filene's Basement, a department store in Boston, ends with the main character saying, "I almost get teary-eyed because we took this completely chaotic consumer event and somebody actually won, actually got exactly what they wanted."

Slide Shows

A slide show allows you to showcase multiple still photographs online. Instead of just posting photos and captions on a Web page, you can use a slide show to display pictures in a specific order, with or without an audio track and text captions. A slide show at its best is an animated photo essay telling a coherent story, not just a collection of interesting pictures in some random order. Some audio slide shows are presented with narration; others just use sound from the people featured in the photos along with natural sound captured on scene, and are essentially nat sound stories that use still photos instead of video.

It's relatively easy to build a simple slide show, using drag-and-drop software that's built into most computers: Macs come preloaded with iMovie and PCs have Movie Maker. Many professional photographers swear by Soundslides, an inexpensive program developed by photojournalist and interactive producer Joe Weiss. Basically, these programs create a video file that plays automatically; the producer decides how long each photo should stay on screen and what audio should accompany each picture. But the user can still pause and restart the slide show, turn the audio on or off and control whether or not to display text captions.

Windows Movie Maker has easy-to-follow instructions (left) for building a slide show with an audio track. You simply drag and drop images and audio files into the timeline (bottom).

Source: Courtesy of the authors.

Captions and hyperlinks can give slide shows depth and context that nat sound stories on TV often lack. Good slide show captions convey more information than newspaper photo captions, which typically are little more than labels to help the audience understand what they're looking at. A slide show caption serves the same function but adds background and context. The Washington Post's "Being a Black Man" series is a good example. In a slide show profiling Eric Motley, a special assistant to President George W. Bush, one photo caption told not just what Motley was doing, but also where he went to school and his connection to U.S. Supreme Court Justice Clarence Thomas. Be aware that writing and fact-checking extended captions like these can take a lot of time.

When using captions in a slide show that also includes audio, be mindful of how the user will absorb the information. You might want to pause the audio track as captions are revealed so the users' attention isn't divided between what they're hearing and what they're trying to read. Or you might choose to show captions only when the user mutes the audio, or when the user decides to navigate the slide show one frame at a time rather than let it play automatically.

GO ONLINE

Module 6: Watch and analyze award-winning audio slide shows.

Outrunning Labels: Eric Motley's Journey   Play slideshow ▸   ≪ PREVIOUS IMAGE | 3 / 36 | NEXT IMAGE ≫

Motley wraps up a day at the State Department. While a student at Samford University, a highly-regarded conservative Baptist school in Birmingham, Motley headed up the school's speakers program, bringing in officials such as Supreme Court Justice Clarence Thomas.   *Photo by Jahi Chikwendiu - The Washington Post*

Well-written slide show captions often add background that would not typically fit in a newspaper caption. The caption for this image from the Washington Post's series "Being a Black Man" reads: "Motley wraps up a day at the State Department. While a student at Samford University, a highly regarded conservative Baptist school in Birmingham, Motley headed up the school's speakers program, bringing in officials such as Supreme Court Justice Clarence Thomas."

Source: "Being a Black Man," *Washington Post,* 2006, www.washingtonpost.com/wp-srv/metro/interactives/ blackmen/blackmen.html (accessed August 15, 2007).

GRAPHICS

Multimedia journalists use graphics of all sorts to enhance their reporting in print, on the air and online. Graphics can make relationships clear and illustrate complex information to make it more understandable. On the Web, interactive graphics allow users to explore information at their own pace and in as much or as little detail as they wish. "The hardest job is getting information into a recognizable form," says John Sculley, the former chairman of Apple Computer, who believes it is well worth the trouble. "In an age of quick information, reading is knowing, but seeing is believing," he says.[10]

While many journalists aren't expected to have the technical skills to build elaborate graphics, they may be asked to create simple graphics for both television and the Web. And even if that's not part of their job description, they should know what it takes to create graphics that will draw a user's attention and provide information in the most useful way.

Why Use Graphics?

The first question any journalist should ask before suggesting a graphic is, "Why do we need it?" Far too often, graphics are a reporter's first recourse when faced with a complex or picture-poor story, but the weakest possible reason for using a graphic is to fill space or cover a black hole for which you don't have video.

The best graphics put information in context and convey it clearly and quickly. On television and online, graphics should help viewers and users grasp the essential point of a story. A graphic can make dry data more understandable and engaging. But graphics that are overdone, crammed with too much information or swirling with pointless animation can be more confusing than helpful. Used sparingly and with a purpose, however, graphics make the complex clear.

Types of Graphics

The type of graphic you choose will depend on what you're trying to communicate. To show change over time, like the rise and fall of gas prices, you might choose a line graph. To compare a set of values, like the time it takes for an ambulance to respond to emergencies in different neighborhoods, a bar or bubble chart would probably work best. Instead of listing the number of apartments and office buildings in an area where more development is planned, you could create a pie chart that shows the relationship between the two.

Graphics can convey basic facts or illustrate a process. If you want to show how air pollution affects the lungs, for example, you might use an animation with no words on the screen. To illustrate the fact that the air is unhealthy in some parts of your community, you'd likely use a map. Online sites like Yahoo! Maps or Google Earth take only seconds to create maps or satellite images that can easily be embedded into Web pages, published in the paper or even used as a full-screen graphic on the air.

Simple Is Better

Avoid graphics that are crammed with too much information. Steve Duenes, graphics director at the New York Times, says it's critical to organize information clearly and eliminate superfluous detail to produce an effective graphic. The audience should be able to look at the graphic and take away one or two basic ideas. "If the story is about someone firing a gun in City Hall, we want readers to look at our diagram and quickly understand where the event occurred in the building, and where the important players were when it happened," Duenes says.[11] On TV, especially, graphics have to be simple because viewers don't have time to study them. A television graphic is a lot like a highway billboard—the driver has to get the key points quickly because in a few seconds the sign is out of view.

Let's say you're doing a story about the state budget. It's now twice as big as it was 10 years ago, and most of the growth has been in the last three years. A simple line graph, animated or static, could make those two facts clear, and you could add more interest to the graphic and reinforce the content by using images of coins or dollar bills. But keep the visual look simple. A multilayered graphic may look terrific when you design it full-screen, but it may just look cluttered on a home television set, computer or mobile device.

Data for Graphics

Make sure you fully understand the story before you develop a graphic.

Sort through any data or premade graphics you've collected during the reporting process and make sure you have material in a form you can use—complete data sets to build a graphic from or legible documents if you plan to scan them.

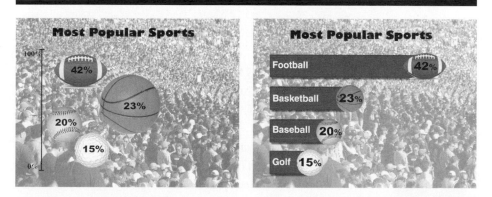

For a story about a survey on the most popular sports in the United States, these two graphics use images that reinforce the content. But the graphic on the left leaves the misleading impression that basketball ranks first, while the bar chart in the graphic on the right makes the order of finish clear.

Source: Courtesy of Lauren Zimmerman.

Convert raw numbers to rates or percentages whenever possible. A graphic full of numbers is almost impossible to understand at a glance and can be misleading. For example, showing that one town has twice as many robberies as another would suggest that it has a higher crime rate, but if the first town has 10 times as many inhabitants the second town would actually have a higher rate of crime. Calculating the rate of robberies per inhabitant would allow you to make a fair comparison.

Writing to TV Graphics

A graphic can serve as a roadblock in a television story if it comes up without warning. Lead the viewer in and out of the graphic by what you say in your track. Make a clear transition from the moving video to the fact-based graphic: "As city budget records show . . ." or "You can see how the budget has grown. . . ."

If you have words in your television graphics, be sure that what you say in the track matches what's on the screen. If possible, write your script before the graphic is created and revise it if necessary before tracking. Some producers make an exception for numbers, so that the graphic might read "5,431" but the narration would say "more than 54 hundred." But when words appear on the screen, people read them. It's human nature. If you don't want the audience to read the screen, don't use words. If you do, make sure the words are large enough and on the screen long enough for people to read them. And don't let the graphic get ahead of your track. If you're listing information—perhaps the items found in a suspect's home— build a graphic that puts the information on the screen, one line at a time, as you say it.

Online Graphics

While many of the same principles that apply to still and TV graphics also apply online, the potential for interactivity adds another layer of complexity. Again, you may not be expected to design interactive graphics on your own, but it's helpful to understand the principles and concepts behind them.

Interactive graphics that let the user explore information instead of just looking at it give them another way of understanding the story. Building an interactive in multiple layers allows journalists to share more data online than they ever could in print or on the air. And interactives can effectively combine different types of graphics, making the data more interesting to navigate. The Los Angeles Times, for example, combined a map of the United States with a timeline to show how laws on same-sex marriage changed over a decade, state by state.

GO ONLINE

Module 6: Explore the variety of online graphic options.

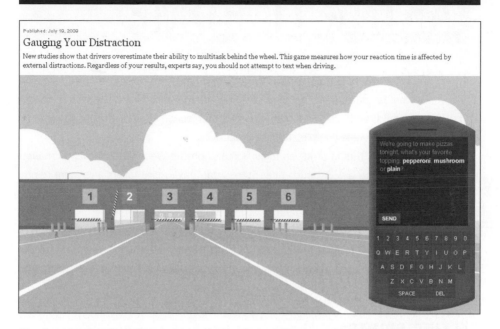

Published: July 19, 2009

Gauging Your Distraction

New studies show that drivers overestimate their ability to multitask behind the wheel. This game measures how your reaction time is affected by external distractions. Regardless of your results, experts say, you should not attempt to text when driving.

Studies showing that drivers overestimate their ability to multitask behind the wheel prompted the New York Times to develop an online game that measures how distractions affect reaction time.

Source: "Gauging Your Distraction," *New York Times,* July 19, 2009, www.nytimes.com/interactive/2009/07/19/technology/20090719-driving-game.html (accessed May 19, 2010).

One way to build interactivity into online graphics is to think broadly about what a graphic can be. The New York Times, for example, created a game to illustrate how texting while driving affects reaction time. American Public Media's Marketplace, among others, gave users a chance to try to balance the federal budget. The Wall Street Journal put together a quiz to show how even "safe" investments could be risky. And USA Today built a searchable database of American casualties in Afghanistan and Iraq to give users a statistical view of the wars' costs, but also a personal view. "People tend to want to find stuff that's sort of about them," says Web producer Josh Hatch. So the interactive lets users sort the casualty list by gender, race, age, hometown and other demographic information to find out if anyone who died is "kind of like me." We'll discuss interactive storytelling tools in more detail in Chapter 8.

TAKING IT HOME

The combination of words, pictures and sounds can add up to powerful and memorable stories in all media, but only if the elements are put together with skill and care. Words and pictures should reinforce but not repeat each other, sound should glue a story together and graphics should make complicated information clear.

The ability to do this in print, on television and on the Web gives today's journalists more avenues to reach a wider audience. Stories can have more layers and more depth. They can be more engaging, using video and audio to help viewers see and hear a story, and they can use interactive elements that let the audience participate in discovering information for themselves. Stories told in multiple media have many entry points, allowing the audience to choose what information they want and the order they want it in. But as exciting as these presentation options can seem to you, don't forget this basic truth: It's all about the story.

TALKING POINTS

1. Watch a network television newscast with the sound off. Can you tell what each story is really about? Listen to a television newscast without watching it. Are you missing anything? If not, does that suggest that video is not being used to the fullest?

2. Watch another newscast to see how reporters write to their video. Are they describing what you're looking at, or using their narration to add context and meaning? What difference does that make to your appreciation or understanding of the story?

3. Find a graphic on a news website. Does it make good use of interactivity? How could a different graphic be developed for the same story with more interactive features?

ONLINE LEARNING MODULE 6

Activate or buy this chapter's online learning module at journalism.cqpress.com to get access to:

- SKILL BUILDING: Consider whether using a graphic would help you tell specific stories better, and if so, decide what kind of graphic you would use.

- DISCOVER: Watch a nat sound story and a slide show to learn how to use these storytelling methods to their best advantage.

- EXPLORE: Find tutorials on working with audio, video, still photos and graphics. View examples of innovative interactive graphics.

- A video tutorial on how to create interactive graphics.

- A digital version of this chapter's text in full color with active links.

Also, continue your work on the ONGOING STORY MODULE. Log raw video and audio for this story, and write a TV package. Learn more about shooting and editing from the photojournalist behind the lens.

7 WRITING FOR THE WEB

The fundamentals of good reporting, writing and ethics apply to news in all media, but to disseminate information most effectively online, additional considerations and skills are needed. This chapter will outline some of the best practices for writing and presenting content on the Web, as well as discuss current standards for adapting broadcast and print styles to meet the needs of the online audience.

Brad Franko gets it. As a journalist in Charleston, S.C., he gets up long before the sunrise to anchor the morning show at WCBD-TV and routinely spends the second half of his day reporting stories for later newscasts. In his relatively small newsroom, Franko also gets the fact that he works for his station online as well as on the air. If a story breaks during his morning shift, he's one of the people who quickly gets the information to the station's website. He posts Web versions of his TV stories too, and routinely updates his blog, Twitter feed and Facebook page.

What Franko gets is that, while the audience has been shrinking for both broadcast and print journalism, the online audience has been growing. According to the Pew Research Center for the People & the Press, more than one in three Americans regularly went online for news in 2010 compared to just one in 50 more than a decade ago. If you add in cell phones, podcasts, e-mail and social media, 44 percent of Americans are routinely using Internet or mobile digital sources for news.[1] Serving this growing news audience is forcing many traditional news organizations to rethink the way they gather and present the news and to retrain their people to work more effectively on the Web and in social media.

Obviously, to do a good job in any medium a journalist must understand the audience. For example, in television, it's understood that most people don't really watch morning news programs; instead, they listen to them. So broadcast journalists working on morning shows have been advised to write in a way that puts less emphasis on the visual elements of a story. Since the writer can't count on the audience seeing what is on the screen, the story has to make sense without any visual support.

In the newspaper world, more people read the paper on Sunday than on any other day of the week, so when journalists do special stories that they hope will get lots of attention, those stories will often run first in the Sunday edition. People also tend to spend more time reading the paper on Sunday, so longer stories are generally more acceptable in a Sunday paper.

Because people have been using print and television as sources of news and information for a lot longer than they have the Internet, our understanding of the online news audience is still evolving. But current research offers insights into what people want from a news organization's website, and you can use that information to tell your stories more effectively by producing online content that will satisfy their needs.

HOW PEOPLE USE THE WEB

Since Web-based news sites first appeared on the scene in the 1990s, a myriad of studies have been done on Web usability—in other words, how people use websites. Though each study may say something slightly different, there are some universal principles for Web use. Typical Web readers do the following:

- Skim content. Online users are often skimming or scanning the content of a site, particularly when they first log on. That doesn't mean they won't read every word of an article that deeply interests them, but initially they're most often looking for information that grabs their attention. That's why headlines, for example, become so important on the Web.

- Look for points of entry. With the Web's bottomless news hole, it's tempting to go wild and write long when you're writing for online. As a general rule of thumb, an 800-word online story is plenty long enough. Users tend to look for entry points in your story—places to jump in and start reading—rather than starting at the top and going through to the end. Think about using multiple sub-headlines or breaking up your text with bullets and frequent paragraph breaks. The technique will help long stories seem less daunting and will help users find what interests them most, even in shorter stories.

- **Look for more.** In addition to readers who skim the content of a site, the online audience includes people who are actively seeking information about a particular topic that interests them. For example, let's say your station airs a story about a tuberculosis outbreak at a local school. At the end of the story, the news anchor could encourage viewers to go online for a list of the disease warning signs and preventive measures. At other times, you might be giving online users access to additional information through links to other useful websites or reminders of previously posted, relevant stories that are still available on your own site.

One ongoing Web usability study has focused specifically on the use of news websites. Since 2003, the Poynter Institute, the Estlow International Center for Journalism and New Media, and a company called Eyetools Inc. have been studying Internet users and literally looking through their eyes at various news websites using "eyetracking" technology. Each test subject spends time reading news sites and multimedia news content while being observed. The two key findings from the 2007 study are the following:

FIGURE 7.1 ONLINE READER FOCUS

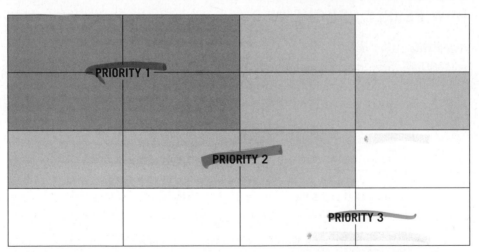

The EyeTrack III study tracked the eye movements of 600 readers in 15-minute online sessions in four U.S. cities. The researchers observed that on news homepages, readers look first at the flag/logo and top headlines in the upper left. This graphic shows their priorities, according to the study.

Source: The Poynter Institute, www.poynterextra.org/eyetrack2004/main.htm (accessed October 22, 2010).

1. When people click on a story, they read most of it. In fact, users read to completion 63 percent of the stories they selected.

2. Online readers can either be methodical in their reading or simply scan the copy. About half read the stories in a more linear way, from top to bottom, while the other half jump around—reading parts of the story and looking at photos—in no particular order. In both cases, users read about the same amount of the text.

WRITING FOR A BLOG

When blogs were first introduced in newsrooms, many journalists found that writing them posed significant challenges. In an effort to be edgy, some forgot all about the principles of good journalism. Others were so stodgy and stilted that they read like the minutes of a city council meeting. Now blogs are an accepted feature on many news sites, and some of the best practices have emerged:

- Keep it conversational but stay professional. Blogs should remain true to your news organization's core journalistic principles, even when you're writing in first person. Some expert bloggers suggest that you think of yourself as a guest on a radio talk show and write as you would if you were just chatting on the air.

- Keep it narrow. Too many blogs are all over the place with their content. It will be difficult to develop a following unless your blog speaks consistently to a particular audience. This will be easier if you work a beat and can blog daily about the area you cover.

- Make it interactive. There's little point in using the blog format unless you're trying to engage your audience. Ask questions, respond to comments from readers and share your opinion unless it will violate some journalistic principles—for example, stating your view that the defendant in the trial you're covering is guilty.

- Finally, don't be afraid to keep it short. If you have new information, but don't have the time to write a full-fledged post, put it out there. You can always revisit the subject later, and comments from your readers may help you find a new angle.

TRADE TOOLS

Another interesting finding from the EyeTrack research involved story form. The study found that alternative story forms like Q&As, timelines, short sidebars and lists helped users better understand the content. During a follow-up interview, participants who accessed these alternative forms correctly answered more questions about the content than their colleagues who didn't have those alternatives.[2] Keep this finding in mind as we talk about the production and presentation of Web content in the next two chapters.

WHEN NEWS ON THE WEB FALLS SHORT

Despite what we know about Web usability, not every site takes advantage of the research. Many news organizations publish what's commonly known as "shovelware" on their sites. They essentially take the stories that were published in that day's paper or aired on that day's newscasts and post a text version online. What type of problems do you think might arise when a site simply repurposes content produced for another medium? As you can imagine, what works in one medium might not in another.

Broadcast Shovelware

As you know, most television stories are written with video references. The script might say, "You can see how the flames ate away at the building for most of the night." The problem is, when a Web user simply reads the script, the video references don't make sense. In addition, video also provides important information for the viewer. For example, a TV reporter covering a story about the effect of an overnight freeze on the Florida orange crop wouldn't have to describe the rows and rows of trees laden with ice-covered fruit because the viewers could see that for themselves. But in the Web version, an important element of the story might be lost if the reporter doesn't include a description of how the trees looked in the video. Of course, the Web allows you to post video clips online, but you can't be sure that someone will take the time to view them. That means your text must provide enough information for the online reader to fully understand your story without screening the video.

Simply posting a text version of your broadcast script can also lead to confusion when time references, such as the words *today* or *tonight,* are included. A story might refer to a meeting that happened "tonight," and thereby confuse users who might be reading the story on the day after the meeting.

Part of the problem is that few television news sites have large Web staffs, and a good number rely on producers and reporters to add Web postings to an already long list of job duties. Sometimes the Web work just doesn't get done or sites are left with outdated or incomplete versions of stories and little unique content.

Print Rehash

Newspapers have their own online problems as well. Many newspapers have computer systems that automatically feed the paper's content onto the Web, but these systems have limitations. For example, automatic feeds can sometimes create version control problems. Let's say a Web producer updates a story on the site with new information after the paper's deadlines have passed. That's great, but when the automation kicks in overnight, the more current copy can be blown out by the older version of the story.

Shovelware can create other problems too. A headline in the printed publication may be too long for the Web format, so some systems will just lop off the end of it. Because of that you can get headlines that simply don't make sense, for example: "Mayor Heads to Buffalo to Compare" instead of "Mayor Heads to Buffalo to Compare City Costs."

Many news organizations are coming to realize what you probably already know from reading this text; online users want something on the Web that is a little different from what they are getting on the air or in the newspaper.

WRITING FOR THE WEB

It's almost certain that all journalists will need to know how to write for the Web in the future. Mary Alvarez, former news director for WCNC-TV, the NBC affiliate in Charlotte, N.C., says that every future journalist should be learning everything possible about working with the Web. "Our reporters are required to write a Web version of every story they work on for the day," Alvarez says. "We're breaking stories on the Web, we're not waiting until 11:00 to run a story that we know about at 8 p.m., so reporters have to get used to putting the Web first."

Fortunately, many of the techniques you've learned as a broadcast or print journalist will help you succeed online; however, there are some additional things you need to know.

Grab Attention!

People often come to the Web to see what's new in a breaking or ongoing story—the immediacy of online attracts them to the Web much as it does to broadcast news. That means the opening of your online story has to be much like a good broadcast lead. A good online lead jumps out at users and makes them want to read more. Check out this example:

> Omaha State University is canceling classes for an entire week. The school's computer room flooded yesterday, shutting down the network and making it impossible for the university to operate.

If you're a student at Omaha State, that lead sentence will clearly capture your attention. Even if you don't attend the school, canceling classes for a week is unusual enough that it's likely a user will read on. When you write a lead sentence, you need to tell us what the news is and present it in a way that will encourage as many people as possible to read more.

Use Time and Tense

Whenever possible, tell users what's happening right now or what's expected to happen in the future. Web stories can and should be updated whenever information changes. For example, the flooding mentioned above happened yesterday, but the news is that Omaha State has decided to cancel classes for a week.

This sounds simplistic, but to write in present tense you have to know what is happening right now. To write in future tense you have to think about what's expected to happen soon. So, in the example above, a future tense lead might look something like this:

> Omaha State students won't be sitting in classrooms as usual next week. The university's computer room flooded yesterday, shutting down the network and making it impossible for the university to operate.

Specific time references can also add to a sense of urgency online:

> Omaha State University is canceling classes next week. The school's computer room flooded yesterday, shutting down the network and making it impossible for the university to operate.
>
> At 2 p.m. today, school administrators will meet to figure out how to make up the instructional time lost. They are considering a shorter December holiday break. That could disrupt vacation plans and leave some businesses without part-time workers.

One word of caution here: If you are using specific time references and even present or future tense, it is critically important that you stay on top of the story and remove those references when they become outdated. For example, at 8 p.m. you don't want a story online that looks ahead to a 2 p.m. meeting that has already occurred.

Be Relevant

After the lead, it's important to explain why the story matters. Sticking with the flood example, the next lines might read like this:

> Omaha State University is canceling classes next week. The school's computer room flooded yesterday, shutting down the network and making it impossible for the university to operate.

At WSPA-TV in Spartanburg, S.C., the goal is to capitalize on the Web's immediacy. Note the multiple uses of present and future tense in the story about a helicopter crash, along with a promise of more information to come.

Source: Courtesy of WSPA-TV.

At 2 p.m. today, school administrators will meet to figure out how to make up the instructional time lost. They are considering a shorter December holiday break. That could disrupt vacation plans and leave some businesses without part-time workers.

The school's decision will have an impact on many people, including students and university personnel and their families who may be planning celebrations or vacations. Even businesses counting on holiday help may be affected.

In this situation, the first and second paragraphs give the basic facts of the story, and the third paragraph explains why this story might be relevant to more than just the students.

Be Concise and Conversational

For both the lead and the body of the story you want to use the same kinds of writing techniques we discussed in Chapter 5. It's particularly important for Web stories to use short, declarative sentences. This technique should help you be clear and concise. It's also good practice to stick to one idea per sentence, so that means avoiding long clauses and passive writing. Remember, readers are often scanning your copy, so this short and declarative style of writing may help hold their attention.

Also keep in mind that you're not writing to impress your audience, you're writing to inform your audience. You can be even more informal online than you might be on the air. "Write like you're dashing off an e-mail note to a friend," says Scott Atkinson, news director at WWNY-TV in Watertown, N.Y. For example, Atkinson's Web story about a predicted snowstorm that never came opened with this line: "OK. We were wrong." Write clearly and with context, he says, but use an intimate style, which seems well suited to the Internet. Here's another example:

Don't say: "The state Department of Health has added 172 rivers and lakes to the list of Florida water bodies that contain fish with harmful levels of mercury."

Do say: "The state says 172 more rivers and lakes in Florida are full of fish with too much mercury."

Web users want to get the news quickly, and conversational writing makes content easier to absorb.

Conversational does not mean sloppy. It's absolutely essential that your online copy follow all the rules of good journalism. You need to be accurate, you need to attribute information, you need to be grammatically correct and so on. Online readers are no different from TV audiences or newspaper readers; they expect their sources of news to be credible, no matter what the medium.

Write for the Scanners

Remember what we said earlier about the way people use the Web? You need to make things easier for the skimmers. Whenever possible, you should break up the text:

- Use subheads. Smaller headlines in the body of the story describe for the reader what that section of the story is about.
- Try bullet points. If you have a series of ideas you need to communicate, try laying them all out in a list for the reader.

TRADE TOOLS

WEB WRITING STYLE

For broadcast writers in particular, the online writing style has a lot of similarities to the way you already produce copy. But don't forget that writing for the Web involves thinking about the unique characteristics of the medium:

- Grab attention with your first line of copy.

- Be sure to use present or future tense in the opening line whenever possible.

- Make sure you're explaining why the story is relevant to a general audience.

- Use short, declarative sentences to make the copy easier to read and absorb.

- Use a conversational style that capitalizes on the intimacy of the Internet.

- Mind the fundamentals—good grammar and punctuation, accuracy and ethics.

- Write for the scanners; use subheads, bullets and short paragraphs.

- Keep paragraphs short. We've already described the need for short, declarative sentences, but even the paragraphs should be brief in an online story, with no more than one to two short sentences in each.

Most of what we've just described about writing for the Web should be somewhat familiar to you, but you'll probably decide which of these techniques and stylistic approaches to apply depending on which medium you're writing for. Multimedia journalists, on the other hand, use all of them in almost every story they tell online.

GO ONLINE

Ongoing Story Module: Write a Web version of the story applying the concepts learned in this chapter; then check it against the authors' version.

CONVERTING STORIES FOR THE WEB

Whether you write a new version of your story for use on the Web or adapt a story from another medium, the same basic rules for online readability apply. So let's put all of this into practice by looking at some examples.

Print to Online

The following story was published online after it was adapted and modified from a print piece.

SURVIVING TORNADO SEASON

By Grant Robertson

It's tornado season in Mississippi and Saturday night's storms left dozens homeless and took 10 lives. The outbreak was a grim reminder of the dangers of twisters and their destructive potential.

In the wake of the tornado disaster that struck Yazoo City, some in Oxford are wondering what they can do to protect themselves and their families from severe weather.

Oxford resident Sherri Riffe thinks she has the answer. The mother of two said the most important thing is preparedness.

"I don't wait for tornado season," Riffe said. "I'm ready for storms year round."

Riffe said the first thing to do is buy a weather radio because it is invaluable when it comes to getting real-time updates on severe weather events.

Jimmy Allgood, Emergency Management Coordinator for Oxford, said he couldn't agree more.

"The weather radio is one of your best protections," said Allgood.

Allgood has been serving as Emergency Management Coordinator for Oxford since 2001 and knows all too well how dangerous and unpredictable tornadoes can be. He was in charge when a twister ripped through an area just north of the city in February 2008, damaging or destroying several businesses.

Allgood stressed the importance of having emergency supplies in place for your family should a devastating tornado strike the Oxford area.

Your Tornado Kit

An emergency-preparedness kit should consist of enough food, water and other basic necessities to last for three days for the entire family, Allgood said. The National Weather Service also suggests the following:

- One change of clothing and shoes per person.
- One blanket or sleeping bag per person.

o A first-aid kit, including prescription medicines.

o Emergency tools, including a battery-powered weather radio, portable radio, flashlight and plenty of extra batteries.

o An extra set of car keys and a credit card or cash.

Allgood said having a tornado kit for your family helps take pressure off of local resources and gives time for agencies such as the Red Cross to step in and provide assistance.

Your Safe Place

Just as important is creating a "safe place."

If a tornado warning is issued the ideal place to be is a tornado shelter, however, most residents in the mid-South do not own shelters. In that case, the next best place to be is an interior room on the lowest floor of your house, Allgood said.

Riffe is one of the fortunate few who do own a tornado shelter, which was paid for, in part, by a government grant provided to some local homeowners after the 2008 tornado outbreak.

"The shelter is set in concrete and is able to withstand an F5 tornado, so I feel very safe in it," Riffe said.

Oxford may have dodged a bullet with this last tornado outbreak but the residents should stay vigilant, Allgood said. In fact, he said he is already monitoring another front moving through the area this weekend, which could constitute a new tornado threat.

As you can see, the writer added subheads to help readers scan the story for relevant information. The story includes bullet points with important details and links to additional content. The opening line is present tense and in active voice, the writing is conversational and the sentences and paragraphs are concise. The story is packed with good information, but it's broken down in a way that makes it easy for the online user to follow.

Broadcast to Online

TV scripts require special attention when being revised for use on the Web. Cory Bergman of LostRemote.com, a website about television news and new media, says broadcast writing style and script formatting have to be changed for stories to read well online. His suggestions:

- Combine copy. If you're modifying a package script, combine the lead-in, body of the package and tag all on the same page. Delete redundancies. Make sure the story starts off with a strong sentence, not a tease line.

- Remove extraneous information. Strip out computer coding, including director, editing and graphics notations.

- Fix capitalization. If you use all upper case for your scripts, convert to upper and lower case, correctly capitalizing as you go along.

KNOW AND TELL

SOCIAL MEDIA WRITING TIPS

Jeff Cutler calls himself a social media journalist. He is the author of the Society of Professional Journalists' newsroom training module on social media, and he travels the country offering advice to writers using social media for their work. Here are his top tips for sharing via social media:

Source: Photo courtesy of Jeff Cutler.

1. Ask questions in your social media engagements. People will respond to questions long before responding to "statement" status updates.

2. 120 characters is the outside limit you should use if you wish your Twitter update to be retweeted (RT). This leaves room for your Twitter handle in the RT.

3. Keep Twitter updates to one thought and one link. They're easier to digest and more memorable.

4. Follow the 65 percent/35 percent rule when using Twitter. Follow a similar ratio when using Facebook (65 percent of the time just be a person talking about life, 35 percent of the time share your products and links).

- **Add quotes.** Change the sound bites to quotes, adding the correct punctuation and attribution.

- **Form complete sentences.** Drop unnecessary punctuation like ellipses and hyphens, and convert sentence fragments into complete sentences.

- **Remove video references.** Delete any language that makes a direct reference to video and audio, but add appropriate description to bring a visual element to your copy.

GO ONLINE

Module 7: Watch a video tutorial on how to write effectively for social media.

5. Be aware that if you have a pay wall in place for your content, you should not hand out links to that content in your Twitter updates or status messages. This only sets your outlet up for a fall when readers hit that wall and cannot get to the stories you planned to share.

6. To ensure folks find you and your news outlet, be strategic in tagging your photos in Facebook, Flickr and other services where photos can be "tagged." Also, endeavor to tag specifically. Don't say "dog in a swimming pool" when you could garner more follows by saying "golden retriever in Des Moines Central High School swimming pool—photo by Register reporter Joe Smith."

7. When leaving comments on blogs and videos, don't go link-crazy. Your profile link is the main way people will find you, so make sure the link is accurate and just share genuine and smart thoughts in the comments.

8. Blog-post titles should be search engine optimization (SEO)-focused. If you are able to create blog-post titles, make sure you put rich information in them. No— "Hair Today!" Yes—"Boston Salon Holds Haircut Fundraiser—See Exclusive Boston.com Photos!"

9. Take a moment to perform a Google search on each reporter at your news outlet. See whose results are most impressive. Then learn from that to get the entire team well placed in search results.

- Beef up the story. Add important details. Web copy should deliver more information than 20-second TV stories deliver (with the possible exception of breaking news).

- Bring it all together. Make sure the story reads well from beginning to end.

- Add interactivity. Finally, add links to any relevant materials.[3]

The script below is an example of a standard broadcast package script. After you read it, we'll use the steps outlined above to convert the copy to a Web story.

Anchor Introduction:

NEIGHBORS SAY IT HAPPENS ALL THE TIME. THIS AFTERNOON PHOENIX POLICE DISCOVERED A HORSE TRAILER PACKED WITH 79 ILLEGAL IMMIGRANTS, ONE JUST FOUR MONTHS OLD. (Map showing location.) AN OFFICER PATROLLING NEAR 14TH STREET AND POLK AVENUE SPOTTED THE TRAILER AND SAW THE DRIVER TAKE OFF. JAMMED INSIDE—68 ADULTS AND 11 CHILDREN.

Anchor Package Script:

(Bob Brunelle/Business Owner) "It's weekly like I said. You see vans pull in here, drop 'em off, and then the guy drives off and the people just disperse in the neighborhood."

BOB BRUNELLE SAYS HE'S OWNED A DISCOUNT AUTO BUSINESS IN THIS PHOENIX NEIGHBORHOOD FOR 30 YEARS. JUST RECENTLY, HE SAYS HE'S SEEN THIS COMMUNITY BECOME A DUMPING GROUND FOR ILLEGAL IMMIGRANTS.

(Brunelle) "I've called before and told them there was a van in the alley here with a lot of people in it, well, you'll have to contact so-and-so, and by the time they get contacted, the van's gone!"

THIS TIME BRUNELLE DID NOT HAVE TO MAKE A CALL. A PHOENIX POLICE OFFICER SPOTTED THE HORSE TRAILER, INVESTIGATED AND FOUND 79 PEOPLE INSIDE. AFTER TWO DAYS IN AN UN-AIRCONDITIONED TRAILER, EVERYONE WAS THIRSTY AND HUNGRY, BUT NO ONE WAS SERIOUSLY ILL.

(Brunelle) "I'm glad they did something about this. It's too bad there were those two babies in there, they took a hell of a chance."

IMMIGRATION CUSTOMS ENFORCEMENT LOADED EVERYONE ON A BUS, HAULING THEM TO THE TEMPORARY HOLDING FACILITY IN DOWNTOWN PHOENIX. BRUNELLE SAYS HE'S GLAD TO SEE IT.

(Brunelle) "I don't think they'll drop them off in this neighborhood again for awhile."

Anchor Tag:

AN IMMIGRATIONS CUSTOMS ENFORCEMENT SPOKESPERSON SAYS HE EXPECTS MOST OF THE ILLEGAL IMMIGRANTS TO BE SENT BACK HOME TONIGHT.

Now let's follow the guidelines set out by Cory Bergman of LostRemote.com to see what kind of Web story we can create from our package script.

Immigration Bust: 79 People Packed in Horse Trailer

An Immigrations Customs Enforcement spokesperson says he expects dozens of illegal immigrants to soon be on their way back home.

This afternoon, Phoenix police discovered a horse trailer packed with 79 illegal immigrants, one just four months old.

An officer patrolling near 14th Street and Polk Avenue spotted the trailer and saw the driver take off. He found 68 adults and 11 children jammed inside.

Bob Brunelle is a business owner in the neighborhood. He says this incident is nothing really new.

"It's weekly like I said. You see vans pull in here, drop 'em off, and then the guy drives off and the people just disperse in the neighborhood," said Brunelle.

Brunelle says he's owned a discount auto business in the neighborhood for 30 years, but just recently, he says the community has become a dumping ground for illegal immigrants.

"I've called before and told them there was a van in the alley here with a lot of people in it, well, you'll have to contact so-and-so, and by the time they get contacted, the van's gone," said Brunelle.

This time Brunelle did not have to make a call. A Phoenix police officer spotted the horse trailer, investigated and found the 79 people inside.

After two days in an un-air-conditioned trailer, everyone was thirsty and hungry, but no one was seriously ill.

"I'm glad they did something about this. It's too bad there were those two babies in there, they took a hell of a chance," said Brunelle.

Immigration Customs Enforcement loaded everyone on a bus, hauling them to the temporary holding facility in downtown Phoenix.

Brunelle said he was glad to see it: "I don't think they'll drop them off in this neighborhood again for awhile."

GO ONLINE

Module 7: Practice converting a television news package script into an online text story.

That actually took about 12 minutes to rewrite and spell check, but we're left with a credible story that pulls together the anchor intro, package script and tag into a solid textual presentation. With a little more time, we could enhance the story further with links to relevant information, a map, still photos and other multimedia elements that would add depth to the story without adding length.

LostRemote's Bergman says he now believes it's better to start from scratch every time you write a Web story. He thinks it's easier to write a more effective online piece if you start with a fresh page and do a complete rewrite. Whichever approach you use, these text versions of your TV stories should be a point of pride for you as a journalist—if your name is on it, you'll want it to be as good as it can be.

SEARCH ENGINE OPTIMIZATION

Now that you've learned how to prepare text versions of your stories for the Web, you need to make sure that people are actually going to read them. You don't have to be a Web expert to know that search engines, such as Google, Yahoo, Bing and others play a critical role in helping people find news and information online. Savvy journalists know a little something about what's called search engine optimization, or SEO, to help people find their stories as opposed to someone else's.

According to Webopedia,

SEO is the process of increasing the amount of visitors to a website by ranking high in the search results of a search engine. The higher a website ranks in the results of a search, the greater the chance that that site will be visited by a user. It is common practice for Internet users to not click through pages and pages of search results, so where a site ranks in a search is essential for directing more traffic toward the site. SEO helps to ensure that a site is accessible to a search engine and improves the chances that the site will be found by the search engine.[4]

If that sounds complicated, it is and it isn't. There are some simple things you can do to write Web headlines and copy that are more likely to show up high in the search engine results.

Key Words Matter

If you've ever googled anything, you've used key words. Essentially, key words are those that an individual would use to search for a particular story, topic or piece of information. Before you post your copy to the Web, you'll want to think about the words someone would be using if they were searching for a story on your topic, then you'll want to be sure those words are included in your headline and in the first sentence of your story. If you do that, your story should show up higher in the search engine results, which means more people are likely to click on it.

The Washington Post once published a story about high-tech gadgets that were revolutionizing fishing, in some cases altogether replacing the need for traditional bait such as worms. In the newspaper, the headline "Wormed Out" worked well. It was supported by a subhead that read, "Technology Is Replacing Some Traditional Fishing Practices," and it included a graphic of a fish, hook and worm. Online, the producers knew "Wormed Out" wouldn't make sense without all that supporting material, so they changed the headline to read, "Technology Replaces Worm."

But that headline may have led some people to believe it was a story about computer viruses. If you were searching for this content, what's the one key word you think most people would use in looking for this story? If you guessed *fishing,* we think you're right. A stronger Web headline might look something like this: "Fishing Better with High-Tech Worms."

WEB HEADLINES

As we've indicated, headlines play a critically important role on the Web, and not just for the part they play in search engine optimization. Just as in newspapers, people often make decisions on whether or not to read an online story on the basis of the headline. But headlines do function in a slightly different way online than they do in a newspaper. As we described in the fishing story example, a clever layout that includes a photo with a caption, a headline and a subhead may work just fine in print, but this arrangement may fall flat on the Web. For broadcast journalists, writing headlines may be something you learned a little about in a print reporting class, but you probably don't feel like you're much of an expert. This next section looks at how to write effective online headlines and summaries.

The best headlines are straightforward, using action verbs and indicating exactly what the story is about. Remember, Web users are often skimming for information, and they want to know what they're getting into before clicking on a headline to read the complete story.

TRADE TOOLS

WEB HEADLINE TIPS

Charlie Meyerson is news director for WGN Radio in Chicago and a former senior Web producer for ChicagoTribune.com. He and his online colleagues have come up with a list of recommendations for creating what they believe are effective Web headlines:

1. Place the most interesting word or phrase as close as possible to the start of the headline.

2. Avoid use of proper names except for the very famous and well-known.

3. Don't rule out simple, direct headlines that say exactly what the story is about.

4. Questions can work, for example, "Who was Deep Throat?"

5. "How-to" or "Why" headlines may be effective.

6. Directly address the user, for example, "Check state's list for your name."

In addition to being the founder and editor of LostRemote.com, Cory Bergman is the director of new product development at msnbc.com. To give you an idea of how important a headline can be, Bergman says he's seen the number of people clicking on a story double when a poor headline was replaced with something more specifically designed for the Web. Online producers at the Richmond Times-Dispatch are well aware that headlines matter. The newspaper headline over a story about a football game that Virginia Tech lost to Auburn read, "Maroon & Blue." It was meant to be a clever reference to Tech's team color (maroon) and the fans' feelings (blue), but it wouldn't have worked online. So the newspaper's Web producers changed the headline to "Va. Tech falls to Auburn despite 4th-quarter burst." The more literal headline tells the online reader exactly what this story is about.

GO ONLINE

Module 7: See what a headline writing expert has learned about the most effective Web headlines.

For that same reason, you'll need to be careful using the first sentence or two of your story as a summary below the headline. What might work well as an anecdotal lead in your print or broadcast story may very well fail as a story summary on the Web. As a good multimedia journalist, you will need to make sure that you've written a headline and a summary that will help Web users know exactly what your story is about, rather than risk confusing them and losing them.

Take a look at page 202 (top panel) and read the two headlines circled on the home page of Tupelo TV station WCBI's website. One of the headlines is straightforward and tells you exactly what the story is about. The other is a bit of a mystery. What's the health care story really about? In the bottom panel on page 202, you can see the story is about the migration of health problems from cities to rural areas and the leading causes of death in rural America. A better Web headline might look something like this: "More people dying in country than cities." Or this: "Rural America's biggest health risks."

Jakob Nielsen, an expert on Web usability, offers this advice to headline writers on his own website, useit.com[5]:

The copy must be:

- Short (because people typically don't read as much online).

- Rich in information scent, clearly summarizing the target article.

- Front-loaded with the most important key words (because users often scan only the beginning of list items).

- Understandable out of context (because headlines often appear without articles, as in search engine results).

- Predictable, so users know whether they'll like the full article *before* they click (because people don't return to sites that promise more than they deliver).

Bottom line: Web headlines are not teases, they are straightforward and to the point. Your audience should understand what the story is about with nothing more than the headline. And knowing what we know about how people use the Web and the role of search engines, the best Web heads are also crafted to put the story's most important words at the beginning.

Some of these headlines are well written and some are not. What's the "news" in the story about rural health care? We can't really tell from what was posted here on the WCBI television site. The headline about the Republican primary winner is much more straightforward.

Source: Courtesy of WCBI.com, http://wcbi.com (accessed June 22, 2010).

Once you've clicked on the headline about rural health care, you learn that this is a story about a new study that found more people are dying in rural areas than in cities and lists the key causes of those deaths. A good Web headline would have made that clear.

Source: Courtesy of WCBI.com, http://wcbi.com/article.php?subaction=showfull&id=1277237082&archive=&start_from=&ucat=2,45& (accessed June 22, 2010).

WEB EXTRAS

In addition to simply rewriting or changing the presentation of information you've gathered for another medium, working with the Web gives you an opportunity to add more or unique information that will enhance what's been aired or published. We call this additional or unique information "Web extras," and we break them down into three broad categories.

Additional Content

As we discussed in Chapter 1, in a strong multimedia story, each platform supplements the others with unique information. These Web extras offer a way for journalists to include compelling content that they had to cut from a broadcast or print story to save time or space or to keep their story tightly focused. For example, you might interview four or five people for a story and wind up using quotes or sound bites from only three. The Web allows and, in fact, encourages you to use the content that wound up on the cutting-room floor. You can simply rewrite your story to include the fresh voices or use clips from the interviews that didn't appear in your original piece. You can even produce a sidebar element for the Web to supplement your print or broadcast story.

Let's say you have written a piece on the opening day of the state fair. Your story is supposed to be an overview of the event, but while you're at the fairground you meet a fascinating corn dog vendor. He's been coming to your state fair for 60 years, with no plans to retire. Since you can't do the story justice in your overview, you choose to write a profile piece for the Web instead. You have now taken advantage of the power of multimedia—you are providing unique but related content on more than one platform.

As we mentioned earlier in this chapter, providing additional content can also be as simple as including links to relevant websites or documents, or even to your past stories on related topics.

Original Web Content

This is where the true multimedia journalist shines. In more and more news organizations, reporters or photojournalists are encouraged to produce content exclusively for the Web—creating additional types of Web extras. Reporters working for "NBC Nightly News" are encouraged to produce "Web-only" videos that offer unique content that won't be found on the network newscast. For example, NBC's Tom Costello posted an in-depth interview with an expert from the Cornell Food and Brand Lab about the factors that influence what and how much we eat. The interview did not appear in the newscast but was exclusive to the show's website.

There are many instances in which photojournalists have used the Web to tell powerful stories though slide shows of still photos on subjects that were not included in the paper or on a newscast. We'll talk more about producing original multimedia content, including maps, timelines and graphics, in Chapter 8.

Web Interactives

Journalists with few or no Web technical skills can create much of what is posted on the Web. However, some of the most creative news content being produced for the Web does require technical knowledge. We've mentioned the tremendous potential of interactivity on the Web and some of the most sophisticated Web extra content is called just that—an interactive. Interactives, as described in Chapter 6, allow users to enter or select information and receive customized responses. For example, the Orlando Sentinel newspaper has an interactive that helps users learn how to protect their homes during hurricane season. By clicking on each area of a house—from the landscaping to the shutters to the roof—you learn about the best methods for minimizing damage in the case of a severe storm. The hurricane interactive provides an entertaining way for people to learn critical information about staying safe during storm season. The average online journalist might not be able to create such an elaborate interactive after coming up with the idea, but partnering with an expert or a team of experts could make it happen.

The goal for you as a multimedia journalist should be to stay current with what's going on with the Web and interactivity. Stay on top of the technology and the techniques being used to create a valuable user experience on the best websites. You can do that by checking out award-winning websites, such as those honored by the Online News Association, the Radio Television Digital News Association (RTDNA), Editor & Publisher magazine and several others. In addition, there are websites devoted to online journalism, such as www.cyberjournalist.net, which link to some of the best work in the industry. In Chapter 9 we'll explore various types of interactive content and how they can enhance your multimedia storytelling.

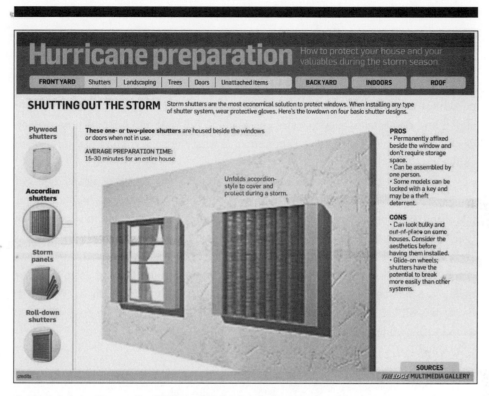

A Flash interactive on the Orlando Sentinel website lets the user explore ways of protecting a house from a hurricane, including the pros and cons of different types of shutters.

Source: Hurricane house preparation, *Orlando Sentinel,* www.orlandosentinel.com/news/local/sfl-edge-hurricane-preparation-house,0,4494935.htmlpage (accessed July 14, 2010).

TAKING IT HOME

For several years, as the online news audience grew, there was a lot of hand-wringing in newsrooms. Some experts asserted that print would soon be dead, and that traditional, over-the-air news broadcasts might not be far behind. While that may eventually be true, traditional news outlets now expect to ensure their survival by building new audiences and finding new sources of revenue online.

Research indicates they're making some progress. As we've indicated in earlier chapters, the Internet is the only part of the mainstream news business that is consistently growing audience. The RTDNA/Hofstra University 2010 survey found that 99.7 percent of television stations have websites and many are hiring people specifically to staff them. On average, television stations have 2.8 full-time and 4.5 part-time employees identified as Web staff; that's about double what the survey found just three years earlier.[6]

For those embarking on a career in journalism today, all this likely means there will be job opportunities in online news. So today's journalists must have a solid understanding of the Web and how people are using it for news consumption, and they must apply that knowledge to their writing and storytelling online. It's no longer enough simply to cut and paste content from another medium onto a website and expect users to accept what's there. At a minimum, your Web stories should be formatted to fit online users' expectations when it comes to style—from language to paragraph length to headlines. Writing for the Web is different from writing for broadcast or print, and good multimedia journalists embrace the online style.

TALKING POINTS

1. Think about your favorite news website. What do you like best about it? Log on to it to see if you can find any evidence that the site's producers are trying to take advantage of the ways in which people use websites. List at least three things the site is doing well and three things it could do better to capitalize on website usability.

2. Go online to your favorite news website. Find a headline that looks intriguing enough for you to click on it and read the story. Was the headline true to the story's content? What was it about the headline that enticed you to click through? Is the subject matter inherently interesting to you? How did the headline writer make sure that someone interested in this topic would click on it? Can you suggest a better headline that might invite more people to read the story?

3. Brainstorm a list of three Web extras for a story about your school system's plan to do away with recess in the elementary schools. Your TV story includes interviews with the superintendent, a teacher, a parent and some kids outside playing during recess. What could you do to enhance this story online?

ONLINE LEARNING MODULE 7

Activate or buy this chapter's online learning module at journalism.cqpress.com to get access to:

- SKILL BUILDING: Convert a standard television script into a Web version and then review what the reporter who covered the story published online.

- DISCOVER: Examine expert analysis of what makes a good Web headline and summary. Learn more about how to create successful headlines and summaries on your own.

- EXPLORE: Peruse new research on the way people use the Web for news information and more great Web writing advice.

- A video tutorial on how to write well for social networking sites.

- A digital version of this chapter's text in full color with active links.

Also, continue your work on the ONGOING STORY MODULE. Write a Web version of this story, using the techniques outlined in the chapter you've just read. See one approach to telling this story online.

CHAPTER 8 PRODUCING FOR THE WEB

Interactivity is at the heart of what makes the Web such a rich environment for news content. Whether you plan to work as a multimedia journalist or specifically as a Web producer, it will be essential for you to understand what it takes to create compelling online news and information. This chapter introduces you to some of the interactive tools available for online storytelling and explores how the Web has changed newsgathering and dissemination strategies in newsrooms around the country.

Online journalists are a varied bunch. Some come from traditional journalism backgrounds, having worked in print or broadcast media before transitioning to the Web. Others have strong technical expertise in Web production but have little journalism experience. Within the last few years, it's become more common for journalism students to set their sights on working with the Web while still in school, applying for online journalism jobs as a first choice rather than as a fallback.

Throughout this text, we've been sharing tools and strategies that any journalist might use to produce strong content across media platforms. But those of you who are excited about the possibilities of working more specifically as online journalists are more likely to need a slightly different skill set, though it will be based on all of the fundamentals you've been learning so far.

THE SKILL SET

What does it take to be a successful online journalist? The Online News Association (ONA) surveyed working online journalists in 2006 on the skills most needed in online news organizations and found widespread agreement on the most important skills.

Survey respondents included both managers and producers for online news sites who were asked to rate the importance of 35 job skills. According to the ONA report, managers were defined as those who oversee operations or content production, or both. Managers were asked to rate each skill based on whether they believed it was an essential requirement for a job applicant. Producers were defined as those who "create, edit or package online content," and they were specifically asked to rank the skills based on how often they use them on the job.

Four skills topped the list for both managers and producers, though not in the same order.

The need to multitask, communicate, work under pressure and pay attention to detail were fairly universal—in fact, there aren't many jobs in journalism that would not require these skills. Web producers stated that they also used the skills of headline writing, story combining and shortening and caption writing for the Web frequently or every day. In earlier chapters we've highlighted some of these skills, particularly headline and caption writing. Both producers and news managers also emphasized the importance of news judgment and an understanding of grammar and style—skills that are critically important for any journalist, of course.

Production Tools

One of the most interesting findings of the survey dealt with online production tools. With so many software programs and a variety of standards and tools that journalists could

TABLE 8.1 SKILLS FOR ONLINE JOURNALISTS

Managers	Percent considering it requirement for job	Producers	Percent using this skill frequently/ every day
Multitasking ability	91.9	Attention to detail	94.9
Attention to detail	90.7	Ability to work under pressure	94.9
Communication skills	85.2	Communication skills	94.9
Ability to work under time pressure	84.3	Multitasking ability	94.4

Source: C. Max Magee, "The Roles of Journalists in Online Newsrooms," Medill School of Journalism, released by Online News Association, November 1, 2006, http://journalist.org/news/archives/MedillOnlineJobSurvey-final.pdf. Reprinted with permission.

learn, it's difficult to determine which are essential. The Web producers who responded to the survey said the emphasis should be on three skills:

1. Use of a content management system
2. HTML
3. Photoshop

A content management system (CMS), according to Webopedia, is "software that enables you to add and/or manipulate content on a Web site."[1] Many students are familiar with Blackboard, a content management system common at many universities. When instructors post an announcement or a link to an assignment, they are using a content management tool whether they know it or not. Two of the most widely used content management systems are Drupal and WordPress. Many news organizations develop their own content management systems for their websites. All of these systems are generally quite similar and designed to be user friendly, making it easy for people to post simple text, video or audio files and to create links to additional content. Web producers obviously learn how to use the software to a much fuller extent, but every multimedia journalist should have some familiarity with what a CMS is and how to use it.

You've probably at least heard the term *HTML* at some point, even if you're not entirely sure what it means. HTML is an acronym for hypertext markup language. At its most basic level, HTML enables Web producers to create documents that can be accessed, viewed and used on the Web. HTML also creates simple links to other Web pages, and it's one of the tools used to develop more complicated interactive features, such as games, polls and apps. Though content management systems often make it possible to use simple cut-and-paste templates and shortcuts to post Web content, anyone considering a career as an online journalist should make the effort to learn HTML. It's also important to have a basic understanding of CSS (cascading style sheets), which are used to set colors, fonts and other design attributes for Web pages.

Adobe Photoshop is another essential online production tool, according to the professional journalists surveyed by ONA. There are other photo-editing software packages available, but Photoshop is the most common in the industry.

Web producer Crystal Lauderdale agrees that a basic understanding of Photoshop is essential for today's journalists. "Any type of photo editing makes you a stronger content producer," says Lauderdale, who oversees video and multimedia for the New York Times' websites at its 16 newspapers and one television station in Florida. She first started reporting across platforms for the Tampa Tribune, WFLA-TV and TBO.com. More than anything else, Lauderdale says those working in multimedia need "writing and image composition skills." In fact, Lauderdale would say that all journalists should know how to build a basic website, including some HTML: "You have to communicate with online producers; you have to know their language."

GO ONLINE

Module 8: Check out links to easy-to-use tutorials for developing your photo editing and other multimedia skills.

Other Proficiencies

Two additional skill areas are considered essential for many online journalism jobs today: fluency in social media and search engine optimization (SEO). Writing for the Online Journalism Review, multimedia journalist Robert Hernandez summed up the top skills required for a Web journalist this way: "Solid news judgment, strong ethics, thrive under deadline, accuracy and a mastery of the AP Stylebook. Other skills I include are knowledge of HTML, experience with CMS, working understanding of SEO, being social in Social media and the willingness to try new technologies."[2]

Alan Murray, executive editor of the Wall Street Journal Online, says he looks for journalists who will "get engaged in finding their audience." Marketing is a big part of what online journalists do, he says, whether it's called that or not, and he expects his staff to promote their work using Twitter and other social media.[3]

CONTINUOUS PRODUCTION MODE

Whether your primary job is to produce your news organization's website or you are a TV or print journalist who must produce multimedia stories, you need to realize that the Web has radically changed the news production cycle in newsrooms around the country.

Most local newspapers publish just one print edition a day. Most local television newsrooms produce an average of about 5 hours of news each weekday, at

ONLINE TUTORIALS

W3C is an international consortium working to develop standards, protocols and guidelines "to ensure long-term growth of the web." Check out World Wide Web Consortium's guide for newcomers to HTML at www.w3.org/MarkUp/Guide.

Dozens of tutorials are available to help guide you through the use of Photoshop. Some of the best come from the software maker at www.adobe.com/designcenter.

There are also websites that aggregate tutorials for a variety of multimedia tasks. Check out one free resource providing tips and tutorials for working with video, audio, graphics and more at www.mediacollege.com.

TRADE TOOLS

specific times. But an online news site is more like an all-news radio station or cable news channel, staffed around the clock—always on, with the potential to operate in what could be called a continuous production mode.

What does that mean for you as a multimedia journalist or someone hoping to become a Web producer? It means changing the way you think about presenting the information you gather.

Breaking News Redefined

A significant amount of research indicates that breaking news is one of the major motivators for people to log on to a news site. During the day, when most people are at work or school, it's often easier to check a cell phone or access a computer than to turn on a television set or a radio to find out what's going on.

But what is breaking news, anyway? According to researcher Andrea Miller of Louisiana State University, traditionally, "breaking or non-routine news is defined as hard, unplanned news that takes the newsroom by surprise, such as a plane crash or earthquake. Breaking news cannot be predicted."[4] But most television news organizations have expanded (some say distorted) that definition to include stories that simply contain new or recently obtained information.

On the Web, it's essential to provide new information and constant updates on developing stories, however you label them. Amanda Zamora, multimedia editor for the Huffington Post Investigative Fund, says that multimedia journalists and Web producers should "recognize that if people are reading the Web, it generally means they expect the latest information available."

What that means for you is that even a predictable story update may have value on the Web. For example, let's say you're attending a regularly scheduled transportation board meeting where you know they plan to release a list of the roads slated for repair in the next six months. For your television news story, you plan to talk to some of the people affected by the announcement, including those who are getting their streets repaired and those who are not. If you wait until you have done all of that reporting before you post a brief story with the list of roads on your station's website, you've missed a great opportunity to keep your audience informed about a developing story.

Strategies for Constant Updates

Though the Web is always on, most news sites get most of their traffic during the day, specifically during working hours. But for years, most reporters produced Web content after they completed their TV stories or filed their print articles—generally after Web traffic had died down for the day. So some news organizations and individuals have developed strategies to provide more frequent postings to the Web.

Smartphones have made it possible for reporters in the field to file short video updates on stories as well as text so they can be posted quickly on the Web. Live streaming video can also be fed in via smartphone for use online. At WIBW-TV in Topeka, Kan., for example, every reporter-photographer carries a video-equipped cell phone and uses it to stream video to the Web while using a separate camera to shoot better-quality video for television stories.

Andrew Pulskamp, digital executive producer for the website of WGAL-TV in Lancaster, Pa., says producing content for the Web has undergone a metamorphosis at his station and others owned by its parent company, Hearst Television, Inc.

"All reporters have been outfitted with iPhones, laptops, air cards, webcams and a few other gadgets. The expectation is that they feed the Web throughout the day with all of this new equipment—and they do," Pulskamp says. "The communication stream between the Web and the field has exploded, as has the amount of content we receive."

Pulskamp says it is now routine for crews in the field to send in raw sound and video, as well as multiple digital still pictures, within minutes of arriving at a breaking news scene. "The days of waiting for a live truck to feed back video are gone for the Web. We get information nearly instantly. We also talk to reporters much more to flesh out the details of what we're getting," he says.

And it's not just breaking news that's getting immediate attention; Pulskamp says reporters feed content to the Web for all their stories, throughout the day: "We don't have deadlines. Instead, we've made all of the reporters and photographers aware of the Web's peak hours—10 a.m. to 2 p.m. They try to hit that big window when we have the most viewers, but they aren't limited to that window. Instead of deadlines, we work on an 'as soon as you can' type of model, which is frankly how we've done it on the Web for years. Essentially, when a story is happening and you are there, your deadline is 'now.'"

This strategy might not work in every newsroom, but news organizations are looking for journalists who know how to keep the Web top of mind and how to incorporate frequent Web updating into their workdays.

Webcasts

The continuous production mode means that Web producers may also be asked to produce online newscasts. At one time, lots of TV stations and some newspapers were producing brief video updates for the Web several times a day. While that seemed like a good idea, it turned out that many computer users couldn't or wouldn't watch the updates during business hours, so the production of scheduled webcasts was scaled back.

That said, there are still times when webcasts are a great way to provide information to your audience. Some stations produce special online newscasts while carrying regular programming over the air. For example, on primary election nights, stations may choose to cover local races in a live webcast rather than interrupt entertainment programs.

When preparing these online newscasts, remember to think about the way that video works online. As we indicated in Chapter 3, researchers in the area of Web usability have found that video clips work best when they're short, and they also say it would be wrong to assume that an online story with video is always better than one without.[5]

Accuracy Matters

One of the things that worries some journalists about the continuous production mode is that it gives them less time to double-check information, so the chance of reporting an error is greater. That's an important concern. If you don't have enough verified information to write or call in a Web story, you must make that clear to your news managers. They're likely to agree that missing a Web update in order to make sure you have your facts straight is a worthwhile trade-off.

A great deal of Web work is done by a single individual. A reporter on a weekend shift might post a story without anyone else reviewing it. A Web producer might watch a feed coming in and not realize that it's file video. If your newsroom doesn't have an approval process for Web content, it's imperative that you develop one on your own. Ask someone whose news judgment you trust to double-check your story for you. One more set of eyes should significantly reduce your risk of getting the story wrong.

If it's really just you, Web producer Crystal Lauderdale suggests you do two edits of your own work. "First you do a quick edit, then a quality edit," she says. Once the time pressures ease, Lauderdale recommends going back to take a look at what you've published to make sure that errors don't get repeated or go uncorrected.

GROWING WEB AUDIENCE

In Chapter 7 we defined search engine optimization (SEO) as a process to make a website more accessible to a search engine, which improves the chances that the site will be found by an audience. Web producers and those interested in getting the largest audience possible for their work will want to gain an understanding of SEO beyond the role of headlines and key words we've already discussed.

More SEO

Search engines are critically important to help people find your content online. It's estimated that more than a third of Web traffic comes to a news site through search engines. In addition to creating headlines for stories that are direct and loaded with key words, using links is an essential way to drive Web traffic.

When a website or individual pages on a site have a lot of inbound links, Google will give preference to that site in search results. Lots of incoming links generally mean that lots of people are recommending the story or the site. Social media can also play a part in your linking strategy; when people click to your site from Facebook or Twitter, for example, it boosts your Google rankings.

Of course, the best way to get lots of incoming links is to have great content that people want to see. Pulskamp says his station tries to educate its staff on what stories drive Web traffic.

"We try to give a lot of feedback to the crews in the field. We share numbers showing what worked, what the audience wants and what they typically don't consume. That has already led to a shift in what the crews provide the Web," Pulskamp says.

But that doesn't mean that stations should ignore important news that the public needs to know. Instead, Web analytics can be used to help push reporters to find more compelling angles or better ways of telling important stories online.

Tagging

Related to key words and links is the concept of tagging or metadata. Tags allow Web producers to categorize content based on the topics that content relates to. For example, an online article about a hurricane forming in the Gulf of Mexico might have tags such as: hurricane, storm, category, landfall, wind speed, the name of the actual storm and the locations in its path. Tags help users see what the content relates to and help them find additional relevant content. If you click on one of the tags for the hurricane story, you would find a list of other related information that carries the same tag. Just about any online content can be tagged, including text, podcasts, audio, photos and video. The benefit is a wider distribution of your content and more opportunities for those seeking it to find it.

Geotagging is growing in popularity as well. The process involves tagging content with geographical information to make it easier for users to find location-specific information on your website. For example, if you are visiting a new city and are looking for vegetarian eating options, a site that has its restaurant reviews geotagged can help you find a desirable eating place nearby. Services like FourSquare and Yelp also use geotagging to help people find information and services. We'll talk more about how news organizations are using geotagging when we discuss mobile delivery of news in Chapter 9.

Social Media

Social networks like Twitter, Facebook and YouTube are also tailor-made for sharing news content with a wider audience that might never visit an online news site otherwise. Embedded links in posts and tweets send users to the source website to read more. Many newsrooms have set up Facebook pages where they post updates throughout the day, and they also have multiple Twitter feeds so users can follow those that meet their specific interests. Twitter is often used as a kind of micro-blog to cover breaking news in real time.

Many news organizations also have their own YouTube channels where they post video. Some even allow those videos to be embedded on other sites so they can expand their audiences. And many media organizations provide bookmarking tools on their websites, making it easy for users to share stories on multiple social networks.

Social media are also important sources of information, as we mentioned in Chapter 2. During protests over presidential elections in Iran, Twitter was invaluable. While censors kept vital information out of newspapers and off the air, thousands of ordinary citizens were reporting on the violence in that country in real time. At its peak, there were 200,000 tweets per hour coming out of Iran. News organizations monitored Twitter as a critical source of information on the story, using traditional verification tools to ensure accurate reporting. By linking to or embedding Twitter streams on important stories like this, Web producers can draw repeat visitors to their news sites.

Digital news manager Chip Mahaney says social media should be an integral part of any news website. "It's all tied together with producing online content, text and video, and showcasing same on our sites," says Mahaney, director of digital content at E. W. Scripps, a media company that owns television stations, newspapers and their related websites across the country. "We've even hired our first producer who's focusing most of her day on managing her station's presence on social media, as well as connecting the social community to our site and to our on-air product as well."

Social networks are not a one-way street. Journalists who respond to their followers find it pays off in readership and story tips. "Journalism is a conversation, it's no longer a broadcast or top-down approach, but a back-and-forth dialogue," says online journalist Vadim Lavrusik.[6]

KNOW AND TELL

SOCIAL MEDIA JOURNALIST

Amanda des Roches graduated from college in 2006 and went right to work as an online journalist for Media General's interactive media division. Now she's called a "Product Owner for Social Media and Video."

"Basically, it means that I am a go-to person as far as the social media and video strategy for the company," says des Roches.

Des Roches uses Facebook Connect as an example of a company-wide social media initiative. Facebook Connect allows users to log on to social media and have seamless access to content on Media General websites.

Source: Photo courtesy of Amanda des Roches.

"Everybody knows that social media has taken off, and we need to be where our audience is," she says. "In addition, we need to get to an audience that we've never been able to reach before. Facebook Connect makes it easier for people to share our content, so we can reach those untapped audiences."

So how did des Roche get her new position?

"I'm not a social media expert; I don't think anybody can be and have a job at the same time," says des Roches with a laugh. "The way the other social media product owner and I can keep on top of things is to devote an hour to an hour and a half each morning to read all the news related to social media. We read about new tools and features. We read what other sites are trying, and we compare notes to see if it's something that we think we should try to implement here."

Des Roches recommends that all journalists familiarize themselves with as many social media platforms as they can.

"We are in the space all the time," des Roches says. "We are on Facebook and Twitter all day every day, even on weekends."

Des Roches says she's always looking at new gadgets too. Her office has a couple of iPads that all her co-workers use to try out new apps.

"We download and test it out and review it and submit our thoughts to the VP to help the company decide if it's something we should try," des Roches says. "Part of the job is getting to play with social media, which is my favorite part."

For TV news anchor Amy Wood, social media is not an afterthought or an extra burden—it's her first priority. "It's a powerful way to reconnect with viewers," she says. "It creates an engaging conversation that draws them in."

INTERACTIVE TOOLS

The number one law of multimedia is "make it interactive," says Al Tompkins, the Poynter Institute's group leader for broadcasting and online. "Let the user manipulate the page, select what part of the story he/she wants to explore."

Earlier in the text we discussed creating "clickable" maps or timelines that allow users to click on or scroll over a graphic to get more information about a given topic or location. To create those and other kinds of Web "interactives," you sometimes need specialized skills, such as knowing how to use software programs like Flash or JavaScript. To learn those skills, you might take a course or teach yourself through online tutorials, some of which are included as links on the website accompanying this text. But it's now possible to create interactives without much specialized knowledge.

In recent years, widgets have turned even technophobes into Web-savvy content creators. According to Webopedia, "Web widgets are pieces of code that you can embed right on to your Web page, or personal publishing space such as Blogger or WordPress. Web widgets work like a mini-application that you use to provide information to visitors. . . . Web widgets are easy to use and require you only to copy and paste a snippet of code to display the widget, which is hosted on the developer's server."[7]

Widgets can be used to embed search boxes, games, maps and other interactive elements directly in a Web page.

There are widget directories, such as Widgetbox and Snipperoo, that enable you to search for a specific type of widget, customize it for your own use, then copy and paste the code to your own pages.

Whether you use a widget or write your own code, multimedia journalists need to know what's possible in terms of interactivity online.

Searchable Data Sets

Because space on the Web is almost unlimited, news organizations can offer users access to complete sets of data behind the news, like the restaurant inspections list we mentioned in Chapter 1. But data sets are most useful when they're searchable or sortable, which usually requires some work. Even if the data are available electronically, journalists still have to decide how to let users manipulate the data. Should they be able to sort that list of restaurants from cleanest to dirtiest? Or should they be able to search the list by name, location, food type or quality rating?

The Washington Post created a searchable data set for its project "Top Secret America." According to the paper's website, the project, two years in the making, was designed to describe "the huge national security buildup in the United States after the Sept. 11, 2001, attacks." As part of that effort, the Post developed an "Explore Connections" page, which allows users to interact in a myriad of ways with much of the information the paper gathered.

Searchable data sets like this one created by the Washington Post for a story on government secrecy are particularly valuable for stories that will have a long shelf life, something users can access over time and use repeatedly.

Source: Courtesy of washingtonpost.com, http://projects.washingtonpost.com/top-secret-america/network/#/overall/most-activity (accessed July 31, 2010).

For example, if you're interested in border patrol issues, with a couple of clicks you can find out just how many government agencies are involved in top-secret border patrol initiatives and which private companies are working for them. You can drill down and search those companies by location, amount of revenue, number of employees, number of government clients and so on. You can search through the government agencies to get a list of the types of top secret work they do and how many companies they're paying to work with them.

Creating and updating this kind of database is time-consuming, but once you've created a template you can provide a valuable tool for the audience and you can use it over and over again for a variety of stories.

Clickable Maps

Clickable maps allow you to organize information about multiple locations and put it in perspective for the audience. ESPN.com, for example, created a clickable map for a story about the potential hazards of eating stadium food. The sports network looked at health department inspection reports for facilities providing food and beverages at all of the arenas and stadiums that host professional football, basketball, hockey and baseball teams. At more than a quarter of the 107 stadiums, multiple concession stands or restaurants had at least one "critical" or "major" health violation.

With the interactive map you could explore which venues had the highest percentage of violations, and by rolling over each stadium or arena icon you could read the actual health inspection reports for that location. The interactive was produced in conjunction with ESPN's "Outside the Lines" television show, which did a series of video reports on the issue as well. Obviously, the TV program could not provide the level of customization of content that could be offered online. For example, a viewer in Green Bay may not care if the venues in Florida are filthy and vice-versa, but an interactive map online lets users get personally relevant information with the click of a mouse.

Simple interactive maps can be created relatively easily with widgets through sites like Google Maps or QuickMaps.com.

GO ONLINE

Module 8: Watch a video tutorial on creating a Google Map.

Interactive Timelines

Interactive timelines help to put stories that develop over time in context for the audience. For example, when an oil rig explosion in the Gulf of Mexico sent millions of gallons of oil spewing into the surrounding waters, many news organizations tracked the ongoing story using timelines. Each time the rig's owner, British Petroleum, or government agencies did something significant, it was plotted on the timeline. Some of these timelines were quite elaborate,

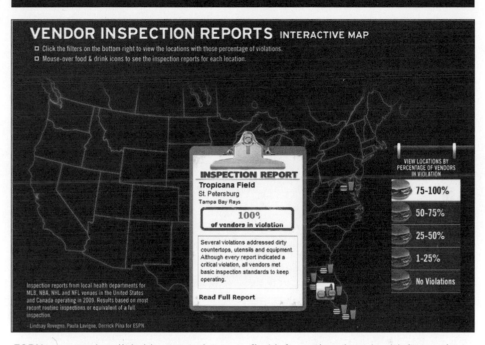

VENDOR INSPECTION REPORTS INTERACTIVE MAP

☐ Click the filters on the bottom right to view the locations with those percentage of violations.
☐ Mouse-over food & drink icons to see the inspection reports for each location.

INSPECTION REPORT
Tropicana Field
St. Petersburg
Tampa Bay Rays

100%
of vendors in violation

Several violations addressed dirty countertops, utensils and equipment. Although every report indicated a critical violation, all vendors met basic inspection standards to keep operating.

Read Full Report

Inspection reports from local health departments for MLB, NBA, NHL and NFL venues in the United States and Canada operating in 2009. Results based on most recent routine inspections or equivalent of a full inspection.

- Lindsay Rovegno, Paula Lavigne, Derrick Piña for ESPN

VIEW LOCATIONS BY
PERCENTAGE OF VENDORS
IN VIOLATION

75-100%
50-75%
25-50%
1-25%
No Violations

ESPN.com used a clickable map to let users find information about health inspections at more than 100 professional sports venues. This type of individualized content is a core strength of the Web.

Source: Courtesy of ESPN.com, http://sports.espn.go.com/espn/eticket/story?page=100725/stadiumconcessions (accessed July 31, 2010).

as was the case for the Guardian newspaper in Great Britain. The Guardian's presentation included timelines for specific elements of the story, such as the environmental impact and human stories, as well as images and links to additional content for every development.

Timelines can also be integrated with maps to show how a situation has changed over time in different places. That's what the PBS "NewsHour" did in producing an interactive that allows users to track the history of nuclear proliferation around the world from 1945 to the present.

For journalists who don't have the coding skills necessary to create such an elaborate presentation, the Vuvox widget may come in handy. Users simply upload content, including text, stills, video and audio, and then drag and drop different elements into the presentation. News organizations such as the Washington Post and the New York Times have used Vuvox to add interactivity to stories on their sites.

Widgets make it easier for those working on the Web to produce specialized online content with limited production skills. This interactive timeline on the Floridian Hotel in Tampa was created for TBO.com with the Vuvox widget, which allowed the producer to easily incorporate stills, text, video and audio into the presentation.

Source: Courtesy of TBO.com, www2 .tbo.com/static/special_reports_news/ tbocom-special-report-news-floridan/ (accessed July 31, 2010).

Online Calculators

Creating an online calculator for a story can take a mundane discussion of a new tax rate and turn it into a fun, interactive learning process. USA Today created a calculator that lets users plug in their current salaries to see how much of it goes to taxes, where that tax money is being spent and how that compares to an equivalent salary going back to 1940. Several news organizations have used calculators as a way of explaining stories about money in a more personal way. For example, msn.com posted a "Retirement Planning Calculator" to help people figure out what they will need to live comfortably after they stop working and how much they will need to save while they're still on the job. When a user enters numbers into the boxes provided, the online calculator begins tabulating and comes up with personalized, estimated amounts.

Calculators can also be used effectively in stories about subjects other than money. Several news sites have embedded body mass index calculators on their health pages. The Dallas Morning News developed an interactive calculator that showed what a person's blood alcohol content level would be based on their weight, type and number of drinks consumed, and time period over which they were consumed.

INTERACTIVE GRAPHIC GUIDELINES

Research conducted by the Department of Media Studies at the University of Trier, Germany, suggests these guidelines for producers of interactive graphics:

- Avoid information overload: If you put too much information into a single graphic, users are unlikely to find it all.

- Keep users' expectations in mind: There's no one standard for embedding links in online graphics, so users tend to expect everything to be clickable. Don't include buttons, legends, keys or points on a map just as decoration or to fill space.

- Be careful with animation: Animation can attract or distract users. Blinking, flashing or fading arrows, dots and circles are guaranteed click magnets. "If there is text competing with animation, the text will lose," says Trier's Peter Schumacher.

- Let users control the interaction: Give users clearly marked buttons to start, stop and restart interactive graphics.

Source: Peter Schumacher, "User Feedback Drives Five Principles for Multimedia News on the Web," Online Journalism Review, September 15, 2005, www.ojr.org/ojr/stories/050915schumacher.

TRADE TOOLS

Polls, Questionnaires and Quizzes

You've likely seen Web polls that ask you to answer a question or series of questions and then allow you to click to see the current poll results. This works well for stories about topics on which people have strong opinions. For example, you might ask people whether school uniforms are a good idea for students or not. This is one of the easiest types of Web interactives to create, thanks to a number of polling widgets such as Poll Daddy. But beware: The information should not be used as a scientific representation of how people feel on a given topic. So if the Web poll shows most of the respondents are opposed to school uniforms, you can't be sure that most people in the community are opposed to the uniforms without doing a more scientific survey. It's a good idea to include a disclaimer about the validity of any poll you report to be sure that people know how to evaluate the information.

Questionnaires and quizzes are also useful ways of adding interactivity to a news site. If you're doing a story about depression, for example, you might post a quiz that would help people determine if they're at risk or already suffering from the illness. The highly regarded Mayo Clinic offers a depression self-assessment online. News organizations often pull quizzes or questionnaires from expert sources like this one. If you use a quiz or a questionnaire from another source, be sure to provide appropriate credit.

Interactive Storytelling

Creating multilayered interactive online content takes a great deal of expertise and time, but the results can be impressive. Interactive storytelling breaks the bounds of linear narrative and allows users to explore information at their own pace in the order that interests them most.

Students at Ohio University's School of Visual Communication have been experimenting with interactive storytelling through a project called "The Soul of Athens." Each year, the students explore various dimensions of the college town and surrounding areas. In 2010 the students reported on five themes, including one they called "Shelter," which among other stories featured a narrated slide show about people choosing to live with as little technology as possible.

The site also includes a Twitter feed that references Athens and a Facebook page with more than 1,100 fans. According to the "About" page, "We are also providing richly featured interactive PDFs, a mashup feature called 'Soul Mixer' and the site is optimized for mobile phones."

The presentation invites users to choose only the content that interests them; it is truly nonlinear in that you don't have to experience the site in any particular order to have it make sense. It is an excellent example of the ways in which the online medium can lead to new forms of storytelling in which the user is able to contribute to the story.

Ashley Wells, executive creative director at MSNBC.com, believes too many online news sites forget the importance of storytelling and don't engage users in a way that helps them relate to the story. "Interactive stories that incessantly nag the user to 'click to continue' become cumbersome," says Wells. Instead, he wants to "make them forget the mouse is there. When I want them to use it, I'll tell them why and show them where."[8]

This type of interactive storytelling is generally used only on major projects for which a news organization commits a great deal of time and resources. For more examples, check the Online News Association's site, interactivenarratives.org. The site's goal is "to highlight rich-media content, engaging storytelling and eye-popping design in an environment that fosters interaction, discussion, and learning."

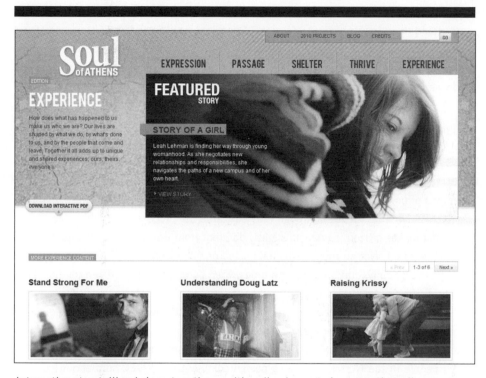

Interactive storytelling brings together multimedia elements in a way that allows users to control and contribute to the content experience. Since 2007, students at Ohio University have been producing the Soul of Athens project as an experiment in interactive storytelling.

Source: Courtesy of School of Visual Communication in the Scripps College of Communication at Ohio University, http://2010.soulofathens.com/experience (accessed July 31, 2010).

USER-GENERATED CONTENT

User-generated content (UGC) is exactly what it sounds like. It is news and information produced by people who use the medium or service to which they are contributing. Facebook, MySpace, Flickr, Picasa, YouTube, LinkedIn and Twitter are all examples of user-generated content sites. News sites also routinely display user-generated content, like photos solicited from and submitted by readers.

At News8 in Austin, Texas, senior Web producer Anna Gonzalez finds user-generated content to be a real asset, but journalists have not always embraced UGC.

"People were initially scared of bloggers and citizen journalists, saying they just don't understand the integrity of the profession," Gonzalez says. "Sites like Twitter have proven the audience will correct false information quickly. I've learned we must always have an editor, and having multiple voices to contribute to a story can only enhance our mission of delivering relevant information."[9]

Citizen Journalism

A citizen journalist is someone who actively participates in the newsgathering and reporting of content. At the very start of this text we talked about interactivity as one of the key strengths of online journalism, and on one level, citizen journalism is about inviting the audience to interact with you through the newsgathering process.

What makes citizen journalism slightly different from user-generated content in general is the intent. Not all the information posted on Facebook or YouTube is meant to be used journalistically, and there will be times when people become citizen journalists by accident.

When a Harrier jet crashed in the Arizona mountains near Yuma one summer, the only pictures of the jet going down were shot by a bystander with a cell phone camera. When she shared that video with local news stations, she became a citizen journalist. When people in the Norfolk, Va., area posted comments on WVEC.com about local gas stations that still had power in the aftermath of a hurricane, they were acting as citizen journalists—gathering and reporting information. From these examples, you can see the benefits of citizen journalism. In these situations, citizens were providing valuable information that news organizations would have otherwise been unable to report.

But citizen journalism has its messy side too, as Gonzalez mentioned. Some news organizations are resistant to the idea of allowing citizens to post content directly on their news sites because of a concern whether citizens know enough about journalistic standards. Let's say a local high school student died in a drive-by shooting and friends set up a memorial outside her home. A trained photojournalist would know that it's inappropriate to move some of the flowers closer to the young woman's photo to create a better picture, but a citizen journalist might not understand why that shouldn't be done, that it distorts the truth of the situation. Similarly, most trained journalists understand that it's important to keep one's own opinion out of a story, but most citizen journalists are only motivated to report on issues or events that matter deeply to them, so they may find it difficult to keep biases in check.

Fact-checking is also an issue in citizen journalism. Jay Rosen of New York University has been a leader in the area of public journalism for more than a decade. Answering questions for a Slashdot.org forum, Rosen said, "To simply pass along unchecked reports received from strangers over the Net would be fantastically dumb."[10] The difficulty is that many newsrooms don't have the staff to do extensive fact-checking on the work of citizen journalists.

But the value of user-generated content is so great that most newsrooms are using it in some way. CNN is one of the biggest players, with its iReport project. The network solicits stories and opinions and creates assignments for iReporters to fulfill. CNN says the best content is vetted and used on the air.

Mike Toppo, senior director for news operations and production for CNN.com, says iReports are all about "passion." With nearly a half-million iReporters around the world, Toppo says CNN is using these folks to tell stories differently. Pointing to a piece in which

News organizations are always looking for ways to connect with new audiences. Incorporating user-generated content into their storytelling is one way to do that. CNN's iReport is one of the most successful UGC initiatives in the United States.

Source: Courtesy of CNN.com, http://ireport.cnn.com (accessed July 31, 2010).

the band Vampire Weekend was interviewed by fans who had sent in video questions via iReport, Toppo asks, "What's better, an interview with Vampire Weekend with some reporter asking the same old questions or questions from passionate fans?"

CNN tries to address the concern about the accuracy of iReports by posting this disclaimer on its site: "The stories in this section are not edited, fact-checked or screened before they post. Only ones marked 'CNN iReport' have been vetted by CNN."

Local stations also are making use of citizen journalists. KMPH-TV in Fresno, Calif., for example, has a "community correspondent" page with more than 13,000 registered users. The station posts assignments or topics on which it is seeking video, photos or stories from users.

Crowdsourcing

Another form of participatory journalism is crowdsourcing, which the Online Journalism Review defines as "the use of a large group of readers to report a news story." Unlike citizen journalism, in which one individual's item or photo may stand on its own, crowdsourcing brings multiple pieces of information together to produce a complete story. Crowdsourcing is often described as "pro-am" journalism because it's the result of a collaboration between professionals and amateurs.

News organizations have used crowdsourcing to cover breaking news stories like severe weather and election fraud. The Washington Post, for example, used the popular open-source software at Ushahidi.com to track clean-up efforts after a massive blizzard. Readers were invited to send updates from their neighborhoods that the newsroom then plotted on an online map. The Guardian newspaper in London used crowdsourcing in a different way when it asked readers to help review a massive public release of formerly classified documents detailing five years of expense claims from every member of Parliament. About 20,000 volunteers weighed in, helping the newspaper find and report the biggest scoops quickly.

PLANNING THE MULTIMEDIA STORY

All of the skills and elements we've described so far come together in multimedia stories, whether you are working on your own or with others. Good multimedia stories require an understanding of what each medium does best. You need to gather more and different content for your stories than you would for a single medium, and you need to think about how the execution of the story will be different on each platform.

Jane Stevens, who teaches multimedia journalism at the University of California–Berkeley Graduate School of Journalism, divides multimedia stories into two categories: reporter-driven and producer- or editor-driven.[11]

According to Stevens, a reporter-driven story is "usually a daily beat story, a feature or part of an investigative series or special project." The reporter or reporter-photographer team gathers all the elements of the multimedia story—everything from video and audio to the information that will go into text and graphics. The story is in the head of the reporter, and that's who "makes the basic decisions on how to assemble the pieces that make up the whole."

In contrast, the editor- or producer-driven story is generally breaking news or a special project. The editor or producer assigns individuals to produce pieces of the story and may ask a photojournalist for stills and video, send one reporter to do interviews in the field and another to gather information by phone, and assign a graphic artist to produce maps or illustrations.

In either situation, you'll want to make sure you have an idea of what you want your finished multimedia story to look like as you proceed with reporting and producing it.

Develop the Plan

There are few stories that don't evolve and change over the course of your reporting. You may have started out doing a story about rising home prices and then discovered a bigger story—that the city was backing out of a plan to build a number of subsidized apartments for low-income families. Your reporting on home prices might be saved for another day or used as a Web element for a multimedia package.

You will want to review the information you've gathered in your reporting to be sure you have what you need to produce unique content for each medium involved. We've said it before—multimedia will not be as effective as it could be if you are simply doing the exact same story on more than one media platform. In our housing story example, you may have just what you need—both a solid story on the city's decision to drop its plan to build the low-income apartments and a Web-only element on housing prices in your area.

Storyboards

In Chapter 6 we talked about making a list of all the video, audio, still photos and other multimedia elements you've gathered as part of your story plan, but some multimedia journalists also like to use storyboards to help them plan their stories. A storyboard is

TRADE TOOLS

STORYBOARDING QUESTIONS

The following tips are excerpted from the Multimedia Reporting and Convergence website created by Jane Stevens:

- Decide what pieces of the story work best in video. Video is the best medium to depict action, to take a reader to a place central to the story or to hear and see a person central to the story.

- Decide what pieces of the story work best in still photos. Still photos are the best medium for emphasizing a strong emotion, for staying with an important point in a story or to create a particular mood. They're often more dramatic and don't go by as quickly as video.

- Does the audio work best with video, or will it be combined with still photos? Good audio makes still photos and video seem more intense and real. Avoid using audio alone.

- What part of the story works best in graphics? Animated graphics show how things work. Graphics go where cameras can't go, into human cells or millions of miles into space.

- What part of the story belongs in text? Text can be used to describe the history of a story (sometimes in combination with photos), to describe a process (sometimes in combination with graphics) or to provide first-person accounts of an event.

Source: Jane Stevens, "Storyboarding," University of California–Berkeley Graduate School of Journalism, http:// journalism.berkeley.edu/multimedia/course/storyboarding.

a visual blueprint of what a Web project will look like online. It typically includes both words and sketches, showing where the elements would go on each page and how the user would navigate through the site.

Storyboards help you think through the pieces of your story and can make it easier for you to decide how to use the information, video, audio and stills you've gathered most effectively. You should start by listing every element you want to include in your multimedia package, and then think about how to present the information in a way that will engage your audience.

For example, you might have considered using video alongside a text story, but during the process of storyboarding you might decide to produce a slide show instead. For the fifth anniversary of the September 11 terrorist attacks on the United States, the Atlanta Journal-Constitution created a slide show that rotated between photos shot on September 11, 2001, and present-day images from the same scene. The comparison was much more striking in still photos than it would have been in moving video.

GO ONLINE

Ongoing Story Module: Create a storyboard for your multimedia approach to the coverage and then view what the authors created.

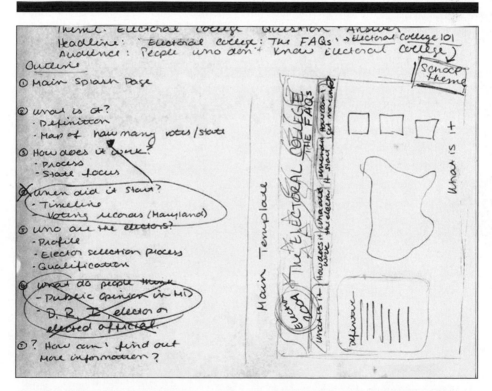

The storyboard above was used to rough out a plan for a Web project about how the Electoral College works. It includes an outline of the content as well as a sketch of how that content might appear on the page.

Source: Courtesy of Lauren Eshkenazi, BaltimoreSun.com.

Teamwork

Teamwork is another important skill for online journalists. Teamwork is considered essential by more than 80 percent of both online news site managers and producers, according to the Online News Association study.[12] At USA Today, major projects are typically produced by a team of five: a designer, programmer, producer, IT person and database editor. Obviously, communication skills are essential for anyone working in a multimedia team.

Some multimedia projects are developed across platforms by teams of journalists from different media. For example, a television station might work in partnership with a newspaper and a jointly operated website to produce stories for all three. In this situation, the team members would each have expertise in broadcast, print or online, and the group would go through a three-step process of determining

GO ONLINE

Module 8: Explore a multimedia project and analyze which elements worked well and which could be improved.

KNOW AND TELL

MULTIMEDIA PLANNING

The best multimedia projects devote a good chunk of time to planning, says Peter Howard, former vice president of news and content for Media General's Interactive Media Division. He's come up with six steps to help ensure a multimedia project's success:

Source: Photo courtesy of Peter Howard.

- Set goals. Howard says you have to ask, "What am I trying to achieve?" Too many people skimp on this step, he says, thinking the answer is obvious, but defining the goals of the project can clearly help shape the content.

- Collaborate. According to Howard, it's important to talk extensively and often with others to determine how you can achieve your goals. Web developers, reporters, photojournalists and anyone else you might need on the project should be included in meetings from the get-go.

- Define the audience. This may or may not be a part of your goal-setting exercise, but it's an important step in the planning process. Determining who you will target

content, sharing resources and developing a presentation plan to arrive at the finished products for each platform.

Putting It All Together

As you might imagine, storyboards are used most often for major multimedia projects, which can take days or sometimes even weeks or months to plan and execute. But many of the same concepts we've just discussed can be used to plan any content you would produce online in conjunction with a daily broadcast or print story. Once you've listed all the elements you want to provide and have decided which medium is the best fit for the content, you continue on to produce your TV or print story and to post your own Web content or provide the online content to a Web producer.

with the project will also have an impact on the content you gather and the way in which you present the information.

- **Develop a timetable.** Howard maintains that this step in the process is critical. "Set realistic deadlines for the collection of material, and be sure to factor in development time," he says.

- **Select tools.** Think about what tools can be used to present the content most effectively and to invite audience participation. Is a poll or a forum the best approach? What about a slide show or a video? "Page views shoot up for photo galleries," says Howard. "But be aware that about half your audience won't be able to hear an audio slide show, so using audio plus captions is probably the best way to go."

- **Establish a presentation plan.** Finally, you have to determine what your project will look like online. Howard suggests you start with a storyboard—sketching out what the audience will be presented with first, then the next scene and the next. "It will help you see gaps in your presentation a lot quicker," he says.

Howard says project planners should also consider what they already know about their audiences and their sites: "One thing we've found is that a text story will get about five times more hits than a video story." Some forms of interactivity work better than others, he says. For example, "It's hard to get people to write, so polls may work better than forums at times."

At WSOC-TV in Charlotte, N.C., coverage of a summer heat wave included several examples of multimedia enhancements online. The story featured a weathercast, slide shows with advice on how local people and pets were combating the heat and links to additional weather information, including a heat advisory map showing which parts of the viewing area were experiencing dangerously high temperatures. The station's meteorologists were predicting severe thunderstorm activity, so the story also provided a link to the station's interactive radar feature, which would make it possible for the audience to track the storms even if they did not have access to a TV.

In this example, use of the Web allowed the station to provide far more information and interactivity than ever would have been possible with a video or text story alone.

TAKING IT HOME

One of the most exciting things about online journalism is its possibilities. Whether you choose to work exclusively as an online journalist or you are simply using the online medium as another vehicle for your storytelling, today's journalists have the opportunity to innovate like never before. For every broadcast journalist who wants another minute of time, for every print journalist who wants to show the readers what happened and for every online journalist who needs more resources, multimedia reporting can be an extremely powerful tool.

By reporting online we are engaging our audiences in a two-way conversation; we are allowing them to explore the information we've gathered to help them make sense of the news on a personal level; and we have been given the opportunity to provide more depth and detail, more context and perspective than we have in the past.

However, the Web's potential as a news and information source has still not yet been fully realized. You are in a unique position to discover new ways of storytelling and to help reinvigorate the importance of journalism in public life. Be creative.

TALKING POINTS

1. People in your community have been arguing over a plan to build a new stadium for the local football team. At 8:30 a.m., you get word that at 1 p.m. today city leaders will announce what they've decided to do. Create a story plan for the Web.

When will you post your first story, and what will it include? How will you keep the story updated throughout the day, and with what information?

2. Go online and find a blog entry from a news organization that has received 25 or more comments. What is it about the entry that promoted so much feedback? Do the comments give you any ideas about future stories you might do on this issue? How would you respond to these comments if you were the reporter who wrote the original post?

3. Choose a story you've produced recently for a single medium. Now you're being asked to take a multimedia approach to the content and to develop a presentation plan across platforms. What unique elements would each platform have to offer? Would the print, TV or Web story be published first, and why?

ONLINE LEARNING MODULE 8

Activate or buy this chapter's online learning module at journalism.cqpress.com to get access to:

- SKILL BUILDING: Follow a video tutorial and create an interactive map.

- DISCOVER: Check out how one news organization covered an important ongoing story online. Analyze the project to determine what else might have been done.

- EXPLORE: See examples of award-winning multimedia journalism and tutorials on developing your HTML or photo-editing skills.

- A list of customizable widgets and instructions on how to use them to create interactivity in your multimedia stories.

- A digital version of this chapter's text in full color with active links.

Also, continue your work on the ONGOING STORY MODULE. Develop a multimedia plan for this story and create a storyboard for the project. Review the authors' multimedia approach to the content.

CHAPTER 9
PRODUCING FOR MULTIPLE PLATFORMS

In this chapter, we'll share what multimedia journalists need to know about the job of producing for TV and mobile devices. We'll also offer some advice about working effectively with producers, and we'll explore the ways in which multimedia journalism is changing TV newscasts now and into the future.

Few people are more important to the success of a newsroom than its producers. The best producers are organized, love to write and always want to be the first to know everything. Toss in some great journalistic instincts, managerial skills and graphic design and you have a great producer.

In most television newsrooms, producers are truly at the center of the action. They work with the assignment editors to make sure the best stories of the day get covered, they work with reporters and photographers to discuss what elements of the story should be included and they work with the production team to determine how to present the entire newsroom's work to the viewers.

From a multimedia perspective, many television newscast producers play a vital role in funneling and posting content to their stations' websites and mobile and social media sites, especially in breaking news situations when reporters and photographers are out in the field and may be unable to post directly to the Web. In addition, producers are involved in promoting the online elements that enhance the stories airing in their newscasts.

Reporters and photographers who understand the producer's job and work to make it easier will generally see a payoff in the way their stories are showcased and promoted. Print reporters who are asked to go on television may also have a better experience if they understand the way broadcasts are put together and can speak the producer's language.

THE JOURNALIST PRODUCER

It's important to remember that a producer is first and foremost a journalist. Although producers may not often go out into the field to report, they play a major role in determining which stories will be included in a station's newscasts each day.

Producers, like all journalists, need to be informed, and not just about what's happening locally, nationally and even internationally. In this highly competitive news environment, it's critical for producers to know a great deal about the station's goals as a news organization. This knowledge will help you evaluate which are the most newsworthy stories of the day.

No matter what job you do for the newsroom, it's important to know your station's news philosophy, but it's critically important for producers. Is your newsroom committed to covering education better than anyone else in town? Is breaking news the number one priority? Does your station brand itself as a viewer advocate? Unless you know what your news organization is trying to achieve each day, it's difficult for you to help decide which stories should be covered and with what emphasis.

Ask if your station does audience research and if the news managers will make some or all of it available to you. Keep an eye on user comments on the Web and Facebook. If your site allows users to rate stories, check which ones are most popular or most e-mailed. It's important to know what the audience is saying about your news and what kinds of stories viewers would like to see on the air and online. Research and feedback should not be used as a substitute for good news judgment, but they can help guide some of your decisions.

At the same time, don't be afraid to throw out all the rules. If you know in your heart of hearts that an important or interesting story needs to be told, champion that story idea. Write up a story proposal, including the people to interview, the visual elements and the relevance to your audience. Some of the best stories ever told on television got on the air because someone was passionate about the idea.

SHOW CHOREOGRAPHY

After producers, reporters and photographers leave the morning meeting, they naturally become very focused on the individual jobs they have to do. But no one in a newsroom works in a vacuum, and understanding what it takes to produce a newscast can help reporters and photographers do a better job of executing their stories.

Once producers have a good idea of what stories are available for the day's newscasts, they begin the process of crafting their shows. You will most often hear this referred to as *show stacking*, but the term *show choreography* seems to reflect the more thoughtful, creative approach that good producers take when they are putting their newscasts together. When WSOC-TV's Jennifer Coates sits down to produce her newscast each day, she says she focuses on the audience first. "I think about what story or stories will affect the most people," she says.

Jennifer Coates got her first producing job at a small station right out of college. She's now at WSOC-TV in Charlotte, N.C., a Top 30 market. Coates says she learned early what was essential to success on the job—keeping viewers top of mind.

Source: Photo courtesy of Jennifer Coates.

Keeping your viewers top of mind throughout the process is essential to good producing, but there are other important factors to consider.

The Lead

As you might expect, the lead story is generally considered the most important story in the newscast. But here's the tricky part —often the lead is whatever you say it is. On many days, there's no obvious story that must air first in the newscast. On those days, a producer's showcasing and writing skills really come into play. Producers are essentially "selling" the viewers on their story choices.

Unless the news breaks very late, a reporter will usually have been assigned to the lead story earlier in the day. That means the producer should spend a fair share of time working with the reporter, photojournalist, graphic artist, director and others to make sure that the story is executed as well as possible.

Echo Gamel, producer for WTVQ-TV in Lexington, Ky., says that when she crafts a newscast, the show's lead story is her top priority. "The first thing I think about is my lead— how can I really make this sing? What elements do I need to tell this story?" she says. "I work closely with the reporters to find out how I can best showcase and tell their story with graphics, video and breakouts. I stay in contact with them throughout the day in case things change and I need to adjust."

Producers need to know everything they can about the story—why it deserves to be the lead, what are the best pictures, the most emotional sound, why the viewer should care. Armed with that information, they need to decide the best way to tell the story. Should the reporter be live, or is the story better told as a straight package? If the live shot won't add important information, it may be better to go without a live element. Can the story be developed beyond a single package? The best lead stories often include breakouts or sidebar information for the anchor to read. Those additional elements can add depth and perspective to the important lead package.

PRODUCER SKILLS

Jennifer Coates' list of the "Top 7 Skills" for producers:

1. Is well-organized.
2. Is able to multi-multi-multi-task.
3. Is able to communicate well.
4. Stays cool under pressure.
5. Is open-minded.
6. Enjoys writing.
7. Is able to be a leader.

TRADE TOOLS

A NEWS DIRECTOR'S EXPECTATIONS FOR PRODUCERS

Angie Kucharski is a former producer who moved up to become a news director in Denver and later managed media strategies for CBS-owned television stations. She thinks producers are the heart and soul of a newsroom. She calls them the coaches, the compasses, the glue, the leaders and the future.

Source: Photo courtesy of Angie Kucharski.

High praise—and it comes with high expectations. At a Poynter Institute seminar, Kucharski said producers have to be focused. This means, above all, being selective. Know what you want and how to get there. Of your many story options, know which one should play today. Know when to use graphics and video—and when not to. When resources are limited, decide what to do well, and leave the rest alone.

Kucharski wants a producer who can delegate. You aren't expected to write the entire newscast yourself. News directors understand that producers are responsible for all the

Multimedia producers will also ask if there are additional elements to the story (such as links, video or pictures) that can be posted on the station's website to drive viewers online.

Producers may decide to showcase a story by using great video or a powerful sound bite right off the top in what's called a "cold open." Special graphics and sharp writing can grab viewers' attention immediately and leave them wanting to know more about the story.

Reporters and photographers can help the producer think these decisions through and, in the process, help themselves do their own jobs better. For example, the focus of a reporter's package is often sharpened when part of a story is turned into a breakout element for the anchor to read. The payoff is that a good lead story, properly executed, may keep the viewer engaged.

details—not just the journalism, but the technical stuff too. So ask for help from managers, anchors, photojournalists, anyone with a spare moment. Let them write. Trust them to pull their weight.

When you're in the booth, Kucharski wants the producer to focus on the anchors, the director and the viewers. Give your full attention to the people who matter most to what's going on the air right now.

Focus early, Kucharski says. Decide during your drive to work what you'll do well that day. Stake your claim early and marshal the resources you need to do good work.

Kucharski wants you to walk in and say, "This is what I wanna do with my newscast today!" She wants you to generate story ideas—lots of them. She wants you to disagree with her—and then convince her that you're right. She wants you to stop by her office—accost her if necessary—to tally the day's successes and review the opportunities for improvement. She wants you to take risks.

Above all, she wants you to be a "doer." Enlist aid, line up resources and set up deals with other producers to make things happen without her supervision. Start conversations about ethics. Produce surprising stories. Put your signature on your newscast.

Source: Adapted from Robin Sloan, "Being the Brightest and Best: A News Director's Expectations for Producers," PoynterOnline, September 6, 2002, www.poynter.org/content/content_view.asp?id=9500.

Flow

This is one of the most controversial aspects of producing. For the most part, producers are taught to create "flow" in their newscasts by placing stories on similar topics together in the show. For example, on a day when a local school system releases new numbers on student test scores, many producers would also place stories concerning a new study about dropout rates and new ways to get college scholarship money immediately adjacent to the test-score story. The argument is that it's easier for an anchor to transition between those stories. For a rundown of what those stories might look like, see Table 9.1.

TABLE 9.1 STORY FLOW

Page #	Anchor	Story name	Story form	Length	Backtime
		SHOW OPEN		:20	
1	Bill	Test Scores	PKG	1:25	
2	Meg	Dropout Rates	V/O	:25	
3	Meg	College Cash	PKG	1:15	
4	Bill	Animal Abuse	V/O-SOT	:35	
5	Bill	Previous Charges	RDR/FS	:20	
6	Meg	Toss to WX	—	:10	
7	Paul	1st WX	—	:45	
8	Meg	State Fair	V/O	:20	
9	Bill/Meg	Tease 1	V/O	:15	

Note: The stories on student test scores, dropout rates and college scholarship money are airing one after another. This is an example of creating flow within a newscast.

To make the stories flow, the producer might write copy like this to transition between the end of the test-score story and the beginning of the dropout story:

Meg: "With great test scores like those, it's hard to understand why so many students continue to drop out of high schools around the state. . . ."

And then the transition to the scholarship story might be written this way:

Meg: "If you do stay in school, it might now be easier for you to get to college. The state has just created a new scholarship fund. . . ."

The goal is to help the viewer see the connections among these three stories, all of which are education-related. However, some research has shown that grouping like stories together can end up confusing the viewer. The researchers say that information can get jumbled when a series of stories with a similar theme are run back to back.[1] For example, the viewers might walk away from the newscast we just described thinking the new scholarship fund is for dropouts or that the test scores are down when they're actually up.

Some newsrooms speak in terms of "clustering" instead of flow. It probably seems logical to cluster stories on similar themes, so that one airs right after the other. But additional problems can occur when you air too many similar stories together—more important stories may be pushed later in the newscast, and you risk losing those in the audience who aren't interested in the cluster topic. For example, you might have a strong lead story about crime, followed by a series of four other crime-related stories. But if your newsroom has produced an important package about a huge issue facing local schools, airing the school story second and moving the other crime stories down to air later in the newscast may better serve your audience.

No matter how your newsroom approaches flow or clustering, you will be expected to write good transitions between stories that allow the show to move seamlessly from one element to another. Reporters must also be sensitive to this issue; they should be cognizant of where their stories appear within a news block and should be able to write an anchor intro that helps move the newscast along.

When creating transitions, writers need to be sensitive to both the anchors and the viewers. You don't want to create content transitions that are difficult for them to handle. Take another look at the rundown in Table 9.1 on the facing page. Our anchor, Meg, is reading a story about college scholarship money, so it makes sense to have Bill read the next story about animal abuse. If Meg were reading both, you might get stuck with an awkward transition like this one:

> Meg: "The school superintendent expects next year's test scores to be even higher, thanks to the new teacher initiative at area high schools.
> Tonight investigators are at the scene of what some call one of the worst cases of animal cruelty in Macon history!"

That's a tough read—the anchor has to go from delivering a positive story to telling people about animal abuse. Abrupt topic changes are sometimes unavoidable, however, especially in newscasts that rely on a single anchor. In those situations, an over-the-shoulder graphic, or OTS, can help a single anchor shift from one story to another. Turning to a different camera, with or without a graphic, can also add separation that makes it more comfortable for both anchor and viewer. In any case, the writing should help the anchor make a smooth transition between unrelated stories:

> Meg: "The school superintendent expects next year's test scores to be even higher, thanks to the new teacher initiative at area high schools.
> In tonight's Crime Tracker report, investigators are at the scene of what some call one of the worst cases of animal cruelty in Macon history."

There are certainly other transitions that would work just as well, but you get the idea. You want to ease the anchor and viewer from one topic to the next. Some producers like to think in terms of emotional shifts for both the anchor and viewer. Are you asking them to make too large an emotional change? If so, you may want to put your stories in a different order, making them easier for the anchor to deliver and for the audience to understand.

Pacing

Another slightly less controversial producing technique involves pacing. Many producers believe it's important that a show has a rhythm, and those rhythms may change from newscast to newscast. For example, many late evening newscasts are faster paced—they include shorter stories and more of them—than 6 p.m. newscasts. In contrast, a more traditional "newscast of record" at 6 would include longer stories with a great deal of depth and detail on the most important events and issues of the day.

Whether a show is fast paced or a little more deliberate, many producers believe that you shouldn't air multiple packages back to back because it slows down the show. In our sample newscast rundown in Table 9.1 on page 242, we created pacing by varying the story format often—we didn't run any packages back to back. But other producers will tell you that compelling content and energetic anchor delivery will keep a newscast moving even if a show includes a series of packages in a row. Suffice it to say that, in general, content is more important than either pacing or flow. If you have urgent, important information that directly affects your viewers, they'll watch.

Newscast Blocks

Newscasts are divided into segments, often called "blocks," of news. Between each block of news, you will typically find a commercial break. In the past, the lead and the other first-block stories could be compared with the front page of a newspaper. The most important or attention-grabbing stories were included in the first block.

But as competition grew along with understanding of how viewership patterns work, producers had to adjust their thinking to create highly interesting segments throughout the show. The second, third, fourth and perhaps even fifth block had to include compelling content as well, to give viewers a reason to keep watching.

Now there is no block of the show that's considered unimportant. As producers work to keep the audience involved from one segment of the show to the next and from one news program on the station to another, every block must be produced to keep the audience watching. Reporters will sometimes argue to get a good story placed higher in the newscast, but they should know that great stories are often more valuable to a news organization if they can be used to pull viewers deeper into a newscast.

GO ONLINE

Module 9: Create your own newscast, then compare it to what others have done with the same information.

Tease writing is another essential tool that helps producers achieve the goal of keeping the audience watching. We'll explore tease-writing strategies in detail a little later in this chapter.

Timing

You've probably heard the expression, "Timing is everything." Timing a show is an important part of the producer's responsibility.

Producers need to keep track of how long every story and tease, every weather and sports segment and every commercial break will take. That's called a running time. Before the newscast begins, those running times are simply estimates, so part of a producer's job will involve copyediting stories to make sure they aren't too long or too short, or negotiating with weather and sports anchors to agree on how long those segments will last. Reporters and photographers will often argue with producers over running times for their stories. There's nothing wrong with fighting for a few extra seconds to help tell a compelling story, but understand that producers are responsible for the big picture. If three reporters beg for more time, that may force a producer to drop another important story from the newscast.

Because commercial breaks are generally *not* negotiable except in extreme circumstances, producers must develop strategies for filling or cutting time when the unexpected happens once the show is on the air. Many producers will identify stories that can be dropped from the show if another segment runs long, and some will even write an extra story or two to add into the newscast if something runs shorter than expected or has to be dropped because it isn't ready.

AUDIENCE AND RATINGS

The need to keep viewers watching throughout the entire newscast is driven by the fundamental way that television news makes money. As you already know, advertising supports the news departments at commercial television stations. Advertisers buy commercial time on stations based on the number of people or the specific types of people watching a particular station's programs.

For example, politicians often buy time during programs like "Wheel of Fortune" or "Jeopardy" because they know that many older viewers are watching those shows. Because older voters turn out in much greater numbers than any other demographic, those programs deliver an important audience for political ads.

News producers don't have to worry about selling ads, of course, but they do have to worry about creating newscasts that viewers will want to watch. If enough viewers are watching, advertisers will want to buy time during the newscasts. There are several things producers need to know about how newscast audiences are measured and the producing strategies used to maximize audience.

Demographics

Advertisers target different groups depending on which audience they feel will be most receptive to their product, whether it's a candidate or a car. Advertisers look for television programming that provides a significant number of people in that targeted group. For example, many newscasts have traditionally targeted women aged 25 to 54 because that's a demographic traditionally coveted by many advertisers. Women in that age group are believed to make many of the buying decisions within a household. Producers at stations targeting these women try to include stories that will make them want to watch the newscast. In turn, the hope is that advertisers interested in targeting these women will buy time in the newscast. Other stations have different demographic targets, so knowing who your station is trying to reach is an important part of producing.

Diaries and Meters

There are more than 200 television news markets around the country—each ranked by size, based on population. In about three-quarters of those markets, the audience is measured solely through the use of "diaries." A diary is simply a written record of what the people in a particular household were watching over a particular period of time. Diaries are only as accurate as the people filling them out, and they are collected just four times a year during what are called "sweeps months." Sweeps or ratings periods include the months of February, May, July and November, but in some of the largest television markets, the measurement is year-round.

That's because in most big markets a combination of diaries and electronic meters is used to measure audience. The meters track television viewing all year, but the results do not usually include the kind of demographic information that the diaries provide. Meters tell you that a television set was tuned to your newscast, but they don't tell you anything about the person who's watching.

That has already changed with the advent of the Nielsen People Meter, in use in the 25 largest markets as of mid-2010. People Meters measure both what is being watched and who is watching. According to Nielsen, each family member in the sample household is assigned a personal viewing button on the People Meter. Whenever the TV is turned on, a red light flashes reminding viewers to press their assigned button, which records the viewer's age and gender. This more advanced kind of meter is likely to become widespread in local news markets as the cost of the technology behind it decreases, giving producers more detailed information, more often, about who's really watching their newscasts.

Ratings and Share

Producers strive to produce highly rated shows with as large a share of the audience as possible. According to Nielsen, a rating is a percentage of all the homes that have television sets in a given market. So, if you have a 10 rating for your newscast, 10 percent of all the homes with television sets in your market are presumed to be watching your show. A share is the percentage of people watching a program in households using television at the time the program airs. Therefore, if your show has a 20 share, that means 20 percent of the homes that actually had their television sets on at the time of your newscast chose to watch your show. Take a look at Figure 9.1 to help understand the differences between rating and share.

FIGURE 9.1 TV RATINGS/SHARES

Rating = The percentage of ALL persons or homes tuned to your station. For example . . .

Total TV households: 10

Households tuning in: 3

RATING = 30

Share = The percentage of homes or persons USING TV who are watching your station. For example . . .

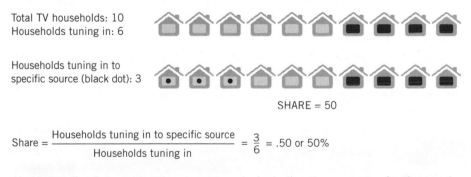

Total TV households: 10
Households tuning in: 6

Households tuning in to specific source (black dot): 3

SHARE = 50

$$\text{Share} = \frac{\text{Households tuning in to specific source}}{\text{Households tuning in}} = \frac{3}{6} = .50 \text{ or } 50\%$$

Understanding how newscasts are measured—including the concepts of ratings and share—is critically important for any multimedia journalist, especially newscast producers.

Strategic Producing

Producers employ many different strategies to keep people watching. We've already described how story selection may be geared to target certain demographics. In a metered market, the newscast may also be choreographed to take advantage of the way most meters record viewership. The relatively new People Meters track what viewers are watching minute by minute, but most meters track the audience in 15-minute increments beginning at the top of the hour. That means you have a chance to beat your competition every 15 minutes. If you can get people to watch your show for the first seven-and-a-half minutes of the quarter hour before switching to another station, your show is credited with a "win" for that particular quarter hour. Even if the viewer switches to watch six minutes of another newscast, you get the credit for the quarter hour of viewing.

Producing "for the demos" or "for the meters" is a controversial practice because it can lead to story decisions that have less to do with journalism and more to do with making money. The best producers are able to do both—take important stories and present them in a way that attracts viewers and keeps them watching.

In addition to developing specific newscast strategies, producers are also heavily involved in most stations' overall strategies for success, including any sweeps month or ratings period plan.

TEASES

Another major tool in your producing arsenal is the newscast tease. Teases alert viewers to what will be airing later in the program and encourage them to continue watching through the commercial breaks.

A newscast tease is essentially a mini-advertisement for an upcoming story. It's different from a headline because it doesn't summarize the story; it generally leaves some intriguing questions unanswered or promises a payoff to the viewer who sticks around to watch the story.

GO ONLINE

Ongoing Story Module: Write a tease for the story, then see what the authors did and why they think it works well.

Tease copy is some of the most important and the most difficult broadcast writing to do well. Many producers hate to write teases, so they may delegate that job to an associate producer or to the anchors. If you are assigned to write a newscast tease, here's the number one rule: Don't wait until the last minute to write it! Give yourself time to play with the copy and make it as compelling as possible.

Know the Story

Too often tease writers will rely on a cursory glance at the reporter intro or the first few lines of the story before they begin to write. To effectively promote content, you have to thoroughly understand what you are writing about.

Knowing the story includes knowing the video. The best thing to do is to watch the video for the story you're teasing. If you can't do that, at the very least, talk to someone else who has seen the video—preferably a video editor or photojournalist. There may be times when the video for a story is so poor that you decide not to tease the story rather than risk losing viewers with boring or irrelevant video. On the flip side, great video can help convince a viewer to stick around to watch, especially if you can incorporate great natural sound or sound bites into your tease.

Armed with all this information, you must still keep your copy concise. "Still to come," "More on that when we come back," "Right after this"—all these phrases send one signal to the viewer: "Commercial coming! Commercial coming!" Commercials are one big reason why viewers change channels, so avoid using those phrases. You also don't want to give the whole story away, so writing tight can help you focus on "teasing" the viewer with what's to come.

At the same time, you can't assume that the viewer knows as much about the story as you do. Be sure that someone tuning into your broadcast for the very first time will be able to understand the story you are promoting. For example, check out this tease:

> Air Tran's heading east, but what about those flying west? See how Fair Fares search for a discount carrier's going, coming up.

The problem with that tease is that it assumes people know what the "Fair Fares" program is all about. Consider this alternative:

> Half of the country is already covered—now see what the airport is doing to help you get cheap air fares nationwide.

The second version is short and to the point, and you don't have to have as much background on the story to understand the tease.

Weather and Sports Teases

Although weather is consistently considered a primary reason why people watch local TV news, many producers never speak to their meteorologists or weathercasters before writing teases for the weather segments. That's why we too often hear teases like this: "How long will today's severe weather last? Paul has the forecast next." That's just plain lazy. The tease writer needs to get a handle on the day's weather story. Here's an example:

> The thunderstorms are moving out, but there's more trouble behind them. Paul's up next with an important change in the forecast.

The story was that skies would be clearing, but high winds were expected for the following day. Your station's weather expert prepares two to three minutes of weather content for the newscast every day and can help with writing an effective weather tease.

If weather teases are bad, sports teases are generally even worse. They often give the story away and leave little for those who aren't sports fans to care about at all. Here's an example of a typical sports tease:

TYPICAL TEASE:

Coming up in sports, our Athlete of the Week Award goes to a local high school softball team that has been one of the big surprises in the Class 4A playoffs.

Also tonight, the Pineville Lady Rebels gear up to face the team that eliminated them last season in the playoffs. We'll have that story and much more coming up in sports.

That wasn't so much a tease as a menu of what was to come. Here's one way you might have given this tease some pizzazz:

ALTERNATIVE TEASE:

It's Ladies Night in sports.

The Athlete of the Week Award goes to an entire team of women who are surprising everyone in the 4A playoffs.

Plus the Lady Rebels are gearing up for a grudge match.

The second version also has the advantage of being much less wordy (:12 versus the original :18). To write an effective sports tease, you'll probably need to take the time to talk to the sports anchor about what's in the show that night or, at the very least, check the sports rundown—there may be a story with wide appeal that will make a better tease element.

Plenty of producers love to write teases. They see promoting the content in their shows as a challenge, and they like the idea of convincing viewers to keep watching.

The ability to write a well-crafted tease can set you apart as a valuable newsroom employee.

Stand-Up and Live Teases

In some news organizations, reporters are asked to do live or taped on-camera teases. Most reporters look at this assignment as an annoyance rather than an opportunity. They produce teases that are little more than headlines for the story.

At WLOS-TV in Asheville, N.C., a reporter once recorded this stand-up tease:

A Spindale woman fights off an attack by a fox and is now getting tested for rabies.

Now that all the viewers know the most important facts of the story, the reporter has given them little reason to keep watching. Consider this alternative:

For the first time in 20 years, health officials are worried about rabies in Rutherford County.

The second version is based on another element of the reporter's package—the fact that county health officials say they haven't had a rabies investigation there for two decades.

It's also important for reporters and producers to communicate about teases. For this same fox attack story, the reporter produced a second stand-up tease. This time, she asked her photographer to start out by shooting the porch of the house involved and then to zoom out to show the reporter in the shot as she said the following words:

You won't believe what ran across this lady's porch and forced her to get treatment at the hospital.

This version is a little better tease, but unfortunately, the producer chose to add the words "Fox Attack" as a super on the bottom of the screen. So much for that tease! Producers can also spoil the surprise of a story with a careless tease. For example, a reporter and photographer might be trying to create suspense in a story about a dog trapped in a sewer pipe. Their story might be told chronologically, showing the rescue from start to finish, leaving the question of whether the dog survived unanswered until the very end. If the tease shows a happy, tail-wagging pup, the story will lose its punch.

Reporters and producers, working together to create compelling teases, should keep in mind all of the principles of tease writing that we've outlined in this chapter.

GO ONLINE

Module 9: Check out examples of effective multimedia teases.

Teasing Pitfalls

In addition to the missteps mentioned above, you should be aware of a few other pitfalls to avoid when promoting the stories in a newscast.

One of the most common mistakes is teasing a story that doesn't deliver. The producer may have written a compelling promotion for the story, but viewers will feel cheated if the story doesn't live up to the tease's promise. This happens often when you promote a story that's little more than a :20 voice over. There's usually not enough information in a story that short to make viewers feel that sticking around was worthwhile.

Another common problem is the tease that uses the exact same sequence of video that we see at the start of the actual story—especially if that story airs in the block

KNOW AND TELL

WORKING WITH NEWSCAST PRODUCERS

Even if you have absolutely no interest in ever becoming a producer yourself, as a multimedia journalist you will probably find yourself working with one someday. By now, we hope you have a better appreciation of the tough job they have to do, and you can probably anticipate their needs a little better as well.

Producers are important to reporters and photographers because they often have a strong voice when it comes to deciding what stories go into their newscasts, which means they have a big say-so in the stories that reporters and photographers are assigned to each day.

Source: Photo courtesy of Lane Michaelsen.

Lane Michaelsen, former director of photography at KARE-TV in Minneapolis, Minn., is now vice president for news and content at WTVJ/NBC Universal. When he was working as a photojournalist, he used what he called the "pennies in a jar" approach to working with producers. Basically, he believed that if you cheerfully do all the assignments that producers need completed but no one else wants to do, you get a "penny in the producer jar" each time. When Michaelsen really wanted to do a story he had to sell to a producer, he'd "cash in the pennies." At that point, he says, he had to start building them up again.

immediately following the tease. That's generally the result of lazy editing; whoever's cutting the video is just pulling the first few shots from the story rather than looking for a way to make the tease video different.

Producers and reporters will also want to avoid tease clichés. For example, some writers love to start teases with a question such as: "Would you like to find an easy way to get your kids to study more?" The problem with a question tease is that too often the viewer's answer is No! What about all those people who don't have children in school? You've basically told them the upcoming story is not going to be of interest to them.

Other clichés involve using phrases such as: "You won't believe . . ." or referencing the "shocking video." Yes, you are "selling" these stories, but good tease writers find a way to make their copy relevant through content rather than hype.

He also talks about "getting over the wall before it's built." By that he means that you have to anticipate roadblocks when pitching a story. If you can get a producer excited about having the story in the newscast, you have an ally when it comes time to convince the news director and others that it's a good story to do.

Michele Harvey is a multimedia journalist in Charlotte, N.C., who has worked with newscast producers for more than 20 years. She says that first and foremost, reporters and photographers need to realize that, in the field, they are producers too.

"Keep in mind that the producer can't see or hear what you do in the field. You need to let them know about the most exciting video, the most exciting sound. You need to help them by saying, 'This is the sound bite I will use to write my story around and I have a similar one that you can use to promote or showcase the story,'" says Harvey.

Harvey says this collaboration process with the producer starts the minute the story is assigned. "It's not about us and them. You need to leave the morning meeting with everyone in agreement on a vision for the story. If you find the vision doesn't work, you need to let them know how it's changed and offer solutions for any problems that develop," she says.

Harvey says your producer should have confidence in you: "They'll learn to count on you and send you out on the tough stories, the good stories, the stories that will lead the newscast."

NEWSCASTS OF THE FUTURE

One of the big questions out there right now is how does the traditional newscast fit into an increasingly on-demand, interactive, nonlinear world? Beyond pushing people to a station website for multimedia content, can a newscast itself be a multimedia or interactive experience? Some people believe the answer is yes, and research suggests that many Americans would be interested in a new kind of newscast.

The Radio and Television News Directors Foundation (RTNDF) conducted a survey in 2006 to determine where news might be headed. The study found that more than 60 percent of people surveyed would like to "interact with TV news." The researchers defined interacting as "pressing a button to get more information on something you see in a newscast." The study also found that about 40 percent of people would be interested in assembling their own newscasts, although 46 percent had no interest in doing that.[2]

Interactivity

These ideas aren't just theoretical. At KCAL-TV in Los Angeles, while anchor Sandra Mitchell presents the day's top stories, she also chats online with viewers and responds to their questions. In Columbus, Ohio, WCMH-TV tore up the format of its 5:30 p.m. newscast to make it less formal and more interactive. The anchors roamed from their desks in the newsroom to the control room, followed by a handheld camera. Reporters discussed their stories in live Q&As. If news was breaking, an anchor might trot up to the assignment desk to ask what's going on.

"We want to bring our customers inside our process and let them peek behind the curtain," says Ike Walker, the station's director of digital journalism. Like other stations around the country, WCMH is using social media to try to involve viewers in the news, asking for feedback and questions for newsmakers via Twitter and Facebook. Incoming comments are featured in a regularly scheduled segment on the restructured 5:30 newscast.

Web-enabled television sets have the potential to allow for even more interactivity, letting users create their own playlist of stories from a menu provided by the news organization.

Portable Pieces

Terry Heaton is senior vice president for Audience Research and Development, a company that consults for news organizations. He believes these changes aren't going far enough yet, and that the traditional TV "News at 6" is going away.

"All news and information is moving to real time, which doesn't bode well for the packaged 6:00 news. What we do in real time—how well we meet our community's needs there—will determine our relevance in the future," Heaton says.

According to Heaton, stations need to be focusing their attention on the Web and delivering content to mobile devices, rather than trying to create a new kind of television newscast. He suggests that a station might hire people with "deep knowledge of important niches in the community" and train them to be reporters. The stories they produce could be used as content for online businesses. Heaton gives the example of a real estate agent hired to report on the local market; the agent's stories could be part of an advertising-supported online real estate site.

At WCMH-TV in Columbus, Ohio, the station's website, NBC4i.com, encourages the audience to interact with newsroom personnel via Twitter and Facebook, sometimes putting user comments on the air.

Source: WCMH-TV, Columbus, Ohio, www2.nbc4i.com/social_networking/ (accessed August 5, 2010).

With more viewing moving to handheld devices, Heaton says content must be created in easily digestible chunks of information versus produced in a full-blown newscast. "Portable and in pieces; that's the model," he says.

Heaton says the challenge for television stations right now is that they have to continue to produce newscasts while they try to figure out what the future might look like. "As I heard someone once say, it's a little like fixing a car while you're driving."

MOBILE NEWS

Many experts believe the future of broadcast journalism lies in a three-screen strategy—TV, Web and mobile. Brian Bracco, vice president of news for Hearst Television Inc., says the audience already is using all three, and they want something different from each.

"Here's a good example—during the Winter Olympics, on my BlackBerry I got an alert about Lindsay Vonn's medal in the downhill. I immediately went on the Web, read about it and saw a picture. Then I couldn't wait to get home that evening and watch her run on my 52-inch high-def set," Bracco says. "While I was watching, my heart was still pounding even though I knew the result. These are three different experiences—the consumer at this point is in charge; we need to be on all those different platforms."

So while newsrooms are still trying to manage the Web as a news outlet, there's also a sense of urgency to figure out how to capture the mobile audience as well. According to the Pew Research Center for the People & the Press, one-third of all cell phone users in the United States accessed news on their mobile phones in 2010. That mobile audience presents a major opportunity for news organizations; it also requires today's multimedia journalists to think about how producing for cell phones changes the delivery of news.

Stephen Quinn, who studies mobile journalism at Deakin University in Australia, says cell phones bring a "new notion of mobility" to journalists and news consumers. "Our concept of news is broadening—if I can get there, it's news," he says. He also suggests that these new capabilities change audience expectations: "They know we can get there and expect to get the info."

In response to these expectations, many news organizations have developed mobile-friendly versions of their websites to make it easier for people to view the content on handheld devices. These are basically stripped-down versions of the site that load more quickly and provide more basic functionality. And some news outlets are experimenting with producing unique, mobile-friendly content through mobile applications.

Mobile Apps

Unlike mobile websites, which are browser-based and can be displayed on different operating systems, mobile apps must be designed for specific operating systems. That's why an iPhone app won't work on a smartphone running the Android system. But it's worth the trouble to design apps for the most popular systems because they allow a news organization to reach a younger audience, which is critically important to the industry's survival. According to NPR's Alan Stone, the network's typical radio listener is over 50 and the typical user of the NPR website is over 40, but the typical mobile news consumer is in his or her 30s.

Vice president/managing editor for the Associated Press Lou Ferrar says that in the mobile space, the consumer really is king. "If you don't deliver for them, you don't get them," Ferrar says. He describes what AP has learned about the mobile news audience:

- They're impatient, so speed is crucial. That means no waiting for a slow app to load.

- They're vocal. They will readily share with others their dislike of a poor user experience.

- They dislike ads, but they still want the content for free.

- If you don't deliver, they'll drop your app and find another.

And that's not all we know about the mobile user. Information about weather and traffic is highly sought after, so the mobile news app for the Indianapolis Star newspaper allows users to view dozens of live traffic cameras on major roadways throughout the city. Commuters can get real-time information for the specific routes they plan to use.

USA Today's news app makes the paper's popular Snapshot feature interactive for mobile users. USA Today Snapshots are those statistical graphics that present information on various issues and trends in a visual form. The Snapshots feature of the app allows users to scan through the day's graphs and to vote on a poll question for each. Then users can view responses by city and state to compare their choices to those of other users.

David Rencher, interactive media director for the Media General—owned station WKRG in Mobile, Ala., thinks mobile offers amazing potential for news organizations to respond to audience needs. "During events like a hurricane, mobile phones may be the only way a user is able to get information," he says. So a station could easily customize its mobile app to prominently display storm-related information.

Making content more easily accessible to mobile users is the strategy behind the application developed for WKRG in Mobile, Ala. It was created to be easily customizable in the event of breaking news.

Source: WKRG-TV, Mobile, Ala.

Location Apps

In Chapter 7 we briefly discussed the concept of geotagging content. Geotagging is expected to become increasingly important as news organizations look to provide location-based information to their audiences. Companies like Gowalla, FourSquare and Google Latitude provide location-based apps that allow you to check in with your social network from wherever you are. On a mobile phone, the app uses the Global Positioning System (GPS) to plot where you are, then allows you to check in at the location and share a message about where you are and why you're there. Most of the apps are also games that let you earn points by checking in, so you can compete with friends and earn virtual prizes.

From a news organization's point of view, mobile location apps can be used to create unique content. The Austin American-Statesman partnered with Gowalla, for example, to provide eight "trips" around Austin built around the newspaper's geotagged content. Users who check in at locations on the trip earn virtual stamps and pins. The newspaper's social media editor says the value for the newspaper is to "go wherever our audience is."[3]

GO ONLINE

Module 9: Create your own location-based "trip" for a local audience.

Other potential uses include the news organization setting up its own "branded" location near the site of a news event and asking people to check in with reports of what they see. For weather coverage, geotagged apps could become a source of micro-local information.

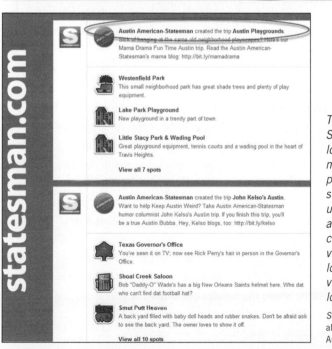

The Austin American-Statesman is using the location-based information service Gowalla to produce interactive trips, such as this one featuring unique places to play around the city. Users collect points and win virtual prizes by downloading the app and visiting designated locations.

Source: Gowalla.com, http://gowalla.com/statesman (accessed August 5, 2010).

Podcasts

One of the earliest forms of mobile content was the podcast. A podcast is simply a pre-recorded program that's posted online and usually made available for download, so users can listen to or watch it on their own computer or mobile device whenever they want. Most news organizations offer podcasts of existing on-air programs, but some also produce content for online listening or viewing only. These podcasts often cover specialized topics like politics, the environment or technology, which may be of less interest to viewers in general but appeal to niche audiences who will seek them out online. And people do seek them out.

When WNYC, a public radio station in New York City, launched the first podcast of an NPR program in 2005, the show doubled the number of listeners it reached online in just four weeks.[4] NPR quickly became a leader in podcasting, making its programs across the board available for download. NBC News believes it has expanded its audience by offering free video podcasts of "NBC Nightly News" and "Meet the Press."[5]

According to an eMarketer survey released in 2009, "the vast majority of the top-rated podcasts come from recognizable media entities that are using podcasts to expand their existing radio, TV, cable or satellite audiences." The researchers estimated that about 9 percent of Internet users download at least one podcast per month.[6]

Mobile Skills

Today's journalists must be prepared to present the news differently on different platforms. The small screens on most mobile devices are "not great for long-form text," says Chet Rhodes of washingtonpost.com. "It's best to produce short summaries or story nuggets for those." But Rhodes believes that as the screens on mobile devices get bigger, longer video clips and stories with more text will work just fine. The Apple iPad, introduced in 2010, was seen by many journalists as a game-changer. "We'll have young people reading newspapers, we'll have different-looking types of newspapers," said News Corp's Rupert Murdoch.[7]

To deliver news to mobile devices, you'll use many of the techniques you've already learned. For example, the headline writing techniques you learned in Chapter 7 can help you create effective RSS feeds, where the headline is often the only thing the user sees. The procedures we outlined for creating effective webcasts in Chapter 8 also apply to producing content for video-capable cell phones or wireless PDAs.

TAKING IT HOME

The best journalists are those who spend their whole lives learning—they want to know why things happen, how things work and the impact of it all. But they don't always spend as much time studying their own profession as they should. Reporters and photographers who fully understand newscast production and producers who fully understand the news-gathering process are all too rare. But just as you have an opportunity to make a difference in your newsroom with your multimedia skills, you can also be a leader in creating better newscasts with your understanding of the process.

Beyond the newscast, the multimedia responsibilities of all journalists are growing. It's not enough to produce content for television; it's not enough to produce content for the Web—journalists have to understand the habits of news consumers and get the content to them on whatever platform they prefer. For now, the push is to make news and information more mobile-friendly as part of a three-screen strategy.

TALKING POINTS

1. Record a local TV newscast. Is there any indication the producer was thinking about the audience? What else could the producer have done to "put the audience first"? Do you think the right choice was made on the lead story? Was it well developed and showcased? Did you notice anything about pacing and flow?

2. Have someone choose a story from a local TV newscast that was included in a newscast tease. Before you watch that tease, watch the story. Try to write a tease for it that keeps all of the principles of good tease writing in mind. Be sure to include a description of the video you would use. Watch the tease that actually aired. Do you like the original version or your own version better? Why?

3. What do you think about Terry Heaton's assertion that it's wrong to assume that there will always be an audience for television newscasts? If you disagree, describe why. If you agree, how long do you think newscasts can survive? Either way, what should local stations be doing to make sure their newscasts have a longer life?

ONLINE LEARNING MODULE 9

Activate or buy this chapter's online learning module at journalism.cqpress.com to get access to:

- SKILL BUILDING: Produce a compelling newscast by creating a lineup from a list of available stories and formats. Then check your show against the newscast that was actually produced from that content.

- DISCOVER: Check out examples of effective news promotion.

- EXPLORE: Find more information about the role of TV news producers and links to online tutorials for building your own mobile app.

- A video tutorial on how to create your own Gowalla trip.

- A digital version of this chapter's text in full color with active links.

Also, continue your work on the ONGOING STORY MODULE. Try your hand at writing teases for this story, screen our version and learn more about why it was done this way.

10 DELIVERING THE NEWS

At one time, only television and radio journalists had to concern themselves with telling stories out loud. But in a multimedia world, it could be a part of almost any journalist's job. Print reporters and newspaper photographers often narrate online slide shows and videos. Like their broadcast colleagues, they may appear on camera on television programs or webcasts. And in a 24/7 news environment, everyone may have to go live. In this chapter, we'll discuss what it takes to do all of these things well.

All the reporting, writing and editing you've done on your story can be undone if you don't deliver it well. This is the moment of truth, when your journalism must become storytelling. There's a good reason no child ever asks to be read a bedtime article. People respond to stories, and one key difference between a story and an article or a report is the storyteller. As a storyteller, you want to connect with the audience when delivering the news.

It's not easy to make that connection when voicing a story for television, radio or the Web because the audience is faceless and remote. But if you want your stories to have impact, you have to know how to deliver.

VOICING

Vocal delivery is one of the least-discussed elements of multimedia storytelling, but it's critically important to the way a story comes across to the audience. If you're going to tell a story well on the air or online, you first need to write a script that's designed to be read out loud. But that's just the start. It takes skill and practice to sound both authoritative and conversational when you deliver a script.

Not everyone is born with "great pipes," and that's OK. Barbara Walters and Tom Brokaw, for example, had successful television careers even though they both have minor speech impediments. Your goal should be to make the most out of the voice you were born with and to sound natural when you read a story out loud.

TRADE TOOLS

SOUNDING NATURAL

Anyone who's ever tried to read a script into a microphone knows that it's not as easy as it may seem. Here are some tips on how to improve the way you sound:

- Breathe correctly. If you learn how to breathe with your abdomen, you'll have better breath support—that is, you'll have control over the breath you need to make sounds. Then you won't find yourself pausing at the wrong time because you need to take a breath. And you won't sound bored because your voice will have energy. Try not to move your shoulders when you breathe. It's easier to do this standing up, which is why many reporters and even some anchors read their scripts while standing.

- Take care of your voice. As any singer will tell you, the voice is an instrument. To get the most out of it, you need to care for it. Don't smoke; it may artificially lower your pitch, but in the long run, it can ruin your voice and your health. Be careful not to strain your voice by shouting yourself hoarse or clearing your throat excessively. Either can damage your vocal cords. Avoid milk products before you record or go on the air, and breathe through your nose to avoid drying your throat. Drink lots of water—not alcoholic, caffeinated or carbonated drinks. It may sound unpleasant, but warm water is the best way to keep your throat moist.

- Relax. Tension in your body will show up in your voice. A tense voice tends to be higher in pitch, which is probably something you're trying to avoid. Take a few deep breaths and relax your shoulders before you begin.

- Get professional help. If you believe you need help with articulation (the process of forming sounds) or the resonance or tone of your voice, consider taking a class in voice and diction or working one-on-one with a voice coach. Some people may also have heavy regional accents that could prevent them from getting jobs in some parts of the country. A voice coach may be able to help.

Mental Preparation

As you prepare to record your narration, try not to think about the fact that there's a microphone between you and the audience. In fact, try not to think about the audience at all. Your goal is to communicate as if you're having a conversation with just one person.

Lots of broadcast journalists say they have one specific person in mind when they track—often it's someone older than they are, so their voice has a tone of respect, but it's also someone they know well so they can speak comfortably. Veteran NPR newscaster Carl Kasell liked to imagine he was making a phone call to "Aunt Martha."[1] Some reporters find that actually holding a telephone to their ear while they're reading into a microphone gives them a more relaxed sound.

To put yourself in the right frame of mind to tell your story, think about what you've learned that you're now ready to share. You have to sound like you're interested in telling your story or no one will be particularly interested in listening to it. You're not acting and this isn't a performance, but the way you tell the story should match the content. "The criticism I got early on was that all my stories sounded the same," says reporter Boyd Huppert of KARE-TV in Minneapolis, Minn. "Now when I sit in the booth the first thing I do is think, 'What's this about? Is this happy or sad?' You can go overboard, but over time you find what's comfortable for you."

Physical Preparation

The admonition to warm up your muscles before exercising applies to vocal work as well, as professional singers know. First, relax your neck and jaw by doing neck rolls, smiling and yawning. Take several deep breaths through your nose. Then warm up your vocal muscles by doing a few exercises. Ann Utterback, author of the "Broadcast Voice Handbook," suggests repeating these three phrases 10 times each, and "exploding" every ending consonant: Put a cup. Fat lazy cat. Hot and cold.

Tongue twisters are another good warm-up activity. Repeating the phrase, "You see Oz," in an exaggerated manner stretches the mouth and jaw, Utterback says, and will help improve your delivery.

Avoid drinking coffee or anything with caffeine before you record or go live because it can dry out your vocal cords. To get the energy you may think caffeine provides, do what some athletes do and boost your energy level without getting winded by swinging your arms rapidly for a few seconds or walking in place, lifting your knees as high as possible.

When you're ready to voice, stand and deliver. You'll have better breath support standing up rather than sitting.

Intonation

When you read aloud, you want to put more emphasis on some words than others or you'll wind up speaking in a monotone, sounding uninterested and boring your listeners. The trick is to avoid setting up a rhythm with your emphasis that will result in a singsong delivery. Marking your copy will help you find the right intonation.

Scan your script for words that convey important information, usually the subject, verb and object in each sentence, and underline those words. When you read, give those words a little more emphasis than the rest. Utterback says to choose the words that would help someone understand what the story is about if they're in the kitchen, listening to the TV or radio that's on in the next room. For example, in the following sentence, you would emphasize the words in bold: "A 20-year-old **woman** was seriously **injured** in an **accident** this morning on Route 99." Not: "A **20**-year-old woman was **seriously** injured in an accident this **morning** on Route 99."

There are exceptions to the rule, of course. You might want to emphasize an adverb if it explains what happened. "The man was shaking so **violently** that he dropped the gun." Sometimes, you'll choose to emphasize a word because you want to draw attention to a contrast. "The boy was supposed to wait next to the car, but he was found **under** the car." In this case, you would not emphasize "next to" because there's no reason to draw attention to it.

When you come to the end of a sentence, drop the pitch of your voice. A rising intonation is usually used for a question or an incomplete thought.

Your intonation may also be dictated by the sound bites you use. Pay attention to the words each speaker emphasizes, and adjust your inflection to fit. Huppert reads sound bites out loud before he tracks the narration surrounding the bite. "I read the bite the way I remember the person saying it because that gets me in the right frame of mind," he says. To achieve the same goal, other reporters play back a recording of the bites as they read the script aloud.

GO ONLINE

Module 10: Practice marking up and reading a challenging script.

Pacing

Pay close attention to the speed of your read. You want to pick a pace that sounds and feels natural to you and that's comfortable for the audience. If you read too slowly, you'll sound ponderous; too quickly and you'll sound rushed and anxious. If you find yourself racing through your story so you won't run long, go back and cut your copy. If you tend to be a fast talker, write shorter sentences and you'll slow down. Don't make the audience struggle to understand what you're saying.

117   SOT COOKE 3-30048 "Most Christian television that you see is very low quality, it's
118   not very good. And a lot of people have issues with it. And so we want to bring the best
119   of the production world and the best of the media world in with it, and help people do it
120   more effectively and make more entertaining shows."
121
122   NAT: FAITHLIFENOW (DVD) approx 5:00 You want to be successful, God wants you
123   to be successful…
124
125   **VO This program, for example, doesn't look like your typical TV ministry, and**
126   **that's deliberate. The pastors of Faith Life Church in New Albany, Ohio, tape it in**
127   **their living room:** (DVD)
128
129   2-21208 Drenda Keesee "We had someone approach us about doing Christian TV, and
130   we were hesitant /// 21218 We weren't sure we were, quote, TV people, if you know
131   what I'm saying. We met people who said hey, you need to try this, your message is
132   important and people need this message."
133
134   2-21348 Gary Keesee "If you're gonna consider starting TV, it's gonna take you a
135   couple hundred thousand dollars, the first year, to get started. // We were on the line
136   personally for that money. But in the long run, after the first year---we just finished our
137   first year---actually the show is now paying for itself."
138
139   **VO It pays for itself, as many TV ministries do, through donations and product**
140   **sales. The Keesee's daughter Amy does the pitch.**
141
142   FAITHLIFE VIDEO: "To order Open for Business…"
143
144   **VO Sales of books, DVDs and other products--as opposed to direct appeals for**
145   **money--provide a significant portion of the income for many TV ministries. They**
146   **say they have to raise money to stay on the air, just as public television does. But**
147   **that wasn't always the case.**
148
149   SOT 13-210049 Sheen walks into studio
150

*Deborah Potter marked this script before recording the track for a story for the PBS
program "Religion & Ethics NewsWeekly." Notice the squiggly line marking words she
does not want to stress because they repeat what's just been said in a sound bite.*

Vary your pacing according to the content of your story. Remember, you want to sound as if you're having a conversation, not declaiming a speech. Nobody talks at the same pace all the time. If you've written the way we've suggested, putting the most important word in a sentence at the end, you'll naturally slow down and emphasize that word.

Some reporters say "3-2-1" before each chunk of track—a holdover from the days of tape-to-tape editing when a countdown made it easier to find the next section of narration. It's no longer necessary, and in fact can break your rhythm and throw off your cadence. Try reading start to finish and pause at the punctuation marks, leaving a little space for nat sound.

STAND-UPS

Stand-ups have been around as long as TV news itself. In the early days, they were used to establish that "by golly, a correspondent had been on the scene of the news event [he] just reported," said the late Jim Snyder, who ran TV newsrooms in Washington and Detroit. That's still the most basic, legitimate reason for going on camera—to establish your credibility on the subject. It's also a way for reporters to build a relationship with viewers, giving them a face to put with the voice. But these days, most reporters and photographers try to produce stand-ups that add more to a story than simple presence. A good stand-up can help the audience make sense out of something complicated. A bad one can bring your story to a screeching halt, make you look foolish or give the audience a good reason to tune out.

For simplicity's sake, we'll use the term *stand-up* to refer to any on-camera appearance by the reporter, live or on tape. Live shots do pose some different challenges, and we'll address them separately. But all on-camera segments have one thing in common: They're not easy to do well. Talking to a camera is an unnatural act, and you have to make it look like the most natural thing in the world.

Planning a Stand-Up

Too many stand-ups are an afterthought, thrown together at the end of the day just because the news director insists on seeing the reporter on camera in every story, or the newscast producer needs a live shot for pacing. A stand-up should be an essential part of your narrative, adding new information and moving the story forward. Consider these questions before you do a stand-up:

- Why include a stand-up in this story?

- What information would be conveyed in a stand-up?

- Do I have something to show or demonstrate in this stand-up?

- Where and when might I do this stand-up?

- How will the stand-up fit into the finished story?

Stand-ups can serve several different functions, so it's important to know in advance what you're trying to accomplish with an on-camera segment. You might decide to go on camera to demonstrate something rather than just tell about it, or to show a relationship between two locations more clearly than you could with a pan. For example, when Susan Shapiro, a reporter at WGAL-TV in Lancaster, Pa., was covering a story about a woman who'd been killed by her ex-husband, she started her stand-up outside the man's townhouse. "Bottenfield moved

GO ONLINE

Module 10: Watch and analyze effective stand-ups.

WGAL-TV reporter Susan Shapiro is a master of the active stand-up. To demonstrate how close a murder suspect lived to his victim, Shapiro started her stand-up in front of the man's townhouse, then walked across the parking lot to show where the victim lived.

Source: Photos courtesy of WGAL-TV.

WHY DO A STAND-UP?

Because the location is central to the story.

To establish your credibility on an issue.

To demonstrate an action rather than tell about it.

To show a relationship between locations.

To make a transition between locations, characters, time frames or topics.

To draw more attention to what you are saying.

Because you have no pictures (or graphics) to illustrate your point.

into this complex in Denver just a couple of months ago," Shapiro said on camera, looking back and gesturing at the building. "He was living in that end unit." Shapiro then took a few steps across the parking lot as the camera followed her, while saying, "Even though his ex-wife had once filed for a protection-from-abuse order against him, he moved in just across the street from where she lived."

A stand-up can also be used to prepare the audience for a transition between locations, characters, time frames or topics. And a stand-up may be your last resort when there just aren't any pictures or graphics to illustrate a particular point. By going on camera, you can help the audience understand what they can't see.

Before you shoot any stand-up, you need a clear idea of your story structure. You don't need a complete script, but a mental outline is essential. You need to know where your on-camera segment will fit in the story, whether you're doing a bridge in the middle or a stand-up close. What information will the audience already know before your stand-up? What will they learn immediately after the stand-up? Sometimes, it's helpful to shoot more than one version in case you decide to change the structure. The important thing is to plan a stand-up that is integral to the story, not one that repeats the obvious or comes out of left field.

Memorizing

Preparing to go on camera is similar to preparing to record a narration, with one key difference. Unless you're using a teleprompter, you won't be able to read a script because you'll have to look at the camera. The temptation is to memorize what you want to say, word for word, but that's not the most effective approach. If you memorize your script and then start talking, your brain will be fully occupied with remembering it and you won't really be able to focus on what you're saying.

Rather than worry about saying specific words in a particular order, figure out what you're trying to communicate and then just say it. Whenever you can, rehearse a few times before you roll tape or go live, until you feel comfortable with the content. When shooting stand-ups, do as many takes as necessary to get at least two that are usable—one will be a "safety" or backup you can use if there are any technical problems with the first one. Keeping your stand-up short will improve your odds of success.

Use the same techniques as you would when recording narration so that you'll sound interested in what you're saying. When Lesley Stahl covered the White House for CBS News, she often used the phrase "I have to tell you . . ." in her live on-camera reports. It was a simple device to give her stories energy that was natural, not fake.

Action

"The walk to nowhere" has become a cliché, but you still see it all the time—an on-camera segment in which the reporter moves from one place to another for no apparent reason. Active stand-ups are great, but only if they make sense. Let's say you're doing a story about a recall of contaminated spinach and you want to shoot a stand-up at a super-market. You could push a cart through the produce section and talk about the fact that there's no spinach on the shelves, but your stand-up would be more effective if you simply stood in front of the shelf and pointed out the empty space where the spinach used to be.

Think of a stand-up as your chance to serve as the audience's tour guide. "Use the scene, don't just stand with it behind you," says veteran television reporter Kim Griffis. Show the audience something they might miss. Demonstrate how something works. "Just make sure that whatever is coming out of your mouth directly relates to what you are doing with your hands, feet and eyes," says longtime news director Forrest Carr.[2] And don't overdo it. Some active stand-ups are so artificial and contrived that they get in the way of the story and can even damage the reporter's credibility. Consider the case of a reporter who will remain nameless: For a story about red tide contamination in the Gulf of Mexico, he put on his swimsuit and scuba mask and rose out of the water, dripping wet, to do his stand-up. He certainly got the viewers' attention, but not their respect. You're doing jour-nalism, remember, not theater.

While most news directors harp on the need for active stand-ups, there are times when a static stand-up can be appropriate. It's a well-known fact that people respond to a human face—even tiny babies will turn toward a sketch of a face—so going on camera is a good way to draw attention to what you're saying if it's complicated and nonvisual. "Looking the viewer in the eye and telling them something important can be the best way to do it," says Griffis. "You're saying, 'I'm the expert. Trust me.'"

Shooting Stand-Ups

Good stand-ups obviously require close collaboration between reporter and photographer, but sometimes attitudes get in the way. Reporters who stress out about going on camera and photographers who think stand-ups are all about ego may not communicate as well as they should, especially on deadline. So it's important to start talking through the stand-up options well before crunch time. The photojournalist should be involved in deciding what information would be best delivered on camera, choosing a location and determining how to shoot it.

"I love stand-ups," says television photojournalist Scott Hedeen. "It's one of the few things I can control." He's more than willing to shoot lots of takes on a stand-up until he gets one that's as good as it can possibly be.

GO ONLINE

Ongoing Story Module: Write a stand-up bridge for this story and see the authors' version.

You can add visual interest to a longer stand-up by shooting it from multiple angles. This approach allows the reporter to walk the audience through a complex process or demonstrate how something works by illustrating individual steps in a visual sequence. If you wanted to shoot a stand-up showing the correct way to install a child's car seat, for example, you might want a wide shot of the reporter approaching a car and opening the door, a matched tight shot of the reporter's hand opening the door, a medium shot of the door opening, a shot through the opposite door of the reporter putting the car seat in place, tight shots of belts and buckles being threaded and latched, and a medium shot of the now-installed seat.

Stand-Ups with Graphics

Another way to help viewers grasp important details in a story is to combine a stand-up with graphics. By shooting the stand-up with the reporter off center in the frame, you leave space for text graphics or a map to be inserted in the control room. For example, in a story for WCNC-TV about a public hearing on a new school program, reporter Sterlin Benson Webber included graphics in her stand-up outside the high school where the hearing would be held, reinforcing the ground rules for the evening. The words "Sign up when arrive; Limit to 3 minutes; Only issue," came up on the right side of the screen as she explained the plan in these words: "Parents and students will be allowed to sign up to speak when they arrive here at East Mecklenburg High School's auditorium. But all speakers must limit their comments to just three minutes. And the student assignment plan is the only issue that parents will be allowed to talk about tonight." Rather than using a full-screen graphic, which interrupts the flow of the story, this approach connects the reporter, the location and the details on the screen in one visual image.

Solo Stand-Ups

In Chapter 3 we talked about video journalists (VJs), solo journalists (sojos) or backpack journalists—what some newsrooms still call "one man bands." No matter what you call it, when you work alone you have to shoot your own stand-ups, which is not as easy as it may look.

The first challenge is framing. Once you've decided what you want in the background, you need to make sure you're standing in the right place. Mark Carlson of the Associated Press places his light stand, adjusted to his height, where he intends to do his stand-up. That allows him to check framing and focus before hitting record. He also flips the display screen on his camera so he can see it from in front of the lens. "It doesn't take a rocket scientist to see if you've got a good shot," he says.

Graphics can emphasize important information in a stand-up without breaking the flow of the story. Framing reporter Sterlin Benson Webber off-center in her stand-up left room on the right for bullet points about that night's public meeting.

Source: Photo courtesy of WCNC-TV.

Kevin Torres likes to set his camera on a tripod 20 feet away from where he'll stand and crank up the shutter speed to blur the background. And even though he works alone, he often shoots "walk and talk" stand-ups. "I will shoot a tight shot of my feet walking and then shoot another clip of my full body walking and talking. I'll add the tight shot of my feet to the beginning of the stand-up for sequencing and a little bit of natural sound," he says. By planning a sequence of shots, solo journalists can produce effective show-and-tell stand-ups as well.

Because you can't monitor audio while shooting your own stand-up, it's critically important to play back what you've recorded to make sure it both looks and sounds good.

SOLO STAND-UPS

Chris Mitchell spent seven years as a solo journalist for WMBB-TV in Panama City, Fla., but he still vividly remembers his first day as a reporter-photographer as a "baptism by fire."

"Another reporter showed me how to turn the camera on, how to do a white balance and how to put the tape in," says Mitchell. "Basically, that was it."

Mitchell later trained dozens of reporter-photographers for the station, and he shares this advice for shooting stand-ups on your own:

Source: Photo courtesy of Chris Mitchell.

- Set the tripod up at chest height. Once you put the camera on top, it should be just about right.

- Check to see that your camera is level and then focus in on a point that approximates where you'll be standing.

- Deliver your stand-up, and then check it to see if it's in focus and well framed and that you're happy with the content.

Mitchell says he used to "fret about stand-ups," but actually came to enjoy the challenge of being creative all on his own. For example, in a story about beach renourishment, Mitchell remembers talking with residents who were griping about the color of the new sand. "I framed my stand-up so that you could see me scoop up a handful of sand and then put it directly in front of the lens, so it filled the frame," says Mitchell.

His advice to solo journalists doing stand-ups? "Don't panic, you can do it."

LIVE SHOTS

Going live adds a degree of difficulty to doing stand-ups. There's the pressure of knowing that you have only one chance to get it right, and there's often the stress of having to stay within a strict time limit. Beyond that, the decision to go live may not be made for the best of reasons, leaving reporters fumbling for a way to make their live presence on the air make sense.

The best reason to do a live shot is because something is happening or because you will be demonstrating something while you're on the air. When you're live, the viewer can see what's going on and the anchor can ask pertinent questions. Some reporters will use props when they add to the story. For example, if you are going live from the courthouse for a story on the indictment of a local mayor, you might hold up a copy of the indictment as you briefly describe what the grand jury's decision means to the city. It's also common to use live shots for logistical reasons, when there isn't enough time to get a story edited for air. But a so-called black hole live shot from a scene where nothing is happening can seem pointless, and research shows it can actually alienate viewers.[3] Bear that in mind when planning a live shot. Reporters, photographers and producers should all be involved in deciding when and where to go live, and for what purpose.

But be aware that in some newsrooms the producers are required to have live elements in their newscasts, and often the lead story is presented as a live shot whether or not there is a good reason to be live. So how do you handle what's often called "live for live's sake"? The best advice may be to keep your live presence as short as possible. This will help minimize the chance that the audience will get bored and tune out before you can get to the meat of your story.

Content

As with every other story form, content is key in a live shot. For most routine shots, you will simply be introducing or delivering a preproduced V/O, V/O-SOT or package from the field. In these situations, you will most likely have some time to plan what you want to say on camera.

When you know a lot about a subject, it can be tempting to do a data dump during your live shot, but don't try to tell the audience everything. Instead, figure out the one or two points you want to share about the story, in addition to what's in your preproduced content.

Instead of writing a script for a live shot, many reporters make an outline similar to the "jot outline" we described in Chapter 5. You may also want to include specific numbers and direct quotes from people you're likely to mention in your live shot. Use the notes as a reference if you need them but not as a crutch. Hold the notes out of camera range when possible, and if you have to refer to them, do it deliberately. Looking down and reading a phrase or two from your notes can add credibility to your story; reading more than that can make you look unprepared.

KNOW AND TELL

LIVE SHOTS

Mark Becker has been doing live shots for WSOC-TV in Charlotte, N.C., for more than 20 years. He says one way to bring relevance to a "live-for-live's-sake" shot is "simply to take the viewer back, through the reporter's eyes, to the event or the scene that they covered perhaps hours earlier. Very simply, the reporter is telling what he or she just saw—something that may or may not be on tape—the same way they would excitedly tell a friend or co-worker about something they'd just seen."

Source: Photo courtesy of Mark Becker.

For example, if you are live at 6 p.m. on a major street where there was a terrible accident at 6 a.m., Becker says you could start by showing how traffic is moving now, and then explain how it wasn't for most of the morning rush hour, saying something along these lines:

> Anyone who drives home on Main Street knows how brutal traffic can be, even on a good day. Right now both lanes are packed heading out of town. But at least they're moving. Now imagine this morning, when a lot of these same people were trying to get into work, those two inbound lanes were funneled down into one, all because of a truck that lost control.

Becker says one other way to inject energy into a live shot where something is not going on at the moment is to use the show-and-tell approach. "Often they're called 'active' live shots," he says. "This works well where there's been a fire or an accident—where there is something left behind. A reporter can show the damage, or walk and talk to show how a car lost control, moved from the right shoulder to the median, bent a guardrail and flipped over, with the reporter pointing out skid marks or debris along the way."

CNN's Jeanne Meserve holds her notebook out of camera range in case she needs to refer to it during a live shot.

Source: Photo courtesy of Ken Tuohey.

When you're going live, it's important to explain where you are and why you're there at that particular moment. Don't leave the viewer wondering. Begin your live segment with current information—not a reference to something that happened hours ago or that will happen hours from now. When reporter Bridgette Bornstein was covering a bad storm for KSTP-TV in Minneapolis, Minn., here's how she began her live shot: "In just the last few minutes we have seen light flashes across the river, what appear to be transformers blowing. This afternoon we had rain, it changed to freezing rain, changed to hail, and now what we've got is a light snow."

Interact with the environment the same way you would in a stand-up. For example, Bornstein turned to look across the river behind her when she referred to the light flashes. But be aware that you can't

GO ONLINE

Module 10: Watch and analyze effective live shots.

Beginning a live shot with current information lets the viewer know right away why you are where you are. Reporter Bridgette Bornstein started her live report on a snowstorm for KSTP-TV in Minneapolis, Minn., by looking across the river and describing what she had seen there just minutes earlier.

Source: Photo courtesy of Bridgette Bornstein.

control the environment when you're live the way you can on tape, and you can't simply do another take if something unexpected happens. That means you need to explain the unexpected when you're live, not ignore it. If cheers break out in the middle of your live shot about a multicar accident, explain that you're standing near a soccer field and someone just scored a goal. Otherwise, the audience will be wondering what the cheering was about and miss the point of your story.

The Live Toss

If your live shot is leading into a package, don't be redundant by echoing what the anchor says in introducing you or by repeating what you say at the top of your package. Use the live segment to set the scene or put your story in context. CBS News correspondent Dean Reynolds makes great use of his live "tops," even when there's nothing happening in the shot. Here's an example from a "CBS Evening News" broadcast, anchored by Katie Couric:

COURIC: As the crisis in the Gulf enters a 13th week a CBS News poll out tonight finds more than *half* of Americans disapprove of how President Obama is handling it. And his overall job approval rating is down three points, tying his all-time low of 44 percent. National correspondent Dean Reynolds is in Chicago. Dean, this seems to be the summer of our discontent.

REYNOLDS (live): It does, Katie. Pessimism just permeates this survey along with a sense that the man in charge is not doing enough to alleviate it.

REYNOLDS (voice over): In Batavia, Illinois, social worker Cherie Jones Das has a short wish list for the president.

CHERIE JONES DAS: I'd like to see Obama do more, I really would. I'd like to see him do more to promote jobs.

REYNOLDS (voice over): Indeed, in our new CBS News poll, the economy is seen as the biggest problem facing the country by far, and specifically the lack of jobs.[4]

Couric's intro connects this story to the one that preceded it, about an oil spill in the Gulf of Mexico. Reynolds uses his live segment to establish the focus of the story, and what he says leads seamlessly into his taped report.

The Live Tag and Anchor Questions

Sometimes a producer will ask you to do both a live toss and a live tag, and sometimes you will be asked to do a live tag only. Too often, reporters look at the tag or "live out" as a throwaway, so they spend little time thinking it through.

However, if you think of the introduction as the appetizer and the package or other preproduced element as the main course, then the tag should be the dessert. You can use it to provide an additional interesting and relevant fact or detail, or to set the stage for future stories. For example, in a story about a tornado touching down in your viewing area, you might mention that tomorrow the Federal Emergency Management Agency will be announcing details on how residents can qualify for aid, and that your station will post the information on its website as soon as you get it.

Another element of live reporting is the "anchor question." Sometimes at the end of a live shot, the producer will want the anchor to question the reporter who is on the air live. Unfortunately, not all anchors ask good questions, and not all reporters know as much about their stories as they probably should. The most important thing to remember is that it's OK to say you don't know something or to say, "That's a good question; I'll look into it and work on getting an answer." Then be sure to follow up and report the information later.

To avoid this kind of awkward situation, sometimes the anchor or producer will ask the reporter to provide a good question. Again, think of this as an opportunity to get more information into your story. What else would you like viewers to know that you didn't have time to tell them? If you really have nothing more to say, then you need to make that clear to the producer and anchor as well.

Here's an example of a live tag that added more information to a story. In a major section of southwestern Florida, the Southwest Florida Water Management District manages water use—locally it's known as SWFWMD (pronounced "swift mud" by local journalists). On this day, reporter Chip Osowski of WFLA-TV in Tampa was previewing a SWFWMD vote that could allocate $85 million more to the Tampa Bay Water desalination plant.

OSOWSKI (on camera): If "Swift Mud" does vote to give the money for funding it will be on a performance-based basis meaning if the plant does not perform, the deal will be dead. Gayle. . . .

ANCHOR: And so Chip if the plant does get more funding, how will it be doled out?

OSOWSKI: Well it would be doled out in stages, basically the first 25 percent would be upon an acceptance test, a second payment after the plant had pumped 25 million gallons a day for 4 months, and the final payment would come 12 months later if the plant produces 12 and a half million gallons a day for the first year.

ANCHOR: OK, thanks Chip. That vote is scheduled to be taken at this afternoon's meeting of the water district's managing board in Brooksville. The meeting is open to the public.

Live Only

There are situations, particularly during breaking news, when reporters and sometimes photographers are doing "live only" reporting. There is no videotape relief; it is simply you and the camera working together. In this situation it is critical that you know what you're talking about. In a breaking news situation, this can be particularly challenging, especially if the story is still unfolding and you have very little background information.

If there is action behind you, help viewers understand what they are seeing. For example, you can tell them how many fire trucks are on scene and from which departments, or share how high the flames were when you arrived versus the current situation. As WSOC-TV reporter Mark Becker puts it, "Simply tell what you see and what you hear and what you smell and what you feel."

You might also talk about the information you are trying to gather for the viewer. For example, you might say that when you arrived there were only two fire trucks there, but seven more have arrived in the past 10 minutes and you plan to ask the fire chief to explain what's behind the big boost in resources.

Tell what you know and avoid speculating in these situations. Becker says many reporters try too hard to sound like they know it all when they go on live. "Call it an urge to 'over-report'—to say more than you know for the sake of staying on the air, or to guess at the answer to an anchor's question, rather than look dumb," Becker says. He is adamant that reporters should never assume: "It's frighteningly easy to do when the camera's on, and the pressure's on to beat the competition on a story. It's far better to say 'I don't know' than to guess that someone was killed in the fire because you see people crying in their front yard. It could have been their cat—or it could just be people overwhelmed by the moment."

No matter whether you are live on a breaking story or doing a typical toss to a package, remember the expression, "Every mic is a live mic." Most practicing journalists can tell you a story about reporters or anchors being fired or disciplined for saying something they shouldn't have when they thought the microphone was off. As a rule, you should get into your live position, do a standard mic check and then stand quietly until you hear your cue.

Live Technology

Going live on TV used to require a truck and a microwave or satellite signal to get the story back to the station for broadcast. Obviously, that's no longer the case. Now all you need is a webcam or a smartphone, and even a solo journalist can be live on the air or online in seconds.

The first truck-free live shots used WiFi connections and the voice-over-Internet service Skype to send video signals. The quality wasn't great to begin with, but it improved dramatically and is still a viable option. Wireless cards made it possible to send video from a laptop without an Internet connection, and backpack video uplinks using air cards from multiple cell phone providers have been on the market for several years, allowing the transmission of live video while on the move. Now smartphones are equipped with software applications that allow them to stream live video from almost anywhere.

The ease with which anyone can go live online can be a challenge for journalists. "How do we provide Web content—especially live streaming video—and still carve out time for actual newsgathering to provide perspective for what people are seeing?" asks reporter Jason Whitely of WFAA-TV in Dallas, Texas. "For hurricanes, wildfires, floods and other disasters you want to stop around every bend and shoot something quick to send back." At some point, he says, you have to put the camera or cell phone down and go talk to people to get the full story.

TALKING HEADS

An increasing number of newspapers are requiring their reporters to go on camera these days, often without any preparation. There are plenty of good reasons for print reporters to do "talking head" interviews for their own news organizations' websites or for television beyond the fact that the news organization insists on it. For one thing, you can get the news out to a wider and often younger audience. An appearance on TV may drive readers to the paper or its website. And even those who do read the newspaper might care more about the stories if they know what the reporter looks like. You may wind up getting more news tips from people who see you on the air or in a Web video.

For a television station, interviewing a print reporter may enable the newsroom to add expertise on an important story. For example, many small stations don't have a dedicated political reporter, but the local newspaper may have someone who covers nothing but politics and that person may provide valuable insight when a big political story breaks. In addition, TV newsrooms often interview print journalists for stories that the station doesn't have the resources to cover. For instance, the newspaper may have a reporter assigned to cover a trial that's expected to last months, while the television reporter may be in court only on opening day and when the verdict is due. When a surprise witness shows up halfway through the trial, interviewing the print reporter who's been there since the beginning would be an efficient way for the television station to cover the new developments.

But a print reporter being interviewed about a story has to be careful not to look foolish, appear partisan or become a punching bag for an opinionated host. Not only can that undermine your credibility, it could get you sued. In 2005 the Boston Herald was ordered to pay more than $2 million for libeling a judge. Part of the award stemmed from an appearance the newspaper reporter made on television—specifically on the Fox News program "The O'Reilly Factor."

Preparation

Before you decide whether to say yes to an invitation to go on television, do your homework and prepare carefully. Know the program and the plan. Is this a news program or a "shout fest"? Listen closely to the questions producers ask before you are "booked" for clues to the approach. Are you the only guest? If not, you will want to know who else will be included and what perspectives the other participants will provide.

Will you be in the studio with the host or anchor, or will you appear remotely from your newsroom or another location? If you are new at this and have the option, you may find it easier to be in the studio, where you can interact directly with the host or anchor, versus trying to communicate through a camera lens.

Will the interview be live or on tape? Ask if there will be a setup piece or other information preceding your appearance, and whether any tape will be used during the segment. You'll want to know what information is included so you don't repeat what's already been reported and so you can potentially clear up any contradictions before they occur.

TRADE TOOLS

DOING TV

Whether you are a print reporter learning TV or a beginning broadcast journalist, the following advice can help you do a better job on the air, especially if you have to go live:

- Know your story. Decide on the two or three main points you want to make about your story. Use details and anecdotes to reinforce points after you have made them. Stick with what you know and respond to questions based on your reporting. Don't be afraid to say you don't know something. Avoid being drawn into a debate or speculation.

- Know the setup. Use a monitor or ask the photographer how they're shooting you. Will your hands be in the shot? Look directly at the camera unless told otherwise, but feel free to blink and look down every so often to avoid that frozen deer-in-the-headlights look. Ignore anything going on behind or around the camera and avoid shifting your eyes from side to side—it's distracting and it makes you look unreliable.

- Look good. Dress for TV by avoiding white, large or small patterns and flashy jewelry, especially dangling earrings. You want the viewer to pay attention to your story, not your accessories. The trick from the old movie "Broadcast News" really does work—pull down your jacket in the back and sit on it to avoid lumpy shoulders. Comb that hair and consider using some makeup. If you're shiny, you may look nervous. At a minimum, use some powder.

- Tell your story. Be brief and direct. Speak in short, complete sentences. Be conversational, and don't overload your answers with acronyms, facts or "official-speak." Define your terms. Correct misinformation politely, but do it. Otherwise you may appear to be confirming or agreeing with erroneous comments. And if you goof, correct yourself.

- Assess the results. Ask for a tape of the program or record it yourself and watch your appearance afterwards. Ask your colleagues for some feedback. It may be painful at first, but there's no better way to improve.

Lessons Learned

Michelle Bearden of the Tampa Tribune says she learned about doing TV news the hard way. "On my first day of working for the television station, I thought I was going in to get training. The news director at the station had told me that the producers would be giving me plenty of help and training before I actually went on the air. But when I got to the station, they had assigned me a TV photographer and they were sending me to cover a visit by the Mormon Tabernacle Choir," she says. "I remember it took me 37 takes to do my first stand-up, and I wrote my first script without any sound bites or a natural sound. It was four and a half minutes long because I thought I had to tell the history of the Mormon Church. So my first experience with convergence was trial and error—with a lot more error."

Mark Fagan of the Lawrence Journal-World says he also learned a valuable lesson when he first started doing on-camera reports for the newspaper's cable TV outlet:

> I'm out for breakfast at a local restaurant. As I'm getting ready to pay the bill, the waiter mentions how he likes my new sports coat. "Nice jacket," he says, with a wry smile. "Thanks," I tell him. "Got it for my birthday." The waiter smiles, then lowers the boom: "It's a good thing. A bunch of us in the back had been talking about taking up a collection to get you a new one." Wow. Another lesson learned: Own more than one suit, and make sure it fits. People really do pay attention to such things.

PODCASTING

Broadcast journalists may think they have nothing to learn about recording podcasts and vodcasts. They're just different ways of delivering the news you'd normally do on TV, right? Well, not exactly. Consider how the audience receives what you deliver. Many if not most people listen to podcasts on iPods or other MP3 players, which means they are listening through headphones. That makes podcasting even more intimate and personal than radio. Your voice and the bites and sounds you include in your podcast go right into the listener's ears, so you'll probably want to tone down your delivery. Until you have a good sense of what works, listen to your podcast recordings on headphones and watch your vodcasts on a portable player before posting them.

Print journalists who record podcasts of their stories need to take one additional step and either rewrite their copy so it's easier to read aloud or decide to ad-lib the story. Reading a print story word for word into a microphone usually makes for an awkward-sounding podcast. If you decide to ad-lib instead of rewriting, before you start recording make some notes similar to the jot outline we suggest for live shots.

Keep your interest level up as you record; if you sound bored, you'll bore the audience or lose them. If you're ad-libbing a podcast, try to avoid long pauses. "Dead air" is just as deadly on a podcast as it is on the radio, giving the listener every reason to tune out. And don't um and ah if you can help it. It may be natural in conversation, but it's really annoying in your ear. If you do stumble a lot and you can't re-record, just edit out the worst of it. Your audience will thank you.

PRINT POINTERS

Just as print journalists need to understand the fine points of going on camera, television reporters need to understand what's required of them when they're asked to deliver stories for the newspaper. When you're first assigned a story for the newspaper, find out who your editor will be. Talk to that person before starting to write or, if possible, even before reporting. Find out what's expected of the story in terms of content, length, photos and graphics.

Print newsrooms measure story length in column inches, so you need to know what a 15-inch story adds up to in word count. One column inch is about 20 words, so that 15-inch story would run about 300 words. For comparison's sake, the average TV script that runs 1:30 has about 225 words.

Structure

The story structures we discussed in Chapter 5 apply to both print and broadcast, but there are a few terms to remember when you're writing for print. One is the "nut graf," frequently used in newspaper stories. It's a paragraph that usually comes about three or four paragraphs into the story, right after the anecdotal or descriptive lead; it explains the significance of the lead, and it gives the reader a reason to keep going. Some editors call it the "so what" graf. Here's an example from the Washington Post:

> DALIAN, China—Tian Deren is only 58, but poor eyesight means he must be helped across the street. He also has diabetes and is hard of hearing, so earlier this year a son-in-law brought him to a privately run home for the elderly.
>
> Because he is still mobile, Tian isn't relegated to the fourth floor, where the most infirm residents live and where some have been known to throw cups of tea at the staff. His room is clean; the food plentiful. Life is good, he said.
>
> But like many of China's graying citizens, Tian understands that the elderly are now treated differently than they once were, that the country's modernization and one-child-only policy have shifted assumptions about old age.[5]

The third paragraph clearly states what the story is about and explains the point of telling Tian's story—because it epitomizes how China's treatment of the elderly has changed.

Style

Print style used to be substantially different from broadcast style, but newspapers have adapted much of what's best about broadcast writing. Lead paragraphs that used to run on forever are now shorter and snappier. Sentences are shorter too. So don't stop writing crisp, declarative sentences when you're writing for print.

A few differences persist, however. Attribution comes at the end of a sentence in print as opposed to the beginning in broadcast. For television, you'd write: "Police say the man escaped in a red Toyota," but the print version would be different: "The man escaped in a red Toyota, Lincoln County police spokesman Joe Jones said." Notice that the print version uses a name and title you probably wouldn't mention on the air.

Pay close attention to time references if you're writing for the newspaper. If it happened today and you're writing for the next edition of the morning paper, you obviously can't use a "today" reference. The "Associated Press [AP] Stylebook" suggests you avoid using the words *yesterday* or *tomorrow* in stories and instead use the day of the week. It's probably a good idea for a multimedia journalist to own copies or buy access to a searchable online version of AP's stylebook and other handbooks for both broadcast and print reporting.

David Cuillier, a longtime print journalist, now teaches both broadcast and print students at the University of Arizona. Cuillier says he notices that his broadcast students like to use a kind of sign-off on their print stories, such as, "What happens next, only time will tell." That's a weak ending in any medium, but Cuillier says it definitely does not work in print, where a summary ending is preferred: "It should be something that ties back to the lead, but not an editorialized statement. Often a quote that summarizes the story is used in print."

He suggests that writers start the final paragraph with a one-sentence quote, provide the attribution and then end the paragraph with a short quote, something like this:

"They told me over and over not to play around with guns," Smith said. "Now that Bobby is dead I wish I would have listened."

Cuillier also makes the point that broadcast journalists have the advantage of showing people what's going on with visuals, but print reporters need to show people what's going on with words. "This requires using specifics and facts that illustrate and illuminate. Sometimes people get lazy and just tell what is going on, writing about 'The treacherous river . . .' instead of showing with words: 'The river that has claimed 43 lives in the past decade. . . .' This requires more reporting," Cuillier says.

TAKING IT HOME

The goal of a storyteller in any medium is to communicate effectively, so strong delivery skills are essential. For some journalists, the techniques we've discussed in this chapter come naturally, but most of us can improve our delivery with practice.

Get in the habit of seeking out critiques of your work from someone whose opinion you value. Make it clear to that person that you want an honest assessment of what you're doing well and what needs improvement.

And be sure to regularly evaluate your own work. Once you've completed one or more stories or live shots, review what you've done. Look for at least one thing you've done well that you'd like to repeat and at least one thing you'd like to improve. Some reporters keep a record of their self-critiques to track their own progress. If you already know what you need to work on, you will also be more prepared to get the most out of sessions with a talent coach or mentor.

TALKING POINTS

1. Find the script of a story you've already produced and that you still have on tape. Mark your copy, looking for words that convey important information—usually the subject, verb and object in each sentence—and underline those words. Now read your script out loud, giving the underlined words more emphasis. Record yourself doing this if at all possible. Now go back and listen to your old story. Have you improved? Did you notice any other delivery issues? Get in the habit of listening to yourself regularly so you can work on getting better.

2. You are assigned to a story about a new study showing fluorescent lighting is contributing to eyestrain and other concentration problems in many classrooms and offices. Develop several ideas for demonstrative or interactive stand-ups you might do for this story.

3. Choose a story you've already reported and feel you know well. If you were assigned a live shot on this story, which two or three main points would you make? Make notes or create a jot outline for a live shot. Deliver it for an audience and ask for a constructive critique.

ONLINE LEARNING MODULE 10

Activate or buy this chapter's online learning module at journalism.cqpress.com to get access to:

- SKILL BUILDING: Test your delivery by recording challenging copy, and see how marking your script improves the end result.

- DISCOVER: Check out examples of strong stand-ups and live shots.

- EXPLORE: Find resources to help you improve your on-air delivery and write strong stories for print.

- Tips from professional journalists to help you improve your delivery and stand-ups.

- A digital version of this chapter's text in full color with active links.

Also, continue your work on the ONGOING STORY MODULE. Try your hand at writing a stand-up bridge for this story, screen our version and learn more about why it was done this way.

CHAPTER 11 MULTIMEDIA ETHICS

As journalism evolves, so does journalism ethics. With the advent of television, ethical discussions about what video to show and what not to show in a television newscast became part of the routine for broadcast journalists. As the Web and social media took on the role of news and information provider, some old ethical problems became more complicated and some entirely new ethical issues were raised. As we begin our exploration of these issues, it's important to remember that we can never anticipate all the ethical dilemmas a journalist will face. We can only strive to develop a system of ethical decision making.

"Reading about ethics is about as likely to improve one's behavior as reading about sports is to make one into an athlete." The author of that quote, Mason Cooley, was a 20th century aphorist, someone who specializes in summarizing complex truths or ideas in a few words. Though it's doubtful that Cooley was talking about journalism ethics, there is some truth to the idea that you can never become ethical simply by reading about ethics. You have to think about ethics and practice making good decisions in order to behave ethically.

Journalism ethics cannot be compartmentalized into a single course or capsulated in a set of rules. Ethics is and should be an ongoing discussion.

THINKING ABOUT ETHICS

Ethics is sometimes defined as "motivation based on ideas of right and wrong." Take a moment to study that phrase. Notice that it doesn't say ethics is defined as "motivation based on what is right and wrong." It says ethics is motivation based on "ideas" of right and wrong. That's an important distinction because making ethical decisions is not necessarily about coming up with the "right" answer, but rather it's about coming up with a defensible answer.

Ethics Codes

Print, broadcast and online news media share many of the same ethical principles. Most news organizations, regardless of platform, support the Society of Professional Journalists' Code of Ethics:

1. Seek truth and report it. Journalists should be honest, fair and courageous in gathering, reporting and interpreting information.

2. Minimize harm. Ethical journalists treat sources, subjects and colleagues as human beings deserving of respect.

3. Act independently. Journalists should be free of obligation to any interest other than the public's right to know.

4. Be accountable. Journalists are accountable to their readers, listeners, viewers and each other.[1]

GO ONLINE

Module 11: Examine ethics codes and other ethical decision-making resources.

Despite agreement on general ethical principles, organizations such as the Radio Television Digital News Association and the National Press Photographers Association have created their own ethics codes that seek to address some of the specific challenges faced by journalists in the broadcast industry or by photojournalists. CyberJournalist.net, a website that focuses on how the Internet and new technologies are changing the media, has created a Bloggers' Code of Ethics to help guide people using this reporting form. Print organizations like the American Society of News Editors and the Associated Press Managing Editors have also developed codes to help guide print journalists.

The number one principle to seek truth is at the very foundation of all journalism ethics. Journalists should always strive to report the most accurate version of a story possible. At the same time, we must take into account the impact of our work on the people we cover, free ourselves as much as possible from internal or external influences and always be willing to explain our actions to the communities we serve. Though you may not convince your viewer or reader that you made an ethical choice, you must at least be able to explain how you reached your decision. That will satisfy some people and, at the very least, your audience will know that the choice was not made arbitrarily. You can reassure them that a great deal of thought went into the decision-making process.

On the surface, it may not look so difficult to abide by these principles. Of course, journalists should seek the truth and treat their sources with respect. But often the principles themselves are in conflict. Journalists who seek the truth may discover information that will be hurtful to the family of a person involved in wrongdoing. A reporter's membership in a nongovernmental organization may permit that reporter to learn more about a story the group is involved with, but that membership may also compromise the reporter's independence and be difficult to justify to the audience. In many cases, making an ethical decision means choosing not between right and wrong but between right and right.

MULTIMEDIA ISSUES

Along with new storytelling opportunities, multiplatform journalism brings new ethical challenges. J. D. Lasica, former senior editor of the Online Journalism Review, says these can be grouped into three broad categories: gathering the news, reporting the news and presenting the news. In this chapter, we'll look at all three. For example, when you as a multimedia journalist are gathering the news, is it OK to ask permission to record an interview without making it clear that you will also be posting the audio on the Web? You can report the news much more quickly online, but greater speed can also lead to greater risk for error. We'll explore standards of accuracy online and in social media, and the issue of how corrections are handled. Plus, the line between advertising and news is often blurred even more in the online world; we'll look at how sponsorships and other advertising-supported content are handled across platforms.

The operational differences among broadcast, online and print media can affect their ethical decision making. For example, TV and online media both deal with pictures and sound, but the nonlinear capability of the Web lets users choose whether to click through to view a graphic photo or listen to a disturbing audio clip. Broadcast journalists can warn the audience that the pictures they're about to see are graphic, but a newspaper can't alert you to a potentially troubling photograph if it's published on the front page.

The big questions arise when a news organization must decide if its ethical principles are uniform across platforms. If your editorial decision makers believe a graphic is too disturbing to use in the newspaper, is it OK to post it online because the user can choose to view it or not? Or do you need to have ethical policies that are consistent, no matter what medium you use to disseminate the information? This chapter highlights some of the decision-making challenges you'll face as an ethical journalist in a converged media environment.

Corrections

Most newspapers and television stations around the country have policies on how to handle mistakes that make it into the paper or on the air. You're probably familiar with the "corrections box" that occasionally appears somewhere in most newspapers. The goal is to alert readers to any errors that were made in the paper's previously published stories.

KNOW AND TELL

CORRECTING MISTAKES

A wag once said that being a journalist means never having to say you're sorry. Emerson Stone begs to differ. The former vice president for news practices at CBS News says if it's important enough to report, it's important enough to correct when you get it wrong. This is Stone's 10-point plan for stations wishing to develop or fine-tune a corrections policy:

Source: Photo courtesy of Emerson Stone.

1. Welcome all who point out your mistakes. Thank them. That sage old Dean, Jonathan Swift (1667–1745), wisely wrote: "A man should never be ashamed to own he has been in the wrong, which is but saying in other words that he is wiser to-day than he was yesterday."

2. No matter is too trivial to correct. See the New York Times' daily corrections of matters as (supposedly) minor as the spelling of names. Those who hear, see or read the news and, out of their own knowledge, perceive a small mistake that goes uncorrected, must ask themselves, "What larger errors do they make that go uncorrected? Can I trust anything they report?"

3. Don't wait. Make the correction on air as soon as its accuracy has been checked.

4. Correct in equivalent news programs. Evening News corrections go in the Evening News, and so on. (You probably don't have the same audience at 11 p.m. and at 5 a.m., so correcting a late-night error in the morning may not do much good.)

Many TV newsrooms have rules that say a correction must be aired as soon as the mistake is confirmed, and some go as far as to say the correction must air again in the same newscast as the mistake was originally made. For example, if the city budget deficit is reported in error at 6 p.m. on Monday, and the error is discovered at 8 p.m. that same evening, most newsrooms will air a correction in the next scheduled newscast at 10 or 11 p.m.; some will even air the correction a second time at 6 p.m. on Tuesday. The goal

5. Avoid burying corrections. Make the correction as prominent in the broadcast as the original error, not thrown away or glossed over.

6. Be complete. That means full and clear, including the statement that it is a correction, from which broadcast, who made the error and how it came about. Doesn't hurt to add that you regret it.

7. Tell the whole truth. Procedures like the one directly above sound as if you don't want to tell viewers on the air: "I was wrong; here's how, when, and why." On air, of course, is exactly where corrections are most vital. Responsibility is the key word.

8. Be attuned to catching errors. All staff members need to learn to welcome and get full details of any communication, phoned or written, that alleges an error or states a correction. That information then goes to the proper person for checking and action.

9. Respond directly to complaints. A polite response should go to anyone who alleges an error, once the allegation is checked out and has been properly dealt with, regardless of whether the information was right or wrong.

10. Lose the attitude. It is time that we put behind us the days of circling the wagons against claims of error; time to cease those brusque I-haven't-got-time telephone cutoffs or we-stand-by-our-story letters of response. Make some time; get back to the caller promptly, if you really can't talk now. Check out the allegation. Respond by letter if that's the best way. Do the necessary. And again: correct any mistake on the air. (I know: The networks don't do it. Do it.)

Source: "Correcting Mistakes," NewsLab, October 1, 2009, www.newslab.org/2009/10/01/how-to-develop-a-corrections-policy.

is to make sure the correct information reaches the widest possible audience, as well as to let people know that accuracy matters to the news organization.

Online Policies

Things get a little trickier in the Web world. Some online journalism outlets have no formal policy at all for handling corrections. When an error is identified, some organizations simply remove the inaccurate information from the site. Unfortunately, if any online news consumers have read the story earlier in the day, they have been misinformed. Even if they return to the story later, they're not alerted to the fact that what they read earlier was wrong. Most reputable journalism sites do include a correction notice to users somewhere in the story or near it, but policies on how prominent the correction must be vary from organization to organization.

As more and more journalists disseminate information online, the question becomes whether corrections policies should be consistent across media platforms. Take Web archives, for example. Many online newspaper sites archive stories exactly as they appeared in the printed paper's final edition, including any errors. If a correction is necessary, it is indicated at the top of the story or published in a separate box. These news organizations believe that the website archive should be the official record of what was published. But a small number of papers have determined that the online archive should include the most accurate version of the story possible. They have developed systems to make the changes necessary to correct a story in the archive. For example, if a suspect's name is misspelled in the printed publication, it will be spelled correctly in the online archive. At the top of the story is a statement noting that the original published version contained an error that has now been corrected. Sometimes the statement will include specifics on exactly what was corrected, sometimes it will not. This approach minimizes the chance that someone will miss the corrections box or notification and republish or simply read inaccurate information. But the story is now altered; it is no longer a record of what was in the paper. So which approach is the most ethical?

One solution is simply to make your news organization's online corrections policy clear to your users. The San Francisco Chronicle's home page includes a link to "Corrections." This page explains the paper's policy to "promptly correct errors of fact and to promptly clarify potentially confusing statements" and includes an e-mail address for reporting errors. That's being transparent—sharing your news organization's policy with the people using your site.

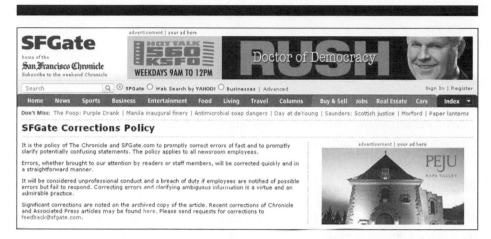

On its website, SFGate.com, the San Francisco Chronicle promises to "promptly correct errors of fact and to promptly clarify potentially confusing statements." The paper notes "significant" corrections on the archived copy of articles.

Source: SFGate.com, www.sfgate.com/pages/corrections (accessed July 8, 2010).

Transparency and Bias

Telling people what you've decided and how you arrived at that decision is one way that news organizations are accountable for their decisions, and it can be helpful in dealing with many ethical dilemmas. Convergence and multiplatform journalism, however, can make things more complicated.

Imagine that you are working in a television newsroom and that your station is a major sponsor of a local golf tournament. Part of the sponsorship agreement is that your sports anchor will have exclusive, pretournament access to interviews with the big-name golfers coming to town. First of all, is there anything wrong with that? Is this an example of paying for a news story? There are no restrictions on what can be asked or used from the interview, but is this an ethical way to gather the news? What if the station's newspaper partner asks your anchor to write a print story from the pretournament interview with star golfer Tiger Woods? Does the station need to make sure the paper knows why the sports anchor is getting an exclusive? Do the viewers and readers need to know? If you don't reveal the nature of the sponsorship agreement, and it eventually comes to light, how

GO ONLINE

Ongoing Story Module: Handle an ethical problem that may require you to change a major part of the story you've created.

might the audience react? This scenario is not at all far-fetched, but the audience is rarely made aware of situations like this when they occur.

If you make the details of a sponsorship agreement clear to everyone involved—both those within the news organizations and the audiences—then you remove the risk of being accused of deception. As an added bonus, the mere act of revealing the arrangement to others may force people in your own news organization to question whether this is an appropriate agreement. That process can help you defend your position if you receive criticism after the arrangement is revealed.

Interview Agreements

Most television reporters have had the experience of spending hours, or even days, coaxing someone into giving them an interview, just to hear this: "Oh, you're not planning to put me on TV, are you?" In fact, it's not even unusual to conduct an entire interview with lights, camera and microphone and then have the interviewee say, "Now, this isn't going on the air, is it?" Some television reporters have developed a habit of prepping interviewees on the front end by making it clear that the information provided will be used in a newscast. That way the reporters don't waste time and effort getting someone to agree to an interview they might not be able to use on the air.

So, in a multiplatform world, do we owe our interviewees the courtesy of informing them of all the ways that we will be using their words and actions? Print reporters sometimes ask interview subjects for permission to record the audio of an interview. When the interview subject OKs the recording, do you think it is with the understanding that it could be used for more than just taking notes? In fact, those recordings could be posted online or aired on a news broadcast. Should the reporter make that clear to the interviewee?

Should TV reporters who plan to write an online version of their television story make their intent clear to everyone they talk to? It's certainly possible that someone would be willing to talk to a local TV station but not want friends or relatives in other cities to be aware of that fact. However, if the story is posted online, it's accessible to anyone with a computer and Internet access. For example, a lesbian may be quite open about her sexuality with friends and co-workers in Dallas, Texas, but she may not have discussed the issue at all with her family in Little Rock, Ark. If she doesn't know the story is going online, she may feel it's safe to talk to a local news organization about her feelings as a lesbian regarding a proposed same-sex marriage amendment. But she might be quite disturbed to learn that the story is available online where it can reach a much wider audience, including people back home in Arkansas.

If you consider that two of journalists' primary ethical principles are to minimize harm and to be accountable, it seems clear that multimedia journalists should provide the people they cover with as much information as possible about the ways in which the information they share will be used.

Links

The nature of online journalism also makes it necessary to discuss the ethics of linking the user to information that's been created by others—some of which may be biased. Let's say you're doing a story on the increase in hate crimes in your community. One of the people included in your story is a member of the Creativity Movement, which believes Caucasians are meant to rule the world. Do you link to the organization's Web page to offer people more information about it? If so, do you also need to link to a site that condemns such groups? Would you embed the links in your news story or place them in a box along-side the text? News organizations have different policies about what types of links they will and won't provide. Many believe the best solution is to clearly identify each link for users and provide a warning if it links to potentially offensive content to make sure users know where they are going and what they'll see when they click on it. At that point, the user can make an informed choice.

ADVERTISING AND PUBLIC RELATIONS

To attract viewers and readers as well as advertisers, news must be credible. But good journalism and economic goals can sometimes conflict. News organizations risk damaging the foundation of their business if they produce or avoid news stories to please sponsors, or solicit or place advertising or PR content in a way that weakens the integrity of their news operation. Holding the line to protect the integrity of the news product has become increasingly challenging in the digital world.

Infomercials and Advertorials

Both television stations and newspapers may sometimes produce special products simply as advertising vehicles. Broadcasters create programs, such as back-to-school specials, to attract advertising dollars to the station, and they use the resources of their news staffs to produce the specials. The advertisers typically have no direct control over the content, but the show will certainly feature content that is advertiser friendly. The program most likely will not include any hard-hitting investigations.

In the newspaper business, many papers hire writers from outside the newsroom to produce the content for their special sections, and in that way they avoid any appearance of having their newspeople writing paid content. But the line between advertising and news copy can be blurry in print. The Los Angeles Times drew criticism in 2009 for letting NBC buy a front-page ad for the TV show "Southland" that was written and designed to look like a news article. About 100 Times employees signed a petition protesting the ad.[2] The controversy eventually led to the resignation of the newspaper's executive editor. A year later, the paper sold its entire front page to the Walt Disney Company to promote the movie "Alice in Wonderland." The ad featured a photo of the actor Johnny Depp superimposed on what appeared to be the front page of the newspaper, complete with masthead, headlines and copy that were actually fake. The editorial board reportedly opposed the ad but was overruled by business executives.[3]

But what happens in a converged environment? Is it OK for the newspaper's education reporter to appear in the sponsor-driven television special? Although most print, broadcast and online journalists strive to be ethical, what's acceptable in one medium may or may not be in another.

Most traditional media have very strict policies regarding the presentation of advertising content. Many television stations air "infomercials"—programs devoted to promoting some product or service to the viewers. Some are even designed to look like news programs, but viewers are often notified throughout the show that they are watching paid programming—in other words, not something produced by the station's news staff.

On the print side, there are "advertorials"—advertisements that are designed to look like a news article or editorial regularly published in the paper. These advertorials are identified with a line of type at the top of the story that usually says "Advertisement," although the size of the type may be so small that it's easily missed.

On the Web, the rules appear to be a little less clear. Take the case of a $10 million Web advertorial campaign paid for by Sony. According to Sony, the stories were written by freelance journalists, and they featured real consumers describing how technology was affecting their everyday lives. One thing that made the content controversial was the "Related Links" section. As Consumer WebWatch discovered, users who clicked to find out more about the technologies described in the articles found themselves exposed to Sony products only. Some of the sites that posted the content published it under the heading of "News," identified it only with the words *feature by Sony* and didn't use the word *advertising* at all.[4] So is it OK for a news site to post this kind of content? Should there be specific guidelines about where the content should appear and how it should be

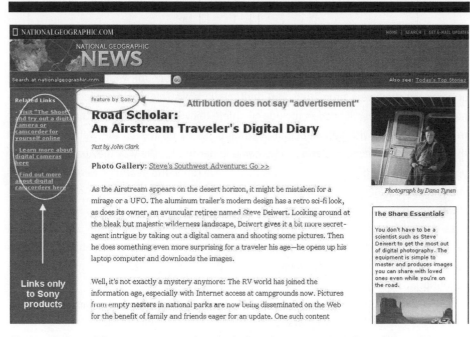

Nationalgeographic.com was one of several sites that ran content from Sony without noting that it was a paid "advertorial." All of the links in what was described as a "feature" led to Sony products.

Source: Nationalgeographic.com, http://news.nationalgeographic.com/sonydigitallifestyles/ (accessed July 8, 2010).

identified? The American Society of Magazine Editors suggests this guideline: "On all online pages, there shall be a clear distinction made—through words, design, placement, or any other effective method—between editorial and advertising content."

Now that most news organizations are on the Web as well as in print or on air, it's probably time for them to develop converged editorial guidelines, so that identification of editorial versus advertising content will be as consistent as possible across platforms. In the case of the TV education special, for example, such guidelines would require that the program's sponsorship be clear to the viewer and to the newspaper's education reporter. If an online product was created in conjunction with the special, the sponsorship would be clearly identified there too. The goal would be to define the line between advertising and news content as clearly as possible for all involved.

Multimedia News Releases

Journalism isn't the only profession trying to understand and capitalize on the power of multimedia. For many years, public relations practitioners have blanketed newsrooms with paper news releases in the hopes of getting positive coverage for whatever event, product or company they were promoting. But multimedia news releases are becoming increasingly common. These kits often include complete television news stories that stations are free to run, along with supplemental information to be posted on the Web or printed in the newspaper. Television stations have come under fire for the way they have used video news releases (VNRs). In some cases, stations have run VNRs as if they were regular news stories, without any attribution at all. And the problem is not unique to broadcast newsrooms; there are plenty of examples of newspapers printing press releases without changing a word. Of course, the problem with this is that the news organization usually has not verified the information in the story or alerted the audience to the fact that the story is coming from a nonjournalistic source, leaving the news organization open to charges of deception.

The Radio Television Digital News Association's Code of Ethics and Professional Conduct states that professional electronic journalists should "clearly disclose the origin of information and label all material provided by outsiders." The group has also created a series of guidelines to help news organizations determine when it's appropriate to use VNRs and when it is not.[5] One of the most important is that news organizations use VNRs only when there is no other way to get the video and the story has clear news value.

Many news organizations have also developed their own policies, which usually include a requirement that the source of the story be clearly identified both verbally and visually. For example, in a story about a new kind of poultry processing, you might not be allowed inside the plant to shoot your own video. In that case, you might include the following line of copy in your story: "As you can see in this video from Tyson Foods, the new machines will change the way each chicken is cleaned." In addition to the verbal reference, you would also want to add a graphic "super" over the video, which would identify the source: Tyson Foods. If you were to use the video online, attribution would be important there as well.

This kind of transparency is essential because it alerts the audience to the fact that you have been unable to verify the accuracy of what you're showing them. What if the machine malfunctions routinely? Certainly, that would not be a part of the news release, so sharing the source of the video allows viewers to apply a healthy amount of skepticism to what they're seeing.

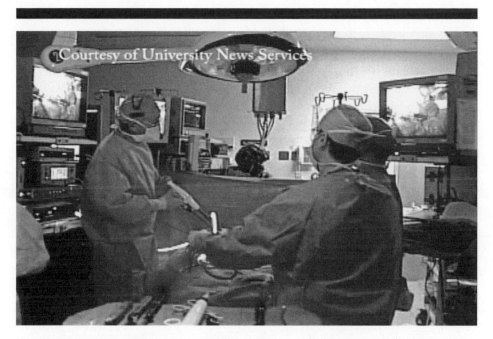

The student-produced newscast at Virginia Commonwealth University has a strict policy of identifying the source of any video not gathered by students involved in the show.

Source: Courtesy of Virginia Commonwealth University School of Mass Communications.

PLAGIARISM AND COPYRIGHT

Although plagiarism is clearly not unique to online journalism, it's so easy to cut and paste information found on the Web that it may be tempting to steal another person's words. However, one word will always protect you from this most egregious of journalism's sins: *attribution*. Make sure that any time you pull information from another source you identify the source for your reader.

At Emory University in Atlanta, the journalism program has a plagiarism statement on its website:

> In journalism, source citations are included in the body of the story. The credit should include the name of the person or source, a person's affiliation, and any other information that provides necessary context. The journalist provides attribution for all direct and indirect quotes and paraphrased information and

statements. Quotation marks are used even if only a word or phrase of a statement is used. Journalists attribute to specific individuals, organizations or sources and do not create composite sources.

Both direct quotations and paraphrases require attribution. A good paraphrase expresses the ideas found in the source (for which credit is always given) but not in the same words. It preserves the sense, but not the form, of the original. It does not retain the sentence patterns and merely substitute synonyms for the original words, nor does it retain the original words and merely alter the sentence patterns. It is a genuine restatement. It is briefer than its source.[6]

KNOW AND TELL

FIGHTING PLAGIARISM

The Poynter Institute's Roy Peter Clark has been tracking plagiarism cases in journalism for more than 20 years. He offered this background and advice in an online column:

The word plagiarism means "kidnap," and each word-snatch has its own peculiar characteristics. But some patterns repeat themselves time and again.

Source: Photo courtesy of Kenny Irby.

1. Almost all cases of serious plagiarism are intentional.

2. Serious plagiarism by adults is a moral flaw, not an ethical one.

3. Not all cases of plagiarism are equal.

4. With guidance, supervisors can exercise discretion and match punishments to the severity of the crime.

5. There are special cases in journalism that require special attention, the articulation of standards and practices, and, yes, training.

6. The Internet complicates all of this. Veteran journalists from Spain complained to me of younger reporters who practiced a kind of cut-and-paste journalism from the comfort of their computer chairs.

Suzy Hansen reports in the New York Times that 40 percent of college students admit to Internet plagiarism.

Students know that plagiarism can lead to grades of F or expulsion from school; professional journalists should know that plagiarism can lead to firing and disgrace.

Fair Use

In addition to understanding how to properly attribute material, you should also familiarize yourself with the laws surrounding the use of copyrighted material. Essentially, anything that appears in a broadcast or is published is considered copyrighted. So if you pull information from another news source, you are using copyrighted material. That's not

So what's an editor to do?

1. Announce to your staff that plagiarism is a serious problem in all of journalism, and that you assume there will be cases in your newsroom.

2. Insist that serious plagiarism is a firing offense.

3. Publish these, review them every year, make them part of any orientation of new staffers.

4. Develop training sessions on "the tools of originality," with particular attention to note taking, file keeping, methods of attribution and the Internet.

5. Without creating a "rat squad," let staffers know that they can blow the whistle on malpractice in confidence.

6. Train editors how to act on such complaints from both inside and outside the newsroom.

7. Consult with a company about using computer technology to conduct random plagiarism checks on reporters' work.

8. Pray.

9. Pray.

10. Pray.

11. Pray.

Source: Adapted from Roy Peter Clark, "The Global War on Plagiarism: Fighting the Pirates of the Press," Poynter-Online, August 26, 2004, www.poynter.org/content/content_view.asp?id=70511. Used with permission of Roy Peter Clark and the Poynter Institute Website: www.poynter.org.

always illegal, however. The United States Copyright Office states on its website that the doctrine of "fair use" permits news organizations to use copyrighted material from an outside source without permission, but only under certain circumstances.

In general, these factors are used to determine fair use:

- The purpose and character of the use, including whether such use is of commercial nature or is for nonprofit educational purposes.

- The nature of the copyrighted work.

- Amount and substantiality of the portion used in relation to the copyrighted work as a whole.

- The effect of the use upon the potential market for or value of the copyrighted work.[7]

In other words, if your state's governor appears on ABC's "Nightline" and makes a controversial statement about working women neglecting their children, you would clearly want to report that information. If you work for an NBC affiliate, you would obviously want to use the video clip of the governor's statement and the fair use doctrine would allow you to do that. However, fair use would likely not allow you to rebroadcast the entire "Nightline" program on your TV station or website. Most legal experts believe the critical issue is to see that no more of the copyrighted work was used than completely necessary to achieve the news-reporting purpose, so you must keep that in mind when you are taking information from another source, even with attribution.

Creative Commons

Some content producers have made it easier for journalists and others to use their material by making it available under what's called a Creative Commons license. This system was created in 2001 by Lawrence Lessig, among others, who believed traditional copyright laws were too restrictive. The Creative Commons organization offers different types of licenses that allow owners to decide how their work can be used. For example, some content can be used only if it's attributed to the person who produced it, or only for noncommercial uses, or only if the original work is used in its entirety and not modified.

The Arabic news channel Al Jazeera used a Creative Commons license to create a repository of footage available online. It allows other media organizations to use the footage provided they attribute it to Al Jazeera, do not use it for commercial purposes and do not create derivative works or mash-ups using the footage.

DIGITAL MANIPULATION

Just as ethical journalists do not make up quotes or steal other people's information, they do not manipulate photos, video or audio in a way that could mislead the audience. Advances in digital hardware and software have made it easier than ever before to manipulate images and sound in a way that changes the reality of what was there.

GO ONLINE

Module 11: Walk through a series of case studies that will test your ethical decision making.

In August 2006, for example, a freelance photographer who had worked for Reuters for 13 years was fired after it was determined that an image he provided to the news agency had been digitally manipulated to make it look like Israeli war planes had done more bomb damage in Beirut than they actually had. This kind of digital manipulation is often called "photoshopping," and it can be a problem with video as well.

Video

Digital editing makes it easy to reverse an image or a camera move. If you shot a tilt down of a building but a tilt up would work better for your story, many editors think it's OK to reverse the video. But be careful. More than one editor has been caught manipulating images when the words on a baseball cap wound up appearing backwards on the screen.

Using slow motion or other effects can make a statement about your subject that you may or may not intend. For example, some research has found that using slow-motion video makes a criminal suspect look guilty. Your reason for using slow motion may be a lack of video, but you should be aware of the unintended impact. One television editor decided to add a sparkle effect in a story about the recovery of a lost diamond ring. The result was laughable.

The National Press Photographers Association bylaws include this statement about the ethics of digital manipulation:

> As photojournalists, we have the responsibility to document society and to preserve its images as a matter of historical record. It is clear that the emerging electronic technologies provide new challenges to the integrity of photographic images . . . in light of this, we the National Press Photographers Association, reaffirm the basis of our ethics: Accurate representation is the benchmark of our profession. We believe photojournalistic guidelines for fair and accurate reporting should be the criteria for judging what may be done electronically to a photograph. Altering the editorial content . . . is a breach of the ethical standards recognized by the NPPA.[8]

Audio

"Cleaning up" sound bites by taking out "ums" and "ahs" and making internal edits used to be common practice in some newsrooms to save time or to make stories flow better. It's difficult but not impossible to cut audio from the middle of a bite without distorting the meaning. But these days, when the same audio is often available from lots of different sources, it's easy for listeners to compare an edited version to the original. And that can raise questions about why the edits were made.

(top) This photo of the Bluffton University baseball team appeared on page A-1 of the Toledo Blade on March 31, 2007, and on toledoblade.com. It was discovered to have been digitally altered and should not have been published. The photographer digitally removed the legs of a person standing behind the number 19 banner.

(bottom) This is the photograph that should have been published, as it represents a true view of what was happening at the time the photo was taken on March 30, 2007. The staff photographer resigned a few days after the altered photo was discovered.

Source: The Blade's policy is to never alter photographs, and these two photos are reprinted with permission of the Blade of Toledo, Ohio, for instructional purposes.

In April 2007 the Toledo Blade published a full-page explanation of an ethical lapse involving the newspaper. The paper discovered that one of its staff photographers had digitally altered dozens of photos over a period of several months.

The BBC found itself in hot water over its editing of President Barack Obama's 2009 inaugural address. What viewers heard appeared to be one sentence: "We'll restore science to its rightful place, [and] roll back the specter of a warming planet. We will harness the sun and the winds and the soil to fuel our cars and run our factories." An alert blogger noticed that the bite was actually created from three separate sentences in the speech; the segment about rolling back the specter of a warming planet was moved up several paragraphs and inserted between two sentences in an earlier paragraph. Left out was a line that immediately followed that segment: "We will not apologize for our way of life." The clip that aired left the impression that Obama had a more coherent climate policy than he may actually have had in mind.[9]

What if you captured great sound and the picture that goes with it is bad? Is it permissible to use that sound over a different picture? Many journalists would say yes, as long as it does not mislead the viewer. For example, if you used the sound of gunfire over a wide shot taken a few seconds before or after the shooting, the meaning would not change. If you used it over a tight shot of someone crying, the implication would be that the person cried because of the shooting, which could distort the truth of the scene.

Adding sound that wasn't captured on the scene can also be deceptive. One local station used sound effects in a story about a shooting, putting a gunshot in the audio track each time the video cut to a close-up of a bullet hole. The result suggested that the station had been present when the shooting occurred.

Some news organizations see nothing wrong with adding recorded music to a story, but the practice can be controversial. Music tends to evoke emotion, and adding music to a news story can enhance or change its impact. Some newsrooms have guidelines requiring that all sound used in a story must have occurred while it was being shot.

BLOGGING

Not too many years ago, journalists around the country were asking themselves whether it was OK for a journalist to write blogs at all. That was at a time when people were confusing the mechanism with the message. Blogs are simply a way to present information; there is nothing inherently unethical or biased about blogs. Many journalists are now expected to blog on their news organizations' websites in addition to writing news stories. Still, journalists must take care to use blogs properly.

Blogs have helped news organizations be more transparent about their decision making. The editor of the Sacramento Bee, for example, often uses her blog to discuss what goes on behind the scenes. By including comments from readers, these types of blogs give the public an open forum to hold the news organization accountable for its actions.

Style and Content

Blogs are typically written less formally than news stories, often in first person with a distinct voice. Journalists who allow their personalities to come through on blogs often find they get a better response from readers, who begin to see them as "real people" and not just bylines. But it can be a delicate balancing act to show a human side while maintaining enough detachment to avoid charges of bias or unfairness. And too much "attitude" on a blog risks alienating some readers of the core news product.

Many blogs are like opinion columns in a newspaper. According to the book "The Elements of Journalism," you must keep three criteria in mind when expressing opinion or editorial comment:

1. What you report must be verified and truthful.

2. You must make it clear to your audience what your views and biases are.

3. You must remain independent from the people or issues you cover.[10]

So, in the case of a reporter covering a trial, it would be inappropriate for a blog entry to say whether the reporter-blogger thought the defendant was guilty, but the reporter-blogger might be justified in writing about how well the trial was going for the defendant, an observation that would be based on direct observations of the jury's reaction to certain testimony. And that's only if the reporter-blogger had no relationships with any of the people involved in the trial and was not personally vested in the outcome. It might be inappropriate for a journalist to serve on the board of local battered women's shelter and then report on a domestic violence trial. It's a fine line, and one journalists should walk very cautiously.

Personal Views

Many journalists keep personal blogs in addition to those they write for work, raising the potential for conflict of interest. Can a journalist who covers the automotive industry maintain a blog for Corvette lovers, for example? Most ethicists will say it depends. "I think the automotive reporter should be circumspect about what opinions he or she offers on the site," says Gary Hill, former chair of the Ethics Committee for the Society of Professional Journalists. "Clearly the person loves the Corvette or they wouldn't labor on the blog, but does it go further? 'GM is the only American auto manufacturer to ever make a decent muscle car.' If you expressed such an opinion you'd have some explaining to do the next time you had to review a Ford or Chrysler product. Conversely if you decided to write something in your newspaper about a Corvette you would need to disclose that you publish the Corvette blog so readers would know of your love for the car." Again, it comes down to the issue of transparency—making sure that people know of your potential bias.

Many news organizations have developed policies that may prevent employees from having personal blogs on any topic at all, regardless of whether it's on a topic the journalist may cover. Others allow journalists to blog freely about their personal lives, but restrict what they write about news stories. Be sure you ask about your newsroom's policy. If there isn't one, carefully consider whether you are in any way creating an appearance of bias through what you reveal on your personal blog. During the 2008 U.S. presidential election, for example, CNN fired a senior producer for expressing his views about one of the candidates on a blog that did not identify him as a CNN employee.[11] As Hill says, "A reporter should know that anything they blog can and will be used against them if it suits anybody's purpose to do so."[12]

SOCIAL MEDIA

Many of the same issues journalists face in connection with blogging apply equally to social media. The line between professional and personal on these sites may be blurry. Should a journalist accept a Facebook "friend" invitation from a source? What kind of information is OK to share on Twitter? It's important to remember that Twitter messages can be read by anyone, not just your followers. CNN fired a senior Middle East editor after she tweeted her respect for a Muslim cleric who supported suicide bombings against civilians in Israel.[13] And even if your Facebook profile is "private," the content may not be. A young TV reporter in Omaha learned that lesson when she posted a photo of herself with a political candidate and urged her friends to vote for him. She lost her job.[14]

Verification

Social media postings may be a great way to find news, but they can't be taken at face value. Think of Twitter, Facebook and similar sites as tips, not confirmed stories. Journalists need to verify information before passing it on. As David Brewer writes at Media Helping Media, they "should not deal in rumor and speculation. Others tweeting can, but a journalist should not."[15]

Confirming information from Twitter or Facebook accounts can be difficult. After Pakistan's Prime Minister Benazir Bhutto was assassinated, her 19-year-old son was named co-head of her political party and news organizations found comments about Islam on his Facebook profile. Many of them quoted those comments before learning that the profile was fake.[16]

ABC News apologized for this tweet from reporter Terry Moran, which quoted an off-the-record comment by President Obama in an interview with CNBC. The network said it was posted "before our editorial process had been completed."

Source: ToMuse, http://tomuse.com/terry-moran-twitter-obama-kanye-jackass (accessed June 3, 2010).

Journalists who post to social media sites typically do not have to get editorial approval. That means they can share information as quickly as they get it, which can be risky if the information has not been verified. Followers will likely forgive a mistake or two if corrected immediately, but do this too often and your credibility as well as that of your news organization will suffer.

Transparency and Privacy

When contacting someone in connection with a news story, it is important to be clear about your purpose. That means revealing that you are a journalist and explaining why you want the information. But what about using photos posted on a page to which you have access? News organizations may have different standards. The Roanoke Times used photos from Facebook in its coverage of a shooting rampage at Virginia Tech; the Washington Post did not.

Posting a request on a social network for information or contacts for a story means that everyone will know what you are working on, including your competitors. Some news organizations believe the value of the feedback they get far outweighs any risk and that letting users know about upcoming stories is a useful promotional tool. Others forbid reporters from tweeting about stories that have not yet been published.

Most journalists do not condone writing anonymously or using an avatar or username that disguises your identity on a social media site. Most news organizations also would draw the line against creating a fake account to be able to access the profiles of people in social networks. But how much personal information should you share on your Twitter and Facebook profiles? Should you have two profiles—one for work and one for friends? Many journalists do just that, but even on personal pages they won't mention their political views or religious affiliation. On professional pages, however, they may include pets or hobbies so viewers see them as "real people." And they may "friend" news sources, being careful to avoid any perception of bias by including a wide range of people.

KUSA-TV in Denver has a social media policy that urges employees to "use the highest level of privacy tools available to control access to your personal activity when appropriate," but also warns, "Don't let that make you complacent." As TV anchor Melissa Brunner puts it, "People have ways of getting to any page you put out there. If you're not comfortable with your mom and your boss seeing it, don't put it on the Web."

COMMENTS

If interactivity is one of the biggest advantages of digital media, it also raises some thorny issues. Most news websites encourage readers to weigh in by making it easy for them to add comments to online stories. The vast majority of users don't write comments, but they apparently do like to read what others have said. Steve Semelsberger of Pluck, a company that provides social media tools to newspapers, told the San Francisco Chronicle that comments can increase page views by up to 15 percent.[17] But comments can be offensive and discussions can degenerate into hate speech, putting the news organization in the precarious position of appearing to condone those comments.

Filtering

Most news organizations use software to automatically filter out comments that include specific words, such as obscenities and ethnic or racial slurs. Some have learned the hard way that they must also apply the filter to usernames. It's also important to let users know what kinds of comments will not be permitted, either in a "terms of service" statement or a note on every page. For example, here's what the Kansas City Star says: "Lively, open, civil debate is the goal. Please refrain from personal attacks or comments that are racist, vulgar or otherwise inappropriate."

Flagging and Screening

No matter how stringent filters are, distasteful comments can slip through. Most news sites enlist the help of readers to flag or "report as abuse" any comments they find objectionable. The site's editors can then remove comments that violate the terms of use. Some news organizations have set up software to remove a comment automatically if it's been flagged by a certain number of users. And some will ban users who repeatedly violate the site's standards.

Many sites require users to register before they can post comments. Some require all comments to be screened by an editor before posting. Depending on the popularity of the site, that can be a huge undertaking. Many sites charge editors and reporters with reviewing comments on stories after they have been posted and arranging to remove any that violate the terms of service.

MULTIMEDIA SOLUTIONS

In earlier chapters, we discussed in detail how converged journalism can help create more powerful storytelling. It may also help in solving ethical dilemmas. In the linear world of television or print, journalists make most of the choices for the news consumer, so the audience is routinely exposed to the content that a journalist or a group of journalists has deemed appropriate. But in the Web world, the consumer has a great deal more choice, and that gives journalists the ability to bring the audience into the ethical decision-making process.

Graphic Images and Sound

No matter whether they work for print, broadcast or online news organizations, most journalists eventually find themselves wrapped up in discussions about the ethical use of graphic images. There is no doubt that a graphic image can be an important aid in reporting the truth of a situation. For example, though many news organizations have policies preventing them from showing video or pictures of dead bodies, dozens of good arguments can be made for violating that policy when you are showing dead bodies in a story about the costs of war. It's tough to adhere to hard-and-fast rules. Most often, conversations about whether to air or publish graphic images occur on a case-by-case basis and revolve around two central issues: What is the journalistic purpose behind broadcasting or publishing the graphic content? What harm may be caused by airing or printing the graphic material?

GO ONLINE

Module 11: Watch TV stories that raise ethical dilemmas and decide what you would have done.

As we mentioned earlier in the chapter, when the journalistic purpose is strong enough to override the potential for harm, television stations, in particular, have tried to come up with a way to notify the audience when a decision is made to air graphic visuals. The anchor might say: "We want to warn you, the pictures in this story may be disturbing to some in the audience." The station is trying to give viewers the option to change the channel or turn off the TV—especially if they are watching with young children or if they themselves are particularly sensitive to graphic images. Sometimes newspapers will publish less graphic photos on a section front page, and then include a warning about more graphic photos published inside.

However, as we've indicated, on the Web you can go far beyond a warning; you can actually require your audience to take action in order to view a particular photo or watch a video. You can offer links to photo or video files on your site or any other with an explanation of what the user will see; presumably the user will read this before clicking on the link. With this technique, you are allowing the audience to make an informed decision about viewing the graphic images.

And it's not just visuals, of course, that can be controversial. Audio from a 9-1-1 tape of a person's voice describing a situation can be as disturbing as seeing the events unfold. At times, however, the content of those tapes does provide important information on such issues as the preparedness of an individual 9-1-1 operator and response times. To minimize the emotional impact, a television station (and, of course, a newspaper) may choose to use a written transcription of the audio. But, to satisfy those who feel "hearing is believing," the entire audio file could be posted on the Web. In this way, you could minimize the harm to your audience as a whole, yet still serve a journalistic purpose.

Using the Web in this way may not always be appropriate. As in every ethical dilemma, there will be those who offer counteropinions. If the journalistic purpose is not strong enough to warrant publishing a photo or airing a video clip, is it strong enough to justify posting the content online? Should your standards for publication be different for online versus on the air or in the paper? Arguments can be made on both sides. However, it may help to remember that you should be accountable to your audience and that ethical decision making is about coming up with defensible answers. News organizations should discuss the issues and be prepared to share with the public what went into their decisions—ideally through a formal statement published alongside the disturbing content, or informally with members of the public who might contact the news organization about the decisions made.

The online magazine Slate published a slide show of explicit photos of lap dancing. Viewers were warned about the nature of the content and could access it only by clicking on a link.

Source: Courtesy of Slate.com.

Access to Information

One of the most exciting attributes of the Web is that it gives the audience access to customized information. For example, if a newspaper conducts an investigation of fire code violations in your community, it would be impossible for the reporter to include in the article the inspection records for every property. But you can publish the records on the Web, and you can make the records easily searchable so users can look up specific schools, favorite restaurants or the local sports stadiums to check on their safety. This capability goes a long way toward making important stories more relevant for the individual news consumer.

But the capability also raises new ethical questions. There is a great deal of information available online through government and law enforcement agencies. For example, the property appraiser in many communities lists on the Web the owner's name, property value and specific floor plan for every home appraised. A news organization could create a quick link to that information that would make it much easier for casual users to surf the data. What kind of privacy issues does that raise? Has the news organization now made it easier for unscrupulous people to do something illegal, like break into a home? Or because the information is already public, has the news organization done nothing more than make public access easier?

These questions have been asked often in regard to the publication of sex offender registries. Because most states require convicted sex offenders to register their names and addresses with local law enforcement, many news organizations have done stories on how the public can access that information. Some have even gone so far as to make accessing the information easier by creating their own searchable databases.

Kelly McBride, an ethics instructor at the Poynter Institute in St. Petersburg, Fla., believes that many newsrooms simply take the attitude that "if it's legal, we are going to do it." She worries that in the case of the sex offender registry, some readers or viewers might overreact to the coverage, either by retaliating against one of the sex offenders or allowing fears of attack to alter their lives. She says newsrooms "should be obligated to go beyond what is legal and weigh the value of what they are legally allowed to do against the harm or good that can come of it and make a decision on journalistic grounds."[18]

Just because something is legal doesn't mean it's also ethical. Is it our job to give the public easy access to information that's rightfully theirs? Or do we need to act as gatekeepers on some level in order to protect the public? It's a tough call, and one that journalists must routinely make by weighing the importance of telling the truth against the potential for creating harm.

Access to Sources and Content

One fundamental principle of journalism is that we try to gather as many differing viewpoints as necessary to tell the truth. You'll often be told to get "both sides" of a story, but the reality is that there are many sides to most issues. What your producer or editor is really asking is that you avoid telling a one-sided story, particularly in the case of something controversial.

Newsroom partnerships give us the ability to tell many sides of a story by opening up more access to content and sources. When you combine the resources of print, broadcast and online sites, you naturally bring together more journalists—each with personal sources and reporting experiences—that can be tapped into when a colleague is looking for a different way to tell a story.

Sometimes multiplatform journalism can literally provide reporters with access to information they couldn't get any other way. For example, television reporters often have a much easier time snagging interviews with major business leaders than newspaper reporters do. Galen Meyer, who trains journalists who work for Bloomberg News, says there's something about the allure of being on TV that makes these industry players say yes to an on-air interview when they have already repeatedly turned down a print reporter. By working with a TV partner, a Bloomberg print reporter can sometimes get answers to the questions that are needed to tell a fair and balanced print story. Without the television partnership, the print reporter might have been forced to write nothing more than "CEO Bill Parks could not be reached for comment."

One thing we discussed earlier in the chapter was the question of whether the interview subject should be informed that the information provided to one medium might be used in another. To be absolutely ethical, we believe the television reporter in the scenario described above should alert the interviewee to the possibility that the interview will be used in more than one medium.

DIVERSITY

Some of you may be wondering why the topic of diversity is showing up in a chapter about journalism ethics. Aly Colón, who taught ethics at the Poynter Institute, sees diversity as a tool for meeting several of our professional ethical standards:

- Give voice to the voiceless. Diversity can clearly help us achieve this goal. By including people who look different, or think differently, from the population at large, we are giving them voice and diversifying our coverage.

- Act independently. This principle urges us to "seek out and disseminate competing perspectives." In this way, we avoid telling one-sided stories that fail to include minority voices.

- Minimize harm. To achieve this goal, journalists are advised to be compassionate and "treat sources, subjects, and colleagues as human beings deserving of respect, not merely as a means to your journalistic ends." To do that, journalists

TRADE TOOLS

ETHICS RESOURCES

No matter whether you're working on your college newspaper or for the New York Times, for a tiny radio station in Tupelo, Miss., or for NBC News, there will be times when you feel like you need a little help from some ethics experts in order to make an ethical decision. Sometimes it may be a matter of pulling up a list of questions or reviewing a professional ethics code online. The following information might be just what you need to help in making an ethical decision—either in a converged environment or in a single-platform newsroom.

One of the most thoughtful journalists at work today is ethicist Bob Steele of the Poynter Institute in St. Petersburg, Fla. He has come up with 10 questions to help you reach good ethical decisions:

1. What do I know? What do I need to know?

2. What is my journalistic purpose?

3. What are my ethical concerns?

4. What organizational policies and professional guidelines should I consider?

5. How can I include other people, with different perspectives and diverse ideas, in the decision-making process?

6. Who are the stakeholders—those affected by my decision? What are their motivations? Which are legitimate?

7. What if the roles were reversed? How would I feel if I were in the shoes of one of the stakeholders?

8. What are the possible consequences of my actions? Short term? Long term?

9. What are my alternatives to maximize my truth-telling responsibility and minimize harm?

10. Can I clearly and fully justify my thinking and my decision? To my colleagues? To the stakeholders? To the public?

The simple act of asking these questions can help guide the discussion of an ethical dilemma, and help those involved reach an answer that they will feel they can defend to the audience.

At other times it may help to access the professional codes of ethics from highly regarded journalism organizations. We've already mentioned some of them; these URLs will take you directly to the ethics content posted on the organizations' websites.

American Society of News Editors, "Ethics Codes":

   http://asne.org/key_initiatives/ethics/ethics_codes.aspx

Cyberjournalist.net, "Bloggers' Code of Ethics":

   www.cyberjournalist.net/news/000215.php

Poynter Institute, "Ethics":

   http://poynter.org/subject.asp?id=32

Radio Television Digital News Association, "Code of Ethics":

   www.rtdna.org/pages/media_items/code-of-ethics-and-professional-conduct48.php

Society of Professional Journalists, "Code of Ethics":

   http://spj.org/ethicscode.asp

All of these organizations developed their ethics codes and guidelines through years of conversations with professional journalists. Their codes are mandatory reading for anyone considering a career in journalism.

Source: For the 10 questions, see Bob Steele, "Ask These 10 Questions to Make Good Ethical Decisions," PoynterOnline, February 29, 2000, www.poynter.org/column.asp?id=36&aid=4346.

must understand the people they write about and become aware of the different ways their reporting, writing, editing, producing and photojournalism affect people. It requires journalists to learn about diversity in all areas, including race, ethnicity, culture, class, ideology, religion, abilities, sexual orientation, gender and politics.

The link between ethics and diversity is strong, and convergence offers journalists a way to achieve more diversity in their storytelling. Combining the resources of multiple media outlets and the opportunity to partner with ethnic media are just two examples of how this can work.[19]

Diverse Sources

Journalists working on deadline often resort to "rounding up the usual suspects." They wind up going to the same experts and getting reaction from the same newsmakers because they don't have time to seek out new voices. In converged news operations you have the potential for more "feet on the street"—more chances for reporters to encounter people whose ideas or opinions have not yet been heard. And convergence offers more opportunities for reporters to work together to share what they know about covering different communities.

When WFLA-TV, the Tampa Tribune and TBO.com decided to get serious about convergence in 1998, WFLA's news director, Dan Bradley, liked to say he had just added more than 130 journalists to his staff. That's because he felt the partnership gave him access to the reporting resources of the Tampa Tribune and Tampa Bay Online. Though many have argued that convergence will diminish the number of voices in the news, it could actually make it possible for the audience to hear from more people with differing perspectives.

The Web and social media open up a whole new avenue for disseminating diverse perspectives as well. Journalists can solicit input and hear from people who aren't typically included in traditional news stories. News consumers also have the opportunity to view the comments and join in the conversation.

The traditional audiences for each medium may be exposed to more diverse coverage through the use of multiple platforms. For example, a younger person who doesn't usually read the newspaper may benefit from reading content online that's generated by a print reporter. That story may offer diverse perspectives that the user does not typically encounter.

Partnerships

One underused model of convergence involves partnerships with ethnic or alternative media. These news organizations are devoted to providing information to groups of news consumers that are largely underserved by the mainstream media. They feature topics and perspectives that are often missing from mainstream coverage. For example, a study by the National Association of Hispanic Journalists found that less than 1 percent of the stories aired in 2006 on network newscasts featured Latinos as news sources. Yet, according to census data, Hispanics make up more than 15 percent of the United States' population and have now surpassed blacks as the country's largest minority group.

So imagine how helpful it would be for a mainstream news organization that was trying to cover an area with a large number of Hispanics to partner with a Spanish-language television or radio station, newspaper or online site. The two organizations could share information about issues that deserved coverage and access to sources on those stories. The partnership would allow both news organizations to reach new audiences with information providing new perspectives.

The same could be said for partnerships with organizations designed to serve blacks or gay and lesbian people, or any of the underrepresented communities in a given news market.

TAKING IT HOME

Credibility is the most precious asset a news organization or an individual journalist has. Credibility is the difference between the New York Times and the National Enquirer, NBC News and TMZ.com. Practicing good ethical journalism helps you maintain credibility and preserve the audience's trust. A multimedia journalist faces new challenges in ethical decision making as technology expands both what we're capable of covering and the way we deliver news and information. But journalism's core ethical principles have not changed—our goal is to seek truth and report it, to minimize the harm we do, to act independently of outside influences and to be accountable to the public. Within that framework, ethical journalists arrive at decisions they can comfortably defend and explain to the audiences they serve.

TALKING POINTS

1. Create your own policy for handling corrections in online stories. How will you handle errors on the live site and in your archive? Decide whether you will post this policy on your website, and be prepared to explain your decision.

2. The U.S. government has released a series of disturbing photographs that show the brutality done to several U.S. prisoners of war. Your news organization has decided not to air the photos in your broadcast, but you will publish them online behind a link. Your job is to write a brief explanation of why the photographs have been posted online but not used on the air.

3. You know that every story you cover is fair game for your news organization's website. Come up with a good way to alert everyone you talk to for your stories to the fact that what they say may also be used online.

ONLINE LEARNING MODULE 11

Activate or buy this chapter's online learning module at journalism.cqpress.com to get access to:

- SKILL BUILDING: Walk through a series of case studies that will test your ethical decision making. Review what one journalism ethics expert would have done in the same situation.

- DISCOVER: Watch a television story produced in response to an ethical dilemma and one story that created an ethical discussion among the community's news media. Decide what you would have done in both cases.

- EXPLORE: Examine ethics codes and other ethical decision-making resources.

- A digital version of this chapter's text in full color with active links.

Also, continue your work on the ONGOING STORY MODULE. Handle an ethical problem that may require you to change a major part of the story you've created. Find out what the authors decided to do about the issue.

12

GETTING READY FOR THE REAL WORLD

The pace of technological change affecting journalism today is truly unprecedented. As a result, the most important job skill for a journalist may be adaptability. This chapter will explore some of the radical shifts taking place in journalism, including the industry's struggles to find new business models. It will also help you position yourself to apply for the jobs that currently exist, as well as get you thinking about the types of jobs that news companies and journalists themselves might create in the future.

The media world is changing so rapidly that you might find yourself worrying that your skills will be outdated even before you get that first job. What do news managers really want in a new hire these days? Although it's an age-old question, the basic answer hasn't really changed. They want it all. They want smart, committed people with sound judgment and strong skills, willing to work hard for not much pay. That said, some things are different today.

"Five to 10 years ago you were searching for someone who brought one specialty—reporting, photography, weather, sports—to the table," says Jim Garrott, former news director of WEEK-TV in Peoria, Ill. "Now you are looking for people, especially in smaller markets, who can do multitasking."

And not just multitasking, but multimedia, says Virgil Smith, vice president of talent management at Gannett, who heads up that company's recruiting efforts. "Video-editing skills, social media skills, blogging—with industry transformation and emergence of new technology, multimedia is now included in all of our job descriptions," Smith says.

Those of you just starting out or in the early stages of your career need to realize that the training you are receiving as a multimedia journalist is going to make you more valuable in the job market. Although gloomy headlines about cutbacks in both print and broadcast newsrooms may be worrisome, there are jobs for those who enter the profession with a strong foundation in multimedia journalism and a willingness to keep learning.

MULTIMEDIA JOB SEARCHES

Recent surveys of journalism and mass communication graduates show the job market has been tough. According to the Annual Survey of Journalism and Mass Communication Graduates, just over half of 2009 graduates with a bachelor's degree were able to find full-time work within a year of leaving school. That was down almost 5 percent from 2008.[1]

TRADE TOOLS

TRAITS OF TOMORROW'S JOURNALISTS

1. Entrepreneurial and business savvy. More and more journalists are finding themselves "self-employed." The more you know about the value of content and how to run a business, the better.

2. Programmer. Yep, this means knowing Flash and HTML and JavaScript and more. Tomorrow's journalists must be "able to report and present a quality story using multimedia, and having the skills to build and manage the platforms that present the stories."

3. Open-minded experimenter. This may be the toughest one of all. Journalists must learn to be innovative, to take risks—especially when it comes to connecting with audiences.

4. Multimedia storyteller. You have to be able to tell stories in more than one medium and to leverage the strength of each platform for your story.

5. The social journalist and community builder. This type of skill now shows up in job postings. Newsrooms want people who have "the ability to find and connect with communities of interest both online and offline."

The study includes specific data for the fields of print and broadcast. In 2009, 58.7 percent of graduates who had specialized in print journalism had a full-time job. That's compared with 71.7 percent of graduates from two years earlier. For those who had specialized in broadcasting, including broadcast journalism, 51.0 percent of grads were working full time, compared with 67.3 in 2007.[2]

Most of those with full-time jobs said their work involved the Web. Online research was cited as a component of the job by 81 percent, writing and editing for the Web by 58.2 percent, work on social networking sites by 45.5 percent and using the Web in promoting work by 40.4 percent. It probably comes as no surprise that the use of social media was almost twice as common as it was a year earlier.[3]

A couple of other findings in the survey are also worth noting. Of the women surveyed, 62.5 percent found full-time employment; for men, that percentage was 56.9. The disparity

6. Blogger and curator. Mashable says "journalists will have to practice blogging regularly and serve as curators of other content on the Web."

7. Multi-skilled. This sounds a lot like "multimedia storyteller," but the distinction is that being a great writer or being a great on-camera presence may just not be enough in the future.

8. Fundamental journalism skills. Yes, they still matter. You have to have "a marriage between core values and new media skills."

The one thing missing from the list may be:

9. A passionate desire. The job of journalist is no longer for people who thought TV looked like a glamorous way to make a living or who wanted a paycheck while they worked on the great American novel. Developing the traits listed will require a true dedication to the craft.

Source: Adapted from "8 Must-Have Traits of Tomorrow's Journalists," published on Mashable.com, a blog about social media, http://mashable.com/2009/12/09/future-journalist/.

between hiring rates for men and women continues a trend that's lasted more than 20 years. Of greater concern may be the findings for graduates who are members of a racial or ethnic minority: "Bachelor's degree recipients who were members of racial or ethnic minorities had a particularly difficult time in the job market in 2009. The gap between the level of employment of non-minority and minority graduates in 2009 is the largest ever recorded in the graduate survey."[4]

The employment gap between racial and ethnic minorities and nonminorities was 15.3 percent, up from 5.9 percent a year earlier, meaning it has become harder for minorities to find jobs in mass communication. This disparity has been apparent since the survey was first conducted in 1988.[5]

The survey does not offer any explanations for the hiring gaps.

Planning

The planning for a job search begins long before you send out that first link to your online portfolio, cover letter or résumé. If you're still in school, be sure you are taking classes that will expand your skill set, rather than taking the "easy" class or the one that best fits your social schedule.

Perhaps the most important piece of advice to act on while you're still in school is to look for opportunities to get "real world" experience. In many programs, that means an internship. Unfortunately, too often students look at an internship as one more hurdle to clear before graduation, rather than as a launching pad to a career. However, there are countless stories of students who took an internship, made the most of it and turned it into a job offer upon graduation.

Mackenzie Taylor was a broadcast major who interned at Media General's multimedia news operation in Tampa, Fla., right after graduation. "I found I loved doing newspaper stuff as well. I learned I had to collect a lot more information and use a lot more description, but now I really love it," she says.

Taylor went on to be hired as a multimedia reporter for WBTW-TV in the Florence–Myrtle Beach, S.C., market where she also worked for the Florence Morning News and SCNow.com. The three news organizations are owned by Media General, Inc. As a multimedia reporter, Taylor was required to produce a TV, print and Web version of her story every day.

Her advice to journalists who are still in school? "No matter what you major in, that's not the only thing you'll be doing. Be sure you have enough training to know the fundamentals of TV, newspaper and Web," she says.

In addition to an internship, some schools produce their own news broadcasts or websites, and most have a student newspaper. Make no mistake, it's important to get involved in these opportunities to produce stories that will actually be published. The internship and the work samples will become critically important when it comes time to produce your résumé and work portfolio.

No matter how much planning you do or how talented you are, a job search takes a lot of effort. Don't think you can post your résumé on Monster.com and dozens of other online sites or send it by e-mail to hundreds of potential employers and then sit back to wait for job offers to come pouring in. Yes, a few experienced journalists say they've received good offers from employers who just happened to run across their online portfolios. But most people actually have to go looking for work; it doesn't come looking for them.

According to Job-Hunt.org, an online resource for job seekers, relying too much on the Web or e-mail to apply for work is a self-defeating strategy; you can't customize your résumé for specific opportunities, and you have no way of knowing if your e-mail was ever received.[6]

Think of the Internet as just one of many resources to use in your job search, and begin the hunt by figuring out what you're really looking for.

Ask yourself exactly what kinds of jobs interest you most and what you're most qualified for. Consider where you want to live as well as what you want to do. If you can afford it, you might decide to look for an entry-level job at a small organization in a city you'd like to call home as opposed to a more challenging job in a smaller market where it's cheaper to live.

In the past it's been a given that most large news organizations expect more professional experience than small ones. The rule of thumb in journalism used to be that you would start in a small market or newsroom and work your way up, and that's still generally true for would-be reporters, especially in television.

But other job seekers are finding they can leapfrog the smallest markets if they bring the right skills or apply for the right job. Television news producers, for example, are so highly sought after that some small-market news directors say they can't find any to hire, not even right out of school. Inexperienced photojournalists are also commonly hired in larger markets if their résumé tapes show good potential. With the use of solo journalists becoming more common, photojournalism skills can also help reporters find entry-level work in larger markets. Certainly, journalists with strong Web skills can often bypass the small markets to work on major news websites.

Whether your challenge in finding a job will be great or small, taking the right approach can help lead you to the best position and the best news organization for you.

TRADE TOOLS

GETTING THE MOST FROM AN INTERNSHIP

Mackenzie Taylor worked as a multimedia reporter for WBTW-TV, the Florence Morning News and SCNow.com in Florence–Myrtle Beach, S.C. She got her job thanks to an internship, and she offers other interns this advice:

- Ask questions. Taylor says she's naturally inquisitive, as most journalists are. Use your reporting skills to find out as much as you can about the way the newsroom works.

- Find a mentor. Taylor says she was assigned to work in the capitol bureau for Media General's South Carolina properties. She credits bureau reporter Robert Kittle with helping her learn as much as she did.

Source: Photo courtesy of Mackenzie Taylor.

- Offer to help. If you wait to be assigned a task, you might spend a lot of time sitting around or doing work that doesn't interest you. Taylor says she volunteered to write stories for Kittle so often that eventually he let her try it.

- Ask for feedback. Once you get a chance to do some real journalism on your internship, ask your mentor or others to review your work. You won't improve as quickly without constructive criticism.

- Be humble. "Coming out of school, you think you know a lot, but you really don't know what you're doing," Taylor says. Interns need to remember that the newsroom staff can help you or ignore you.

Hunting

There are two basic ways to conduct a job hunt—either look for openings or target places you really want to work. You can begin a general search at these online starting points that offer searchable databases of journalism job openings (find more on this book's companion website):

- JournalismJobs: www.journalismjobs.com

- Mediabistro: http://mediabistro.com/joblistings

- MediaLine: www.medialine.com/jobs.htm

- Variety Careers: www.variety.com/index.asp?layout=variety_careers

As you look through the listings, pay close attention to all the details—required skills, experience, duties and responsibilities. In 2010, for example, WFMY-TV in Greensboro, N.C., was advertising for a "multimedia producer":

> This position requires strong writing and decision-making skills. Teamwork and the ability to work under intense deadline pressure are critical. Our multimedia news producers generate content for our on-air, online and mobile products. Candidates should have a degree in journalism or a related field plus two years of professional experience with a proven track record in a winning news environment.[7]

The listing makes it clear that an understanding of the "three-screen strategy" we discussed in Chapter 9 applies to many types of newsrooms positions. But the posting calls for two years of professional experience, so it's probably not a job for someone right out of school.

This job posting for a "digital journalist" at WBTW in Myrtle Beach, S.C., is much more focused on attracting applicants with specific skills rather than a specific experience level:

> Candidates for this position will have strong writing skills, ability to operate digital video and still cameras and the associated editing equipment and software used in processing raw images into completed content for broadcast, print and web posting. Some newscast producing may also be required with this position. Successful candidates must have strong reporting and interpersonal skills necessary for the development of relationships and unique hyper local stories. Since Digital Journalists often work alone and unsupervised, time management and organizational skills are critical to a candidate's success.[8]

The lesson here is that job titles don't tell the whole story, so make sure you read the full listing before you decide whether or not to apply.

Another approach is to search directly on news media company websites. Corporations like Gannett, Cox, E. W. Scripps and Media General all have job listings on their sites.

Targeting places you really want to work can be even more difficult than sniffing out openings to apply for. You need to figure out exactly what jobs are open and whether you're qualified. It's a good idea to bookmark the websites for the organizations you're targeting and then check those sites daily for job postings.

GO ONLINE

Module 12: Visit job posting sites and learn more about job hunting strategies.

Once you've spotted the right job, you have more to do, says Ernest Sotomayor, assistant dean of Career Services at Columbia's Graduate School of Journalism. "Being familiar with the company is critical," Sotomayor says. He advises learning everything you can about the news organization, the market and the audience before you craft a personal appeal for consideration, making sure you send it to the right person. To improve the chances that your request will get through, you may find that you need to do some serious networking before you make an approach.

Don't rule out a postgraduate internship as an option. Shreeya Sinha got her master's at Columbia University and started as an intern with MediaStorm, a site that showcases innovative multimedia storytelling. "I accepted this internship over a full-time job in broadcast because MediaStorm are pioneers in the multimedia field and there's a greater possibility now to join them full-time in the future," says Sinha.

Source: Courtesy of Shreeya Sinha.

Networking

Contacts are crucial when it comes to finding a job. Use the connections you've made in previous jobs, internships or in school, and look for additional ways to network with other journalists. The next time your instructor brings in a speaker from the industry or a high-profile journalist visits campus, be sure you do everything you can to get some one-on-one time with that person. Ask questions during his or her presentation; introduce yourself afterwards and ask for a business card—then follow up with a thank you and a request to stay in touch. Most people like to help students who impress them.

In addition, some of your instructors may still work for local newsrooms or have significant industry contacts; don't be afraid to ask them for advice.

Don't hesitate to ask for a list of your school's journalism alumni and then use that alma mater connection to contact graduates who are working in a field or in a particular news organization that interests you. Although few of us would feel comfortable doing it, if your Aunt Edna's next-door neighbor's son works for ESPN and that's your dream job, you should seriously consider using that connection to make a contact.

Other options include joining a journalism group—the Council of National Journalism Organizations maintains a list of more than 50 on its website at www.cnjo.org. These groups often sponsor workshops or conferences where you can mingle with news professionals and ask for advice or leads about jobs. Some of these organizations, like the Radio Television Digital News Association (RTDNA), allow job hunters free access to their online listings and let members post résumés. You can also find journalism conferences or workshops to attend by checking www.journalismtraining.org.

But don't confuse networking with asking someone for a job. You need to concentrate on building relationships with people within the profession for other reasons, including knowledge sharing, friendship and mentoring.

Another strategy is to request informational interviews from news managers or other practicing journalists to help you research journalism careers. Never ask for a job during an informational interview, but be sure to take along a copy of your résumé.

DNAinfo.com contributing editor Sree Sreenivasan recommends online networking using LinkedIn (www.linkedin.com), which is sometimes described as MySpace for all kinds of professionals, including journalists. Once you create an account, you can search for people you know who are also members and ask them to connect to you. Their connections then become part of your network, although you can't communicate with them directly. Let's say you're in Sreenivasan's network, and you see that he knows someone at a news organization you'd like to work for. You could send that person a message by way

KNOW AND TELL

GETTING THAT FIRST JOB

Nick Ciletti got his first reporting job at KYMA-DT in Yuma, Ariz., where he also does some anchoring. He shares his best job hunting advice:

Describe how you landed your first job.

I had met my news director a year before I graduated college at a networking conference, the National Association of Hispanic Journalists. After graduation, I heard he had a job opening and I called him (and overnighted my demo reel and résumé!). A few days later, I was hired. I had sent out dozens and dozens of demos before this, and was so relieved to have it finally happen.

Source: Photo courtesy of Nick Ciletti.

What skills do you think gave you the edge over other applicants?

I speak Spanish. My market is right on the border, so knowing Spanish opens up a lot more doors for me as far as stories are concerned. I occasionally cross into Mexico for

of Sreenivasan, but he would decide whether or not to pass it on. "I have declined to forward messages in some cases when the contact would not be appropriate," he says. "In the old days (i.e., last year), I would have just c.c.-ed my contact and the job seeker. I still do that, on occasion, with very good friends, but this way is better so that the contact can decide whether he/she wants to respond, without the job seeker automatically getting hold of his or her e-mail address."[9]

Not everyone finds this process helpful or convenient, but it's one more option to consider to expand your contact list.

JOB APPLICATIONS

When you're looking for a job, you basically have five chances to market yourself: your cover letter, résumé, portfolio, follow-up calls and a newsroom visit or formal interview.

stories, not to mention my market has a very high Hispanic population. I was also an associate producer in a big market first. I think my boss liked the fact that I had some experience in a bigger market before moving to a smaller one.

What skills do you wish you would have had before going out to look for jobs?

Time management! It's one thing to turn a package for class when you have a week to do it—but it's a lot different when you have just a few hours! I also would have liked that "thick skin" early on. It would have softened some of those early blows!

What job hunting strategies could you share for those just graduating now?

Networking, networking, networking! Get to know as many people as possible. You never know who may help you land your next job. Also, try to make a great (but still genuine) impression on people. Sell yourself, but make sure to paint an accurate portrait of your talents and abilities. Don't pretend to be something you're not. Your integrity is everything.

It's important to use each of these chances to your best advantage, but many job applicants don't. News managers say they see the same mistakes over and over—mistakes that land applications in the trash instead of the callback file.

Cover Letters

The quickest way to doom your chances is to send a generic form letter, or get basic facts wrong. Here's an example one TV news director received:

> Dear Prospective Employer,
>
> As a journalist working in the field, on the scene of breaking news working long hours, and always on deadline, I find myself pressed but always cognizant of every aspect of the urgency and accuracy behind LIVE, LOCAL and LATE-BREAKING NEWS.

The applicant clearly hadn't done any research—the slogan belonged to a different television station in the market. "Don't be lazy," says Kevin Benz, a longtime TV news manager in Austin, Texas. Address your letter to a specific individual and spell the name correctly. "Google me! Google the station," he says. "If you want to be a reporter and you can't find out my name, what does that suggest to me about what kind of a journalist you will be?" If you're applying for an open position, explain how your experience matches the job. Don't talk about what the news organization can do for you; instead describe what skills you can bring to the job. Don't exaggerate your abilities, but do make the strongest case you can in your own favor. And use your cover letter to highlight your skill as a writer—every job in journalism will require you to communicate clearly. Just imagine how quickly this applicant's letter hit the wastebasket:

> I want you to no I'm a mature and experienced newsmaker. Above all, my news suaveness put me in a position to receive information in a timely manner, in order to brake news stories.

Use the cover letter to introduce yourself, but don't repeat your entire résumé. You may want to offer some background on your video clips or portfolio, however. It's hard for employers to know whether you shot and edited your own stories, just how much of a newscast you wrote or what your specific contributions were to an online story, so tell them in the cover letter.

Résumés

It's becoming almost standard for job seekers to post an online résumé, but many employers still want to see one on paper. Be specific and candid about your skills and experience. If you're applying for your first job, there may be no reason to submit a résumé that's any longer than one page, but Gannett's Virgil Smith says his company wants résumés that truly showcase the applicant.

"The one-page résumé makes no sense. I want you to tell me who you are, what you know and what sets you apart from other applicants," says Smith. "We have no problem with a résumé of two to three pages."

Many college career centers recommend you put an objective at the top of your résumé, but many news directors say that's a waste of time. Obviously, your objective is to get a job.

Some résumés will follow the objective with a section on education, but that can easily come a little farther down the page. What most news directors really want to know about you is how much journalism experience you've had. If you are already working in the news business, that should be the first thing a news director sees after your name and contact information. If you reported for a student newscast, wrote for the student newspaper or interned for a news website or any other journalism outlet, that kind of information should figure prominently under work experience too. What you don't want to do is load up the experience section with your lifeguard and waitstaff jobs. If you have enough journalism experience, leave those out altogether; at the most, include one or two that demonstrate longevity in a job.

Be specific about your skills, and if you can shoot video, tell what formats you've worked with. If you can edit nonlinear video, name the programs you've used, like Avid, Adobe Premiere or Final Cut Pro. The same goes for your multimedia skills. Describe what you can do and how you've applied your skills on the job or in school, but again, don't exaggerate. Don't say you know HTML if you've only edited tags in Dreamweaver.

Social media skills are growing in importance to employers. Be sure to include your professional Twitter name and a link to a public Facebook page; then keep them updated with relevant content. For example, you'll want to post links to your own stories, and you may want to start tracking and sharing news on industry developments to show a potential employer that you're staying on top of what's happening in the profession.

List references on your résumé, but don't include any letters of reference with your application unless the job listing specifically requests them. Make sure any person you list as a reference is willing to be contacted and will say something good about you. Some recruiters recommend that you have at least one nonacademic reference, so try to include someone off campus who can speak knowledgeably about your work. Many prospective employers won't contact your references until after you've been interviewed, but if you definitely don't want anyone to contact your current employer, say so in the cover letter.

Be aware that any prospective employers who are really interested in hiring you will not check just the references you've listed—they may also call people they know where you've worked or studied. Expect that a future employer will google you, search for a MySpace or Facebook page, a personal blog or comments you've made on social media. Beware of what you post. Kay Miller, former news director at WWSB-TV in Sarasota, Fla., says she's been shocked by what some prospective employees have posted on these sites—everything from pictures of themselves swilling beer to shots of themselves wearing little or no clothing. Miller says she routinely checks these sites before hiring new people, and a risqué page can lose a promising candidate the job. "As a journalist you are only as credible as your last impression you left on your readers or viewers," says Miller. She believes journalists need to do more reputation management for themselves in this age of online access to information.

If you're still in school, it's fine to put your grade point average on your résumé, but only if it's impressive. The same goes for awards or scholarships. Extracurricular activities or hobbies that demonstrate a relevant skill, like foreign languages or travel, are worth including. You can also mention examples that show your leadership abilities or character, but keep the list short.

You may also want to take what you've learned about search engine optimization and apply it to your résumé. Crystal Lauderdale, a Web manager for the New York Times Company in Florida, also helps in hiring. She says these days, many medium and large companies run résumés through an electronic filter before selecting first-round candidates.

"If a news, public relations or marketing company is looking for someone with a background in 'journalism' specifically (and nearly all are, if you look at job listings), a well-qualified graduate may not even make it to the first round if they're lacking just a few key words in their résumé," says Lauderdale. "It's a balancing act between being generic enough to pass through the filters and being unique enough to stand out afterward."

If you want to see what words are getting the most emphasis in your résumé, you might try creating a "word cloud"—a visual representation of text, with the most frequently used terms getting the most real estate. One free Web service can be found at Wordle.net, where you simply cut and paste the text of your résumé into a box and then hit a button to generate the cloud. If the job you're applying for references the need for multimedia skills and the words *education* and *anchoring* seem to dominate the word cloud for your résumé, you may want to tweak the language.

And a word to those applicants with cute or clever e-mail addresses like bootilicious@whatever.com: They make you look frivolous, or worse. Get a different one to use on your résumé. The same goes for a voice-mail greeting with your dog barking or your favorite song playing. When potential employers call, you want them to be impressed, not turned off.

GO ONLINE

Module 12: Review strong video and text résumé examples to help you craft your own.

Video Résumés

For television jobs it's still important to provide a video résumé, although these days most news directors say they'd be happy to receive it as a link to a video-sharing site in an e-mail. If you do send a hard copy, your best bet is to use a DVD unless the job listing specifies a different format.

Understand that news directors are busy, so be sure to make a good first impression. "Don't start with yourself on camera introducing you and your tape," says Chip Mahaney, who spent years as a news director. "This tape is supposed to show me the kind of work

HOW *NOT* TO GET A JOB, IN FIVE EASY STEPS

To make sure your job application is rejected, just follow this advice from Kevin Benz, former news director at News8 in Austin, Texas, and Chip Mahaney, director of digital content at E. W. Scripps:

1. Don't follow directions. If the ad says to apply by e-mail, send a letter. If it asks for a tape, be sure to send a DVD. The instructions in the ad are a first test for applicants, so do what it says and don't blow it.

2. Fake it. Say you're experienced when you're not; list skills you don't really have and include work samples you didn't produce. Do you really think that will help you land a job in a business that's based on facts?

3. Use gimmicks. They'll definitely get you noticed. Like the applicant who sent a candy bar with a note that read, "I will bring you MOUNDS of great stories." Or the one who sent a shoe, to demonstrate a desire to "get a foot in the door." Not a great idea.

4. Stalk the boss. Call every day to make sure your application was received. Twice a day is even better. Show up unannounced to guarantee you won't have a shot at the job.

5. Dress for the tennis court, frat house or nightclub when you come for the interview. If you don't want the job, make sure you don't show up the way the boss should expect you to dress at work. "I can't tell you how many photographers I have not hired because they come in looking like they just got out of jail," says Benz.

TRADE TOOLS

you can do." Begin with a simple slate that runs no more than 15 seconds and that shows your name, phone number and e-mail address.

The video résumé should reflect your professionalism, intelligence and good writing and storytelling skills. For a reporter candidate, most news directors expect to see a montage of four or five creative stand-ups and live shots at the start. "We want to see how you handle yourself on TV," Mahaney says. Dave Busiek of KCCI-TV in Des Moines, Iowa, says he's been known to pop a tape out in as few as three seconds if the applicant shows no

Emily Timm offers potential employers several different ways to check out her work online. She provides links to her Facebook, Twitter and LinkedIn accounts, as well as her own personal website. For her printable and hard copy versions, she should be sure to provide additional details such as her Twitter name and the full URL for her blog to make it easier for those who prefer paper copies to find her work.

Source: Photo courtesy of Emily Timm.

on-camera skills. After that, many news directors like to see a range of stories you've done recently, including spot news, general assignment and possibly a feature. Reporter tapes generally don't need to run any longer than 10 minutes.

Photojournalists should put their best work first. Rocky Dailey, former chief photographer at WXMI-TV in Grand Rapids, Mich., says that, ideally, the video résumé would include general news, a feature, breaking news and possibly an in-depth or series piece. A photo essay is always a good idea—something that showcases the photojournalist's storytelling ability without a reporter. In addition to all that, make certain the stories demonstrate solid shooting and editing skills. So if you have a story with some great editing but a blue stand-up, don't use it! And remember, chief photographers also want to see what you can do on a nonvisual story; anyone can get great video of a house fire.

Both reporter and photojournalist candidates routinely use video-sharing sites such as YouTube or Vimeo to host their résumés. These sites are free and offer a quick and easy way to update your work samples, so you can replace weaker content as soon as you produce something more compelling.

Producers should provide writing samples or an entire newscast if they have one. Many also include self-critiques of their shows. These critiques typically outline what the producers were responsible for in the broadcast, what they thought worked well and what might have been improved. Sometimes a news director will also ask the producer to spell out a personal producing philosophy in this critique.

"No matter what job you're applying for, include only your best work and don't ever pass someone else's work off as your own. I've seen tapes come in where it's clear they're retracking the work of one of the reporters at the station where they interned," says KALB news director Keith Weiss. "I'd rather see something produced by someone a little more green than get a tape from someone who rips off other people's work."

Many news directors agree with Weiss and say they will look past poor video quality if it's the best the applicant can do with the equipment or facilities available. Don't make excuses or cast blame, but feel free to explain the circumstances in your cover letter.

Often reporter candidates' résumé tapes open with a montage of stand-ups that showcase storytelling ability and presence on camera.

Source: Photo courtesy of Jessica Chapin.

Multimedia Portfolios

Many of the same principles that apply to video résumés also apply to multimedia portfolios. Include the best examples of your current work, not everything you've ever done. Don't waste a prospective employer's time. Focus your portfolio on your work, not you. Put just as much effort into creating your portfolio as you did to developing each of the projects you want to highlight, following the principles of clean design and easy navigation.

You need to build "your name dot com," says Dan Bradley, general manager of WCMH-TV in Columbus, Ohio. "And it can't be a static enterprise, either. You need to keep updating it, put in some RSS, make it your little news station, interactive, up-to-date."

At a minimum, your portfolio should include your résumé, contact information, examples of your work along with the publication date and source and links to any blogs or social media profiles you maintain. Ideally, you've saved everything you've done electronically—newspaper stories, Flash videos, audio slide shows and so forth. If not, you'll be reduced to hoping that your work is still online with an active URL, always a risky proposition. If at all possible, create a DVD version of your portfolio; just make sure that whatever you burn will work on both PC and Mac platforms.

Pay particular attention to issues of copyright infringement. If you have signed away all rights to your work, you could be open to legal action by including it in an online portfolio.

GO ONLINE

Module 12: Learn how to build a simple multimedia portfolio that you can easily customize.

TRADE TOOLS

FINDING A SMALL-MARKET TV JOB

Keith Weiss is the news director at KALB-TV in Alexandria, La., a small market where students can often find jobs right out of college. What is he looking for?

- Applicants who understand the importance and power of the Internet and who are willing to make it a priority to post breaking news stories on the website and through social media tools.
- Applicants who can speak clearly and are proficient in the English language.
- Applicants who can function in a "team" work environment and who are willing to help others, as needed.
- Applicants who can take a look at a news story or event and realize the "what's new and what's now" concept of making sure the latest information is told first.
- Applicants who are naturally curious about the world around them and have an interest in a wide variety of topics including civics, history, politics, law and ethics.
- Applicants who can multitask, including editing their own video, shooting their own footage and producing graphic elements to enhance their storytelling skills.
- Applicants who thrive on breaking news and realize that long hours are part of the routine in a newsroom.
- Applicants who can think visually and who are willing to understand the importance of telling a story through the use of pictures and compelling sound.
- Applicants who do their "homework" regarding the job market and have realistic salary expectations.

Interviews

Once you make it to the all-important interview stage, be prepared for what recruiters call the five fundamentals:[10]

1. Tell me about yourself.
2. Why do you want to work here?
3. What are your weaknesses?

4. What salary do you expect?

5. Don't call us, we'll call you.

Use an open-ended invitation to talk about yourself to provide real-life examples of your accomplishments. Share a story that indicates what you would bring to the job. Show that you've done your homework and are familiar with the company, its news philosophy and the product. You're likely to be asked what you think of it, but that doesn't mean you should launch into a full-blown critique. Just be prepared to describe what you saw and say something positive if you can.

When you're asked about your weaknesses, don't try to fudge your answer by focusing on strengths instead. An employer won't see "working too hard" as a weakness. Be brief but candid about what you think you still need to learn and, if possible, describe strategies for how you plan to learn it.

According to Korn/Ferry International, an executive search company, the most common mistake candidates make in interviews is talking too much.[11] Come prepared to ask some questions of your own and listen closely to the answers. The interview is your chance to find out if the job, the boss and the news organization are a good fit for you.

Expect to be asked about your current or previous jobs, but if things haven't gone well don't spend the interview trashing your employer or co-workers. You will be asked why you want to leave, and it's fine to say that you're looking for a new experience or advancement. Just don't say you can't stand your boss, or everyone you work with is a jerk. "We will set traps in an interview to try to draw that out of you," says news director Kevin Benz.

If you're looking for your first job, the initial interview is not the time to raise the issue of salary, benefits or work schedules. The interviewer may bring these topics up, however, so be prepared for questions like, "What kind of salary are you looking for?" One good answer is another question, "What do you generally pay people with my level of experience?" If you've done your homework, you'll have checked the cost of living in the area so you can tell whether their salaries are reasonable. You can also find calculators online to compare the cost of living in hundreds of cities and to estimate moving costs.

Finally, no matter how well or poorly you felt the interview went, always send a brief note or e-mail to thank the person you met with. If you're enthusiastic about the opportunity, say so.

Hiring Tests

When you come in for an interview, you may be asked to take a hiring test. The most common tests cover writing or other skills and current events. The Associated Press hiring exam includes a number of timed writing assignments to see how well applicants work under pressure.

Susie Steimle received a bachelor's degree in journalism from the University of Missouri. To showcase her multimedia skills, she created an online portfolio, which includes examples of her reporting, live shots and her work as a bilingual journalist. The site also includes her résumé and a personal statement to be used in the hunt for a job. A site like this is becoming more and more common because it showcases multimedia skills.

Source: Courtesy of Susie Steimle.

At KALB-TV, the hiring test involves applicants using fact sheets to write stories. Job candidates are told to choose the two most newsworthy scenarios and the most relevant facts, and then decide the format (package, V/O or V/O-SOT) the selected stories should take.

Jim Garrott's current events quiz at WEEK-TV included 10 questions: five based on local stories published on the station's website in the previous week, three involving national news and the other two about major local institutions like Caterpillar. "We allow them to sit at a computer and time them," says Garrott. "At no time do I say they cannot

EMPLOYER PET PEEVES

Many prospective employers have pet peeves when it comes to job applicants. Here are some of them:

- Your voice mail is full. You don't respond to e-mails. "You won't get a second chance if I can't get in touch with you within 24 hours," says J. J. Murray, a former small-market TV news director.

- "Don't send me a glamour shot where you look like a porn star," says Kevin Benz. "Your credibility is gone."

- If you apply, be willing to actually move. "I've had people say they're looking for something closer to home, yet send me a tape anyway," Murray says.

- Don't send stories that are more than six months old. "It shows you're not getting enough practice, doing enough stories, or you're not doing enough good work," says Chip Mahaney.

- "I talk with a lot of college students about positions and they often have trouble articulating why they want the job or why they're interested in television news," says Deana Reece, news director at WICS-TV in Springfield, Ill.

use the Internet to find the answers. In the last three years, I have had only one person get 100 percent." Applicants who think the test is designed to test their knowledge miss the point, he says. "It isn't a college test. You need to use everything available to you to find the answers."

CONTRACTS

Journalism jobs these days often come with contracts attached, either "personal services" or union contracts. According to the 2008 survey by the Radio Television Digital News Association, well more than half of all TV reporters and anchors and just under half of all producers are under contract, and the vast majority of those contracts have noncompete clauses, restricting them from working for a competing station in the same market for a certain period of time.[12]

"About the only contracts I see without noncompetes are in states where it's illegal," says Bob Papper, who conducts the RTDNA survey. Many contracts also include standard language giving stations the right to terminate the agreement at any time for any reason on just 60 or 90 days notice.

Signing a contract is intimidating, especially because most contracts are designed to give all the advantages to the employer rather than the employee. Unfortunately, it's tough to make changes to a contract until you've proven your value as a journalist. For that reason, you should not expect to truly "negotiate" a first contract. It is OK to ask for more salary, additional moving expenses or, in the case of an anchor, a better makeup or clothing allowance, but you might not make any headway. Ultimately, employers have most of the power; if you truly want the job, you will probably need to accept their terms. As you become more experienced and more valuable to a news organization, the dynamics of contract negotiations will likely change in your favor.

Still, there are stations that don't use contracts, especially in the smallest markets. KALB's Weiss says he sometimes uses the lack of contract as a bargaining chip to get people to come to market 179. He says that way people work at the station because they want to, not because they have to.

"The only thing worse than a person who quits and leaves is the person who quits and stays," Weiss says.

TABLE 12.1 STARTING ANNUAL SALARIES

Type of employer	Annual salary
Daily newspapers	$27,000
Weekly newspapers	$25,700
Television	$24,900
Cable television	$26,500
Radio	$29,000
World Wide Web	$31,200

Source: Lee B. Becker et al., "2009 Annual Survey of Journalism and Mass Communication Graduates," University of Georgia, Grady College of Journalism and Mass Communication, August 4, 2010, Appendix Table 35, www.grady.uga.edu/annualsurveys/Graduate_Survey/Graduate_2009/Grad2009MergedB&W.pdf.

Note: These are median yearly salaries for 2009 graduates of journalism and mass communication programs.

You've probably heard this before, but it bears repeating: You really don't need to hire an agent to get your first job. It may be counterproductive, in fact. Many news managers in small markets simply won't talk to agents. Instead, some news directors recommend you have a family lawyer look at the contract; it's cheaper to pay by the hour than by a percentage of what little you may make in your first job.

JOURNALISM ENTREPRENEURS

As you already know, journalism is a profession in transition. The economic model that sustained newspapers and broadcast stations for decades has become shaky, and there's lots of gloom and doom talk about the future of the news industry. But there's also plenty of room for optimism about the future of journalism for those who aren't bound to the old ways of doing things. "I think that journalism today, given the upheaval of multimedia and reader-contributed reporting, really does belong to those reporters and editors with an entrepreneurial spirit," says Robert Niles, editor of the Online Journalism Review.[13]

One way to succeed as an entrepreneur is to create your own specialties, whether it's combining sports coverage with database reporting or photojournalism with entertainment reporting. "The people who create combinations of two or more passions and skills will be inventing new jobs for the industry and security for themselves," says Joe Grimm, author of the "Ask the Recruiter" column for the Poynter Institute.[14]

These entrepreneurs are finding new ways to fund the journalism they think is important. Take Dave Cohn, who launched Spot.us. His idea was to ask the public to sponsor journalists to cover stories they'd like to read about. Some people thought it was either a pipe dream or a recipe for trouble, with funders having too much influence over what gets reported. But Spot.us stories are getting written and published. For example, a Spot.us-funded story about pollution in the Pacific Ocean ran in the New York Times. More than a hundred people gave an average of 10 dollars each to make it happen.

Another example of entrepreneurial journalism is Gothamist.com, which bills itself as "a daily weblog covering New York city's personalities, news stories, and media with humorous photos and running commentary." It started as an online dialogue between two college friends, Jen Chung and Jake Dobkins. Dobkins had a website where he would post links to interesting content and Chung would comment. Their interaction became so popular with readers that there are now 12 Gothamist sites in cities around the country, all supported by advertising dollars and donations.

These journalism entrepreneurs are making a living publishing content they think is important, but they created these jobs for themselves.

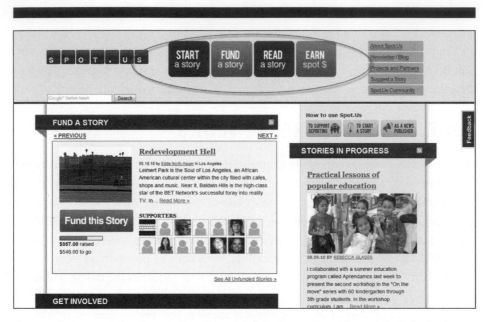

Spot.us is an example of a new funding model for journalism. The public is invited to submit story ideas and to help pay for them. It also offers writers a way to get paid for the stories they want to tell. Its founder, Dave Cohn, is a journalism entrepreneur.

Source: Courtesy of Spot.us, http://spot.us/ (accessed August 10, 2010).

Hyperlocal Sites

As mainstream news organizations are cutting back on coverage, hyperlocal websites are emerging to pick up the slack. Sites like EveryBlock and Patch collect data, including content such as government reports, blog posts, photos from Flickr, content from Craigslist, news stories and more, which they categorize so that users can get very specific information about the neighborhoods that interest them. There are many funding models for these hyperlocal sites; for example, EveryBlock is owned by MSNBC and Patch is owned by AOL and supported by local advertisers. Other sites rely on donations or grant money; an example is the New Haven Independent website, which covers that Connecticut city with a small staff of journalists and user-generated content.

Sometimes individuals launch their own hyperlocal sites, with little to no funding. Jacqueline Dupree's blog JDLand covers the area around the Nationals baseball park in Washington, D.C. About 10 years ago she decided to chronicle the transformation of

GO ONLINE

Ongoing Story Module: Consider how to incorporate user-generated content into the story.

a neighborhood two blocks south of where she lives. When a new ballpark plan was announced, her blog traffic went off the charts.

In addition to a small amount of advertising, JDLand features stories from news organizations, links to original documents and databases, and an interactive neighborhood map along with an extensive photo archive. And Dupree also does a lot of independent reporting, covering government meetings in her spare time that almost no one else attends. "It's 'news over the fence,' what people are talking about," she says. "The paper can't cover all of that. Just because they can't doesn't mean it's not news."

So is Dupree a journalist? Absolutely. She doesn't traffic in gossip, she checks her facts and she keeps her personal opinions to herself.

Branding Yourself

A major part of being a journalist entrepreneur is branding yourself.

"Don't wait for somebody to give you a job. Study personal branding, pick a niche and go for it," says Terry Heaton, senior vice president for AR&D, a news consulting firm.

This idea of branding oneself can rub journalists the wrong way, but Alfred Hermida, who runs the integrated journalism program at the University of British Columbia, says selling yourself is not selling out. "A journalist's identity has always been a part of the job, otherwise why have bylines?" he asks.[15]

But how do you develop a brand while you're still in school? Follow the advice in this text. Get your own domain name and apply SEO strategies to the site so if someone googles your name, the first result is one on which you control the content. Create professional Twitter, Facebook and other social media accounts and use them to show the world what type of journalist you are. Report on content you care deeply about and post it to your website or blog. There are plenty of opportunities for individual journalists to create their own niche-oriented online sites.

Finally, if your program doesn't already require them, take advantage of any business or finance courses available at your college or university. Even if you never go into business for yourself, having an understanding of what it takes to begin and maintain a business enterprise is likely to help you both professionally and personally.

Freelance Opportunities

Entrepreneurial journalists may also create careers for themselves without holding a full-time job at any one news organization. Freelancing is a challenging way to make a living but it has its rewards, including more flexibility to pursue the stories you want to tell. Freelancers spend a fair amount of time searching for outlets for their work and pitching story ideas, so you have to be a good salesperson to succeed at freelancing. Freelancers usually have had some experience working within a news organization, so they understand what editors or producers want. Without that experience, freelancing might be a tough way to make a living right out of school. You should also research the legal issues involved in freelancing, including copyrights and licensing, before deciding if it's really for you.

Look for freelance opportunities by analyzing the news organizations you'd like to produce for. Pay attention to bylines, which can tell you what kinds of stories they buy from freelancers. Come up with story ideas that fit the bill and pitch them directly to the supervisor in charge. "Treat any assignment like gold," says Joe Grimm. "Get details on the editor's requirements and fill them to the letter. It is far easier to establish a continuing freelance arrangement with an editor or two than to have to go through all these steps over and over again as you bounce from paper to magazine to website."[16]

Content farms like Demand Media and Examiner are another online outlet for freelance work. They typically pay a small amount per story or a sliding fee based on Web traffic, and they provide a byline.

Networking is just as important to freelancers as it is to job seekers—maybe even more so. The Freelance Marketplace, hosted by MediaBistro (www.mediabistro.com/fm), is a forum where freelancers can showcase their work and, with luck, land assignments. The Society of Professional Journalists also has resources for freelancers online at www .spj.org/freelance.asp.

TAKING IT HOME

Today's journalists have so many options. From the way we gather, present or deliver the news to the job opportunities available, the term *traditional journalist* is becoming obsolete, or perhaps it is simply taking on a new meaning.

Whether you're just getting into the field or already working in a newsroom, you have the potential to envision new forms of storytelling thanks to the rise of multimedia, the growth of user-generated content and the increased capabilities of mobile devices.

As someone in the job market, you will need to highlight versatility and a willingness to experiment and learn. You can't possibly know it all, but if you can show your employer that you have strong journalism skills, an understanding of how those skills are applied across media platforms and a desire to create, you can set yourself apart from other job applicants.

TALKING POINTS

1. Find an example of a hyperlocal site in your community or a larger community near you. How does the content compare to what you see in the more mainstream media that cover your market? Are they true competitors, or do they provide an entirely different experience? Is one better than the other, or do they complement each other? How?

2. Review the latest survey of journalism graduates at www.grady.uga.edu/ANNUAL SURVEYS. Take a look at the hiring gap between men and women as well as between minorities and nonminorities. What do you think might be behind these disparities? What, if anything, should be done to close these gaps?

3. Go online and find a job opening that interests you. List some of the things you would do before sending off your application materials. Show a classmate or two what you've come up with. What would they suggest?

ONLINE LEARNING MODULE 12

Activate or buy this chapter's online learning module at journalism.cqpress.com to get access to:

- SKILL BUILDING: Learn how to create your own multimedia portfolio using a simple template to post online.

- DISCOVER: See résumé materials created by successful job candidates for both broadcast journalism and multimedia positions.

- EXPLORE: Find resources to help with your résumé and portfolio preparation as well as for the job hunt itself.

- Highlights from the latest research on what skills journalism employers are looking for in today's job applicants.

- A digital version of this chapter's text in full color with active links.

Also, complete your work on the ONGOING STORY MODULE. Brainstorm strategies for incorporating user-generated content into this story and for delivering the content to mobile devices. Review what the authors came up with for the final multimedia presentation of this story.

NOTES

Chapter 1 The Multimedia Mind-Set

1. "Average Person Spends More Time Using Media than Anything Else," Ball State University, www.bsu.edu/up/article/0,1370,32363-2914-36658,00.html (accessed July 3, 2010).
2. Nielsenwire, http://blog.nielsen.com/nielsenwire/online_mobile/three-screen-report-q409/ (accessed June 21, 2010).
3. M. Langeveld, "AP's Ethnographic Studies Look for Solutions to News and Ad 'Fatigue,'" March 26, 2010, www.niemanlab.org/2010/03/aps-ethnographic-studies-look-for-solutions-to-news-and-ad-fatigue (accessed March 30, 2010).
4. Pew Research Center for the People & the Press, http://pewresearch.org/pubs/1469/public-following-haiti-donations-texts (accessed June 21, 2010).
5. Journalism.org, www.journalism.org/analysis_report/how_news_happens (accessed June 21, 2010).
6. Excerpted from "Americans Spending More Time Following the News," Pew Research Center for the People & the Press, October 16, 2010, http://people-press.org/report/?pageid=1792.

Chapter 2 Finding the Story

1. Jim Schaefer, "Nurturing Sources," *IRE Journal* 33, no. 2 (Spring 2010): 29.
2. "Local Characters: How to Tell the Stories You Have to Tell," *Nieman Reports* (Winter 2007), www.nieman.harvard.edu/reportsitem.aspx?id=100122.
3. "Social Media Has 'Central Role in Our Newsgathering,' Says AP's Lauren McCullough," Poynter.org, January 12, 2010, www.poynter.org/column.asp?id=101&aid=175577.
4. "Podcast: Social Media Critical to Reporting a Story," BeatBlogging.org, February 10, 2009, http://beatblogging.org/2009/02/10/podcast-social-media-critical-to-reporting-a-story.

5. Marcus D. Rosenbaum and John Dinges, eds., *Sound Reporting: The National Public Radio Guide to Radio Journalism and Production* (Dubuque, Iowa: Kendall/Hunt Publishing Co., 1992).
6. Debora R. Wenger, Daniel Bradley and Forrest Carr, "Media General Broadcast Group News Operational Guidelines," Media General, Inc., 2003.
7. Gary Hanson and Stan Wearden, "The Accuracy of Local TV News: A Study of News Coverage in Cleveland," NewsLab, www.newslab.org/2004/08/08/the-accuracy-of-local-tv-news.

Chapter 3 Multimedia Newsgathering

1. Regina McCombs, "Shooting Web Video: How to Put Your Readers at the Scene," Online Journalism Review, March 2, 2005, www.ojr.org/ojr/stories/050303mccombs/.
2. Jakob Nielsen, "Talking Head Video Is Boring Online," Jakob Nielsen's Alertbox, December 5, 2005, www.useit.com/alertbox/video.html.
3. Terry L. Heaton, "10 Questions for Lisa Lambden," AR&D, www.thepomoblog.com/papers/10Q8.htm.

Chapter 4 Reporting in Depth

1. Jim Detjen, "The Beat's Basics," *SEJ Journal* (Summer 2003), www.sej.org/resource/index11.htm.
2. Bradley Wilson, "Establishing a Rapport," Journalism Education Association, 1999, www.jea.org/curriculum/writing/tragedies.html.
3. Lori Dorfman and Vincent Schiraldi, "Off Balance: Youth, Race & Crime in the News," Building Blocks for Youth, April 2001, www.buildingblocksforyouth.org/media/media.html.
4. Charlotte Grimes, "Top Ten Hints for Covering Government," http://knightpoliticalreporting.syr.edu/teachingfiles/Top%20Ten%20Hints%20for%20Covering%20Government%209-25-03.pdf.
5. Pat Stith, "A Guide to Computer Assisted Reporting," PoynterOnline, June 3, 2005, http://poynter.org/content/content_view.asp?id=83144.
6. ASCII is computer code that represents text.
7. Bob Steele, "Hidden Cameras: High-Powered and High-Risk," PoynterOnline, October 19, 1998, www1.poynter.org/dg.lts/id.5612/content.content_view.htm.
8. Pam Zekman, "Undercover Reporting Tips," IRE Tipsheet no. 1186, Investigative Reporters and Editors, Inc., 2000, www.ire.org/resourcecenter/viewtipsheets.php?number=1186.

Chapter 5 Writing the Story

1. "Make Every Word Count," www.concernedjournalists.org/make-every-word-count.
2. Robert Krulwich, "Work That Feels So, So Good—and So, So Bad," *Current*, December 16, 2002, current.org/people/peop0223krulwich.shtml.

Chapter 6 Multimedia Storytelling

1. "Q&A with Travis Fox, Video Journalist for washingtonpost.com," Online Journalism Review, September 18, 2006, www.ojr.org/ojr/stories/600916Junnarkar.

2. "Video Even Less Interactive than Print" (comment by Regina McCombs), Teaching Online Journalism, October 29, 2006, http://mindymcadams.com/tojou/2006/video-even-less-interactive-than-print/.

3. "Transcripts: CNN Newsroom," CNN.com, December 16, 2006, http://edition.cnn.com/TRANSCRIPTS/0612/16/cnr.03.html.

4. Mark Bowden, "Narrative Journalism Goes Multimedia," *Nieman Reports* 54, no. 3 (Fall 2000), www.nieman.harvard.edu/reports/00-3NRfall/Goes-Multimedia.html.

5. Tamara Keith, "More Workers Quit Labor Force," NPR.org, July 2, 2010, www.npr.org/templates/story/story.php?storyId=128273018.

6. "Audio-Video Redundancy," in "Annotated Bibliography of TV News Research," NewsLab, www.newslab.org/2008/07/19/tv-news-research-bibliography/#Audio.

7. "Video Even Less Interactive than Print" (comment by Angela Grant), Teaching Online Journalism, October 29, 2006, http://mindymcadams.com/tojou/2006/video-even-less-interactive-than-print/.

8. Ira Glass, "Mo' Better Radio," *Current,* May 25, 1998, www.current.org/people/p809i1.html.

9. Nancy Updike, "The Transom Review," January 24, 2006, transom.org/?p=6676.

10. Warren Watson, "A Primer on Informational Graphics: Package for Design on Small-Newspaper Info-Graphics," American Press Institute, November 28, 2000, www.americanpressinstitute.org/content/p1465_c1390.cfm?print=yes.

11. Steve Duenes, "Talk to the Newsroom," *New York Times,* February 25–29, 2008, www.nytimes.com/2008/02/25/business/media/25asktheeditors.html?_r=1&pagewanted=all.

Chapter 7 Writing for the Web

1. Retrieved from http://people-press.org/report/652/ on November 15, 2010.

2. "EyeTrack07," PoynterOnline, http://eyetrack.poynter.org.

3. Based on Cory Bergman, "How to Write for the Web: Lost Remote's Guide for TV Newsrooms," LostRemote.com, 2007, www.lostremote.com/how-to-write-for-the-web.

4. Webopedia, www.webopedia.com/TERM/S/SEO.html.

5. "World's Best Headlines: BBC News," UseIt.com, www.useit.com/alertbox/headlines-bbc.html (accessed June 23, 2010).

6. B. Papper, "TV and Radio on the Web," www.rtdna.org/media/Section3.pdf (accessed June 22, 2010).

Chapter 8 Producing for the Web

1. Webopedia, www.webopedia.com/TERM/C/content_management_system.html.

2. Online Journalism Review, www.ojr.org/ojr/people/webjournalist/201002/1821 (accessed July 25, 2010).

3. "Alan Murray of the Wall Street Journal on Hiring and Managing Online Reporters," Nieman Journalism Lab, April 4, 2009, http://vimeo.com/4097252 (accessed August 4, 2010).

4. Andrea Miller, "When Cable Networks Break In—and Why," NewsLab, 2006, www.newslab.org/2006/08/04/when-cable-networks-break-in-and-why.

5. "Talking-Head Video Is Boring Online," UseIt.com, December 5, 2005, www.useit.com/alertbox/video.html.

6. Vadim Lavrusik, "The Missing Link in Journalism Curricula: Community Engagement," May 12, 2010, http://lavrusik.com/2010/05/12/the-missing-link-in-journalism-curricula-community-engagement (accessed August 4, 2010).

7. Webopedia, www.webopedia.com/DidYouKnow/Internet/2007/widgets.asp (accessed July 29, 2010).

8. "Interactive Storytelling Demystified," NewsLab, March 2002, www.newslab.org/2002/03/04/interactive-storytelling.

9. Search Engine People, www.searchenginepeople.com/blog/ruud-questions-anna-gonzalez-from-news-8-austin.html.

10. "Citizen Journalism Expert Jay Rosen Answers Your Questions," SlashDot, 2006, http://interviews.slashdot.org/interviews/06/10/03/1427254.shtml.

11. Jane Stevens, "Choosing a Story," University of California–Berkeley Graduate School of Journalism, http://journalism.berkeley.edu/multimedia/course/choose/.

12. C. Max Magee, "The Roles of Journalists in Online Newsrooms," Medill School of Journalism, released by Online News Association, November 1, 2006, http://journalist.org/news/archives/MedillOnlineJobSurvey-final.pdf.

Chapter 9 Producing for Multiple Platforms

1. "Newscast Structure" (bibliography), NewsLab, 2006, www.newslab.org/2008/07/19/tv-news-research-bibliography/#Newscast.

2. "RTNDF's 2006 Future of News Survey: Section 6, How Do People Want to Get to That Future?" Radio and Television News Directors Association and Foundation, 2006, www.rtnda.org/resources/future/section6.pdf.

3. Omar L. Gallaga, "Statesman Teams Up with Gowalla for Austin Virtual Trips," statesman.com, June 3, 2000, www.statesman.com/business/statesman-teams-up-with-gowalla-for-austin-virtual-724228.html?srcTrk=RTR_95649.

4. "Podcast Boosts NPR Show's Audience," CyberJournalist.net, February 9, 2005, www.cyberjournalist.net/news/001903.php.

5. "NBC News Launches Video Podcasts," CyberJournalist.net, November 14, 2006, www.cyberjournalist.net/news/003876.php.

6. "Podcasting Goes Mainstream," eMarketer, March 4, 2009, www.emarketer.com/Article.aspx?R=1006937.

7. "Murdoch: iPad Is 'Game Changer' That Will Get Youth Reading Newspapers," Associated Press, August 5, 2010, www.editorandpublisher.com/Headlines/murdoch-ipad-is-game-changer-that-will-get-youth-reading-newspapers-62214-.aspx (accessed August 6, 2010).

Chapter 10 Delivering the News

1. Marcus D. Rosenbaum and John Dinges, eds., *Sound Reporting: The National Public Radio Guide to Radio Journalism and Production* (Dubuque, Iowa: Kendall/Hunt Publishing Co., 1992).

2. Forrest Carr and Andy Friedman, "Caught on Tape," Radio and Television News Directors Association and Foundation, http://web.archive.org/web/20060602085330/http://www.rtnda.org/members/communicator/52_may.asp.

3. Charlie Tuggle, Dana Rosengard and Suzanne Huffman, "Going Live, as Viewers See It," Newslab, www.newslab.org/2001/12/04/going-live-as-viewers-see-it/.
4. "CBS Evening News," July 13, 2010.
5. Maureen Fan, "In China, Aging in the Care of Strangers: One-Child Policy Changes Tradition," *Washington Post*, December 22, 2006, Sec. A.

CHAPTER 11 Multimedia Ethics

1. "Code of Ethics," Society of Professional Journalists, 1996, www.spj.org/ethicscode.asp.
2. Stephanie Clifford, "Front of Los Angeles Times Has an NBC 'Article,'" *New York Times,* April 9, 2009, www.nytimes.com/2009/04/10/business/media/10adco.html?_r=2&ref=media.
3. Richard Pérez-Peña, "A Cover Ad That Mimics a Newspaper's Front Page," *New York Times,* March 5, 2010, www.nytimes.com/2010/03/06/business/media/06paper.html.
4. "Few Sites Reject Unusual $10M Sony 'Advertorial' Campaign," September 9, 2002, www.consumerwebwatch.org/dynamic/journalism-investigation-sony-campaign.cfm.
5. "RTDNA Guidelines for Use of Non-Editorial Video and Audio," Radio Television Digital News Association and Foundation, April 2005, www.rtdna.org/pages/media_items/guidelines-for-use-of-non-editorial-video-and-audio250.php?p=40?id=250.
6. "Plagiarism Statement," Emory University, Journalism Program, www.journalism.emory.edu/program/plagiarism.cfm, quoting Floyd C. Watkins and William B. Dillingham, *Practical English Handbook*, 9th ed. (Boston: Houghton Mifflin, 1992), 357–358.
7. "Fair Use," United States Copyright Office, July 2006, www.copyright.gov/fls/fl102.html.
8. National Press Photographers Association, www.nppa.org/professional_development/business_practices/digitalethics.html.
9. Bud Ward, "BBC 'Newsnight' Editing of Obama Inaugural Address Prompts Criticisms," February 3, 2009, www.yaleclimatemediaforum.org/2009/02/bbcnewsnight-editing-of-obama-inaugural-address.
10. Bill Kovach and Tom Rosenstiel, *The Elements of Journalism: What Newspeople Should Know and the Public Should Expect* (New York: Three Rivers Press, 2007), 94–98.
11. Sewell Chan, "CNN Producer Says He Was Fired for Blogging," *New York Times,* February 14, 2008, http://cityroom.blogs.nytimes.com/2008/02/14/cnn-producer-says-he-was-fired-for-blogging.
12. Gary Hill, e-mail interview with authors, November 10, 2006.
13. Brian Stelter, "CNN Drops Editor after Hezbollah Comments," *New York Times,* July 7, 2010, http://mediadecoder.blogs.nytimes.com/2010/07/07/cnn-drops-editor-after-hezbollah-comments.
14. Bill Dedman, "TV Reporter Who Supported Candidate Is Out," MSNBC, July 11, 2007, www.msnbc.msn.com/id/19415989.
15. David Brewer, "Editorial Ethics for Twitter Journalists," Media Helping Media, June 28, 2009, www.mediahelpingmedia.org/content/view/401/234.
16. Mike Nizza, "Prankster Playing Bhutto's Son on Facebook Fools News Outlets," January 2, 2008, http://thelede.blogs.nytimes.com/2008/01/02/prankster-playing-bhuttos-son-on-facebook-fools-news-outlets.
17. Ryan Kim, "Comments on News Stories a Double-Edged Sword," May 4, 2009, www.sfgate.com/cgi-bin/article.cgi?f=/c/a/2009/05/03/MNUT17CCM3.DTL.
18. Joe Strupp, "Ind. Paper Stands behind Sex Offender Coverage," PoynterOnline, February 24, 2004, www.poynter.org/column.asp?id=55&aid=61424.

19. Aly Colón, "Connecting Ethics and Diversity," PoynterOnline, November 17, 2003, www.poynter.org/column.asp?id=36&aid=54476.

Chapter 12 Getting Ready for the Real World

1. Annual Survey of Journalism and Mass Communication Graduates, 2009, www.grady.uga.edu/annualsurveys/Graduate_Survey/Graduate_2009/Grad2009MergedB&W.pdf.
2. Ibid.
3. Ibid.
4. Ibid.
5. Ibid.
6. "The Dirty Dozen Online Job Search Mistakes," Job-Hunt.org, 2001, www.job-hunt.org/jobsearchmistakes.shtml.
7. Gannett, www.jobpath.com/Jobs/Gannettbroadcast/Multimedia-Producer-Pm/J3H12F6KLMLOSPST17C (accessed August 6, 2010).
8. Media General, http://jobs.mediageneral.com/JobDetails.asp?varID=BTW-000287 (accessed August 6, 2010).
9. Sree Sreenivasan, "LinkedIn, Anyone? Social Networking for Professionals," PoynterOnline, October 11, 2006, https://www.poynter.org/column.asp?id=32&aid=102953.
10. Michael Kinsman, "Five Fundamentals for Acing Any Job Interview," California Job Journal, June 11, 2006, www.jobjournal.com/thisweek.asp?artid=1726.
11. "Recruiters Reveal Interview Secrets and Employment Gaffes," Korn/Ferry International, May 8, 2006, www.kornferry.com/PressRelease/3421.
12. Bob Papper, "A Run for the Money," *Communicator*, June 2008, www.rtdna.org/media/pdfs/research/Salary_Survey_2008.pdf.
13. Robert Niles (comment), "Teaching the Future of Journalism," Online Journalism Review, February 15, 2006, www.ojr.org/ojr/stories/060212pryor.
14. Joe Grimm writes the column "Ask the Recruiter" for PoynterOnline; the column can be found at www.poynter.org/column.asp?id=77.
15. Alfred Hermida, "Journalism Students Need to Develop Their Personal Brand," MediaShift, August 19, 2009, www.pbs.org/mediashift/2009/08/journalism-students-need-to-develop-their-personal-brand231.html (accessed August 9, 2010).
16. Joe Grimm, "Ask the Recruiter: How Do I Freelance for a Newspaper?" PoynterOnline, October 27, 2006, https://www.poynter.org/column.asp?id=77&aid=112664.

GLOSSARY OF MULTIMEDIA JOURNALISM TERMS

One essential task for a multimedia journalist is to become familiar with some of the key terms each medium uses to describe typical job functions, tools and personnel. Here is a glossary of basic terms used in television/radio, online/social media and newspaper journalism. One word of caution—many newsrooms create their own lingo, so what's called a V/O-SOT in one TV station may be called a VO/B in others. However, we're confident you'll find it fairly easy to translate unique terms once you have a fundamental understanding of the overall concepts.

TELEVISION/RADIO

actuality. See *SOT.*

aircheck. Recording of program for logging, screening or archiving purposes.

anchor lead. What the anchor says on the air to introduce a news package. Also called a *lead-in, anchor intro* or *intro.*

assignment editor. Person who supervises and coordinates the coverage of news events for a newsroom.

B-roll. Often used as shorthand for video.

bird. See *satellite.*

booth. Short for "control booth" or "control room." It houses the producer, director and some other technical staff during the newscast. May be used as a verb to describe a portion of the producer's job, that is, to "booth the show."

cans. Another term for headphones.

capture. See *digitize*.

CG. Short for "character generation," this is a generic term for text, such as the person's name or location, or numbers superimposed on the television screen. May also be called *chyron* or *super*. See also *side CG*. The term *CG* also refers to the character generator device that creates these graphics.

chyron. See *CG*.

cue. Direction to anchor or reporter to begin speaking. May also be used to describe the process of getting audio or video ready for playback, as in "cue the tape."

digitize. To load linear field tape into a nonlinear editing system, thereby converting analog audio or video to digital format; also called *ingest* or *capture*.

director. Person responsible for the technical production of a newscast.

donut. Refers to a story with a live top and tag from the reporter, wrapping around a package or some other pre-recorded visual element.

FS. Short for "full-screen graphic," a graphic that fills the entire screen; often used to display complicated information that the audience needs to read to understand.

IFB. Short for "interruptible foldback," the small earpiece that anchors and reporters wear so they can hear what's on the air as well as directions from the producer or director during a broadcast.

ingest. See *digitize*.

intro. See *anchor lead*.

lead-in. See *anchor lead*.

lineup. See *rundown*.

live shot. Report that has not been recorded but is presented live, often at a news scene.

lock out. See *sig out*.

look live. Recorded "live" shot, when a reporter goes through the motions as if he or she were live. Although this technique is sometimes used when technical issues prevent an actual live shot, it's considered poor journalistic practice and raises serious ethical questions.

microwave. Refers to a type of signal from a live truck.

news director. Person responsible for the work of an entire newsroom staff.

OTS. Short for "over the shoulder," a graphic that appears over the anchor's shoulder during a newscast.

package. Story that is preproduced and presented by a reporter, usually introduced by an anchor.

phoner. Story called in by a reporter and broadcast either live or on tape; may also refer to any interview conducted by phone and aired in a newscast. Usually this is accompanied on TV by a graphic that includes a picture and location. Often used when conventional live equipment is not available.

post mortem. Review or critique after the newscast airs.

producer. Essentially a newscast coordinator, this person determines the order and presentation of stories in a newscast and is responsible for much of the writing as well as for timing the show.

reader. A basic, short television story read by the anchor without video or graphic support. Sometimes called a *tell*.

re-ask. For editing purposes, a reporter may re-ask questions on camera after a single-camera interview. Re-asks raise ethical concerns because it's hard to ask a question exactly the same way twice.

remote. Any live program insert from outside the studio.

rundown. Term to describe the blueprint for the newscast; essentially a list of the stories assembled by the producer, shown in the order they will run. Also designates the length of each story, its format and which anchor will read it. Also may be called a *lineup*.

satellite. Term for another type of live shot; involves bouncing a live signal from a specially designed truck to a satellite and back to the television station's receiver. This can be done from almost anywhere, but it is expensive. Sometimes referred to as a *bird*.

satellite window. Refers to a block of satellite time; typically purchased in blocks of five to 15 minutes.

side CG. Used to describe a graphic look that incorporates text or numbers, or both, on one side of the screen while keeping the anchor or reporter's face or video on the other side of the screen.

sig out. Term used for the last few words a reporter says in a story. Typically includes the reporter's name, the station name or brand and often the story's location. May also be called a *tag out* or a *lock out*.

slot. Position of a story in a newscast; making slot is good, missing slot is bad.

SOT. Stands for "sound on tape," and is another expression for *sound bite*. It is a portion of a taped interview that has been selected to air. On radio, often called an *actuality*.

sound bite. See *SOT*.

split screen. Refers to a production technique that divides the television screen in half with something different in each half. Often used to transition between the studio and a live reporter or to keep the anchor's face on screen while video is rolling in another window on the screen.

stand-up. Reporter's on-camera appearance in a news story, usually not live.

sticks. Term commonly used to describe a camera tripod.

straight live. Reporter simply stands and talks or answers questions from the anchors.

super. See *CG*.

tag. What the anchor says after the news package airs, or what a reporter says live at the end of a package.

tag out. See *sig out*.

technical director. This person pushes the buttons that change cameras and puts tapes and graphics on the air; oversees camera angles, lighting and other technical aspects of a program.

tell. See *reader*.

throw. See *toss*.

toss. Anchor's introduction to a reporter's live shot; sometimes called a *throw*.

VNR. Short for "video news release"; denotes video provided by a public relations firm, company or government agency. Using a VNR without disclosing the source raises ethical concerns.

V/O. Stands for "voice-over." Used in scripting to indicate what portion of narration is covered by video; also used to refer to a story that includes a short video clip, narrated by the anchor or a reporter, usually live.

V/O-SOT. A story, usually read live, with both voiced-over video and a sound bite. Sometimes called a "V/O bite."

vox pop. Short for the Latin "vox populi," meaning "voice of the people"; a gender-neutral term used to refer to what is sometimes still called man-on-the-street, or MOS, interviews.

ONLINE/SOCIAL MEDIA

app. Short for "application"; a program or tool that runs inside another service such as a website.

blog. Short for "weblog"; a series of entries to an online journal, posted in chronological order, that can be written by an individual or a group. Video versions are sometimes called *vlogs*.

blogosphere. Term used to describe all blogs on the Internet collectively.

citizen journalism. News and information gathered and reported by citizens, rather than by professional journalists. Also called *participatory journalism* or *grassroots journalism*.

clip. Segment of audio or videotape that's posted on the Web.

CMS. Stands for "content management system," a software system used to manage the content of a website; popular examples include Blogger, WordPress, Typepad and Drupal.

cookie. Computer file that attaches to the hard drives of visitors to a website; it tracks what people are doing on a particular site and stores information that allows the site to remember the visitors if they return.

CPC. Stands for "cost per click," a pricing model in which advertisers are charged based on the number of clicks their ad receives.

CPM. Cost per thousand impressions (M is the Roman numeral for 1,000); it's the rate advertisers will pay to have an ad displayed on 1,000 page views.

crowdsourcing. Term often used in conjunction with "citizen journalism"; users submit information that is collected into a larger data set for reporting a story. Sometimes called *open source reporting*.

CSS. Stands for "cascading style sheet." See *style sheet*.

dashboard. The administration area on a blog that allows you to perform such tasks as creating posts, uploading files and managing comments.

direct message (DM). A private message sent from one user to another on a social networking site.

download. To take files from another computer or server for use on your own.

embed. To place a specific piece of content from one Web page on another, typically by pasting in HTML code.

encoding. Process of changing analog audio or video into a digital file to be read and displayed by a computer.

Facebook. Popular social networking site established in 2004 that allows users to create and customize their own profiles, add friends and socialize with other users. Many news organizations have Facebook pages.

flaming. Act of posting personal attacks to an online forum or blog.

follower. Twitter term that refers to a user who follows or subscribes to another user's posts, or tweets.

freeware. Software that's available at no cost for users, generally available for download over the Internet.

friend. To add someone as a friend or contact on a social networking site like Facebook.

FTP. Stands for "file transfer protocol"; a program used to upload files and Web pages to a server.

geotagging. The process of adding geographic location data to an image, video or address, allowing it to be easily displayed on a map. Also called *geocoding.*

grassroots journalism. See *citizen journalism.*

hits. Term used to describe a request for a file on a Web server; when you click on a photo or link or answer a poll question online, it's counted as a hit. Sometimes hits are used to measure Web traffic, but measuring unique visitors is more useful.

HTML. Stands for "hypertext markup language"; a language used to format content so it can be displayed on a Web page.

hyperlinks. Text on a website that can be clicked on to take you to another Web page or a different area of the same Web page; often called "links" for short.

JavaScript. A Web scripting language used to enhance websites by making them more interactive without requiring a browser plugin.

JPEG. Stands for "joint photographic experts group"; the most common type of picture file on a website, with the file name extension .jpg. Other common picture file extensions are .gif and .png. Pictures must be created or converted to formats like these to display properly on the Web.

lurker. Person who reads discussions on a message board or chat room but rarely participates.

mash-up. Term used to describe a Web page that mixes two or more different types of information or services into something new; for example, a mash-up might involve an overlay of traffic data on a Google map.

metadata. Data attached to information on the Web that describes when, how and by whom the information was collected.

microblog. Short text updates to a blog, usually filed by text-message-enabled cell phone or social network.

mobile. Umbrella term in technology that was long synonymous with cellular phones but has since grown to encompass tablet computing and netbooks.

MySpace. Social networking site founded in 2003 that allows users to create profiles, upload photos and socialize with other users.

open source reporting. See *crowdsourcing.*

open source software. Software that is usually free and allows users to see the original source code so they can modify it more easily.

page view. Request for a single page of a website; each page view may translate into multiple hits, which is why measuring hits can be misleading.

participatory journalism. See *citizen journalism.*

pay wall. Process that blocks access to Web content unless users have paid to read it.

peer-to-peer. Direct interaction between two people in a network.

photosharing. Act of uploading images to a social networking site.

platform. Hardware or software that other applications are built upon, such as Facebook or WordPress.

podcast. Multimedia file distributed over the Internet for playback on mobile devices or personal computers; video versions are sometimes called *vodcasts.*

PPC. Stands for "pay per click"; an advertising system such as Google's AdWords/AdSense, where advertisers pay each time a reader clicks on their ads.

profile. Information, such as interests and hobbies, provided about one's self on a social networking site. Some profiles may also include photos and other special features such as polls and music.

retweet. To repost another user's message on the social networking site Twitter. This is often abbreviated "RT."

RSS. Method for distributing Web content to another website or online application such as a news reader on a cell phone. Some say RSS stands for "rich site summary," and others say it's "really simple syndication."

search engine. Computer software used to search data for specified information; also a site such as Google or Yahoo! that uses such software to look for specific words and display the information for the user.

SEO. Stands for "search engine optimization." The process of improving the visibility of a website or Web page in search engines.

server. Usually refers to a computer connected to the Internet that is part of a network shared by multiple users.

shovelware. Publishing stories from one medium to another, usually to a website, without changing the content significantly, if at all.

social media. Internet-based applications that allow users to create and exchange video, audio, text or multimedia, such as a blog, forum, wiki or video-hosting site.

social networks. Online sites where users can create profiles for themselves and socialize with others using a range of social media tools including blogs, video, images, tagging, forums and messaging.

status update. Quick comment, often posted on social networks, on what the user is currently doing or thinking about.

style sheet. Set of instructions that tells Web browsers how to display various elements on a Web page; style sheets can dictate font styles and colors, where photos and graphics are located on the page and other elements concerning the way a Web page looks when viewers access it.

tagging. Way to associate a posting with key words that can be found by search engines.

thumbnail. Small graphic usually included as an online image link to a larger external image.

troll. Person who posts to an online forum or blog to provoke a hostile response from other readers.

tweet. Text-based posts of up to 140 characters sent via the social networking site Twitter.

Twitter. Social networking and microblogging site that enables users to send and read messages known as tweets. A collection of tweets by a user or about a specific topic is called a Twitter stream.

unfriend. To remove someone as a friend on a social networking site.

unique visitors. Number of people who have visited a particular website during a fixed time period (typically 30 days).

upload. To transfer files from your computer to another computer or server.

vlog. See *blog*.

vodcast. See *podcast*.

wall. Part of a social network profile where other users may write messages or comment on statuses.

webcast. Video or audio broadcast that's transmitted over the Web.

widget. Useful application, such as a weather report widget, that allows users to turn personal content into dynamic Web apps that can be shared, or embedded, on just about any website.

wiki. Web page or set of pages that can be edited collaboratively. Wikipedia, for example, is an encyclopedia created by online contributors worldwide.

XML. Extensible markup language; a language much like HTML but designed to describe online data. It allows you to structure, store and send information.

NEWSPAPERS

banner. Headline extending across the entire page.

body type. Type used for text.

boxcars. See *skyboxes*.

breakouts. Words, phrases or text blocks used to label part of a map or diagram (also called *callouts* or *factoids*).

broadsheet. Standard newspaper page size.

budget. List of news stories scheduled for the next issue of the newspaper.

callouts. See *breakouts.*

caption. See *cutline.*

character. Typeset letter, numeral or punctuation mark.

column inch. Way to measure the length of text or ads; it's an area one column wide and 1 inch long.

copy block. Small chunk of text accompanying a photo spread or introducing a special package of text.

copy editor. Person who edits news copy for content, style and grammar. Copy editors also write headlines and cutlines, and they design pages.

credit. Identifies source for story; for example, Associated Press or Media General News Services.

crop. To indicate where a photo should be trimmed before it runs in the newspaper; usually done by making crop marks in the margins of the photo.

crosshead. See *subhead.*

cutline. Line or block of type providing descriptive information about a photo; also called a *caption.*

dateline. Line in all capital letters at the beginning of a news story that says where the story took place. Originally this also included the date the story took place, hence the name.

deck. Smaller headline that sometimes comes between the headline and the story.

desk. General term to describe the people who edit and design the newspaper.

double truck. Two facing pages on the same sheet of newsprint that are treated as one unit.

dummy. Small, detailed page diagram showing where all elements go; also, the process of drawing up a layout.

extra. Additional edition of a newspaper published at a time other than the usual scheduled publication times; extremely rare since the introduction of Web editions.

factoids. See *breakouts.*

flag. Name of a newspaper as it's displayed on Page 1; also called a *nameplate.* Sometimes mistakenly called the *masthead.*

full frame. Entire image area of a photograph.

graf. Newsroom slang meaning "paragraph."

infographic. Short for "informational graphic"; any complex map, chart or diagram used to analyze an event, object or place.

jump. To continue a story on another page; text that's been continued on another page is called the "jump."

layout. The placement of art and text on a page; to lay out a page is to design it.

lede. Another spelling for "lead," the first few lines of an article that introduce the story.

liftout quote. Graphic treatment of a quotation from a story, often using bold or italic type, rules or screens; sometimes called a *pull quote.*

mainbar. The lead or top story in a package of stories on the same topic.

managing editor. Person responsible for all aspects of the news department and has supervisory responsibilities for all the editors.

masthead. Block of information, including staff names and publication data, often printed on the editorial page.

measure. Width of a headline or column of text.

morgue. Newsroom library.

nameplate. Name of a newspaper as it's displayed on Page 1; also called a *flag.*

nut graf. Paragraph that explains what a story is about; most often used in news features, the nut graf comes within a few paragraphs of the lead.

pagination. Process of generating a page on a computer.

penetration. Percentage of households in the newspaper market that subscribe.

photo credit. Line that tells who shot a photograph.

press run. Total number of copies printed.

promo. See *teaser.*

proof. Copy of a pasted-up page used to check for errors; to check a page is to proofread it.

publisher. Chief executive responsible for all departments of the newspaper.

pull quote. See *liftout quote.*

rack sales. Papers sold by the single copy either from vending machines or by stores. Also called *street sales.*

rail. Teasers that run in a single column on the left or right side of Page 1.

refer. Line or paragraph, often given graphic treatment, referring to a related story elsewhere in the paper or in another medium, for example, the newspaper's website. Sometimes spelled "reefer."

rules. Lines used to separate columns on a newspaper page.

sidebar. Story accompanying a bigger story on the same topic.

sig. Small standing headline that labels a regularly appearing column or feature.

skyboxes, skylines. Teasers that run above the flag on Page 1. If they're boxed (with art), they're called *skyboxes* or *boxcars*; if they use only a line of type, they're called *skylines.*

street sales. See *rack sales.*

stylebook. A newspaper's standardized set of rules and guidelines for grammar, punctuation, headline codes, design principles and so forth.

subhead. Heading within the text or story or article, often used to break columns of type into smaller sections and make the page more attractive or easy on the eye. A crosshead is centered in the column; a subhead is usually set left.

tabloid. Newspaper format that's roughly half the size of a regular broadsheet newspaper.

teaser. Eye-catching graphic element, on Page 1 or section fronts, that promotes an item inside; also called a *promo.*

INDEX

Tables, figures, boxes, photos (or screen shots) and notes are indicated by t, f, b, p and n, respectively, following the page number.